PENGUIN BOOKS

THE LIFE OF RAYMOND CHANDLER

Frank MacShane was born in Pittsburgh, Pennsylvania, and received an A.B. from Harvard College, an M.A. from Yale University, and a Ph.D. from Oxford University. He was a Fulbright professor in Chile in 1957 and in Nepal in 1962, and in 1974 he held a Guggenheim Fellowship. Among his previous books are a widely praised biography, *The Life and Work of Ford Madox Ford*; two anthologies of Ford's writings, *Critical Writings of Ford Madox Ford* and *Ford Madox Ford: The Critical Heritage*; two anthologies of travel writings, *Impressions of Latin America* and *The American in Europe*; and an art-history and travel book, *Many Golden Ages*. He was also the co-editor of *Borges on Writing* and has translated many books of Miguel Serrano. Frank MacShane is presently chairman of the writing division at Columbia University in New York City, where he lives with his wife and son.

(Courtesy of John Engstead)

THE
LIFE
OF
RAYMOND
CHANDLER

Frank MacShane

PENGUIN BOOKS

Penguin Books Ltd, Harmondsworth,
Middlesex, England
Penguin Books, 625 Madison Avenue,
New York, New York 10022, U.S.A.
Penguin Books Australia Ltd, Ringwood,
Victoria, Australia
Penguin Books Canada Limited, 2801 John Street,
Markham, Ontario, Canada L3R 1B4
Penguin Books (N.Z.) Ltd, 182–190 Wairau Road,
Auckland 10, New Zealand

First published in the United States of America by
E. P. Dutton & Co., Inc., 1976
First published in Canada by
Clarke, Irwin & Company Limited 1976
Published in Penguin Books 1978

LIBRARY OF CONGRESS CATALOGING IN PUBLICATION DATA
MacShane, Frank.
The life of Raymond Chandler.
Reprint of the 1976 ed. published by Dutton, New York.
Includes bibliographical references and index.
1. Chandler, Raymond, 1888–1959—Biography.
2. Authors, American—20th century—Biography.
I. Title.
[PS3505.H3224z7 1978]   813'.5'2   [B]   77-16644
ISBN 0 14 00.4791 3

Printed in the United States of America by
Offset Paperback Mfrs., Inc., Dallas, Pennsylvania
Set in Linotype Palatino

Grateful acknowledgment is made to the Houghton Mifflin Company and Hamish Hamilton for permission to
reprint an excerpt from *Raymond Chandler Speaking*
(1962), edited by Dorothy Gardiner and Kathrine Sorley
Walker. Grateful acknowledgment is also made for permission to print unpublished material by Raymond
Chandler owned by Mrs. Helga Greene, executrix of the
Raymond Chandler estate.

FOR LYNN AND NICHOLAS

CONTENTS

The titles for chapters 5, 6, 8, 10 and 11 are taken from Raymond Chandler's list of possible titles for future work.

INTRODUCTION
AND
ACKNOWLEDGMENTS

The first thing I should like to say is that in this book I am treating Raymond Chandler as a novelist and not simply as a detective-story writer. This is how Chandler looked at himself, and with justice. Therefore, except for such references as are necessary about crime writing, and Chandler's relationship to it, the book contains no extended consideration of mystery writers past or present, aside from Chandler himself.

Insofar as possible, I have tried to let Chandler tell his own story and have quoted extensively from the hundreds of letters he wrote. In the notes at the back of the book I have cited the letters individually and have described their source and degree of reliability. In order to make the book as readable as possible, I have not indicated omissions in the passages quoted, but I have in no way distorted the author's intention. The only omissions made are passages that are irrelevant to the main purpose of the citation.

The origins of this book go back to 1961, when I was living in California. Someone said, "If you want to know what California is like, read Raymond Chandler." This I did and became an immediate enthusiast. The time was not then right for a biography of Chandler, but subsequently Mrs. Helga Greene, Chandler's heir and executrix, together with her son, Graham Carleton Greene, proposed that I write this book. Mrs. Greene gave me access to all the Chandler letters, papers, manuscripts, and photographs in her possession and let me borrow most of them while working on the book. She also spent a good deal of time talking to me and giving me such assistance as I needed. Her associate, Kathrine Sorley Walker, the coeditor of Raymond Chandler Speaking, was also most generous with her time. The book as it now stands simply could not have been written without their help.

Next, I wish to thank Chandler's English publishers, Hamish Hamilton and Roger Machell of Hamish Hamilton Ltd., for allowing me to keep at hand the file of Chandler's correspondence with them between 1939 and 1959. I also wish to thank my agent, Carl Brandt, for letting me keep the entire Chandler file from Brandt and Brandt, which includes an extensive correspondence between Chandler and his father and between Chandler and Bernice Baumgarten.

I wish to record my gratitude to the many institutions and the individuals in those institutions, where named, who helped me gather information about Chandler. In particular, I should like to thank the Administrator of National Banks in Washington; the records office of the Admiralty in London; the Alleyn Club and its secretary, Mr. T. E. Priest; the American Academy of Motion Picture Arts and Sciences; the Atlantic Monthly; the Bank of Montreal and its archivist, Mr. Freeman Clowery; Miss Pamela Döerr of Barclays Bank in San Francisco; the Mugar Library of Boston University; the British Museum; Miss Mary Esworthy of the Civil Service Commission; the Daily Express; Dulwich College and its librarian, Mr. Austin Hall; Houghton Mifflin and Company and in particular Mrs. Ellen Joseph, Mr. David Harris, and Mr. Austin Olney; the Houghton Library of Harvard University; Alfred Knopf, Inc., especially Mr. William Koshland; Miss Elfrieda Lang and Mr. William Cagle of the Lilly Library of Indiana University; the Ministry of Defence in London; the Air Historical Branch (RAF); the Information Service of the Ministry of National Defence in Ottawa; Mr. F. J. Dallett of the University of Pennsylvania Archives; the Public Archives of Canada; the Very Reverend Howard Lee Wilson, dean of St. Matthew's Cathedral in Laramie, Wyoming; the Screen Actors Guild; the Research Library of the University of California at Los Angeles and especially Miss Hilda Bohene and Messrs. James Mink and Brooke Whiting of the Department of Special Collections; Mr. David Farmer and the Humanities Research Center of the University of Texas; Universal City Studios, Inc.; Mr. Alan Rivkin and others on the staff of the Writers Guild; and Mrs. Judith Feiffer and Mr. Mort Lichter of Warner Brothers.

I should also like to thank the many individuals who took the trouble either to write to me about Raymond Chandler or to answer questions personally. I am especially indebted to Mrs. Vera Adams, Mrs. Ruth Babcock, Mrs. Kay West Bockott, Mrs. Nicolas Bentley, Miss Leigh Brackett, Mrs. Ruth A. Cutten, Miss Jean de Leon, Miss Dorothy Gardiner, Mrs. Jean Bethel (Erle Stanley) Gardner, Dr. Evelyn Hooker, Mrs. Juanita Messick, Mrs. Ruth Morse, Mrs. Marian Murray, Mrs. Sonia Orwell, Miss Dilys Powell, Miss Jocelyn Rickards, Mrs. Meta Rosenberg, Mrs. Hana M. Shaw, Mrs. Katherine Sistrom, Mrs. Stephen Spender, Mrs. Marjorie Suman, Miss Jessica Tyndale, Messrs. John McClelland Abrams, Eric Ambler, Dwight Babcock, W. T. Ballard, Nicolas Bentley, Walter Bruington, James M. Cain, Teet Carle, Edgar Carter, Whitfield Cook, George Harmon Coxe, Keith Deutsch, Ernest L. Dolley and Mrs. Dolley, Messrs. Patrick Doncaster, William Dozier, Philip Durham, William E. Durham, José Ferrer, Steve Fisher, James M. Fox, Frank Francis, Philip Gaskell, William Gault, Michael Gilbert, Maurice Guinness, E. T. Guymon, Jr., John Houseman, Christopher Isherwood, Jonathan Latimer, Gene Levitt, Dr. Paul F. Lloyd, Messrs. Daniel Mainwaring, Kenneth Millar, Robert Montgomery, Neil Morgan, E. Jack Neuman, Lloyd Nolan, Frank Norman, Sir Alwyne Ogden, Dr. Solon Palmer, Messrs. Eric Partridge, S. J. Perelman, George Peterson, Milton Philleo and Mrs. Philleo, Messrs. Robert Presnell, Jr., J. B. Priestley, Steve Race, James Sandoe, Joseph T. Shaw, Dr. Francis Smith, Messrs. H. Allen Smith, H. N. Swanson, Julian Symons, Cecil V. Thornton, Harry Tugend, Irving Wallace, Dale Warren, Hillary Waugh, Billy Wilder, Maxwell Wilkinson, Prentice Winchell, John Woolfenden, Leroy Wright and the late Sir P. G. Wodehouse.

Others have assisted me in a variety of ways, and I should like to thank the following for their courtesy and helpfulness: Mrs. D. Beach, Miss Patricia Blake, Mrs. Bernice Baumgarten Cozzens, Miss Patricia Highsmith, Miss Barbara Howes, Mrs. John Steinbeck, Messrs. Michael Avallone, Jacques Barzun, J. Frank Beaman, Harry Boardman, Carl Brandt, Richard S. Bright, Pliny Castanian, Howard Dattan, Commander A. R. Davis, Messrs. Michael Desilets, Digby Diehl, Osborn Elliott, John Engstead, Donald Gallup, Arnold Gingrich, Hercule Haussmann-Smith, Dan Hilman, Alfred Hitchcock, E. J. Kahn, Jr., Jascha Kessler, David Lehman, Clifford McCarty, Theodore Malquist, William F. Nolan, John Pearson, Ross Russell, Bernard Siegan, Ted Slate, Lovell Thompson, and Timothy Williams. I apologize to anyone whose name has been inadvertently omitted from this list.

I owe thanks to Robert and Susan Nero, who helped me in my researches in California, especially when I was unable to look up material myself. Their assistance was invaluable to me. I am also grateful to

Mr. James Neagles, who did some research for me in the National Archives in Washington.

Several books containing hitherto unpublished material by or about Chandler have already been published, and I am naturally indebted to them. I should like to mention in particular *Raymond Chandler Speaking*, edited by Dorothy Gardiner and Kathrine Sorley Walker (Hamish Hamilton and Houghton Mifflin, 1962). Matthew Bruccoli has edited two small but useful books: *Raymond Chandler, A Checklist* (Kent State University Press, 1968) and *Chandler Before Marlowe: Raymond Chandler's Early Prose and Poetry 1908–1912* (University of South Carolina Press, 1973). The pioneer study of Raymond Chandler's work is Philip Durham's *Down These Mean Streets a Man Must Go* (University of North Carolina Press, 1963): I am indebted to both the book and its author.

I wish also to thank Helga Greene, Kathrine Sorley Walker, Ursula Vaughan Williams, Seymour Lawrence, William Jay Smith, and my wife, Lynn, who read the typescript of this book in whole or part and who were kind enough to make suggestions for improvements and whose encouragement was most welcome. I want to record my indebtedness to my publishers as well: Graham Carleton Greene and John Macrae III.

Finally, I must thank the John Simon Guggenheim Foundation, whose fellowship made the book possible simply by giving me the time to write it.

Now at the end I must also pay homage to the landscape and ambiance of an Italian island where in peace and isolation I was able to complete the book. The experience there was almost magical, so I shall say no more about it, except to record it.

THE
LIFE
OF
RAYMOND
CHANDLER

1.

NEBRASKA
TO
DULWICH

———◆———

Two years before he died Raymond Chandler wrote to his London solicitor: "I have lived my life on the edge of nothing." He experienced life with great intensity, and this helped make him one of the finest novelists of his time, with an emotional range few of his contemporaries could approach. As the foremost exponent of the "tough guy" school of mystery writing, Chandler was also a romantic poet. During his lifetime he became world famous as a novelist, and the hero of his books, Philip Marlowe, was known to millions of readers. Yet the emotional sensitivity that made this literary achievement possible also made him miserable as a human being. The Welsh writer Jon Manchip White, who met Chandler at the Connaught Hotel in London, where he often stayed toward the end of his life, described him as "an exceedingly complex and obviously deeply unhappy man. There was no resignation in his character, and he was unable to accept the fact that none of us, and especially artists, ever find what we are looking for and must ultimately settle for what we have and are." Chandler was temperamentally incapable of this sort of acceptance. "I suppose all writers are crazy," he wrote, "but if they are any good, I believe they have a terrible honesty."

Chandler was honest in the way he perceived ordinary existence,

1

but he also had a sense of human possibilities and aspirations. He was in part a dreamer, a poet of the ideals of love and beauty and generosity. Because he was so aware of the gap between these two levels of reality, he suffered greatly. He was also torn by contradictory impulses, which he controlled as best he could by the exceptional orderliness of his mind. It is no surprise that this exponent of "hard-boiled" fiction lived a withdrawn and unusually private life. He was shy and retiring, suspicious of strangers and even hostile until he found out that he could trust them. On secure ground, he was charming and witty, as funny as his books. But like his fictional detective, he was usually on guard and at the same time quite aware of his own peculiarities. "I'm strictly the background type," he wrote Hamish Hamilton, his London publisher, in response to an invitation to a dinner party in his honor, "and my character is an unbecoming mixture of outer diffidence and inward arrogance."

Cynical enough to look on life as "today, a pat on the back; tomorrow, a kick in the teeth," he was also extraordinarily sentimental. Whatever he felt he felt passionately. It took him nearly fifty years to learn how to bring together the opposed impulses of his nature in a work of fiction, but when he finally did so he created works of lasting value and pleasure. At sixty-five he wrote: "I hope I have developed, but perhaps I have only grown tired and soft, but certainly not mellow. After all I have fifty per cent Irish blood."

He probably had more than that. His mother, Florence Thornton, was wholly Irish, having been born in Waterford, and his father, Maurice Benjamin Chandler of Philadelphia, also had Irish blood in his veins. He was descended from Quakers who came from Ireland to settle near Philadelphia in the seventeenth and eighteenth centuries. Earlier, during the Cromwellian period, the Chandlers had gone from England to Ireland, where many of the old estates were sold for a pittance to settlers, or Adventurers, as they were then called.

Maurice Chandler was born in 1859, and in 1880 he matriculated as a special student in engineering at the Towne Scientific School of the University of Pennsylvania. Maurice lived alone in boarding houses during his stay at the university, and the records contain no mention of his parents. After two years he obtained a certificate of proficiency from the Towne School but did not receive a university degree.

He then went to Chicago, where he worked for one of the Western railway companies, probably the Union Pacific. He moved back and forth along the line from Chicago. In Omaha, which at the time was a great railway center requiring the services of young engineers, he met Florence Dart Thornton, who had gone out from Ireland to nearby Plattsmouth, Nebraska, to stay with her sister Grace, who had married a man called Ernest Fitt. Chandler's friendship with Florence matured, and in 1887 they were married in Laramie, Wyoming, which was also on the Union Pacific line. The ceremony was performed at St. Matthew's Episcopal Church by the Reverend George Cornell, and the only witnesses were William and Nettie Comley, who were also transients in this frontier town where hardly a tree had been planted to soften the barrenness of the new wooden buildings.

Maurice and Florence Chandler set up housekeeping in Chicago, and there, on July 23, 1888, two days short of a year after their marriage, Raymond Thornton Chandler was born. "I was conceived in Laramie, Wyo.," Chandler later observed, "and if they had asked me, I should have preferred to be born there. I always like high altitudes, and Chicago is not a place where an Anglophile would choose to be born." With Maurice often away on business, Florence and her son spent the summers in Plattsmouth, where they stayed with the Fitts. Years later Chandler recalled some of his experiences there:

"I remember the oak trees and the high wooden sidewalks beside the dirt roads and the heat and the fireflies and walking-sticks and a lot of strange insects and the gathering of wild grapes in the fall to make wine and the dead cattle and once in a while a dead man floating down the muddy river and the dandy little three-hole privy behind the house. I remember Ak-Sar-Ben* and the days when they were still trying to elect Bryan. I remember the rocking chairs on the edge of the sidewalk in a solid row outside the hotel and the tobacco spit all over the place. And I remember a trial run on a rail car with a machine my uncle invented to take on mail without stopping, but somebody beat him out of it and he never got a dime."

Chandler also had a sharp eye for the people he encountered, including his uncle Ernest Fitt, who was "a minor politician—crooked, if I am any judge of character." Chandler recalled him as "a boiler inspector or something, at least in name. He used to come home in the evening (in the Plattsmouth period), put the paper on the music rack and improvise while he read it. My uncle had talent, but no musical education. He had a brother who was an amazing character. He had been a bank clerk or manager in a bank in Waterford, Ireland (where all my mother's people come from but none of them were Catholics), and had embezzled money. He cleaned out the till one Saturday and, with the help of the Masons, escaped the police net to the continent of Europe. In some hotel in Germany his money was stolen, or most of it. When I knew him, long after, he was an extremely respectable old party, always

* Ak-Sar-Ben—Nebraska spelled backward—is a middle-class social and philanthropical society.

immaculately dressed, and of incredible parsimony. He once invited me to dinner and to the Ak-Sar-Ben festivities. After dinner he leaned over and in a confidential whisper said: 'We'll each pay for our own.' Not a drop of Scotch blood anywhere either. Pure middle-class Protestant Irish."

Chandler never said much of his own childhood in America except that at the age of seven he had scarlet fever in a hotel. "I remember principally the ice cream and the pleasure of pulling the loose skin off during convalescence," he wrote. Perhaps his reticence comes from memories of discord between his mother and father. Often absent, his father also drank a good deal. In due course the inevitable separation and divorce took place. Chandler rarely spoke of his father except occasionally to call him "an utter swine." His complete disappearance from Chandler's life and his failure to provide support for his former wife and for his child made him reprehensible, and Chandler never forgave him for the burdens that were inevitably imposed on Florence.

Despite the family disruption, Chandler's memories of the Middle West reveal a certain delight in the modest and informal life of Platts-mouth. It was easygoing and relaxed, and at the same time a breeding ground for confidence tricksters. The Nebraska of Chandler's youth seems to have been a highly suitable preparation for the Los Angeles he eventually was to describe.

Following the divorce, Florence and her seven-year-old son sailed for England, where they moved into a house in Upper Norwood in the suburbs south of London, near the site of the Crystal Palace. The house had originally been provided by Chandler's uncle Ernest Thornton, a solicitor in Waterford, as a place where his mother might live after her husband's death. The home in Ireland had not been happy, for the family itself was not a happy one. "All the girls but one," Chandler later wrote, "were beauties and all but one (the same one) made poor mar-riages to get away from home." The one plain sister now lived alone with her mother in Upper Norwood, and neither one of them welcomed Florence and her child with much enthusiasm. In later years Chandler recalled the various petty humiliations imposed on his mother by her sister Ethel and by her own mother: at dinner time, sitting at the head of the table, Chandler's grandmother would offer wine to everyone except Florence. It was a way of reminding her of her dependent position, and perhaps also of her former husband.

Between them, Grandmother Annie and Aunt Ethel ran a strict household. South London had once been a fashionable section of the city, and some great houses were built there. But in time these properties were sold off into small lots and were developed in the nineteenth century as row houses of a dreary if respectable kind. The neighborhood had propriety but no style, and for a young boy straight from the casual atmosphere of Plattsmouth and Chicago, it must have been a shock. At first, sent to a local school and involved in the usual routine of childhood, he probably did not realize how profound a change had come upon his life, but it did not take long to be felt. Living in a matriarchal household, he could never fully relax. He was the man of the house. No one stood behind him; there was no one to guide him in the way that only fathers can. Forced into a position of responsibility long before he was capable of accepting it, he became aware of how alone he was. Abandoned by his father, he developed an extraordinary sense of loyalty to his mother, and a sense of justice that became a central part of his character and gave him the attitudes he was to express later through his character Philip Marlowe.

During the summer holidays Chandler and his mother would visit Waterford, where Uncle Ernest presided over the family business of I. Thornton and Son, Solicitors and Notaries Public, with offices in Cathedral Square, Waterford, as well as in Dublin. Uncle Ernest despised the law but felt obliged to carry on the firm, a mistaken attitude that led to much of the tension in the Thornton family. "What godawful snobs!" Chandler exclaimed about them in later years. "My grandmother referred to one of the nicest families we knew as 'very respectable people' because there were two sons, five golden-haired but unmarriageable daughters and no servant. They were driven to the utter humiliation of opening their own front door. The father painted, sang tenor, built beautiful model yachts and sailed a small yawl all over the place." Compared to this genial confusion, the Thornton household bristled with hostility and self-consciousness. The housekeeper, Miss Groome, sneered at Uncle Ernest behind his desk because he was not a barrister but only a solicitor. For her, there were but four professions—the Church, the Army, the Navy, and the Bar. But Miss Groome also suffered. As Chandler noted: "Outside Waterford in a big house with gardens and gardens lived a Miss Paul who occasionally, *very* occasionally invited Miss Groome to tea on account of her father had been a canon. Miss Groome regarded this as the supreme accolade because Miss Paul was County. It didn't seem to bother Miss Paul but it sure as hell made a wreck of Miss Groome.

"It would be some comfort to add that she was a capable housekeeper, but she was not. My uncle had a succession of awful Irish Protestant maids and cooks and so on—always Protestants, as they and the Catholics had little or nothing to do with one another on any level. I remember playing in a cricket match with one of my cousins and one of the boys was a Catholic from some probably rather important family. Anyhow he came in a carriage with a coachman and footman and after the game immediately departed without even having tea with the teams. My uncle was a man of rather evil temper on occasion. Sometimes when the dinner did not suit him he would order it removed and we would sit in stony silence for three quarters of an hour while the frantic Miss Groome browbeat the domestics belowstairs and finally another meal was delivered to the master, probably much worse than the one he had refused; but I can still feel that silence."

Chandler's Irish experiences marked him for life. He was an American, a boy whose father had gone to the bad, but his background also gave him a sharp eye for social distinctions and the effect of the Anglo-Irish class system. His American sense of freedom made him ridicule the rigidities of his relatives, but he was by no means free of snobbery himself. He did not like to be referred to as Irish-American, because that usually meant Catholic and working class. In discussing the matter later with his publisher, Blanche Knopf, he explained that "professional classes in Southern Ireland are and always have been largely non-Catholic. Those few Irish patriots who have had brains as well as spite have also been non-Catholics. I should not like to say that in Ireland Catholicism reached its all-time low of ignorance, dirt, and general degradation of the priesthood, but in my boyhood it was bad enough."

Chandler's attitude toward Ireland and the Catholics in particular reveals his way of thinking—the intensity of his feelings and at the same time his awareness of himself. "I grew up with a terrible contempt for Catholics, and I have trouble with it even now," he once observed. But he also kept his eyes open in observing the Anglo-Irish and the Catholics among whom they lived. Of these he wrote: "It does the Irish great credit that out of this flannel-mouthed mob of petty liars and drunkards there has come no real persecution of the non-Catholic elements."

At issue was not religion but class and education. Churchgoing was a part of the weekly routine, and Chandler remembered that he had been an acolyte and was confirmed by the Bishop of Worcester. "As a young man," he wrote, "I was very high church and very devout. But," he added, "I was cursed with an analytical mind."

By 1900 the Thornton-Chandler household moved to a house called Whitfield Lodge at 77 Alleyn Park in Dulwich. The building no longer stands, for it was bombed in World War II, but it must have been substantial, since it served for five years as the premises of the Dulwich College Preparatory School. The move to Dulwich was probably made so that Chandler could attend the college, which was only a short distance away, across the playing fields from his house. By the end of the nineteenth century Dulwich had begun to emerge as one of the better Public Schools in England. In 1870 a large block of new buildings constructed in Victorian Gothic was opened by the Prince of Wales half a mile from the old school, which had been founded in 1617 by Edward Alleyn, an Elizabethan theater manager and courtier. Alleyn had bought a 1,500-acre valley called Dulwich Manor, and as he was a religious man he established a foundation called the College of God's Gift in thanks for his good fortune. For some 250 years Dulwich was an obscure village school, but under A. H. Gilkes, who was headmaster for nearly thirty years, including the years Chandler spent there, it increased in numbers and stature. Socially Dulwich was not, as Chandler himself recalled, "quite out of the top drawer as public schools go," and was not in the same class as Eton, Winchester, and Harrow. Academically, however, it was sound, winning more than its share of Oxford and Cambridge scholarships and introducing educational reforms such as courses of study in engineering and commerce, which were thought to be useful for the predominantly middle-class boys who attended it.

In the autumn of 1900 Chandler entered the First Form of Dulwich and was given his school number, 5724. Like all the other boys, he wore a black coat and waistcoat, a dark blue and black tie representing the school colors, and an Eton collar. Matriculating in the autumn term, he had a school cap which he replaced in warmer weather in the spring with a straw boater. Chandler was one of twenty-eight boys in his form, and at the end of the term he placed second among them. In addition to mathematics and music, which he took under special masters, he was taught Latin, French, divinity, and what were called English subjects. These included the history of England from William the Conqueror to King John and a study of Lawson's *Geography of the British Isles*. During the spring term, in the Upper Second, he maintained his position in the form and kept to much the same curriculum he had begun with.

In the autumn and winter afternoons Chandler played Rugby; in the spring, cricket. As a day boy he was less intimately involved with school life than the boarders were, but he undoubtedly watched the school matches and attended the Christmas concert in the Great Hall, where Mendelssohn's *Elijah* was performed, as Dulwich was renowned for its musical activities. Chandler was probably too young to belong to the School Corps, which gave basic military training to half the boys under the guidance of a retired sergeant major from the Grenadier Guards, but he must surely have turned out with all the other boys to greet Lord Roberts, the hero of the South African war, when he paused at the school in May on his way to visit the Crystal Palace.

There are now few people alive who were at Dulwich with Chandler, and only one of these remembers him. Sir Alwyne Ogden, a form mate, recalls that Chandler always insisted on using his first name, Raymond, in the American way, rather than his initials, R. T., as is the English custom. Also, he carried a small notebook with him in which he would jot down items of interest as they occurred to him. Sir Alwyne never discovered what use this information was put to but surmised that it revealed a thirst for knowledge.

During his second year at Dulwich, Chandler switched over to what was called the Modern Side, a course of study that was planned, in the words of the school's announcement, for "boys who are intended for business." This course of study did not prepare one for the university but had more practical purposes. The classics were dropped, and in their place came instruction in French, German, and Spanish, with an emphasis on conversation and correspondence. In their final years boys enrolled in the Modern Side would take courses in political economy, commercial history, and geography. Here Chandler maintained and even improved his performance and was ranked at the top of his form, the Modern Upper Third. He won a prize for general achievement and also a special prize in mathematics.

By the spring of 1903 Chandler had changed back over to the Classical Side. His form ranking does not appear in the Dulwich records, which suggests that he may have had to make up work in Latin and Greek in order to qualify. He may also have been ill, for he was a somewhat sickly child, subject more than most to childhood ailments. He suffered a number of attacks of follicular tonsillitis, which would sometimes take as long as three weeks to cure. Chandler seems to have been a highstrung and somewhat nervous boy, studious, energetic, and somewhat impulsive. In sports, for example, as he later recalled, "I played rugger a bit, but was never first chop, because temperamentally I was the furious type of Irish forward and didn't have the physique to back it up. I never weighed more than about ten stone in those days, and you have to be made of steel springs at that weight to survive." It was the same with cricket; he bowled a fair offbreak but admitted that he "didn't have the control."

Chandler's third year was a memorable one for the school. The new library, built in honor of old boys who had lost their lives in the South African war, was opened. The college was also exceptionally successful in football, even defeating Merton College, Oxford, and playing two victorious matches against L'École Albert le Grand—one in Paris, the other in Dulwich. Finally, on Founder's Day, the headmaster was able to announce that Dulwich boys had won seventeen scholarships to Oxford and Cambridge, rather more than usual.

Chandler stayed in the Lower Fifth during the autumn term of 1903 and proceeded to the Upper Fifth in the following spring. In each he showed his capabilities in the classics, for he was respectively first and second in his form. Aside from mathematics and German, which he carried over from the Modern Side, he read, in Latin, Caesar, Livy, Ovid, and parts of Vergil's *Aeneid;* in Greek, Thucydides, Plato, and Aristophanes; in divinity, the Gospel of St. Mark (also in Greek) as well as some lectures in theology; in French, various grammar exercises and Alfred de Vigny's *Cinq-Mars;* in English, Shakespeare's *Henry V,* Addison's *Spectator Papers,* Milton's *Comus,* and some of his essays, and Roman history, in particular accounts of the Second Punic War and the Macedonian and Syrian wars.

During his last year at Dulwich, Chandler was in a form called the Remove, intended for boys not proceeding to the university, and his form master was H. F. Hose, a man who taught at Dulwich for thirty-five years. Again Chandler was not placed in the form list, which suggests that he may have suffered from periods of illness. The school records show that Chandler left Dulwich in April of 1905, in accordance with the family decision to send him abroad for further studies in foreign languages.

Chandler had great respect for the education he received at Dulwich, especially his training in the classics. Like others in the school, he was also affected by the atmosphere of the place. The headmaster, Gilkes, whose influence was unusually pervasive, believed that literature was a source of moral instruction. "Cicero," he told the boys, "had a large plant of conceit growing in his heart, and he watered it every day." Gilkes hated self-assertiveness, and he was painfully upright. The boys invented a personal motto for him: *Magna est veritas et praevalebit.* For Gilkes and generations of Public School masters, the subjects taught were part of a moral order, which was basically Christian with an infusion of Greek and Roman virtues, especially public service, honor, and self-sacrifice. The Bible and the classics illustrated these virtues, and the Public School gentleman was someone who lived by a code embodying them. Manliness meant forgetfulness of self: as Gilkes put it, a man of honor is one who is "capable of understanding that which was good; capable of subordinating the poorer part of his nature to the higher part." This code, familiar to generations of middle- and upper-class families who attended Public Schools in England, certainly affected Chandler. It helped mold his own character, and, transplanted to America, it helps explain the behavior of Philip Marlowe, Chandler's fictional hero.

The moral tone of schools such as Dulwich did not preclude aesthetic concerns. Indeed, Gilkes was unusual among headmasters for his passion for English literature and for being a published novelist. He would often read one of his favorite passages to the boys and then ask them whether they liked it and why. The boys sometimes thought this instruction useless, since it had nothing to do with examinations; but later most realized they were learning something fundamental. Gilkes was also a stickler for clear prose. He would require essays of his students and then go over them, sentence by sentence, making them cast out unnecessary adjectives and break up long, involved sentences. Another common exercise in the mastery of language used widely at Dulwich was to have the boys translate, say, a passage from Cicero and then, a week or so later, put their English versions back into Latin.

Whether Chandler was influenced by Gilkes to any degree is unknown. P. G. Wodehouse, who preceded him there by a few years, doubted it and denied any on himself. Certainly Chandler showed no signs of literary ability while he was at the school. Nevertheless, the training he received there definitely affected him, as he acknowledged. "I am not only literate but intellectual, much as I dislike the term," he wrote. "It would seem that a classical education might be rather a poor basis for writing novels in a hard-boiled vernacular. I happen to think otherwise. A classical education saves you from being fooled by pretentiousness, which is what most current fiction is too full of." Having spent his time at Dulwich reading dead languages wholly lacking in immediate practicality, he was able to look at later literary fads with some skepticism. "In this country," he wrote of the United States, "the mystery writer is looked down upon as sub-literary merely because he is a mystery writer rather than, for instance, a writer of social-significance twaddle. To a classicist—even a very rusty one—such an attitude is merely a parvenu insecurity." Yet there was also a practical result. When he first read Chandler, J. B. Priestley noted: "They don't write like that at Dulwich." To that, Chandler commented: "That may be, but if I hadn't grown up on Latin and Greek, I doubt if I would know so well how to draw the line between what I call a vernacular style and what I should call an illiterate or faux naïf style. That's a hell of a lot of difference, to my mind."

If Chandler's intellectual attainment is there for all to see, what his private life was like, living alone in a household of women with no older men, is hard to know. John Houseman, who knew Chandler in Hollywood in the 1940s and who went to a similar Public School, Clifton, thought that "the English Public School system which he loved had left its sexually devastating mark upon him. The presence of young women —secretaries and young women around the lot—disturbed and excited him. His voice was normally muted; it was in a husky whisper that he uttered those juvenile obscenities at which he would have been the first to take offense, if they had been spoken by others." Yet Chandler in the 1940s was not the same young man who was a schoolboy at Dulwich. Even as a child he was precocious: "Very young I belonged to a neighborhood gang (not criminal in any way) and found myself paired up with a nice little girl, whom I used to undress up to a point, purely out of curiosity, and she rather expected it. I also used to take down the drawers of a cousin of mine in Nebraska, about my age, and since her four year-old brother was with us, we used to take down his pants just to get him into the act and make him feel he was not excluded. The curious thing, as it seems to me now, was that I wasn't in the least interested (so far as I knew) in her genital organs, but only in her nice firm round backside. I suppose it was a dawning sex feeling in a way, but it never appeared to me as anything but naughty and rather nice. I think I was a strange boy in many ways, because I had an enormous personal pride. I never masturbated, thinking it dirty. (I had plenty of wet dreams, however.) The headmaster, who ran the pre-confirmation interviews, clearly, to me, never believed that I had never masturbated, because practically all the boys did. I got hold somehow of a curious idea, must have read or heard it somewhere. 'When you do that, you think you are holding in your arms a beautiful and unattainable woman. When you get one really, you will find it very disappointing.' "

Chandler's self-control, or the "personal pride" he mentions, may have come partly from the sort of ignorant notion about masturbation that he cites. Another source was probably his solitary position as the only responsible male in the Thornton-Chandler household. He could not take risks: he had his mother to look after as soon as he was able, and in a way he almost had to be his own father. He did not fill himself with sexual fantasies partly because of this sense of duty and partly because of his ignorance and fear. "When I was about sixteen," he wrote, "I had an infatuation for a girl, but was too shy even to speak to her about it. I used to write letters to her. It would have been an ecstasy to hold her hand. A kiss would have been almost unthinkable." Sublimation seems to have been the answer, a common solution for Public School boys at the end of Victoria's reign—children who had also been assiduously taught the virtues of self-denial.

Dulwich affected Chandler far more deeply than it normally would a man of his intelligence. The Public School code, which is now so widely derided for inhibiting the natural development of the whole person, was an element of stability in Chandler's life, mainly because he spent most of it in the formless world of California, where anything goes. In the rigidly class-structured society of England, its influence was more complex. Dulwich certainly made him a snob as far as the Irish were concerned. One rich family near Waterford he described in this way: "Later on when I was about seventeen, I think, I was invited over to their house to play tennis. They were rather gaudy people, except the father. A number of the guests were very young girls and young men, all expensively dressed, and several rather drunk. I was in no way expensively dressed, but far from feeling inferior I realised at once that these people were not at all up to the standard even of Dulwich, and heaven knows what Eton and Rugby would have thought about them. The boys and girls had gone to private schools, but not the right kind. There was a little something about their accents, and more than a little about their manners. (One sicked up in the drawing room.) During the course of an afternoon of rather studied courtesy on my part the family dog chewed up my straw hat with the school ribbon on it. When I left, the head of the family, a very nice little man in some kind of 'trade' in the City, insisted on paying for the hat. I coldly refused to accept his money, although in those times it was quite usual for the host to tip a schoolboy at the end of a visit. But this seemed to me different. This was taking money from a social inferior: not to be thought of. Yet they were kind people and full of fun and very tolerant and, as I look back on it now, probably much more worth knowing than my stupid and arrogant grandmother."

Like all snobbery, Chandler's youthful attitude reveals an insecurity about himself and his future. His uncle had the sense to send Chandler to Dulwich, and he was the only Thornton relative to attend an English Public School. There he acquired the intellectual equipment with which to judge the nature of English society and to prosper in it. But what frustrated Chandler was that he could not advance any further. He had performed well enough at Dulwich to go on to one of the universities, as the leading boys on the Classical Side normally did. But there was no money. When he left Dulwich he wanted to become a barrister, but Uncle Ernest had no intention of paying the necessary fees for training in law at Oxford or Cambridge and for the additional preparatory work in one of the Inns of Court. Instead the family decided that he would go into the civil service, where it was believed he would eventually fashion a respectable career, and where the values he had learned at Dulwich would keep him comfortable and undisturbed.

Chandler seems to have taken the decision without much fuss. University training was not widespread, even among those who had attended Public Schools, and there was the glamorous prospect of a year's living in France and Germany in preparation for the civil service examinations. "I was a bit passive about the whole thing," he wrote later, "since I wanted to be a writer and that would not have gone down at all, especially with my rich and tyrannical uncle."

Chandler was only seventeen when he reached Paris for the first time. Intellectually, he was well equipped, for he had done well in French and German at school, but he was probably more innocent than most young Englishmen crossing the Channel alone for the first time. He put

up at the Pension Marjollet at 27 Boulevard St. Michel. He was near the
Musée Cluny and the intersection of the Boulevard St. Germain, not far
from the Sorbonne, the Ile de la Cité, and Notre Dame. He enrolled in a
business college and concentrated on learning commercial French. He
was enough of a rebel, however, to imagine himself a comparative
philologist, and on his own he dabbled in such recherché languages as
modern Greek, Armenian, and Hungarian. Over his bed at the pension
he also kept a chart of the 214 key ideographs of Mandarin Chinese.

Like any other young man in Paris for the first time, he explored
the city from Montparnasse to Montmartre, but his inhibitions and the
habits of suburban London prevented him from enjoying himself as he
might have done. "During my year in Paris," he later wrote, "I had run
into a good many Americans, and most of them seemed to have a lot of
bounce and liveliness and to be thoroughly enjoying themselves in
situations where the average Englishman of the same class would be
stuffy or completely bored. But I wasn't one of them. I didn't even speak
their language. I was, in effect, a man without a country." Undoubtedly
Chandler visited Smith's English Bookshop in the Rue de Rivoli and read
as widely in French literature as he could, but his stay appears to have
lacked the verve charactertistic of a later generation of Americans in
Paris. "When I was a young man and very innocent," he wrote, "I lived
in a pension on the Boul' Miche and was very happy wandering around,
with very little money, but a sort of starry-eyed love of everything I
saw. The only thing that upset me was the whores at the door of the
apartment building if I happened to be out a little late. And I was so
innocent that I didn't realise that there were two girls at the pension that
couldn't keep their feet off mine and were offering themselves to my
innocence and I never knew it."

Chandler always had great respect for the French but little personal
feeling for them. He realized that "you didn't exactly have to like the
French to be at home in Paris"; but given Chandler's sense of intellectual
competence, it probably irritated him that he could never completely
master the language. "French one never speaks well enough to satisfy a
Frenchman. *Il sait se faire comprendre* is about as far as they will go,"
he remarked years later.

After completing his course in Paris, Chandler moved to Germany,
which he seems to have preferred, perhaps because he was working with
a tutor rather than attending a school, and also because at the time his
German was better than his French. He settled in Munich for the most
part but also visited Nuremberg and Vienna. "I did like the Germans
very much," he later wrote, "that is, the South Germans. But there
wasn't much sense living in Germany, since it was an open secret,

openly discussed, that we would be at war with them almost any time now. I suppose it was the most inevitable of all wars. There was never any question about whether it would happen. The only question was when."

In the spring of 1907 he returned to England and once again took up suburban life in South London. He called on his old schoolmaster, H. F. Hose, who helped him prepare for the civil service examination. On May 20, 1907, he was naturalized a British subject in order to be eligible for a position in the civil service. It was easily arranged, for, as Chandler later wrote, there was a law which stated that "the British-born widow of a foreigner, after five years residence in the U.K., regained her British nationality automatically, and that her minor children became of the same nationality." Of course at the time there was no mention of divorce. "So the Home Office, after a rather perfunctory investigation, simply handed me a Naturalisation certificate. I made no court appearance, had no interview with any official except a brief talk with a Scotland Yard detective, but I had to swear an oath of allegiance to the British, which I did before a family friend who was a J.P."

This act caused Chandler considerable trouble later in his life, but for the moment it enabled him to sit for a special civil service examination being held for openings in the Supply and Accounting Departments of the Admiralty. These appointments were made outside of the usual Class I and Class II civil service clerkships, but were open competitions of the same sort. In addition to the special language qualifications Chandler had fulfilled abroad, they required mastery of a considerable body of knowledge. The examinations took place in June of 1907 and took six days to complete. Chandler was examined in mathematics, English, German, Greek, English history, and French, and he placed third among the six hundred candidates and first in the examinations in the classics.

By 1907 Chandler's mother had moved to 35 Mount Nod Road in Streatham, a less attractive part of suburban South London than Dulwich. The move was brought about by the death of Chandler's grandmother, which meant that the larger house was no longer necessary. The Streatham building, a three-story red brick structure, had a small front garden and shade trees. It appears to have been intended from the beginning as a small block of flats, as there are six separate entrances. Mount Nod Road is an attractive street with a number of individual and semidetached houses set back from the tree-lined road. But the brutality of lower-middle and working-class suburbia becomes apparent as soon as you turn the corner into Hailsham Avenue, a treeless stretch of row cottages that leads down to the High Road and Streatham Hill Station. It is not likely that in 1907 the shops along the High Road were any less dismal than they are today, and this was the landscape that Chandler passed through daily as he went up to the West End.

His work at the Admiralty began early that year. According to the Imperial Calendar, R. T. Chandler was employed under the Controller of the Navy as Assistant Store Officer, Naval Stores Branch. The job was clerical and involved keeping records of the transfer of naval supplies and ammunition from the depots to the fleet stations. Chandler's ability with figures and his concern for accuracy, which were characteristic of him for the rest of his life, indicate not only an orderliness of mind but also a desire to establish control over his world. This was only natural, since up to this time he had really no say in what happened to him. It was also a sign of the mental discipline with which he kept his emotions under control.

Once installed in the Admiralty, Chandler began to realize what a mistake he had made. As a young man with no very clearly articulated ideas, he had gone along with Uncle Ernest's plan because he thought he could turn the job into something else. "I wanted to be a writer," he later explained, "but I knew my Irish uncle would not stand for that, so I thought perhaps that the easy hours in the Civil Service might let me do that on the side." But the job was utterly dull, and the main office passion was a bitter struggle against the use of carbon paper, which was then being introduced. But the real problem was social. "I could have had a life-long and perfectly safe job with six weeks' vacation and ridiculously easy hours," he later wrote. "And yet I thoroughly detested the civil service. I had too much Irish in my blood to stand being pushed around by suburban nobodies. The idea of being expected to tip my hat to the head of the department struck me as verging on the obscene." After six months in the Admiralty, Chandler resigned from the civil service, an act that enraged his uncle and appalled nearly everybody connected with him.

He had by this time discovered some of his old friends. He joined the Alleyn Club, the old-boys society of Dulwich, and even did some substitute teaching at the college from time to time. His mother's apartment in Streatham was convenient to his school friends, but undoubtedly the stiff collar and bowler hat, the morning and evening train rides into Charing Cross or Victoria, were constricting for a man of Chandler's temperament. After leaving the Admiralty, he said that he "holed up in Bloomsbury."

Chandler had begun his literary career the year before as a poet. "My first poem," he later wrote, "was composed at the age of nineteen, on a Sunday, in the bathroom, and was published in Chamber's Journal. I am fortunate in not possessing a copy." We are less fortunate. Here is the opening stanza of "The Unknown Love":

> When the evening sun is slanting,
> When the crickets raise their chanting,
> And the dewdrops lie a-twinkling on the grass,
> As I climb the pathway slowly,
> With a mien half proud, half lowly,
> O'er the ground your feet have trod I gently pass.

Seven stanzas later the poem ends:

> When the last great trump has sounded,
> When life's barque the point has rounded,
> When the wheel of human progress is at rest,
> My belovèd, may I meet you,
> With a lover's kiss to greet you,
> Where you wait me in the gardens of the blest!

Here, to paraphrase J. B. Priestley, is how they did write at Dulwich —and in dozens of literary papers and magazines in Edwardian England. The less said of Chandler's early poems the better, except to note the deep strain of romanticism they contain. The twenty-seven poems he published between 1908 and 1912, all but one of them in the *Westminster Gazette*, are cloying and saccharine. Whether intended or not, they are conventional in the worst sense. They are full of sadly noble subjects and sentiments like death, fairyland, melancholy, art, and meditation. As for many late Victorians and Edwardians, poetry for Chandler was an escape from the reality of daily life. It was a world populated by knights and ladies who achieve happiness only in death. These poems reveal a yearning for something higher, something that engages the soul more vividly than shifting naval stores or taking the 5:10 to Streatham Hill Station.

Chandler seems to have been quite unaware of the literary revolution underway in England at the time he began to write, represented by the work of Pound, Wells, Ford, Yeats, Lewis, Lawrence, Conrad, and even Hardy and James from an earlier generation. The literary taste of Dulwich, which presumably formed his own, was that of the old guard, and Chandler chose to write in this tradition, apparently without any sense of dissatisfaction. Undoubtedly he read the more "substantial" magazines—the *Academy*, the *Athenaeum*, and the *Saturday Review*. These papers were still influential though literarily moribund, but Chandler does not seem to have known or cared about that. Moreover, Chandler's introduction to writing was journalistic rather than literary.

Having given up the Admiralty, he had to secure some other means of support. First he worked as a reporter for the *Daily Express*. "I was a complete flop, the worst man they ever had," he admitted years later. "Every time they sent me out on a story I would get lost. They fired me. I deserved it." From there he moved to the *Westminster Gazette*, then edited by J. A. Spender and the best evening paper in London. Chandler got the job through the intercession of a friend of his uncle's, "a wonderful old boy named Roland Ponsonby Blennerhasset, a barrister with a House of Lords practice, a wealthy Irish landowner (he owned some fabulous number of acres in Kerry), a member, as I understand from my uncle in Waterford, of one of those ancient untitled families that make earls and marquesses appear quite parvenu."

The *Westminster Gazette* was a leading Liberal paper, and next to the *Times* was probably the most respected and widely quoted English journal. Aside from the leading article, which appeared on the first page, the paper was put together in the helter-skelter fashion typical of English and American newspapers of the time. The paper published news reports from all over the world, but with its book reviews, poetry columns, feature stories, satirical articles, and cartoons by the famous F C Gould, it was rather like a daily magazine. Spender employed Chandler as a general reporter on European affairs and put him up for the National Liberal Club so that he could browse through the French and German papers in search of "odd paragraphs and news items which could be translated and adapted for a column the *Westminster Gazette* ran." Chandler later recalled that Spender "was the first editor who ever showed me any kindness," but his prediction that Chandler would soon be earning six guineas a week was exaggerated. In fact he rarely made more than three. He would send in his work, and the paper would either return it or send him proof. "I never corrected the proof," Chandler recalled, "didn't even know whether I was expected to. I simply took it as a convenient form of acceptance. I never waited for them to send me the money but appeared regularly on a certain day each week at their cashier's office and received payment in gold and silver, being required to affix a penny stamp in a large book and sign my name across it by way of receipt."

Since most of Chandler's contributions to the *Westminster Gazette* were anonymous, it is impossible to know how long he continued with them or how much he published there. Chandler wrote that, in addition to items for anonymous columns, he contributed a considerable number of poems, "most of which now seem to me deplorable," as well as "sketches, most of a satirical nature—the sort of thing that Saki did so infinitely better." The link with Saki (H. H. Munro) is important, because he was Spender's most famous contributor. Saki was also an early model for Chandler, one from whom he eventually had to escape, making an extraordinary leap from the turn-of-the-century prose of Saki's

London to the vernacular of 1930s Los Angeles without stopping anywhere in between. In the meantime, Saki probably helped Chandler
realize the importance of writing for the wide and unselective audience
of a newspaper rather than for the little magazines of the avant garde.
Saki's humorous and satirical tone was also obviously influential.

With inadequate income from the *Westminster Gazette*, Chandler
had to turn elsewhere, often in a surprisingly enterprising fashion. "I
suppose I have told you of the time I wrote to Sir George Newnes," he
recalled in a letter to Hamish Hamilton, "and offered to buy a piece of
his trashy but successful weekly magazine called *Tit-Bits*. I was received
most courteously by a secretary, definitely public school, who regretted
that the publication was not in need of capital, but said that my approach had at least the merit of originality. By the same device I did
actually make a connection with *The Academy*, then edited and owned
by a man named Cowper, who had bought it from Lord Alfred Douglas.
He was not disposed to sell an interest in his magazine, but pointed to a
large shelf of books in his office and said they were review copies and
would I care to take a few home to review. I wonder why he did not
rather have me thrown down his murky stairs; perhaps because there
was no one in the office who could do it, since his entire editorial staff
seemed to consist of one placid middle-aged lady and a mousy little man,
named Vizetelly, who was (I believe) the brother of another and more
famous Vizetelly—the one who was arrested in New York in connection
with an obscenity complaint over the American publication of *Madame
Bovary*."

The *Academy* was less political than the *Westminster Gazette*. It
was a literary weekly that featured general essays, book reviews, travel
articles, and long biographical pieces. Frank Harris, Hilaire Belloc, and
Arthur Machen were contributors, but under Cecil Cowper's direction
the paper was traditional in outlook and noncontroversial. Cowper himself stayed in the background, and most of the articles were unsigned.
During Chandler's time the most forceful contributor was Richard Middleton, who uttered such sentiments as these: "There are two kinds of
poetry, good and bad. Minor poetry is a phrase used by incompetent
critics who dare not oppose their judgment to the possible contradiction
of posterity." Chandler later remembered Middleton as a "tall, bearded,
and sad-eyed man" who, shortly after they met, "committed suicide in
Antwerp, a suicide of despair, I should say."

In 1911 and 1912 Chandler published twelve articles and reviews in
the *Academy*, and for the most part they reveal the sharp critical side of
his nature, so different from the tone of his dreamy verses. The first
article, "The Genteel Artist," was signed but was accompanied by an

editorial caveat: "We much admire the satire of our esteemed contributor but in the opinion of some his salad may be thought to be a little
too sharp—we wonder."

In his essays for the *Academy* Chandler seemed to be preoccupied
with literature and the career of writing. His first essays deal with
realism and with the way writers approach their material: he has two
scornful articles entitled "The Literary Fop" and "The Phrasemaker."
Looking over these pieces in later years, Chandler rightly noticed that
"they are of an intolerable preciousness of style, but already quite nasty
in tone." Noting that he rarely got the best books to review, he added:
"Like all young nincompoops I found it very easy to be clever and
snotty, very hard to praise without being ingenuous."

Nevertheless, it is evident that Chandler was trying to work out his
own position as a writer. His main concern was that a writer must have
something to say, a vision worth expressing. In an essay called "Realism
and Fairyland" he attacked scientific realism: "Of all forms of art
realism is the easiest to practice, because of all forms of mind the dull
mind is commonest." He believed that scientific inquiry and its results
do not touch the inner person. Science seems to solve problems but only
changes the circumstances. For Chandler, the subject should never control the author (as in social realism), but the writer the subject. Therefore the only writers who matter are idealists rather than realists,
because "they exalt the sordid to a vision of magic; and create pure
beauty out of plaster and vile dust."

The idealistic view, according to Chandler, deals with human possibility; it does not merely record facts as in a sociological catalog. One of
his essays deals with old houses, abandoned in the suburbs during bad
times. He describes the dilapidated mansions, the cobwebbed windows,
the gate hanging from a single hinge, the tangle of overgrown rose
bushes. "The effect," he concludes, "is like that of a fine etching, colour-
less but full of suggestion, with a faint flavour of the sordid—but it is
the romance of sordidness."

Here is the origin of Chandler's Los Angeles. The essay is not
unrealistic in the sense of failing to record unpleasant phenomena, but it
records them so that the reader can feel them emotionally, in terms of
human joy and sorrow. This is the poet's vision and is central to
Chandler's aesthetic and moral stance as a writer.

At this early point in his life Chandler was unable to express his
literary intentions. Whenever he tried to in his poetry, he produced
impossibly sentimental verses, for the idealist's great trap is sentimentalism. In his one published story of this period, "The Rose-Leaf Romance," which is really more tale than short story, ending with a Saki-

like surprise, he is too literary and self-conscious to be successful. He uses sarcasm, the antidote to sentimentalism, too freely, and the story is unconvincing.

Chandler understood the need for a literary vision, but he did not have one himself. There was little use pretending he was a successful young writer. He was depressed by Richard Middleton's suicide because the man had been so talented: "If he couldn't make a go of it, it wasn't likely that I could." Looking about him in London, Chandler observed that "there were clever young men who made a decent living as free lances for the numerous literary weeklies and in the more literary departments of the daily papers. But most of the people who did this work either had private income or jobs, especially in the civil service." But Chandler had thrown up his job and had no money of his own. He was trained and educated, but there was nothing for him to do that engaged his interest or gave him necessary support. The relative success of others also rankled, and he began to think of himself as a failure. "I had the qualifications to become a pretty good second-rate poet," he wrote years later, "but that means nothing because I have the type of mind that can become a pretty good second-rate anything, and without much effort."

The prospect was grim. He may have had a room in Bloomsbury, but he probably also lived with his mother, who by 1909 had moved to 148 Devonshire Road, S.E., in Forest Hill. This was a semidetached house up a long street that rises gradually from the village and over-looks a railway line in the back. Forest Hill is pleasanter than Streatham, and closer to Dulwich, but Chandler cannot have been much cheered by the atmosphere. In an essay called "Houses to Let" he speaks of "the paramount *bourgeois* spirit, seeing through front windows the inevitable delft bowl on a *table d' occasion*, the outline of laboured family portraits, the most recent improvements in gas fittings or electric light shining hardly on those clean, smug bookcases, which seem to cry aloud that they have as little as possible to do with literature or learning."

To make things worse, there seems to have been a girl and a love frustrated by his failure. This is only conjectural, and it is notoriously dangerous to base biographical assumptions on works of the imagination. Nevertheless, there is a poem written in 1932, just as he was beginning to write the stories that led to his ultimate success. Called "Nocturne from Nowhere," it is thematically central to his fiction and also seems to have had basis in fact. The poem, written in free verse, describes a nighttime revery

> *In which mingle visions of a woman*
> *I once loved*

> With the visions of a country I have loved
> Almost as well.

There are revisions which are impossible to decipher, but the key lines
are these:

> There are no countries as beautiful
> As the England I picture in the night hours
> Of this bright and dismal land
> Of my exile and dismay.
> There are no women as tender as this woman
> Whose cornflower-blue eyes look at me
> With the magic of frustration
> And the promise of an impossible paradise.
>
> . . . . .
>
> So for a little while in the night hours
> Let me go back
> Into that soft and gorgeous future
> Which is not past,
> Never having happened,
> But yet is utterly lost—
>
> . . . . .
>
> Into some quiet garden
> Where towards dusk she will come down a path,
> Walking as gracefully as a rose sways,
> And stop, and with eyes half closed
> And a voice a little muted
> Say nothing of any great importance.
> Only the music of all life and all love
> Shall be in her voice,
> And in her eyes shall be
> Only the light of all youthful love
> Which we put away,
> With a sort of wry smile,
> Knowing there is no such thing,
> And if there was,
> It would not agree with the urgent necessity
> Of making a living.
>
> I do not think I shall touch her hair,
> Nor lay groping fingers on her unforgotten eyes.
> Perhaps I shall not even speak to her,
> But presently turn away, choked with an awful longing,

> And go off under the grave English trees,
> Through the gentle dusk
> Into the land called Death.
>
> And going I shall wonder a little
> How much it profits the courses
> Of the various sidereal universes
> That I could not be permitted to be happy
> With the woman I loved
> In the land that I loved
> For a few brief butterfly hours
> Before the deep dark
> Came to crown and anoint me with the opulent splendor
> Of oblivion.

This is not a good poem, but its directness of expression and feeling suggest that it may derive from actual experience. At least the girl does not sound like the conventional figures of his earlier poems. Moreover, its themes recur in Chandler's work. The girl with the cornflower-blue eyes is the unattainable blonde whom Philip Marlowe frequently encounters but never wins. The idea of the future that never happened and never would emphasizes the sense of loss that Chandler felt when he returned to America. Despite his nationality, it was second best and would always be so.

There was one last chance for financial success which Chandler described himself: "I think my most startling experience in those days was the result of an introduction to Horace Voules, then editor of *Truth*, whose chucker-out (*Anglice* bouncer) was a suave Cantabrigian in a cutaway coat and the usual striped pants, and this gentleman advised me to write newspaper serials at six guineas a week. Said it was easy, you just kept on until they made you stop and then you started a new one. Imagine me then in a blue-chalk-striped flannel suit cut by a West End tailor, wearing an old school tie and an old school band on a natty straw hat, carrying a cane and gloves, and being told by this elegant fellow to write what then appeared to me the most appalling garbage ever slung together in words. I gave him a sickly smile and left the country."

Without possibilities for a decent future in England, and with what sadness we can only guess at, Chandler approached Uncle Ernest and borrowed five hundred pounds from him so that he could go to America. He noted later that "every penny of it was repaid, with six per cent interest." It was 1912, and he was twenty-three. In five years he had published twenty-seven poems, seven essays, and a handful of reviews, not counting the anonymous paragraphs in the *Westminster Gazette*. It was not an impressive production for a young man of Chandler's brains and competence. "America seemed to call to me in some mysterious way," he remembered afterward. Only there really was no mystery.

2.
THE
RETURN
TO
AMERICA

———◆———

Chandler's return to America began in sadness and frustration, but for the next twenty years he was to be involved in a life of action that would never have been possible had he remained in England. There his activities would always have been restricted by the conventions of his class and education. He was disappointed by his failure to become a successful writer in England, but in America he gained the experiences that made it possible for him to write his novels.

Moreover, the return to America was in itself an adventure, and the neat young man with a handsome profile and dark hair parted down the middle, wearing rounded stiff collars, a school tie, and tweeds, was soon doing things he certainly never contemplated at Dulwich. Nor were the Americans he encountered so barbarous as he may have imagined them to be. On the steamer going to New York he met the Warren Lloyd family from Los Angeles, who, unlike most shipboard acquaintances, were to be very important in his life. They were upper middle class with money from the oil business, and at the same time had intellectual interests similar to Chandler's. Warren Lloyd, the father, was a Ph.D. in philosophy from Yale; his wife, Alma, was a sculptor. They had three children, of whom the eldest, Estelle, was thirteen. The family had just

spent a year or so in Germany and were therefore also in a sense
American expatriates. Undoubtedly they were a comfort to the young
man returning to the unknown country of his birth after so many years.
They invited him to visit them in California, and within a short time he
did.

Chandler later wrote that at this time he "had no feeling of identity
with the United States" yet did not feel English. Disembarking in New
York, he declared himself to be an American citizen despite an "English
accent you could cut with a baseball bat." He took the train to St. Louis
and got a job there "where the canaille referred to me as Lord Stoopen-
takit, which didn't bother me in the least, but the climate did, and there
seemed a great deal of spitting going on, which we didn't do in England.
A crusty old boy informed me with an immense fraudulent dignity that
'the American gentleman did not spit.' I said, 'Good, perhaps I'll meet
him some day.' This didn't go over good either."

Chandler's next stop was Nebraska, where Uncle Ernest and Aunt
Grace Fitt lived. It is possible that Chandler intended to settle there for a
time, since in the Dulwich College address book he listed as his own his
uncle's address at 3924 North 29th Street, Omaha. The raw Middle
West seemed extraordinarily alien to this class-educated Anglo-Ameri-
can. He later recalled a relative, Harry Fitt, who lived in Omaha and
worked in a hardware store. "Since I was fresh out of England at the
time," he noted, "and a hardware store was 'trade' I could hardly be
expected to get on terms of anything like familiarity with him. Boy! Two
stengahs, chop chop!"

From Nebraska, Chandler moved on to California "with a beautiful
wardrobe, a public school accent, no practical gifts for earning a living,
and a contempt for the natives which, I am sorry to say, has in some
measure persisted to this day. I had a pretty hard time trying to make a
living. Once I worked on an apricot ranch ten hours a day, twenty cents
an hour. Another time I worked for a sporting goods house, stringing
tennis racquets for $12.50 a week, 54 hours a week." Such alien employ-
ment must have given Chandler many moments of despair, living alone
as he probably did, in anonymous boarding houses wherever he landed.
He may have been too exhausted physically to absorb his American
experiences with any detachment. Nevertheless, with his sensibilities
attuned to the structured society of England, there is no doubt that he
learned very thoroughly what it was like to live in America without
privilege. The words did not come out for twenty years, but they were
probably being formed unconsciously at this time.

By 1913 Chandler listed his address with Dulwich as care of Mrs.
Warren E. Lloyd, 713 South Bonnie Brae Street, in Los Angeles. He
probably did not actually stay with the Lloyd family but used their

house as a more certain mailing address than the furnished rooms he occupied. By this time Chandler had decided to use his brains instead of his muscles and began a straight business career as a bookkeeper, relying in part on his experience in the Admiralty. "As I knew nothing about bookkeeping, I went to a night school and in six weeks the instructor asked me to leave; he said I had done the three years' course and that was all there was." Chandler later claimed that his subsequent "rise was as rapid as the growth of a sequoia," but in fact he did not attain any prominence as a businessman until after the war. In the meantime, he worked as an accountant and bookkeeper at the Los Angeles Creamery, a job he obtained through the intercession of Warren Lloyd, who was legal counsel to the company and whose first cousin was married to its treasurer.

Keeping account of milk shipments cannot have been more interesting than watching over naval stores in London, and Chandler must have been aware of the similarity of the two positions. In the meantime, he was a protégé of the Lloyds and belonged to what was probably as agreeable a society as could then be found in Los Angeles. The Lloyds' house was the center for Friday evening meetings at which philosophical and literary subjects were discussed by the guests. Warren Lloyd had many interests beyond the law and was coauthor of a book called *Psychology Normal and Abnormal*. This was a period of great interest in the occult, and one of the topics that most engaged the Lloyds and their guests was Indian culture and philosophy. They were influenced by Madame Blavatsky and also read fictional works that stressed psychic phenomena, such as Bulwer-Lytton's *Zanoni*. Chandler's contribution to these gatherings seems to have been mainly literary, and there is one poem entitled "To-morrow" written jointly by Estelle Lloyd, Warren Lloyd, and Chandler, although Lloyd penned in "with accent on Chandler." There is a note saying that it was "composed for the use of Optimists"—which may have been the name of their group—on "June 14th, 1914, on the road between Hollywood and Burbank," then open country.

There were also musical evenings, for Alma Lloyd had a good voice and had trained as a singer in Berlin. Another participant and friend was Julian Pascal, a distinguished concert pianist and composer, who was born in the West Indies as Goodridge Bowen but who used Pascal both as a social and professional name. He had been a professor at the Guildhall School of Music in London, where his most famous pupil was Myra Hess, but ill health had driven him first to New York and later to Los Angeles, where he continued giving piano lessons.

The Lloyds' literary and musical evenings were not in the least bit formal or pretentious. In an era before movies and the radio, they were simply the way intelligent people entertained one another. The informality of the arrangements between the various families and individuals participating tended to eliminate the barriers that so often separate generations. On Sundays, Warren Lloyd would play a ritualistic game of chess with his contemporary Julian Pascal, and the whole house would be silenced so as not to disturb them. At the same time, after movies began to be shown, Chandler would go to the theater with Warren Lloyd, who was twenty years his senior, where they would sit on opposite sides of the hall. First one would start laughing, then the other would take it up, alternatively, until they had everyone doing the same, regardless of the subject of the film. It was partly a joke, partly an experiment in psychology.

By 1916 Chandler was living at 311 Loma Drive in the old residential section of Los Angeles that stretches for a mile or two to the west and northwest of Pershing Square. This is no longer an attractive part of the city, except for some apartment buildings, but it was then a typical middle-class section, with streets lined with palm trees and single or double houses set back from the road and sidewalks with small front lawns. The houses were mostly wooden, but here and there were bungalow courts in a vaguely Spanish design with red tiled roofs and stucco walls. There was little style to these neighborhoods, but they were agreeable and unpretentious, quite unlike the later sections of Westwood and Beverly Hills, which were built after the Hollywood boom.

By this time Chandler's mother had come over from England to live with him; and with the Lloyds and Pascals nearby they were part of an easy community that made up for many of the things they must have missed in England. But distance and other customs tend to mute comparisons, and Chandler was probably far more interested in what was going on around the corner on Seventh Street where, as he later recalled, Kid McCoy shot his estranged wife—"a procedure," he noted, "which has become almost standard in California now."

Yet whatever tranquillity Chandler may have felt was disrupted by America's declaration of war in 1917. As an American, he had not joined up in 1914, but in August of 1917, together with Gordon Pascal, Julian's son, he went up to Victoria, British Columbia, and enlisted in the Canadian army. After the war he told some of his friends that he had tried to join the American army, only to be rejected for bad eyesight; but it is more likely that he preferred the Canadians because, as he admitted, "it was still natural for me to prefer a British uniform," which his dual nationality permitted. Moreover, the Canadian army paid a separation allowance to his mother, which the American would not do, and this was an important consideration. Upon his enlistment he was given a service number of 202571 in the Fiftieth Regiment, known also as the Gordon

Highlanders of Canada, a unit that was amalgamated with the Victoria Fusiliers in 1920 to form the Canadian Scottish Regiment.

His first training took place near Victoria, the regimental headquarters. Wearing his kilt, Chandler occasionally went into the town, but he found it "dullish, as an English town would be on a Sunday, everything shut up, churchy atmosphere and so on." The war was going badly for the Allies, and Chandler's training was brief. Only three months after he enlisted, he was sent east for embarkation on a troopship from Halifax. The ship sailed on November 26 and reached Liverpool on December 7. At this point Chandler was transferred to the British Columbia Regiment and sent to their depot at Seaford, on the Sussex coast, not far from Beachy Head and halfway between Newhaven and Eastbourne, convenient for embarkation to France. At night it was a frightening place, since the light from front-line bombardments could be seen in England, and even the roar of artillery sounded across the Channel.

On March 18, 1918, Chandler was assigned to the Seventh Battalion of the Canadian Expeditionary Force (known also as the Canadian Corps) and sent to France. The Seventh was one of four battalions in the Second Canadian Infantry Brigade, which in turn was one of three in the First Canadian Division. At the time of Chandler's arrival in France, the four divisions of the Canadian Corps, nominally under the command of Lieutenant General Sir Arthur Currie, were under the unified command of Marshal Foch.

Chandler's battalion had already served in France for three years and had participated in some of the fiercest trench fighting of the war. Just before he arrived, the battalion had successfully defended Vimy Ridge from a German attack and had emerged victorious from the bloody battle of Passchendaele. The winter months had been quiet, with both sides preparing for new encounters. When General Ludendorff began his spring offensive, he bypassed the Canadians at Vimy Ridge, so Chandler and his companions were spared this assault. The Germans were not finally stopped until June at Chateau Thierry.

During the spring the Seventh Battalion remained for the most part behind the lines in a reserve position. Stationed on either side of the road that linked Arras with Cambrai, the troops underwent extensive training and maneuvers with tanks and airplanes in preparation for the August push that eventually ended the war. In the London press the Canadians were criticized for not being directly involved in the German spring offensive, but there were domestic political reasons for holding the Canadians apart, and they also needed the training.

For Chandler, as for most soldiers brought so quickly to the front, his experiences were too overwhelming to digest. He rarely spoke of his service in France, saying that it was a nightmare he preferred to forget. Despite the battalion's reserve position, Chandler's unit was engaged in heavy action. He soon rose in the ranks and in later years referred obliquely to his experiences. "Courage is a strange thing: one can never be sure of it," he wrote. "As a platoon commander very many years ago I never seemed to be afraid, and yet I have been afraid of the most insignificant risks. If you had to go over the top somehow all you seemed to think of was trying to keep the men spaced, in order to reduce casualties. It was always very difficult, especially if you had replacements or men who had been wounded. It's only human to want to bunch for companionship in face of heavy fire." The psychological effect of this brutal war was to make Chandler block out memory of it, except for an occasional remark, such as "Once you have had to lead a platoon into direct machine-gun fire, nothing is ever the same again."

In June, Chandler's service in France ended abruptly when an artillery barrage of eleven-inch German shells blew up everyone in his outfit, leaving him the sole survivor. The explosion concussed him, and he was taken behind the lines and shortly afterward returned to England. Perhaps because the bombardment was not as unbearable a memory as leading other men to their deaths in an infantry attack, Chandler tried to write an account of what happened in a short piece called "Trench Raid," but it is just a sketch and he never touched the subject again:

"The strafe sounded a lot heavier than usual. The candle stuck on the top of his tin hat guttered from something more than draught. The rats behind the dugout lining were still. But a tired man could sleep through it. He began to loosen the puttee on his left leg. Someone yelled down the dugout entrance and the beam of an electric torch groped about on the slimy chalk steps. He swore, retied his puttee and slithered up the steps. As he pushed aside the dirty blanket that served for a gas curtain the force of the bombardment hit him like the blow of a club at the base of the brain. He grovelled against the wall of the trench, nauseated by the din. He seemed to be alone in a universe of incredibly brutal noise. The sky, in which the calendar called for a full moon, was white and blind with innumerable Very lights, white and blind and diseased like a world gone leprous. The edge of the parados, lumpy with the dirt from a recent housekeeping, cut this whiteness like a line of crazy camels against an idiotic moonrise in a nightmare. Against the emptiness [word uncertain] of the night, a nose cap whined down nearby with a slow intimate sound, like a mosquito. He began to concentrate on the shells. If you heard them they never hit you. With a meticulous care he set himself to picking out the ones that would come near enough to be reckoned on as a possible introduction to immortality. To these he listened with a sort of cold exhausted passion until a flattening of the screech told him they had gone over to the support lines. Time to move on. Mustn't stay too long in one place. He groped round the corner of the bay to the Lewis gun post. On the firing step the Number One of the gun crew was standing to with half of his body silhouetted above the parapet, motionless against the glare of the lights except that his hand was playing scales on the butt of the gun."

By June 11 Chandler was back at the depot of the British Columbia Regiment in Seaford. His military records show that he was now an acting sergeant with pay, a battlefield promotion that was confirmed by his soldier's wages. At this point he decided to transfer and was accepted as a cadet in the Royal Air Force, the successor to the Royal Flying Corps. This change may have been prompted in part by correspondence with Gordon Pascal, who had joined the Royal Flying Corps soon after his enlistment in Vancouver. Flying was popular with the Canadians, and some 13,000 had joined either the RFC or the RAF. "Canadians made wonderful fighters," wrote Colonel George Nasmith in his history of Canadian involvement in the war, "and the majority of the greatest fighters in the R.A.F. were Canadians."

The Royal Air Force has skimpy records on Chandler, since the end of the war cut short his service with it. Officially, he joined up in July and was posted to No. 6 School of Aviation. This may have been a training center just established in Bristol, but Chandler later remembered being at a place called Waddington, seven miles from Lincoln, "a hell of a place to spend Sunday." His training was cut short by the Armistice, and on December 31, 1918, he was stationed at the London depot of the RAF, waiting for embarkation to Canada. He was never commissioned but set sail for Canada before the end of January. Once returned to Vancouver, he was discharged on February 20, 1919. The records show that he was both an acting sergeant and a cadet, and he was awarded the British war and victory medals. His military career had lasted almost exactly eighteen months.

It is hard to know how Chandler felt upon returning to the United States. At the very least, the war must have made him reconsider his position. Instead of returning to Los Angeles immediately to see his mother, he dallied along the Pacific coast. There is evidence in his writing of familiarity with Washington State and Puget Sound, and at this time he probably became familiar with the region. He may have stayed for a while with a friend named Smythe, a barber from Seattle who was a fellow soldier and "a great rogue and a great comedian. He always announced that if he ever got a wound, he would get shot in the ass. In the spring of 1919 when I was at Seaford awaiting a ship home I found him again, and you guessed it. Right through both cheeks."

Returning to America in 1919, Chandler must have realized that he had advanced little from where he was in 1913. He still wanted to write, and while in the Pacific Northwest he gave it another attempt. What happened he described this way: "I had another feeble fling at writing and almost sold the *Atlantic* a Henry James pastiche, but I didn't get anywhere."

The repeated literary failure left him only with the possibility of making a success in business. Presumably he wanted to be more than an accountant in a Los Angeles milk company. If he could make a name for himself in an overseas branch of an English company he might then be transferred to the head office in London with a proper salary and promotion. Some thought of this kind must have crossed his mind, for he moved down the coast to San Francisco and took a job at one of the two English banks then operating there. These were the Anglo and London Paris National Bank, which eventually became the Crocker Anglo Bank, and the Bank of British North America, which was absorbed by the Bank of Montreal. In whichever bank he worked, he did not find what he was looking for; indeed, he was in for a shock: "I think I there for the first time began to dislike the kind of English who don't live in England, don't want to live in England, but bloody well want to wave their Chinese affectations of manner and accent in front of your nose as if it was some kind of rare incense instead of a distillation of cheap suburban snobbery which is just as ludicrous in England as it is here."

There seems to have been no choice but to return to Los Angeles. By this time, however, Chandler's rootlessness had become habitual. If not changing towns, he was changing houses, as if trying to reject any imputation of bourgeois values. His roaming was useful, however, for it sharpened his sensibilities, making him aware of the plight of so many of his countrymen who lacked security. For Chandler, the instability extended to jobs as well: upon returning to Los Angeles in 1919, he took a position on the *Daily Express*, but stayed for only six weeks.

Chandler's return meant the resumption of his friendship with the Lloyds and with the Pascals. During the time he was in the army, he had listed his address as 127 South Vendome Street, which was the address of Julian and Cissy Pascal. Whether Chandler's mother lived with them during the war is unknown, but it is certainly possible, for the relationship between the two families was close—too close, as would soon be evident. As a returning war veteran in his early thirties, Chandler was considered an eligible bachelor. His natural shyness made him attractive to women, and many members of his circle hoped and expected that a

romance would develop between him and Estelle Lloyd, who was by then
twenty herself. This was not to be: instead, Chandler and Cissy Pascal
fell in love.

The two had corresponded throughout the war—originally perhaps
to share news of Cissy's stepson, Gordon Pascal—but gradually the
relationship developed. The relaxed atmosphere of the Lloyd-Chandler-
Pascal households, where different generations easily mixed, undoubtedly encouraged the romance. Cissy was forty-eight but did not look her
age and was probably more in tune with the younger members of these
families than with the elder. Pascal, by contrast, was a frail and delicate
man who looked older than he was.

The news startled everyone and naturally dismayed Julian. Nevertheless, the participants were emancipated enough to discuss the matter
openly and publicly. They turned to the Lloyds, and especially Warren
as a lawyer and friend, for advice and help. Paul Lloyd, the youngest of
the Lloyd children, remembers how his parents would sit down with
Julian and Cissy Pascal and with Chandler to discuss the situation. The
fourteen-year-old boy was ostensibly playing by the window, but he
overheard a good deal before he was noticed and sent away. Cissy would
say that she loved Julian but that she loved Ray more. What, then, were
they to do? They agonized over it for some time in an open and civilized
way, and in the end it was agreed that Cissy should file for a California
divorce, which she did on July 10, 1919. They were too conventional to
think of a quick divorce in Reno and were resigned to a year-long
moratorium before the divorce was made final on October 4, 1920.

It was in fact Cissy's second divorce. She had been born in Perry,
Ohio, which is near Cleveland, on October 29, 1870, as Pearl Eugenie
Hurlburt, daughter of Eugene Hurlburt and Maria Amanda Gray. She
had one sister, Lavinia, who later lived in California. By the time she was
twenty-one, if not earlier, she moved to New York, where she studied
music and eventually became a proficient pianist. She lived at 333 Lenox
Avenue in central Harlem, which was then still a largely middle-class
white neighborhood. There are many rumors about Cissy's life in New
York (the name Cecilia may have been added at this time). Photographs
show her as an exceptionally beautiful woman with a delicate profile,
soft hair, and a romantic look about her, and she seems to have been a
model both for photographers and painters. When Chandler was writing
films in Hollywood and Cissy was rarely seen, there were stories that she
had modeled for a famous nude painting that once hung in the Plaza or
St. Regis Hotel in New York. Chandler himself owned photographs of
her taken in the nude when she was a girl.

In December of 1897 Cissy married a young man by the name of
Leon Brown Porcher, who was a salesman living on West 123rd Street.

The ceremony took place at the famous marrying church, the Church of the Transfiguration, better known as the Little Church Around the Corner, on East 29th Street. This marriage lasted seven years, and the couple were divorced in May of 1904. Cissy's musical accomplishments undoubtedly led to her meeting Goodridge Bowen (Julian Pascal), whom she married in Greenwich, Connecticut, in April of 1911. Within the year they moved to Los Angeles.

In later years Chandler often referred to Cissy as a New Yorker, by which he meant mainly that she had a greater degree of sophistication and awareness than the people he generally came across in California. She was also somewhat theatrical in her manner. She was stylish and chic and soon won Chandler's attentions. Cissy's appearance in Chandler's life seems to have been a confirmation of his own identity as a man. Because of the great difference in their ages, it has sometimes been said that in effect Chandler "married his mother." But in 1919 Cissy had strawberry blonde hair and a marvelous figure and complexion. She was lively and original and liked to be naked when she did housework. She was also an excellent cook of the old-fashioned kind. By this time Chandler had wandered a lot and was tired from the war. Here was a woman with sexual maturity who also had the brains to be an intellectual companion as well. She seemed just right to Chandler.

Four years went by before Chandler actually married Cissy, although they lived together, at least for periods of time. After her divorce Chandler took an apartment for Cissy in Hermosa Beach and another place for his mother and himself at 224 South Catalina Street in nearby Redondo Beach. Mrs. Chandler disapproved of the proposed marriage because of the difference in ages, so Chandler delayed it until she died in 1924. He was enormously fond of his mother and honored her as a sort of saint for the sacrifices she underwent to bring him up. "I knew that my mother had affairs—she was a very beautiful woman—and the only thing I felt to be wrong was that she refused to marry again for fear a step-father would not treat me kindly, since my father was such a swine."

Toward the end of his mother's life Chandler was living at 723 Stewart Street in Santa Monica, probably to be closer to doctors. Cissy meanwhile had a place at 3206 San Marino, about three miles from the downtown center of Los Angeles in the general direction of Beverly Hills. Chandler's mother endured a long illness with cancer, and at the end her pain was so severe she had to be given morphine. She finally died at the end of January in 1924.

Within two weeks, on February 6, 1924, Chandler and Cissy were married in Los Angeles by the Reverend Carl S. Patton. Undoubtedly, the Lloyds and other friends attended. Cissy listed her age as forty-three—to Chandler's thirty-five—and this was a deliberate deception. She was in fact fifty-three, but as her sister, Lavinia, recounted, she would do anything to disguise the discrepancy of years between them. At first she was successful, for she did not look her age. After the ceremony they moved to half of a double house—which Cissy had already taken some time earlier—at 2863 Leeward, on the corner of Magnolia. The house is bleak and the neighborhood characterless, rows of small houses and bungalow-court apartments lining the streets. It was and still is a mixed neighborhood.

By the time of his marriage Chandler had been employed for at least two years by the Dabney Oil Syndicate, a company whose offices in the Bank of Italy building adjoined those of the Los Angeles Creamery on South Olive Street. Once again, the Lloyd family were responsible for Chandler's employment, for this company had been formed jointly in 1918 by Joseph B. Dabney and Ralph B. Lloyd, Warren Lloyd's brother. Hearing they were in need of a young bookkeeper, Warren Lloyd suggested Chandler, who was again back at the Los Angeles Creamery and in need of preferment.

All the companies that Chandler eventually became involved with stemmed from this original syndicate, which was formed to develop the Ventura Avenue oil fields. The Lloyd family already owned large tracts of land there, but Ralph Lloyd, who had originally been in the paper business in Oregon and was the family member chiefly involved in the business, was glad to be joined by Dabney, a fellow Iowan recently arrived from Aberdeen, Washington, who was also attracted by the oil boom in Los Angeles. The Dabney-Lloyd partnership was formed to drill the Ventura Avenue property, but after a while Dabney sold his share to Lloyd and formed a new enterprise called the South Basin Oil Company. This was a holding company for a dozen smaller firms, among them the Dabney-Johnston Oil Corporation, which was formed with a drilling expert, Sidney Johnston, to develop the Signal Hill oil fields in Long Beach. Over the years the company operated a hundred oil wells, producing 16,000 barrels a day. Signal Hill was one of the greatest oil bonanzas in California history: Shell was the largest developer, with Dabney just behind. The discovery of oil on this site created more excitement than usual, for the surface land had recently been subdivided for houses, and the lot owners were besieged by companies and individuals anxious to lease the oil rights. Thousands of people rushed out to the oil fields in buses and taxis from Los Angeles hoping to buy land or at least invest in companies formed on the spot to drill the oil. Signal Hill eventually became one of the world's greatest oil fields and, with its immediate neighbors at Huntington Beach and Santa Fe Springs, produced one-fifth of the world's oil.

Chandler joined the Dabney Oil Syndicate while Ralph Lloyd was still in partnership with Dabney. He first worked in the accounting department, where he became aware, in October of 1923, of a scandal that in no way involved him, but that opened his eyes and gave him experience that would later be useful to him as a writer. The auditor of the company, W. A. Bartlett, was arrested for having embezzled $30,000 of the company's funds. After a trial which resulted in a conviction, Dabney hired a man from a well-known firm of accountants called Haskins and Sells to take charge of the company books. This individual was a Scot by the name of John Ballantine, and Chandler was named his assistant. More potentially useful experiences came his way when one day Ballantine had a heart attack and died in the office. The police were called, and Chandler, as Ballantine's assistant, accompanied them through the ritual of recording his death, placing the body in the morgue, and performing the autopsy.

Following Ballantine's funeral, Chandler was named auditor of the company, and within a relatively short time rose to become vice-president, in effect the person in charge of the Los Angeles office. His salary rose from $500 to $1,000 a month, a considerable amount for the early 1920s. Chandler handled all the paperwork for the company, the contracts, the mergers and the purchase of such subsidiary companies as the Herndon Petroleum Company, the Dabney-Mills Alloys Corporation, a trucking company, and various firms that produced drilling equipment and other necessities for the operation. The office people realized that Chandler, as Dabney's right-hand man, was an exceptional person. They called him a "genius" for his skill in resolving business problems and were astonished at the ease with which he dictated letters of three or four pages on complicated negotiations which were a delight to read as prose. Chandler also knew how to compress complex issues and write succinct reports for the office staff. Years afterward he discussed some of his experiences there:

"I was an executive in the oil business once, a director of eight companies and a president of three, although actually I was simply a high-priced employe. They were small companies, but very rich. I had the best office staff in Los Angeles and I paid them higher salaries than they could have got anywhere else, and they knew it. My office door was never closed, everyone called me by my Christian name, and there was never any dissension, because I made it my business to see that there was no cause for it. Once in a while, not often, I had to fire someone—not someone I had picked myself, but someone who had been imposed on me by the big man—and that I hated terribly, because one never knows what hardship it may mean to the individual. I had a talent for picking out the capabilities of people. There was one man, I remember, who had a genius for filing. Others were good at routine jobs, but had no initiative. There were secretaries who could remember everything and secretaries who were wonderful at dictation and typing, but whose minds were really elsewhere. I had to understand them all and use them according to what they were. There was one girl, not pretty and not too bright, who could have been given a million dollars in cash, and a month later, without being asked, she would have known the number of every bill and listed it, and would have, at her own expense, taken a safe deposit box to keep the money in. There was a lawyer on salary in our office (I didn't approve of the idea, but was overruled by the Board) who was very acute but also very unreliable, because he drank too much. I found out just how to use his brain, and he said often and publicly that I was the best office manager in Los Angeles and probably one of the best in the world."

But there was also a cocky side to Chandler that the competition of business brought out: "I always somehow seemed to have a fight on my hands. At one time I employed six lawyers; some were good at one thing, some at another. Their bills always exasperated the Chairman; he said they were too high. I always paid them as rendered because they were not too high in the circumstances. Business is very tough and I hate it. But whatever you set out to do you have to do as well as you know how."

Not surprisingly, Chandler made enemies, one of them a man named John Abrams, who married into the Dabney family and worked for a while as an independent oil man in the fields at Huntington Beach. For him, Chandler was the office "martinet" who "began by 'protecting' his boss and even interfered with field operations and employees." Whether Chandler's toughness was exaggerated or not, he was not the sort to settle a dispute amicably over a drink. There is a certain literalness in his solutions to problems that suggests a lonely man who did little consulting before he acted and who was always on guard. Here is Chandler's account of a minor episode:

"I remember one time when we had a truck carrying pipe in Signal Hill (just north of Long Beach) and the pipe stuck out quite a long way, but there was a red lantern on it, according to law. A car with two drunken sailors and two girls crashed into it and filed actions for $1,000 apiece. They waited almost a year, which is the deadline here for filing a personal injury action. The insurance company said, 'Oh well, it costs a lot of money to defend these suits, and we'd rather settle.' I said, 'That's all very well. It doesn't cost you anything to settle. You simply put the rates up. If you don't want to fight this case, and fight it competently, my company will fight it.' 'At your own expense?' 'Of course not. We'll sue you for what it costs us, unless you pay without that necessity.' He

walked out of the office. We defended the action, with the best lawyer
we knew, and we proved that the pipe truck had been properly lighted
and then we brought in various bar men from Long Beach (it took
money to find them, but it was worth it) and [proved] that they had
been thrown out of three bars. We won hands down, and the insurance
company paid up immediately about a third of what they would have
settled for, and as soon as they did this I cancelled the policy, and had it
rewritten with another company.

"Perhaps all this sounds a little hard-boiled. But I wasn't like that
really at all. I was just doing what I thought was my job. It's always
been a fight, hasn't it? Everywhere you go, everything you do—it all
takes it out of you."

The melancholy note Chandler sounds here was eventually to
undermine his life with Dabney, but in the early and mid-1920s he was
comparatively buoyant and happy. He was married and was a successful
businessman with a good salary, a Hupmobile for office business, and a
Chrysler roadster for his own. If he was not a writer, he could still write
poems, which he did with the hope that they might eventually be
published. He was also distracted by being busy. The Chandlers moved
about a good deal: after a year in a three-story Spanish-style apartment
building at 700 Gramercy Place at Melrose Avenue, a neighborhood of
rundown bungalows, they moved to 2315 West 12th Street, closer to the
center of the city. The houses are like the addresses, characterless and
uninspired. Some have front porches; others are shingled or stuccoed,
standing behind small front yards with palm trees and bushes lining the
sidewalk. In 1928 they moved to 1024 South Highland Avenue, further
out toward Beverly Hills, in the vicinity of the Wilshire Country Club.
This was a pink stucco house divided into two apartments, of which
theirs was the upper. Here the neighborhood was more substantial: no
more front porches, but shrubbery and an attempt at decorative gardening instead. Chandler's income was large enough to allow him to live
better than he did, but except for some years toward the end of his life,
he always had a modest house or apartment. He hated showiness and
was aware that his fortunes might suddenly change.

During the early years of their life together, the difference in age
between Chandler and Cissy did not show. Gradually, however, as she
approached sixty, with her husband not yet forty, the discrepancy became evident. Cissy tried to disguise her age by dyeing her hair blonde
and dressing as stylishly as she could. Sometimes she overdid it, wearing
young women's clothes that did not suit her. In her manner, she would
be skittish and unpredictable, sometimes vague and distant. Undoubtedly she was suffering from the realization that she was no longer
convincingly young; accordingly, she exaggerated her femininity. Her

bedroom was full of pink ruffles and Hollywood-style French furniture. It was exotic and stagily erotic.

While there is no doubt that theirs was a real marriage, Chandler obviously became aware of the age difference. For her part, Cissy would often plead illness; some who knew her believed that her ailments were mainly intended to attract Chandler's attention and sympathy, and for a time they did. Usually Chandler went out alone and did not take Cissy to functions that would tire or embarrass her. Chandler was interested in sports, both as participant and spectator. In the autumn he would often go with office friends—Ernest Dolley and his wife or Milton Philleo and his—to the local football games at UCLA or at the University of Southern California. Once a year he and his friends would also go north to Palo Alto or Berkeley to see "the game"—the annual rivalry between Stanford and the University of California. They would leave on Friday afternoon and drive all night. As soon as they arrived, the drinking would start. Sometimes Chandler drank so much he never went to the game. But in the early days, at least, Chandler did not have a serious problem with drinking. There would be an occasional weekend bender, but nothing worse than that.

On other weekends Chandler and his friends often played tennis, again without Cissy's presence. There was a foursome of Chandler, Milton Philleo, Orville Evans (another man from the Dabney office), and Louis Knight (the company's insurance agent) who played doubles on Saturdays. Sometimes they would find a court near Chandler's house; otherwise they would go out to West Covina, where the Philleos lived. Chandler was a good player, and the matches were weekend rituals, relaxing and pleasant for all. They constituted Chandler's main social life. After the tennis there would be cocktails, and Chandler would drink a lot, though usually not excessively. Sometimes, however, he would drink too much and become morose and gloomy, thereby destroying the genial atmosphere of the occasion.

Sometimes the weekend conviviality would be disrupted by Chandler's erratic behavior, which foretold trouble ahead. In addition to the usual sports, Chandler enjoyed flying. He and Philleo would hire a plane for an hour and go up together with a professional pilot. It was the sort of exhilaration Chandler liked, and the risk also appealed to him. If he had been drinking, he was capable of taking extraordinary chances. One day, after the plane took off, Chandler undid his safety belt and stood up in the cockpit. The pilot angrily motioned him to sit down, but he wouldn't. Then the pilot threatened to squirt him with a fire extinguisher, so Chandler sat down quietly with a shrug of his shoulders.

Another time Chandler drove out on a Saturday morning to play tennis with Philleo. When he arrived, he found out that Mrs. Philleo was ill and that her husband wanted to stay at home with her. Chandler, who had been drinking, then went into the bedroom and tried to pull her out of bed. Philleo became very angry and told Chandler to leave the house. He expected to hear Chandler open the front door, but when he didn't he went into the living room, where he found Chandler standing with a gun pointed at his own head. Mistaking the front door, Chandler had walked into a hall cupboard, where he had found a holster and gun. Philleo told Chandler to put the gun down, which he did, and then left. The following Monday, Chandler apologized and they agreed to forget about the incident.

These incidents suggest that Chandler was undergoing considerable strain. The precise cause is hard to determine, but there is no doubt that he was subject to a wild feeling of despair. He was not angry with Cissy, for he may never have known her actual age, and he adored her in many ways. But in the company of the young wives of his friends and associates, he realized that he was missing the quality of youthful love they were enjoying. The toughness he expressed in business dealings did not help him in his own life, and he fell into the opposite mood, a soft feeling of self-pity that arose from the realization that the ideal world of his poems was now more impossible than ever. The drinking, brought on initially by a nervous shyness with other people, which he believed whiskey would diminish, plunged him into a black Irish depression. Sometimes he would go off for days at a time, without telling Cissy or anybody else where he was. He would then phone up the office and say that he was about to jump out of the window of a room in the Mayfair Hotel on West Seventh Street in Los Angeles. These suicide threats became so frequent that after a while his friends ignored them, believing that he was just calling attention to himself in a childish way.

John Abrams, who had no fondness for Chandler, has thrown some light on his attempts to escape from the condition he was in. "He was a loner," he writes. "At the annual oil and gas banquets of 1,000 rollicking oil men at the Biltmore, Chandler was a shadowy figure, stinko drunk and hovering in the wings with a bevy of showgirls, a nuisance." At public occasions such as these where all is forgiven, he perhaps hoped to overcome his Public School scruples and find women who might give him what was not provided in the pink boudoir at home.

Chandler also began to have affairs with the office girls. Here his troubles multiplied, for he misused his powers as office manager for private ends. One secretary who had been hired by Philleo began failing to appear on Mondays, giving contradictory and confusing excuses. Philleo told her she would have to leave the company, but then Chandler came into Philleo's office and said he would take care of the matter. The girl stayed on. What happened was that Chandler had taken an apartment for her where he went on weekends. There they would have such binges that she simply was unable to turn up for work on Monday. As for Chandler, he would not come in until Wednesday. Eventually, the girl quit the job of her own accord.

By the end of his days in the South Basin Oil Company, Chandler began to let everything slip through his fingers. His colleagues tried to cover for him, but he would be away for weeks at a time, and no one knew where he was. Moreover, he was irritable and arbitrary in the office. When the company became involved in lawsuits, Chandler would be acerb and sarcastic with his own attorneys. He was evidently no longer the easygoing office manager he had been before. John Abrams told Dabney about the trouble Chandler was causing: "I phoned 'J.B.,' who said come up to the mountain house where we can discuss it. He was sitting on the porch with his bare belly exposed to the sun, his stocking feet on the rail." Abrams then told him what he thought of Chandler and urged Dabney to fire him. Chandler later heard what had taken place and threatened to sue Abrams for slander, but by this time his position had eroded so much, and he was drunk so often, that he was hardly in a position to do anything. Chandler was given a warning, and then he was finally fired in 1932, at the age of forty-four.

Chandler never denied his dismissal, but he did not give the real reason for it. "My services cost them too much," he once said. "Always a good reason for letting a man go." To an interviewer he remarked: "It was a good job—so good I couldn't hold it. They tossed me out during the Depression."

Of course it was a disaster: his marriage was nearly on the rocks and would have failed completely except for Cissy's own loyalty and her lack of options. As the womanizing and drinking showed, he was miserably unhappy. The dismissal was a terrible blow, for it destroyed his own sense of identity. Exactly twenty years after his return to America he was back where he began, except that he had a bad reputation, fewer possibilities, and less energy than before. It was the worst crisis of his life, but it was a necessary one. In bitter moments he would equate crooks with oil tycoons and regret having wasted ten years "as the factotum of a corrupt millionaire." But both the experience and his failure contributed to his development. The experience gave him insight into the Southern California world he was to write about, and the failure told him about himself. Typical of Chandler's resilience was his remark that the most important thing he learned from being fired was that it "taught me not to take anything for granted."

3.

BLACK
MASK

---◆---

In the immediate shock of his dismissal by Dabney, Chandler went to Seattle, where he still had friends from the army, in order to recover and plan what to do next. During his absence Cissy became ill with pneumonia and had to be hospitalized. Chandler returned immediately and for the next two months stayed with his sister-in-law Lavinia and her husband, Archie Brown. When Cissy recovered, the Chandlers took a place of their own at 4616 Greenwood Place, in the lower part of the Hollywood Hills, not far from Griffith Park. The move in itself was not significant, because after leaving their apartment on South Highland Avenue in 1930 they moved almost annually, and were to continue to do so for years.

Just at this time the Dabney company together with Ralph Lloyd was sued for the misappropriation of oil revenues from the Ventura Avenue fields, which had once belonged to the Lloyd family as a whole. The suit was brought by Edward Lloyd, Warren Lloyd's eldest son, on behalf of his branch of the family. Since he deeply resented being fired by Dabney, Chandler did all he could to help his old friends and gave them whatever information he could remember about the financial manipulations of the South Basin Oil Company.

Partly in gratitude for this help and certainly in sympathy for his plight, Edward and Paul Lloyd gave Chandler an allowance of a hundred dollars a month. They knew well enough that he loathed business and always wanted to write. The money may have been their way of helping him achieve this ambition, although it is possible that they just wanted to help a friend who had fallen into misfortune.

At any rate, Chandler planned to try again, and even listed himself in the Los Angeles Directory as a writer. Once more he began the wearisome process of learning how to write. He had done this earlier in England, where he had taken a correspondence course in short-story writing. All his life he preserved the exercises he then wrote in narration and dramatic setting, of which there were at least four types in the syllabus. Chandler's efforts were marked "A" or "B" or "B+" by the instructor, for they showed verbal facility. As is usual with beginning work, they are overwritten and literary, lacking the vitality of real fiction. Here is the opening of one: "When the darkness had completely fallen he sat very still and watched the leaping flames play among the logs. No movement was to be heard in the house, no sound but the light crackling of wood in the grate, the stirring of curtains, the creaking of a wainscot, the vague stir of some ancient unease sighing in the dim old walls."

The one completed story from this period is about a writer's visit to a famous duchess, who utterly fails to live up to his idea of aristocracy because she herself is a would-be author. It is a Jamesian pastiche, even a parody, and Chandler has his hero utter remarks like "One can only—don't you think?—write with passion about what one has never experienced." It has verbal ease: "Polished leather curved to his delicate instep. He was silk-hatted almost to the eye-brows and, for the rest, swallow-tail-coated admirably." But there is little real life, even for a sketch with the perverse point of showing that there is not much reality in fiction. It is witty and clever, but it lacks substance and style.

In Los Angeles in 1932 Chandler fell under a new literary influence. James and Saki were put aside and Hemingway took their place. The only surviving piece from this time is a short parody entitled "Beer in the Sergeant Major's Hat, or The Sun Also Sneezes." It is "dedicated with no good reason to the greatest living American novelist—Ernest Hemingway." There are two versions of this burlesque, and the second is a genuine improvement. Here is the first page:

Hank went into the bathroom to brush his teeth.
"The hell with it," he said. "She shouldn't have done it."
It was a good bathroom. It was small and the green enamel was peeling off the walls. But the hell with that, as Napoleon said

when they told him Josephine was waiting without. The bathroom had a wide window through which Hank looked at the pines and the larches. They dripped with a faint rain. They looked smooth and comfortable.

"The hell with it," Hank said. "She shouldn't have done it."

He opened the cabinet over the wash-basin and took out his toothpaste. He looked at his teeth in the mirror. They were large yellow teeth, but sound. Hank could still bite his way for a while.

Hank unscrewed the top of the toothpaste tube, thinking of the day when he had unscrewed the lid off the coffee jar, down on the Pukayuk River, when he was trout fishing. There had been larches there too. It was a damn good river, and the trout had been damn good trout. They liked being hooked. Everything had been good except the coffee, which had been lousy. He had made it Watson's way, boiling it for two hours and a half in his knapsack. It had tasted like the socks of the Forgotten Man.

Chandler's talent seemed to be crying out for use. All he needed was a subject and a desire to say something about it. This did not necessarily mean writing from experience, but it meant finding something that he could grasp and express with some feeling, thereby creating the illusion of life, which is what real fiction is. At first, he was inhibited by his own cleverness and by his literary sophistication. J. B. Priestley said that because Chandler was so intellectual, his critical faculties originally prevented him from letting himself go as a writer. Chandler became aware of this later on, when he was more experienced, for he said: "I begin to realise the great number of stories that are lost by us rather meticulous boys simply because we permit our minds to freeze on the faults rather than let them work for a while without the critical overseer sniping at everything that is not perfect."

Chandler began, as all artists do, by imitating others. During the 1930s he read the so-called slick magazines, such as the *Saturday Evening Post*, *Collier's*, *Cosmopolitan* and *Liberty*, always in search of a vehicle for his work. But he never liked them and was put off by "their fundamental dishonesty in the matter of character and motivation." He therefore started to look elsewhere. Driving along the Pacific coast with Cissy, he would pick up pulp magazines, so-called because they were made from wood pulp, in order to have something to read at night. He liked them "because they were cheap enough to throw away and because I never had any time for the thing which is known as women's magazines." With the need to publish becoming increasingly evident Chandler had a thought: "It suddenly struck me that I might be able to write this stuff and get paid while I was learning."

As a man of forty-five with a wife to support, his hand was forced by financial necessity, but he found that the writing in *Black Mask* and the other pulps was "forceful and honest, even though it had its crude aspect." Later on he was more specific: "I should never have tried to work for *Black Mask*, if I hadn't at one time got a kick out of it." He was also philosophical enough to realize that, as he put it, "no writer ever, in any age, got a blank check." He always had to accept certain conditions, whether religious or political or social, or even those imposed by commercial limitations: "No writer ever wrote exactly what he wanted to write, because there was never anything inside himself, anything purely individual that he did want to write. It's all reaction of one sort or other."

Cheap fiction had been published for decades in the United States and Europe, with special magazines devoted to adventure, sports, crime, and other interests. As in the magazines Dickens wrote for in England, this fiction was written exclusively for entertainment. Its readers did not want uplift or information; they wanted to kill time with a good read, and above all they wished to be taken away from the realities of their own lives and to have a touch of adventure and romance. This fiction was escapist, but it imposed a hard duty on those who wrote it. Since it was written only to amuse, it had to be amusing. There was no time for fancy literary effects. The writer had to grip the reader's interest from the beginning and embroil him in a real story. Otherwise, there was nothing.

By the 1920s a large number of pulp magazines were being published, mainly in New York. Their titles indicate their quality and thrust: *Underworld, Dime Western, Dime Detective, Adventure, Argosy, Love Story, Wild West Weekly, Ace Western, Ace Sports, Railroad Stories, The Shadow, Black Mask,* and *Clues.* Most of these magazines relied on what the writer Frank Gruber called a "pulp jungle"—a group of writers mostly living in Greenwich Village or in rented rooms in the smaller hotels off Times Square. Standard payment for pulp writing was only one cent a word, and during the Depression, when competition for acceptance was fierce, these writers suffered a good deal. Gruber has described how he used to go to Bernarr MacFadden's Penny Restaurants, where "you could dine sumptuously for around nine cents per meal. A hamburger steak made of meat-flavored sawdust cost four cents, a good, hard roll was a penny, coffee, two cents (made from dishwater with a dash of chickory), and dessert, two cents. You ate the meal standing up, which was good for your digestion. The food was very filling."

There were about 300 pulp writers in New York, with another 1,000 spread around the country. Their task was to supply the nearly 200 million words that were needed to fill these magazines annually. It was an awesome industry, not unlike television today, and it produced some extraordinary characters. One of these was Arthur J. Burks, who was interviewed by the New Yorker in 1936: " 'And is it true,' we were saying, 'that you write a million and a half words a year?' 'Of course,' Mr. Burks said, adding with contempt, 'a million and a half is so usual. Lots of pulp writers do more than that.' Mr. Burks, it seems, isn't the most prolific writer around, but the most versatile; turns out with equal facility stuff classifiable, he said, as 'detective, animal, Western, mystery, fantastic, terror, airplane, World War, adventure, pseudo-science.' He paused for breath. 'And weird,' he added." Burks seems to have had a sense of pride typical of his fraternity. "I don't feel like apologizing for writing to an audience of twenty-five million people," he said.

Black Mask is conceded to be the best of the pulps that specialized in the hard-boiled school of detective fiction. It was founded in 1920 by H. L. Mencken and George Jean Nathan to help make money to support Smart Set, the magazine they cared about. Mencken had little use for Black Mask, calling it a "louse" because it published only detective stories. Nevertheless, with two other "louse magazines" they owned, it gave the editors sufficient income to conduct their more serious literary venture. Mencken was pleased with its success and conceded that "the readers included many judges, Statesmen, and other Eminentisimos." He understood that even "Woodrow" [Wilson] was among them.

After six months Mencken and Nathan sold their interest in Black Mask to Eugene Crowe, a paper magnate, and Eltinge "Pop" Warner, the head of Warner Publishing Company at 25 West 45th Street. These two, with the help of their circulation manager, Phil Cody, continued the magazine much as before until 1925, when Cody was named editor. Although he was primarily a businessman, Cody brought Erle Stanley Gardner to the magazine, as well as Carroll John Daly, Raoul Whitfield, Frederick Nebel, and above all Dashiell Hammett. After two years Cody was named vice-president of Warners, and a new editor, Joseph T. Shaw, was appointed. Building on what Cody achieved, he gave the magazine a clear editorial position and made it the best-known magazine of its type.

A New Englander and graduate of Bowdoin College, Shaw was not only a writer but also an athlete and man of action who won national championships in sword handling, especially the saber. During the war he was a captain in the army, and after remaining abroad for a while with the Hoover Commission, he returned to New York, where through the intercession of a friend, he was asked to edit Black Mask, a magazine he had never seen or heard of before. But "Cap" Shaw, as he was called, knew enough about detective stories to realize that he was tired of the "crossword puzzle" type which lacked "human emotional values." Looking through back numbers of the magazine, he picked out Dashiell Hammett as one whose stories had originality and authenticity. Through correspondence with Hammett he developed an idea of what he required of his magazine: "We wanted simplicity for the sake of clarity, plausibility and belief. We wanted action, but we held that action is meaningless unless it involves recognizable human character in three-dimensional form." The detective story had certain formulas, but Shaw and Hammett wanted a pattern that "emphasizes character and the problems inherent in human behavior over crime solution."

Shaw's artistic beliefs were the result of his moral character. Returning from Europe, he was appalled by the wave of crime that engulfed the country during the Prohibition era, and by the gangsterism that put the names of Al Capone, John Dillinger, and Dutch Schultz in newspaper headlines throughout the country. He believed that the protection racket and the political scandals that typified the Harding administration were becoming a greater danger to the country than the old-fashioned crimes of passion or revenge. Shaw pointed out that "organized crime has allied politics as a necessary part of its business," and he decided that it was his duty to reveal the connections that existed between criminals and the country's elected representatives, judges, and police. In 1931 he said that "we feel that we are rendering a public service by publishing the realistic, true-to-life, highly illuminating stories of modern crime by such writers as Hammett, Whitfield, and Nebel."

Shaw had a clear idea of the law-abiding reader for whom *Black Mask* was intended, a person who was also the kind of fictional hero he admired. Physically, he pictured this reader as a "pretty stalwart, rugged specimen of humanity—hard as nails, swift of hand and foot, clear-eyed, unprovocative but ready to tackle anything that gets in the way." He is a man "who knows the song of a bullet, the soft, slithering hiss of a swift-thrown knife, the feel of hard fists, the call of courage." This paragon, who has experienced "grim life in the raw," also has a moral code. "He is vigorous-minded; hard, in a square man's hardness; hating unfairness, trickery, injustice, cowardly underhandedness; standing for a square deal and a fair show in little or big things, and willing to fight for them; not squeamish or prudish, but clean, admiring the good in man and woman; not sentimental in a gushing sort of way, but valuing true emotion; not hysterical, but responsive to the thrill of danger, the stirring exhilaration of clean, swift, hard action—and always pulling for the right guy to come out on top."

It is perhaps unfair to quote at length so fatuous a statement, and Shaw had enough sense of humor to report in the next issue that several of his readers had written in to say that he must have had Teddy

Roosevelt in mind as his typical reader. If Chandler read this proclamation, which he probably did, since it was printed during the same year his own first contribution appeared in *Black Mask*, he undoubtedly let it pass by, since he was suspicious of theorizing and would have spotted immediately the ludicrous elements in the statement. It nevertheless has some bearing on him, for although the descriptive language is different in substance, Shaw's ideal reader is not very different from the typified product of an English Public School. He is more vigorous and physical, and certainly less intellectual, but a fundamental similarity remains. This may have made it easier for Chandler to write pulp detective stories than might otherwise be imagined.

When he began, he had no such fancy notions; rather, as he sat down to write, believing he had no natural talent for it, he said that he "just had to learn it like anything else." Having no faith in outside agencies, he believed that "any writer who cannot teach himself cannot be taught by others." The advice he gave to others he followed himself: "Analyze and imitate; no other school is necessary." To begin with, he read widely, at first such writers as R. Austin Freeman, who considered the detective story to be basically a tale of ratiocination. This school derives from Edgar Allan Poe and is concerned more with the unraveling of the mystery and with the intellectual pleasure that can afford than with the emotional impact of the story. Like Hammett and Shaw before him, he was dissatisfied with the deductive kind of story and associated himself with writers who tried to use the detective story to say something about the nature of contemporary life and the injustices that infest it. In this, he echoed G. K. Chesterton's observation that the "essential value of the detective story lies in this, that it is the earliest and only form of popular literature in which is expressed some sense of the poetry of modern life."

As a resident of California who had learned much from his years in the oil business and the Depression he was living through as he began to write, Chandler knew a good deal about the "poetry" of modern American life. He naturally studied his predecessors—above all, Dashiell Hammett. In citing Hammett as the main influence on his own work, he placed himself implicitly in the central tradition of contemporary American letters, for he also thought of Hemingway, Dreiser, Ring Lardner, Carl Sandburg, and Sherwood Anderson as his antecedents. He even went back to Walt Whitman for the basic inspiration for what he and Hammett were trying to do. Chandler's admiration for Hammett was based on two related features of his work—his subject matter and his language. "Hammett," he wrote, "took murder out of the Venetian vase and dropped it in the alley." Unlike English detective stories in which murder was an affair of "the upper classes, the week-end house party and the vicar's rose garden," Hammett "gave it back to the people who commit it for reasons, not just to provide a corpse. He put these people down on paper as they were, and he made them talk and think in the language they customarily used for such purposes."

Chandler was concerned with style. "All language begins with speech," Chandler wrote, "and the speech of the common man at that, but when it develops to the point of becoming a literary medium it only looks like speech. Hammett's style at its worst was as formalized as a page of *Marius the Epicurean*; at its best it could say almost anything."

Most of Hammett's stories were first published in *Black Mask*, and many of his novels, including *Red Harvest, The Dain Curse, The Maltese Falcon*, and *The Glass Key*, were serialized there. Chandler studied Hammett's work with care, and his own grew out of it. "I did not invent the hard-boiled murder story," he wrote to a fellow crime writer, "and I have never made any secret of my opinion that Hammett deserves most or all of the credit. Everybody imitates in the beginning. What Stevenson called playing the 'sedulous ape.' " He must especially have had Hammett in mind when he wrote: "The best writing in English today is being done by Americans, but not in any purist tradition. They have roughed the language around as Shakespeare did and done it the violence of melodrama and the press box. They have knocked over tombs and sneered at the dead. Which is as it should be." What also impressed Chandler was Hammett's attention to detail and his ability to transform a physical observation into something that reveals character. He admired Hammett's narrative ability and said that he'd gladly read one of his novels even if the last chapter were torn out. "It would be interesting enough without the solution," he wrote. "It would stand up by itself as a story. That's the acid test." Yet Hammett lacked Chandler's verbal facility and the vision that illuminated a scene. Here Chandler exceeds him in a fundamental way. Chandler realized that the American language, which belonged to both of them, was capable of saying things that Hammett "did not know how to say, or feel the need of saying. In his hands it had no overtones, left no echo, evoked no image beyond a distant hill."

In the meantime, Chandler had to master the fundamentals. Specifically, he went to school with other writers in the *Black Mask* tradition. One he imitated was Erle Stanley Gardner, to whom he later wrote: "I forgot to tell you that I learned how to write a novelette on one of yours about a man named Rex Kane, who was an alter ego of Ed Jenkins and got mixed up with some flowery dame in a hilltop house in Hollywood who was running an anti-blackmail organization. You wouldn't remember. It's probably in your file No. 54276–88. I simply made an extremely detailed synopsis of your story and from that rewrote it and compared what I had with yours, and then went back and rewrote it some more, and so on. In the end I was a bit sore because I couldn't try to sell it. It looked pretty good." Here Chandler's training at Dulwich deserves some credit, for the work was done in the same spirit as translating Cicero into English and then back into Latin. Chandler realized that it took slow, patient work to become a writer. He always rewrote the story he was working on. "Then I compared it with professional work and saw whether I had failed to make an effect, or had the pace wrong, or some other mistake. Then I did it over and over again." His main problem as a writer came in trying to master his own language, since until then he had always written in British English. "I had to learn American just like a foreign language," he later wrote. At the age of forty-five he had enough experience to write simply. "Thank heaven," he wrote to Charles Morton, of the *Atlantic Monthly*, "that when I tried to write fiction I had the sense to do it in a language that was not all steamed up with rhetoric."

Finally, after spending five months on his first story, "Blackmailers Don't Shoot," he sent it in to *Black Mask*. Upon receiving it, Shaw sent it to another of his writers, W. T. Ballard, with a note saying that Chandler was either a genius or crazy. What Chandler had done was to try to justify the right-hand margin so that his typescript would look as though it had been set in linotype. Despite this naïveté, Shaw recognized Chandler's quality, although he paid him only $180 for the story, the basic rate of one cent a word.

As an editor, Shaw was much admired and appreciated by his contributors. Lester Dent has described his surprise when, after having written a great many pulp stories, he finally approached Shaw in the hope of being accepted by *Black Mask*. He was impressed by Shaw's culture and education and by his seriousness of purpose, for "here was a man who could breathe this pride of his into a writer. Cap didn't think I was a pulp hack. Joe felt I was a writer in step with the future. He thought that of all his writers. He had a way, with this device or some other device, of breathing power into his writers."

When Dent visited Shaw on that first day, he was shown a letter Chandler had written Shaw, which was "so delicate and sensitive and perceptive that it forever moulded my view of Chandler, whom I have never met." Shaw's point in showing the letter was to impress Dent with "the idea that I was not to sit and do a hack hard-boiled piece of pulp for *Black Mask*. I was to believe and feel I was doing a great piece."

Shaw was also an instructive editor: "He would start discussing his writers, their skill, and before you knew it you would find some Hammett or Chandler in your hands along with a blue pencil and Cap would be asking, 'Would you cut that somewhere? Just cut a few words.' The idea, of course, was that there was no wordage fat. You could not cut. Every word had to be there."

Older than most *Black Mask* authors, Chandler was not so dependent on Shaw as others were, although he looked upon him as a "very kind and warm editor" who had the "ability to get better writing out of his men than they could really do." While still an active contributor to the magazine, he wrote that Shaw had "a great insight into writing and he can give a man a buck up when he needs it as nobody else I know can, or does." As an editor, Shaw became actively involved in the work of his contributors. When he received a story that was too full of action, he would say, "To accomplish action it's not necessary to stage a gun battle from start to finish, with a murder and killing in every other paragraph. You can keep it alive through dialogue."

Shaw himself never claimed credit for the work of his authors. "I never 'discovered' an author," he wrote; "he discovered himself. I never 'made' an author. He made himself." He had great respect for Chandler, and almost without exception he placed his stories in the lead position in the magazine. Shaw felt that Chandler "came to us full-fledged; his very first stories were all that could be desired. There was never any question or doubt about Ray's ultimate success."

Chandler had no such confidence, although he had a clear idea of what he wanted to write and why the mystery story was suitable for what he had to say. Looking back on his stories in 1950 he identified their main characteristic as the "smell of fear" they managed to generate. In this, they echoed his own experience, for they were about "a world gone wrong, a world in which, long before the atom bomb, civilization had created the machinery for its own destruction, and was learning to use it with all the moronic delight of a gangster trying out his first machine gun. The law was something to be manipulated for profit and power. The streets were dark with something more than night. The mystery story grew hard and cynical about motive and characters, but it was not cynical about the effects it tried to produce nor about its technique of producing them."

What complicated Chandler's development as a writer was his awareness of the potential for the detective story. He had no intention of remaining a pulp writer, for except by churning out a large number of such stories every year, he could not survive as one. "From the beginning," he later wrote, "from the very first pulp story, it was always with me a question (first of course how to write a story at all) of putting into the stuff something they [the readers] would not shy off from, perhaps even not know was there as a conscious realization, but which would somehow distill through their minds and leave an afterglow." This is just another way of saying that Chandler wanted to write real fiction while using the detective-story form. In this way, he hoped to earn an income and also do something that was worth his while. "Of course I'm peculiar," he wrote some years afterward. "I look on mysteries as writing, demand the same standards as from any novel, and the extreme difficulty of the form to be met as well."

In following the footsteps of Hammett, Chandler knew that he was inevitably part of a group. "We all grew up together, so to speak," he wrote to a fellow pulp writer, "and we all wrote the same idiom, and we have all more or less grown out of it. A lot of *Black Mask* stories sounded alike, just as a lot of Elizabethan plays sound alike. Always when a group exploits a new technique this happens." He knew that he had to make his stories tough, although he later regretted the vast number of murders and violent deaths they contained. These were the conventions of the form. "Some of us tried pretty hard to break out of the formula," he wrote, "but we usually got caught and sent back. To exceed the limits of a formula without destroying it is the dream of every magazine writer who is not a hopeless hack." Specifically, he was anxious to exceed Dashiell Hammett: "I thought that perhaps I could go a bit further, be a bit more humane, get a bit more interested in people than in violent death."

In later years Chandler explained more fully what he meant: "A long time ago when I was writing for the pulps I put into a story a line like this: 'He got out of the car and walked across the sun-drenched sidewalk until the shadow of the awning over the entrance fell across his face like the touch of cool water.' They took it out when they published the story. Their readers didn't appreciate this sort of thing, just held up the action.

"I set out to prove them wrong. My theory was that readers just *thought* they cared about nothing but the action; that really, although they didn't know it, they cared very little about the action. The things they really cared about, and that I cared about, were the creation of emotion through dialogue and description. The things they remembered, that haunted them, were not for example that a man got killed, but that in the moment of his death he was trying to pick a paper clip off the polished surface of a desk, and it kept slipping away from him, so that there was a look of strain on his face and his mouth was half open in a kind of tormented grin, and the last thing in the world he thought about was death. He didn't even hear death knock on the door. That damn little paper clip kept slipping away from his fingers."

Chandler's first story, "Blackmailers Don't Shoot," he later dismissed as "pure pastiche," saying that it contained enough action for five stories and condemning it as a "goddamn pose." The judgment is fair, if exaggerated, given the quality of his later work, but it was only to be expected that his first attempt would be imitative. "Finger Man," his third story, published in 1934, was the first he said he felt at home with. Nearly all his early stories adhere to certain conventions. The private detective is not employed to unravel a mystery or reveal the murderer of the corpse that appears on page one, as in the tales of ratiocination so popular in England. Chandler's detectives become immediately involved in an active world of crime and have to steer a tricky course between the criminals and the police (who are sometimes the same) as well as be circumspect about the women. Chandler experimented with a number of detectives before he settled on Marlowe. Some of the stories are told through an anonymous first person; some are characters observed by the omniscient author. But whether named or not, John Dalmas, Ted Carmady, Johnny DeRuse, Pete Anglish, and Sam Delaguerra are all tough, independent men, aware that society has gone wrong, who try to deflect the corruption a little bit by saving one or two innocent people, usually women who are being blackmailed. The type is set in the first story: "The man in the powder-blue suit—which wasn't powder-blue under the lights of the Club Bolivar—was tall, with wide-set gray eyes, a thin nose, a jaw of stone. He had a rather sensitive mouth. His hair was crisp and black, ever so faintly touched with gray, as by an almost diffident hand. His clothes fitted him as though they had a soul of their own, not just a doubtful past. His name happened to be Mallory."

In Chandler's work the private detective is usually disliked, or at most tolerated, by the police. His very existence is an implied criticism of their incompetence, corruption, or both. The "private eye" as portrayed by Chandler is a fictional hero in the central tradition of American literature. Like so many rebellious and individualistic characters in the novels of Hawthorne, Melville, Cooper, and Mark Twain, he lives by his own code of morality and is at odds with prevailing standards of behavior. The Robin Hood tradition is one of the oldest in all fiction, and its popularity rests on the skeptical view most people have of human institutions.

On the other hand, the detective is not the most important character in Chandler's early work. He is there mainly as narrator and as someone through whom other, far more interesting characters may be seen. These cover the whole range of society, far more so than in the ordinary story that has a fixed setting and class of people. The gangsters range from brutal thugs to polished sophisticates. Those who do the kicking and gouging, the pistol whipping, torturing, and blackjack sapping are usually ignorant hulks with picturesque names like Moose Magoon and Big Chin Lorentz. Mentally deficient, they just follow orders, but Chandler recognizes their humanity. In "Mandarin's Jade" one of the gangsters comes to a bad end, and the detective comments: "He wasn't funny any more or tough, or nasty. He was just a poor simple dead guy who had never known what it was all about."

The men who hire these hoodlums generally live in the shadowy middle world of crime. They sell pornography or drugs, are gamblers or fake spiritualists; they run doubtful clinics or crooked veterinary hospitals. A large number are nightclub operators or owners. As heir to the speakeasy of Prohibition, the nightclub is a natural arena for Chandler's dramas. It is a place where night is turned into day and where people reveal the undersides of their nature. People from all levels of society mingle there. Chandler's nightclub proprietors vary in elegance and style: some are fairly squalid; others are too clever to get their hands dirty. Most of them are typed, wearing dinner jackets and dark glasses, with a pistol in the desk drawer in the back office. Most of them are Italian or Mexican with names like Zapparty, Benny Cyrano, and Canales. Although they give orders to the hoodlums and goon squads, they are really not much above them. They are caught in the middle like Soukesian in "Mandarin's Jade," who "looked like a man who had something to do he didn't relish, but was going to do it all the same."

The police have a similar hierarchy. The tough cops may be honest or dishonest, but all rely equally on force to get what they want. Above them there are some hard-working chief inspectors and detectives, but there are also others, usually with ambition, who become as corrupt as the crooks, making deals for their own advantage. At this point, the corruption is mainly personal. Above comes the level of politics, which, like everything else in Chandler's world, has both its legal and illegal aspects. In "Finger Man" the murder is arranged by a political manipulator, Frank Dorr, who peddles influence and lives off graft from gamblers and others on the fringe of legitimate society. "Politics—even when it's a lot of fun—is tough on the nerves," Dorr says. "You know me. I'm tough and I get what I want. There ain't a hell of a lot I want any more, but what I want—I want bad. And ain't so damn particular how I get it." In another story, "Spanish Blood," the criminal turns out to be the police commissioner, but there is nothing to be done about it. "Downtown," the detective explains, "they like it the way it is. It's swell politics." Though rarely so overt, Chandler's cynicism about society is a pervasive element in his stories. All a decent man has is his individual code of honor. As for society, it offers little to cheer about. At the end of "Smart-Aleck Kill" the detective and the police captain are sitting together. "What'll we drink to?" asks the captain. "Let's just drink," answers the detective.

But Chandler is not interested so much in social justice as in people, even if, like the women, they play somewhat conventional roles. Since there can be no real romance between the detective and the women of the story, because the detective must remain professionally apart and personally uninvolved, the women are mainly decorative. Most of them are beautiful and glamorous, tall, willowy blondes or girls, like Rhonda Farr in "Blackmailers Don't Shoot," with the telltale "eyes of cornflower blue" and "the sort of skin an old rake dreams of"—a phrase lifted incidentally (and probably unconsciously) from his prewar story about the London duchess who had "such skin as an old roué dreams of on his deathbed." Most of these girls require protection: they have got caught up in somebody else's troubles and are victims. "She was just a nice girl in a jam—and she didn't even know she was in a jam," says Marlowe in "Red Wind." Some of the girls are just drifters. Francine Ley, for example, is mixed up with a lot of marginal characters, and although not mischievous herself, she picks up their habits. She is amoral, a pretty girl who is playing with fire and doesn't know how to act. Others are sentimental and warm-hearted, but almost all of them are infected by the atmosphere of crime in which they live. In this cat-and-mouse world they are always afraid, for they are caught up in the drama as much as the men are. The detective helps wherever possible. In "Pickup on Noon Street" he finds the innocent girl he had been looking for everywhere, and when they meet, "the girl stared back at him. Slowly all the fear went out of her face."

Chandler is enough of a feminist to allow some of his women to be crooks, and no one is tougher than Carol Donovan in "Goldfish." She is "a very pretty black-haired, grey-eyed girl" and carries a .32. Even her partner in crime says, "She's too damn rough, Marlowe. I've seen hard women, but she's the bluing on armor plate." Finally, there is the pert, capable kind of girl who doesn't need help but needs love instead. Carol Pride is such a girl, with "a tired, pretty little face under fluffed-out brown hair, a rather narrow forehead with more height than is considered elegant, a small inquisitive nose, an upper lip a shade too long and a mouth more than a shade too wide. Her eyes could be very blue if they tried. She looked quiet, but not mousy-quiet. She looked smart, but not Hollywood smart."

Chandler's characters are really not fully developed in these stories. His avoidance of type figures makes his people seem real, but there are too many characters in each story for any one to be especially memorable. Many are vivid enough, however, to give the impression that they seem to be trying to grow. Chandler's *Black Mask* stories were all about 15,000 to 18,000 words in length, and this format forced Chandler to write more developed pieces of fiction than he had done when, as a young man in London, he wrote short sketches and tales in the manner of Saki. His experience with the pulps was an essential stage in his development as a novelist, for it taught him to mistrust the mind of the short-story writer, which, he later acknowledged, "gets by on an idea or a character or a twist without any real dramatic development." Chandler's stories are quite literally miniature novels.

The best writing in these stories appears in the descriptive passages and the dialogue. Chandler did not succeed in attaining a genuinely original style as he did in his novels, for he was experimenting all the time. Only when he settled on Marlowe and chose to speak through that personality did the language fully cohere. But in the stories there are immensely powerful passages. Here is one at the beginning of "Nevada Gas":

It was raining outside the Delmar Club. The liveried doorman helped Hugo Candless on with his belted white slicker and went out for his car. When he had it in front of the canopy he held an umbrella over Hugo across the strip of wooden matting to the curb. The car was a royal blue Lincoln limousine, with buff striping. The license number was 5A6.

The chauffeur, in a black slicker turned up high around his ears, didn't look around. The doorman opened the door and Hugo Candless got in and sank heavily on the back seat.

" 'Night, Sam. Tell him to go on home."

The doorman touched his cap, shut the door, and relayed the orders to the driver, who nodded without turning his head. The car moved off in the rain.

The rain came down slantingly and at the intersections sudden gusts blew it rattling against the glass of the limousine. The street corners were clotted with people trying to get across Sunset without being splashed. Hugo Candless grinned out at them, pityingly.

The car went out Sunset, through Sherman, then swung towards the hills. It began to go very fast. It was on a boulevard where traffic was thin now.

It was very hot in the car. The windows were all shut and the glass partition behind the driver's seat was shut all the way across. The smoke of Hugo's cigar was heavy and choking in the tonneau of the limousine.

Candless scowled and reached out to lower a window. The window lever didn't work. He tried the other side. That didn't work either. He began to get mad. He grabbed for the little telephone dingus to bawl his driver out. There wasn't any little telephone dingus.

The car turned sharply and began to go up a long straight hill with eucalyptus trees on one side and no houses. Candless felt something cold touch his spine, all the way up and down his spine. He bent forward and banged on the glass with his fist. The driver didn't turn his head. The car went very fast up the long dark hill road.

Hugo Candless grabbed viciously for the door handle. The doors didn't have any handles—either side. A sick, incredulous grin broke over Hugo's broad moon face.

The driver bent over to the right and reached for something with his gloved hand. There was a sudden sharp hissing noise. Hugo Candless began to smell the odor of almonds.

Very faint at first—very faint, and rather pleasant. The hissing noise went on. The smell of almonds got bitter and harsh and very deadly. Hugo Candless dropped his cigar and banged with all his strength on the glass of the nearest window. The glass didn't break.

The car was up in the hills now, beyond even the infrequent street lights of the residential sections.

Candless dropped back on the seat and lifted his foot to kick hard at the glass partition in front of him. The kick was never finished. His eyes no longer saw. His face twisted into a snarl and his head went back against the cushions, crushed down against his thick shoulders. His soft white felt hat was shapeless on his big square skull.

The driver looked back quickly, showing a lean, hawklike face for a brief instant. Then he bent to his right again and the hissing noise stopped.

He pulled over to the side of the deserted road, stopped the car, switched off all the lights. The rain made a dull noise pounding on the roof.

The driver got out in the rain and opened the rear door of the car, then backed away from it quickly, holding his nose.

He stood a little way off for a while and looked up and down the road.

In the back of the limousine Hugo Candless didn't move.

There is an element of burlesque in many of the stories or in portions of them, suggesting that Chandler knew that much of what he was writing was rubbish. One story called "Pearls Are a Nuisance" is a parody from start to finish, with its exaggerated drinking bouts and physical violence. This obligatory aspect of the hard-boiled school was tedious, and so, to amuse himself, Chandler wrote a burlesque of the tough-guy scene in "Bay City Blues." The crooked policeman De Spain gives the hoodlum Big Chin a beating to end beatings, of which this is just a portion:

> De Spain kicked him in the face.
> Big Chin rolled back on the gravel and clawed at his face with both hands and a wailing sound came through his fingers. De Spain stepped over and kicked him on the ankle. Big Chin howled. De Spain stepped back to his original position beyond the coat and the holstered gun. Big Chin rolled a little and came up on his knees and shook his head. Big dark drops fell from his face to the gravelly ground. He got up to his feet slowly and stayed hunched over a little.
> De Spain said: "Come on up. You're a tough guy. You got Vance Conried behind you and he's got the syndicate behind him. You maybe got Chief Anders behind you. I'm a lousy flatfoot with a ticket to nowhere in my pants. Come up. Let's put on a show."
> Big Chin shot out in a diving lunge for the gun. His hand touched the butt but only slewed it around. De Spain came down hard on the hand with his heel and screwed his heel. Big Chin yelled. De Spain jumped back and said wearily: "You ain't over-matched, are you sweetheart?"

Chandler had to be clever with his use of parody because he still wanted his stories to be accepted. For this reason, he often planted his jokes inconspicuously, as in the opening of "Red Wind": "There was a desert wind blowing that night. It was one of those hot dry Santa Anas that come down through the mountain passes and curl your hair and make your nerves jump and your skin itch. On nights like that every booze party ends in a fight. Meek little wives feel the edge of the carving knife and study their husbands' necks. Anything can happen. You can even get a full glass of beer at a cocktail lounge."

In an opening like this, most readers will be carried away by Chandler's genuinely atmospheric sentences and not notice the joke in the last one; but it is there for those who do. Chandler has a wide and varied audience of both kinds of reader.

In dialogue Chandler's object was to write sentences that sounded realistic. But he also liked to joke with word order and diction. Consider this extraordinary colloquy:

> "How did you know that was his window and what would he be doing here at this time of night?"

"Loading up his little needles," he said. "I've watched the guy some is how I know."

"Watched him why?"

The ordinary reader would not notice what Chandler was doing here, with his transference of spoken language to the printed page. He would think it sounded authentic and might find it curiously funny. But Chandler worked hard on these effects: "I'm an intellectual snob who happens to have a fondness for the American vernacular, largely because I grew up on Latin and Greek. As a result, when I use slang, solecisms, colloquialisms, snide talk or any kind of off-beat language, I do it deliberately. The literary use of slang is a study in itself. I've found that there are only two kinds that are any good: slang that has established itself in the language, and slang that you make up yourself. Everything else is apt to be passé before it gets into print."

Chandler's style—at least in the early stories—seems to break into two parts. In dialogue he carefully mimics American speech patterns. The sentences are formless and meandering and the word order is often cockeyed. He was obviously much amused by this practice, and the sentences are often funny. He was also delighted by the richness of the American language and added numerous locutions of his own, as in this passage: "Get dressed, sweetheart—and don't fuss with your necktie. Places want us to go to them."

In all other parts of Chandler's prose, in descriptive and narrative passages, his method is quite different. Here he does not use American patterns of speech, as Sherwood Anderson, Ernest Hemingway, and William Faulkner did, but writes in standard British English, the language that he had been taught to use at Dulwich and that is based on an understanding of Latin sentence structure. Chandler's diction is formal and compound sentences are common. His only mannerism is the overuse of the word "and," which he may have adopted from Hemingway, although in all other respects his style is utterly different from Hemingway's. What gives Chandler his particular flavor is that while using a standard British English sentence structure, he also employs a predominantly American vocabulary. His prose is never boring, because Chandler knows about cadence and pace. It is never dry, because the language is so fresh. This style is a natural product of his personal history. In his novels Chandler developed and refined his writing, but this is the basis from which he worked.

From the beginning Chandler's stories were recognized as being among the best of their type, but the five years that preceded the writing of *The Big Sleep* were not easy ones. Within a year of embarking on his new career, the Chandlers had moved to 1637 Redesdale Avenue, which was not far from Silver Lake. Thereafter they were constantly on the move, sometimes as often as two or three times a year. Chandler was a restless person, and there was always something wrong—noise, children, the traffic, bad neighbors, or climate. He and Cissy would go to Big Bear Lake in the hills above San Bernardino, where they could get a simple cabin for a few dollars a week; then they would go down to La Jolla to get away from the cold in the hills, and then to Riverside, where they had to "stop the doors and windows with wads of rag to keep the dust out, and without success." Harried from there to Cathedral City, the poor relation of Palm Springs, they moved to Pacific Palisades, where they bought some land, hoping one day to build on it. But the wind was so bad they had "to put five stakes around each Dahlia bush to keep it from being blown down." And so they moved on again.

In an interview some years afterward, Chandler told Irving Wallace that his earnings averaged $2,750 a year—but this was after he had begun to write novels. In the 1930s he earned far less, even though he was no longer paid the minimum rate for his stories but probably about five cents a word. As late as 1938, when he sold three stories to *Dime Detective* magazine, whose payment records have survived, he earned only $1,275, about one-tenth of what he earned as an oil executive. The Depression was hard on the Chandlers. They lived always in furnished rooms, having put their furniture in storage to save money. "I never slept in the park," he later wrote, "but I came damn close to it. I went five days without anything to eat but soup once, and I had just been sick at that. It didn't kill me, but neither did it increase my love of humanity. The best way to find out if you have any friends is to go broke. The ones that hang on longest are your friends."

The psychological strain was also great, and he had nothing to rely on but himself, having given up drinking entirely after losing his job with the oil company. Then with the first publication came the cruel realization that at his age he could not produce the thousands of words a day he would need to survive as a writer. Yet with his back to the Pacific, he dug in his heels and endured a lustrum of physical discomfort and isolation.

The miracle is that during these five years his work steadily improved. Every year he became a sharper craftsman and a more vivid stylist. But perhaps it is no miracle: perhaps Chandler needed the misfortunes of this period to force himself to greater efforts. Yet how many moments of doubt there must have been. In a short story about a failed playwright and a failed novelist called "A Couple of Writers," Chandler describes the emptiness that afflicts anyone who takes up creative work. "Jesus, we're the most useless people in the world," muses one of his characters. "There must be a hell of a lot of us too, all lonely, all empty, all poor, all gritted with small mean worries that have no dignity. All trying like men caught in a bog to get some firm ground under our feet and knowing all the time it doesn't make a damn bit of difference whether we do or not."

But with Chandler it was different. He knew he had something to say, and that is why he stuck to it from the age of forty-five to fifty with scant evidence that it was worth anything. His faith in himself may be seen in a remark he made about Shakespeare which, though not immodestly intended, has an autobiographical ring: "Shakespeare would have done well in any generation, because he would have refused to die in a corner; he would have taken the false gods and made them over; he would have taken the current formulae and forced them into something lesser men thought them incapable of. Alive today he would undoubtedly have written and directed motion pictures, plays, and God knows what. Instead of saying 'This medium is no good,' he would have used it and made it good."

In all of this Chandler was supported by Cissy. Her willingness to endure hardships spurred him on as a writer. In Chandler, the artist developed through his own strength and through the knowledge that his wife believed in him. There was a passion that encompassed the thing itself and the artist who created it, working with the help of his wife. The stories and novels that were to follow were, in a sense, their children.

4.
THE
BIG
SLEEP

After writing short stories for five years, Chandler began to plan a full-length book in 1938. Instinctively he knew that the life of a pulp writer was limited. The decision was made partly because Joseph Shaw had resigned as editor of *Black Mask*. Chandler switched his allegiance to *Dime Detective* but did not have the same intimate relationship with Ken White, the editor, or with the publisher of Popular Publications, Harry Steeger.

Chandler admitted a general ignorance of detective novels and said that he hadn't read more than three or four before he actually began to write them himself. He always stood apart from his fellow detective-story writers. "The main trouble with most detective stories, as I see it," he wrote, "is that the people who write them are bad writers." He also found most of them unsatisfactory as literature because "the mind which can produce a coolly thought-out puzzle can't, as a rule, develop the fire and dash necessary for vivid writing." Chandler also considered the traditional deductive novel basically dishonest because it relied on esoteric information or gave misleading information. He believed that "the truly honest detective story or novel of detection (a more respectable term perhaps) is one in which the reader is given all the material for solving the mystery, where nothing significant is underemphasized and nothing insignificant overemphasized, and where the facts themselves carry their own interpretation and do not have to be carried into a laboratory and be analyzed under microscopes to disclose their meaning."

Freeman Wills Crofts and R. Austin Freeman he admired, but for Agatha Christie Chandler had the greatest scorn. Reading *And Then There Were None*, he commented that "as an honest crime story, honest in the sense that the reader is given a square deal and the motivations and mechanisms of the murders are sound—it is bunk." The book annoyed him especially because it relied on a contradiction of character and depended on a man suddenly acting quite differently from the way he had behaved before. He also thought the book showed Christie's "abysmal ignorance of lethal drugs and their action." Despite his irritation with it, Chandler wrote: "I'm very glad I read the book because it finally and for all time settled a question in my mind that had at least some lingering doubt attached to it. Whether it is possible to write a strictly honest mystery of the classic type. It isn't.

"To get the complication you fake the clues, the timing, the play of coincidence, assume certainties where only 50 per cent chances exist at most. To get the surprise murderer you fake character, which hits me hardest of all, because I have a sense of character. If people want to play this game, it's all right by me. But for Christ's sake let's not talk about honest mysteries. They don't exist."

Another aspect of the traditional detective story that irritated Chandler was the elevated social position of the detective. "I don't deny the mystery writer the privilege of making his detective any sort of person he wants to make him—a poet, philosopher, student of ceramics or Egyptology, or a master of all the sciences like Dr. Thorndike. What I don't seem to cotton to is the affectation of gentility which does not belong to the job and which is in effect a subconscious expression of snobbery, the kind of thing that reached its high-water mark in Dorothy Sayers. Perhaps the trouble is that I'm an English Public School man myself and know these birds inside out. And the only kind of Public School man who could make a real detective would be the Public School man in revolt, like George Orwell."

In preparing to write longer fiction, Chandler read a great deal in the traditional literature of detection, but almost everywhere he was disappointed. He believed, for example, that an enjoyment of Sherlock Holmes relied "partly on nostalgia and partly on qualities which did not originally make the interest of the Holmes stories. Doyle understood the uses of eccentricity, but to a person with any knowledge of the police and how they operate his policemen are utterly absurd. His scientific premises are very unreliable, and the element of mystery to a sophisticated mind frequently does not exist."

Jacques Barzun has tried to distinguish detective fiction from the ordinary novel by saying that it derives from the tale, the sort of story written by Poe. In this fantasy world he believes that Chandler's strictures about character and plausibility are simply irrelevant. But it is evident from the beginning that Chandler wanted to write novels, not tales, even though he used the formulas of detective fiction. In later years he wrote that "my whole career is based on the idea that the formula doesn't matter, the thing that counts is what you do with the formula; that is to say, it is a matter of style." As a writer, he therefore took as his models the best of his predecessors and cited his admiration for such works as Merimée's *Carmen*, Flaubert's "Hérodias" and "Un Cœur Simple" from *Trois Contes*, James's *The Spoils of Poynton* and *The Wings of the Dove*, and Conrad's *The Secret Agent*. Knowing that the form he chose was basically melodramatic, Chandler read and studied Dumas and Dickens, who in many ways were his masters. They were useful models, because in melodrama "the potential for emotion is overcharged, the compression of time and event is a violation of probability, and although such things happen, they do not happen so fast and in such a tight frame of logic to so closely knit a group of people." Chandler also had a list of books which for special reasons he admired. They included Maugham's *Ashenden*, Saki's *The Unbearable Bassington*, Borrow's *Lavengro*, Stevenson's *The New Arabian Nights*, and *The New Humpty Dumpty* "by a man named Chaucer, of whom I never otherwise heard," who was in fact Ford Madox Ford.

As Chandler began to write longer fiction, he faced a real challenge. The compression of the short story allowed him to rely on action, but in the novel he had to portray his characters fully and give an authentic sense of their world. Unlike Hammett, who had been a Pinkerton detective, Chandler knew little about crime. He did little direct research with the police, because, as he told an interviewer, "cops are pretty dumb people." Mainly he relied on reading. He owned Major J. S. Hatcher's *Textbook of Firearms* and a pamphlet called *1,000 Police Questions Answered for the California Peace Officer* by Judge Charles W. Fricke. Also on his desk were books on forensic medicine, cross-examination, and toxology. He also relied on his memory. If he wanted to portray a seedy hotel and didn't have it quite right, he would go and sit in the lobby of one of them for half a day, listening and watching. He would notice what the desk clerk wore, what he said; he would observe the walls, the pictures or calendar hanging by the desk, the furniture, the hotel guests. But generally he made no special effort at research. Like most novelists, he was alert and aware of his surroundings, and he would use whatever came to hand. A newspaper article about a secret purveyor of pornographic books would set him off, and his imagination would transform this person into A. G. Geiger of *The Big Sleep*.

The expansion of Chandler's material from the short story to the novel also allowed him to convey a real sense of Los Angeles. From the beginning, as a Spanish colonial town, it was a tough place, whose first building was the jail. After the Mexicans were dispossessed by the Yankees in the 1850s, with a chicanery that is typical of the place, it remained for the next twenty years the worst frontier outpost in the West, with whorehouses, weekend murders, and frequent lynchings of Chinese and Mexicans. The Protestant churches even closed down and abandoned the city to the devil—and the Roman Catholic Church.

The railways opened up California at the end of the century, and the great corporate battles between the Southern Pacific and the Santa Fe (described in Frank Norris' novel *The Octopus*) set a pattern of land manipulation that has persisted. The Los Angeles Chamber of Commerce, the first in the country, advertised the city as heaven on earth, and to the delight of land speculators, hundreds of thousands of people poured in from the Middle West.

Believing that Los Angeles would flourish only if its labor force were less well paid than the workers of San Francisco, the businessmen of the city, under the leadership of Harrison Gray Otis, the owner of the *Los Angeles Times*, formed the Merchants and Manufacturers Association to fight the closed-shop movement. There was virtually open warfare between the two sides, which ended when several bombs exploded in the *Times* offices, killing twenty people and destroying the building. When it was proven in court that the bombs were planted by union agitators, the ensuing outcry ended the possibility of socialism and vigorous unionism in Los Angeles. The city fell under a right-wing coalition so repressive that it had no equal elsewhere in the country. Underneath a benign surface, the hard hand of the businessman directed the elected officials and the police. Violations of free speech and assembly were common: the "Red Squad" drove dozens of teachers and clergymen from their jobs, forced censorship of reading in the schools, and led to the "zoot suit" riots of World War II in which white sailors on leave together with other vigilante groups attacked and stripped hundreds of black and Mexican citizens, destroying their clothes and beating them up, while the police looked on, occasionally arresting a black or Mexican.

Police lawlessness has been more prevalent in Los Angeles than in most American cities. Growing up in a tradition of brutality, the police relied heavily on arbitrary arrests made merely on suspicion of criminal activity and wholly lacking in evidence or legality. Ernest Hopkins, writing in 1931 in *Our Lawless Police*, said that the Los Angeles police officers he encountered expressed an open hostility to constitutional guarantees and spoke publicly in favor of "the criminology of violence, the denial of individual rights, and the infliction of cruel punishments." The rubber hose was most frequently used, since it left no visible marks. The beatings usually took place during third-degree grill sessions, another illegal practice, in which the police tried to force confessions from arrested persons.

Los Angeles is the largest American city that is predominantly Protestant. With so many of its citizens coming from Iowa and Kansas, it has a strong puritanical streak, which makes it possible for the public to accept summary police proceedings and the harassment of minorities with unpopular opinions. This repression in turn explains much of the craziness associated with Southern California—the religious cults and the quackery. Lacking legitimate outlets for protest and even free expression, people find bizarre solutions to their problems. This is why Southern California is at once the most conservative part of the country and also the most egalitarian.

The strange customs of Los Angeles have attracted many commentators, especially from abroad. Aldous Huxley's *After Many a Summer*, which is a loose parody of William Randolph Hearst's life, and Evelyn Waugh's *The Loved One*, which satirizes the local attitude toward death, have attracted much notice. But these two books were just raids on Los Angeles. In choosing overt absurdities, the authors neglected the main subject. Also, they removed themselves physically or spiritually from the place.

With Chandler, it was different. He was American and had lived in California for years, working in an office and intimately aware of its commercial life. Given his background and education, he could not take it seriously, nor could he escape it. This is the comic and tragic aspect of California of which Chandler takes account in his work. Moving to Los Angeles from some older, more settled place, you think it's absurd. But every morning you wake up and you're still there. It's funny, but it's also your life.

When Chandler went to Los Angeles in 1912, he found a provincial city and, in the comfortable household of the Warren Lloyds, a society of intelligent people. But gradually, as the city grew in size and he grew up in it, it was transformed into what is now called urban sprawl. The old center of Los Angeles ceased to have meaning before it fulfilled itself, and the wide, flat basin that stretches from the Pacific to the mountains is essentially a conglomerate of villages and small cities. Los Angeles is just a name: the reality is Westwood or Pasadena or Beverly Hills for the rich; Watts for the poor blacks; East Los Angeles for the Mexican Americans; and the characterless streets that stretch from West

Hollywood to the beaches for the hundreds of thousands of immigrants who came from other parts of the country to have a few square feet in the sun. Neighborhoods are completely segregated from one another. By the time San Fernando Valley had nearly a million white inhabitants, only eighteen black families lived outside of Pacoima, the ghetto arranged by the developers for blacks with moderate incomes. There is no real center to Los Angeles and little feeling in one section for another. The city lacks an identity of its own and the buildings show it. There is no native architecture, as in New York. In the richer sections the houses are modeled on Italian or Spanish villas; below that come ordinary wooden houses that might as well be in Illinois or New Jersey; then comes the anonymous mass architecture of flat-roofed bungalows and apartment buildings.

Yet life in Los Angeles is by no means dull. Its vitality comes from its extraordinary contrasts. It also has the energy of an unfinished city and a creative spirit that is wholly absent, for example, in the superficially more attractive museum city of San Francisco. As Joseph Dabney's vice-president, Chandler undoubtedly visited this millionaire's house at 420 South Lafayette Place and saw there the rough style of first-generation riches. Los Angeles was anonymous enough for him to go anywhere, and he was obviously uninhibited in his exploration of the city, becoming familiar with the old section of Bunker Hill, the nightclubs on the edge of town in Santa Monica and Glendale, the rundown hotels in districts gone to seed. Above all, the relaxed atmosphere and unpretentiousness of the place, like the endless sunshine and warmth, so different from the formality and gloom of London, made it attractive to Chandler. In his fifth novel, *The Little Sister*, a disillusioned Marlowe reminisces about the days Chandler himself must first have known in Los Angeles. "I used to like this town," he says. "A long time ago. There were trees along Wilshire Boulevard. Beverly Hills was a country town. Westwood was bare hills and lots offering at eleven hundred dollars and no takers. Hollywood was a bunch of frame houses on the inter-urban line. Los Angeles was just a big dry sunny place with ugly homes and no style, but goodhearted and peaceful. It had the climate they yap about now. People used to sleep out on porches. Little groups who thought they were intellectual used to call it the Athens of America. It wasn't that, but it wasn't a neon-lighted slum either."

There is something appropriate in Chandler's choosing the detective story as his vehicle for presenting Los Angeles, and not only because a real detective, William J. Burns, became the hero of the ruling powers for discovering the union agitators who blew up the *Los Angeles Times* building. The detective story, so peculiar to the modern city, can involve an extraordinary range of humanity, from the very rich to the very poor, and can encompass a great many different places. Most of Chandler's contemporaries who wrote "straight" fiction—Fitzgerald, Hemingway, and Faulkner, for example—confined themselves to a special setting and a limited cast of characters. The detective story, however, allowed Chandler to create the whole of Los Angeles in much the same way that such nineteenth-century novelists as Dickens and Balzac created London and Paris for future generations.

When Chandler began to write *The Big Sleep* in the spring of 1938, he decided to use some of the stories that had already appeared in pulp magazines as the basis for his novel. "I had a bunch of old novelettes full of material—and it looked like pretty good material to me—and they were, so far as I could then see, as extinct as a dodo." Chandler called his custom of rescuing earlier work "cannibalizing," and it bears some examining because of its peculiarities. Ordinarily, a novelist would avoid the tedious method of combining two or three short stories to make a longer work. Most novelists could not bear the analysis required and would find it far easier to start again with new characters and situations. But Chandler did not have this narrative abundance. He found it hard to tell a story and therefore used a method similar to that of a playwright who has in mind a number of scenes he wants to string together. "When I started out to write fiction I had the great disadvantage of having absolutely no talent for it," he later wrote. "I couldn't get characters in and out of rooms. They lost their hats and so did I. If more than two people were on a scene I couldn't keep one of them alive. This failing is still with me, of course, to some extent. Give me two people snotting each other across a desk and I am happy. A crowded canvas just bewilders me."

In using the earlier stories, Chandler did not tinker with them, fitting one scene beside another or revising in the ordinary sense of adding or eliminating phrases. He worked out more or less what he wanted to say in his head, and then he began all over again, being careful not to be tied down by his preconceptions and remaining open to chance. Chandler believed strongly in spontaneity and in being relaxed. "All good writing takes skill and devotion," he wrote. "Sometimes it comes hard and is no good. Sometimes it just floats in and says, 'Here I am'" In cannibalizing his stories, he tried to combine his analytical gifts, which were purely intellectual, with the organic or physical ingredient that determines the emotional quality and value of a book. "I do my plotting in my head as I go along," he wrote, "and usually I do it wrong and have to do it again." Chandler's dislike of deductive detective stories made him disparage plots: "The plot thickens and the people become mere names." But he also had a special attitude toward his own plots, which is simply a part of his attitude toward writing generally:

"With me a plot, if you could call it that, is an organic thing. It grows and often it overgrows. I am continually finding myself with scenes that I won't discard and that don't want to fit in. So that my plot problem invariably ends up as a desperate attempt to justify a lot of material that, for me at least, has come alive and insists on staying alive. It's probably a silly way to write, but I seem to know no other way. The mere idea of being committed in advance to a certain pattern appals me."

The Big Sleep, written in a short spurt of three months, is derived from two stories: "Killer in the Rain," which was published in 1935, and "The Curtain," which appeared the following year. These stories have certain similarities which made it natural that they be combined. In each there is an older father with a rich and irresponsible daughter; Chandler turned the two men into General Sternwood of the novel. He also took the two women, Carmen Dravec of "Killer in the Rain" and Mrs. O'Mara of "The Curtain," and made them sisters. Certain other characters are combined or transferred whole into the novel. He also borrowed small portions of two other stories, "Finger Man" and "Mandarin's Jade."

Chandler wrote The Big Sleep as an entirely new work, but he was helped by a memory that permitted almost total recall, even of phraseology. It is as if the creation of the original images required the sort of emotional energy that makes a poet remember his lines years after he first wrote them down: they were there for Chandler whenever he wanted them. Chandler's novels therefore have the wholeness that comes from fresh creative effort. He had already recorded the world of Southern California that fascinated him, but he had not yet given it the form—or perhaps completed his conception of it—until he began writing full-length books. The difference between the stories and the novels is mainly one of feel. The stories have a certain brittleness, a tentative quality that vanishes in the novels.

This development is a matter of literary authority and does not derive from technique so much as from a genuine comprehension of the subject. Details of setting, for example, can be used just to give the reader some necessary information, or they can help set the mood and reveal the theme of the whole work. In "The Curtain" Chandler introduces Mrs. O'Mara's room in the general's house with nothing more than utilitarian details: "This room had a white carpet from wall to wall. Ivory drapes of immense height lay tumbled casually on the white carpet inside the many windows. The windows stared towards the dark foothills, and the air beyond the glass was dark too. It hadn't started to rain yet, but there was a feeling of pressure in the atmosphere."

The same scene in The Big Sleep is more leisurely, and Chandler uses physical details—especially the contrast of white with ivory and the "bled out" image—to suggest indirectly that something is very wrong in the house and that Mrs. Regan (the name is changed) knows it: "The room was too big, the ceiling was too high, the doors were too tall, and the white carpet that went from wall to wall looked like a fresh fall of snow at Lake Arrowhead. There were full-length mirrors and crystal doodads all over the place. The ivory furniture had chromium on it, and the enormous ivory drapes lay tumbled on the white carpet a yard from the windows. The white made the ivory look dirty and the ivory made the white look bled out. The windows stared towards the darkening foothills. It was going to rain soon. There was pressure in the air already."

The main reason for the higher quality of Chandler's novels is his decision to use Philip Marlowe as his first-person narrator. He had experimented with other methods and characters with different names, but eventually he settled on Marlowe. At first, Marlowe was an ordinary *Black Mask* character: tough, strong, attractive to women, an honest man in a crooked trade. This kind of hero is common in American literature and seems to represent a faith in the incorruptibility of at least part of the population. The early Marlowe's antecedents are Natty Bumppo, Huckleberry Finn, and Hemingway's Nick Adams.

The use of a first-person narrator has great disadvantages, especially in a mystery story, where a lot must happen when the detective is not on the scene. It is difficult to provide this information without boring the reader. Chandler was aware of the problem, and in making Marlowe witty and alert he got away with it as much as possible. Having a first-person character tell the story also has advantages: it enriches the texture of the writing and gives it a personality that cannot be provided by the omniscient narrator. Joseph Conrad discovered this when he used the character Marlow to tell his tales; so did Chandler when by coincidence he used a man with the same name. But instead of the portentousness that comes with Conrad's narrator, Philip Marlowe lightens the tone. The wisecracks create the quasi-cynical, quasi-romantic atmosphere that envelops the books. Most detective-story narrators are colorless: Hammett's Sam Spade is tough and clever, but he is not a person at all. For Chandler, Marlowe was something quite different: through his voice comes what Chandler called the "controlled half-poetical emotion" that is at the heart of the work.

To a degree, Marlowe evolves from Chandler's own character. Certain personal qualities, such as Marlowe's tolerance for physical abuse, belong to the formula of the hard-boiled detective, but Chandler actually dissected his own character as objectively as possible in order to apply what was appropriate to Marlowe. There is a kind of absurdity in the procedure that must have amused him. Nevertheless, as is shown in his famous characterization of the fictional detective in "The Simple Art of Murder," there is also a good deal of the real Chandler: "He has a sense of character, or he would not know his job. He will take no man's money dishonestly and no man's insolence without a due and dispassionate revenge. He is a lonely man and his pride is that you will treat him as a proud man or be sorry you ever saw him. He talks as a man of his age talks—that is, with rude wit, a lively sense of the grotesque, a disgust for sham, and a contempt for pettiness."

Some readers, knowing a little about Chandler's own nature, have imagined that he created in Marlowe an idealized concept of himself, making up for his own deficiencies. Such a procedure might have appealed to a young writer bent on self-expression, but Chandler was fifty when he began *The Big Sleep* and no longer a child. He had the far more difficult problem of investing a type of person he probably never even met with attributes that would make him bearable as a narrator yet realistic as a character.

After creating the fully drawn Marlowe of the novels, Chandler realized that although Marlowe was closer to being a real detective than the heroes of Dorothy Sayers and Agatha Christie, he was still a long way from being realistic: "The real-life private eye is a sleazy little drudge from the Burns Agency, a strong-arm guy with no more personality than a blackjack. He has about as much moral stature as a stop and go sign." A person as intelligent and sensitive as Marlowe would simply not work as a detective. Chandler put it succinctly by saying that the private detective of fiction "does not and could not exist. He is the personification of an attitude, the exaggeration of a possibility." Moreover, the conventions of detective fiction impose other unreal attributes. "The whole point," Chandler observed, "is that the detective exists complete and entire and unchanged by anything that happens, that he is, as detective, outside the story and above it, and always will be. That is why he never gets the girl, never marries, never really has any private life, except insofar as he must eat and sleep and have a place to keep his clothes. His moral and intellectual force is that he gets nothing but his fee, for which he will if he can protect the innocent, guard the helpless and destroy the wicked, and the fact that he must do this while earning a meagre living in a corrupt world is what makes him stand out."

The limits these conventions impose show how different most detective fiction is from ordinary fiction. In most novels the reader associates himself with the central character, but with Marlowe that would be an exercise in empty fantasy. Chandler was well aware of the problem he was dealing with when he observed that the ordinary mystery novel had "the elements of tragedy without being tragic, and the elements of heroism without being heroic. It is a dream world which may be entered and left at will, and it leaves no scars." Chandler's ambition was to bridge the gap between detective fiction and ordinary fiction by imbuing his characters with attitudes and feelings that do in fact leave scars.

In his early fiction in particular, Chandler thought of Marlowe as a catalyst, a means of bringing to the foreground the other characters who are the real substance of his fiction. This was an act of compromise, as writing so often is; but it was an original and important one, for in effect it was an attempt to give real substance to a popular form of literature. If fantasy and reality are blended in Chandler's work, another pair of opposites were equally necessary. "There must be idealism," he wrote, "but there must also be contempt." The balancing act this attitude requires affects Marlowe as narrator. Although he is a creature of fantasy, he also serves as a guide for the reader. Marlowe is like Vergil in Dante's *Divine Comedy:* he says what the reader might say about the world of Los Angeles were he to encounter it himself. The reader cannot sensibly associate himself with Marlowe as a character in the novel, but he readily accepts his voice. Because it is casual, witty, and forthright, he naturally likes to identify himself with it. This is one of the reasons for Chandler's popularity as a writer.

Chandler's longer fiction also enlarges his focus. Where in his shorter fiction he limited his range to those immediately involved in the criminal world, in *The Big Sleep* he points his finger at those who are responsible for the corruption of society or who live off it, often unaware that they are parasites. Chandler was not in the habit of condemning whole classes of people, and was attracted to upper-class life. But his hatred for such people as his wealthy Irish uncle and the millionaire Joseph Dabney comes out in Marlowe's outburst against Carmen, General Sternwood's younger daughter. "To hell with the rich," he says. "They make me sick." They disgust him because they misuse their power and are careless about other people, which shows how corrupt they are as human beings. In *The Big Sleep* Chandler is more overt in his social commentary than he is in his later novels; it's as though, at the outset, he thought he ought to make it clear where he stood, not quite trusting the story to make the point for him. In an interview toward the end of the book, Marlowe listens to Captain Gregory of the Missing Persons Bureau, whose view of society is similar to Chandler's own:

"I'm a copper," he said. "Just a plain ordinary copper. Reasonably honest. As honest as you could expect a man to be in a world where it's out of style. That's mainly why I asked you to come in this morning. I'd like you to believe that. Being a copper I like to see the law win. I'd like to see the flashy well-dressed mugs like Eddie Mars spoiling their manicures in the rock quarry at Folsom, alongside of the poor little slum-bred hard guys that got knocked over on their first caper and never had a break since. That's what I'd like. You and me both lived too long to think I'm likely to see it happen. Not in this town, not in any town half this size, in any part of this wide, green and beautiful USA. We just don't run our country that way."

This somber note is sounded again at the end of the book when the action is over: "What did it matter where you lay once you were dead? In a dirty sump or in a marble tower on top of a high hill. You were dead, you were sleeping the big sleep, you were not bothered by things like that. Oil and water the same as wind and air to you. You just slept the big sleep, not caring about the nastiness of how you died or where you fell."

Despite these dark thoughts, *The Big Sleep* is a comedy—a comedy of human futility. Chandler was not interested in making social statements: he was just eager to write an extended story and have the jokes come off. He succeeded because he wrote the book quickly and because its serious side is expressed obliquely. The energy of the narrative and the wit of the dialogue are what the reader remembers. Cities and society in decay are notably capable of giving off this energy—their corruption is vivid and picturesque—whereas it's far more difficult to write about honest and high-minded people.

Chandler had no elaborate pretensions about the book. "My story," he wrote, "is just another detective yarn that happens to be more interested in people than in plot, to try to stand on its own legs as a novel with the mystery a few drops of tabasco on the oyster." As is natural with a first novel, it has faults. There are some tiresomely explanatory passages (although Chandler was proud to have avoided one at the end), and, as he admitted, he worked the similes to death. But beyond everything lay his delight in language. "I guess maybe there are two kinds of writers," he mused afterward; "writers who write stories and writers who write writing." He was not in the least apologetic about writing a detective novel instead of a "straight" one. His ambitions were quite different: "The thing is to squeeze the last drop out of the medium you have learned to use. The aim is not essentially different from the aim of Greek tragedy, but we are dealing with a public that is only semi-literate and we have to make an art of a language they can understand." Critical illiteracy that rates the arts according to subject matter irritated Chandler, however, because his artistic ambition was to do something with the detective novel that had never been done before. He therefore had no interest in the traditional detective-story fan. "Our target is not the mystery addict," he wrote to his publisher. "He knows nothing, remembers nothing. He buys books cheap or rents them. It all goes in one ear and crosses the vacuum to the other." This is why he later kept apart from other detective-story writers and disliked being considered in their company. "Very likely," he wrote of several of them, "they write better mysteries than I do, but their words don't get up and walk. Mine do, although it is embarrassing to announce it."

In 1939 Chandler's self-confidence was not so secure as these later comments suggest, but the reception of *The Big Sleep* justified his hopes. The book was placed with the firm of Alfred A. Knopf, Inc., Dashiell Hammett's publisher, by Chandler's agent, Sydney Sanders, who was familiar with *Black Mask* authors and later employed Joseph Shaw in his office. Before publication Chandler was naturally apprehensive, having so much riding on the success of this first book. Knopf urged him to get on with his next, but Chandler wanted to wait until the results were in. The reviewers immediately recognized him as the newest member of the Hammett school, but several thought that his work was nasty and perverted. "I do not want to write depraved books," Chandler protested to Knopf. "I was aware that this yarn had some fairly unpleasant citizens in it, but my fiction was learned in a rough school, and I probably didn't notice them much." He was cheered by an enthusiastic review in the *Los Angeles Times*, however, and added that "I don't feel quite such a connoisseur of moral decay as I did yesterday."

Actually, Chandler did very well with this first novel. Innes Rose of John Farquharson Ltd., working as Sanders' London representative, placed the book with Hamish Hamilton and thereby embarked Chandler on a lifelong relationship with that firm. American sales of *The Big Sleep* justified Knopf's faith in Chandler, and he offered him a contract for his next book with a 20 per cent royalty for the first 5,000 copies sold and 25 per cent afterward—all based on wholesale prices. Comparing his English and American sales, Chandler often noted that Hamish Hamilton invariably did better by him than his American counterpart. The answer lies in the reading habits of the two countries. The English library system ensures considerably larger hardcover sales than normally occur in the United States. By contrast, American paperback sales are almost always several times greater than those in England. *The Big Sleep*, which sold over 10,000 copies in the original Knopf edition, did remarkably well for a first novel. According to Frank Gruber, an expert on the subject, "the average mystery novel sells in America less than 2,500 copies; between 15 and 20 of every year's offerings sell from 5,000 to 10,000 copies and a meagre six or eight, more than 10,000. These figures pertain to the regular $2 editions only, for the better-selling authors are also published in larger, cheaper editions." Chandler was one of these, for Grosset and

Dunlap, then the chief publisher of reprints made from the original plates, brought out a one-dollar edition that sold nearly 3,500 copies. Despite his grumbling, much of it justified, Chandler was right when he observed: "You work hard for ten years without getting anywhere, and then in ten minutes you 'arrive.' "

His success did not come a moment too soon, even though its material results were meager at the beginning. Fortunately, like most pulp writers, he had grown accustomed to a simple style of living. Over the years while writing for *Black Mask*, Chandler gradually became acquainted with some of his fellow detective-story writers, notably Dwight Babcock, Erle Stanley Gardner, Norbert Davis, Cleve Adams, W. T. Ballard, and George Harmon Coxe. The relationships began through correspondence, and he soon met those within reach. As a group lacking in literary reputation or pretensions, pulp writers were more friendly toward one another than most writers are. Two of them, Ballard and Adams, founded a group called the Fictioneers. There were about twenty-five members; all pulp and movie writers, who met once a month at Steven's Nikobob Café at the corner of Ninth Street and Western Avenue in Los Angeles, where they had a private dining room. The meetings were always informal, and their real purpose, Ballard recalls, "was to get comfortably drunk and then en masse attend one of the local burlesque theatres." The meetings also had a certain literary importance for its members since they provided a sense of identity. "The Fictioneers had been thoroughly pulp oriented," Ballard writes, "and one of the things that held it together was that most of us were working in the same markets. In the east there was a lot of backbiting among competitors, but in Hollywood because we were three thousand miles from our markets, we clung together, passing on any information which might help the other fellow." Chandler attended these meetings frequently, but Ballard never got to know him well. "He was a very retiring person who would sit at the dinners after the table had been cleared, sucking on his pipe and offering very little comment. Most writers like to talk about their own work (which is the only reason for a writers' club). Ray seldom did."

Another *Black Mask* writer who knew him then, Dwight Babcock, says that although they met from time to time, "I could never get close to him." He describes Chandler as "a professorial type, more of an intellectual than most of the other pulp writers I knew. He was a quiet man at that time, did not drink, and was older than most of the rest of us."

Of the group of *Black Mask* writers he knew, Chandler was probably closest to Cleve Adams, who was his contemporary in age. Chandler and Cissy often dined with the Adamses, but Chandler always remained somewhat apart. He was admired for what he had accomplished in a short period but was not intimate with anyone. The Chandlers lived near another pulp writer, John K. Butler, in Pacific Palisades, and the Butlers tried to bring the Chandlers into the group of young writers they knew, many of whom even lived together when times were bad. But Chandler kept his distance.

At the parties he attended Chandler would consume many cups of coffee and smoke his pipe, talking little with the other guests. Ruth Babcock, Dwight Babcock's wife, remembers his partiality for cats. "At one of our parties," she writes, "he seemed to be more interested in our cat than he was in the other guests. Our cat had been exiled to our trailer for the festivities, but Chandler insisted I take him to visit her. He spent quite some time comforting and consoling her at being displaced for the evening. I sensed he was more comfortable in our one-to-one conversation than the lively party going on inside."

To this same party Chandler brought a young writer whom he knew slightly. Unfortunately, the man got drunk and so Chandler took him home, throwing him over his shoulder like a sack of potatoes. Mrs. Babcock recalls the incongruity of "someone as dignified as Chandler" having to make his exit in such a way. Despite his reserve, Chandler could be outspoken, and he refused to be imposed upon. Once Mrs. Babcock gave a party for the Chandlers to which she invited Craig Rice, who at the time was well known as a detective-story writer. Mrs. Rice was a great admirer of Chandler's, but at her husband's insistence she spent much time at the party reciting her own poetry and playing her own compositions on the piano. At a later date Mrs. Babcock proposed another evening with the Rices, but Chandler refused. "If that woman is going to be there, I'm not coming," he said. He didn't care in the least that Craig Rice thought highly of his work.

Living standards among pulp writers were modest though decent. "A family of four could live comfortably on fifteen dollars a week," recalls W. T. Ballard, presumably referring only to the cost of food. If any one of the group had a successful sale, he would give a party and invite all the others. "Most of us were not secure financially," Mrs. Babcock recalls, "but very secure in our friendships. Even the wives, thrown together by their husbands' professions, were congenial."

Once a special dinner was held for those connected with *Black Mask*. It took place on January 11, 1936, and seems to have been arranged in preparation for a trip Joseph Shaw was planning to make to California. A group of ten writers gathered together and had their photograph taken. They then wrote their names on a piece of the tablecloth and sent both to Shaw in New York. The group included W. T. Ballard, Horace McCoy (author of *They Shoot Horses, Don't*

They?), and a number of others, of whom the most important were Chandler and Dashiell Hammett, who was then working in Hollywood. It was the only time Hammett and Chandler met, and in later years Chandler briefly recalled the occasion, saying that Hammett was "very nice-looking, tall, quiet, gray-haired, fearful capacity for Scotch, seemed quite unspoiled to me." It is somehow typical that these two men, who had more to say to each other than anyone else had at the dinner, never talked again.

Chandler's shyness made it difficult for him to know how to act with others. What social ease he may have developed in the oil business he lost in the solitude of his apprenticenship as a writer. In 1940 George Harmon Coxe visited Los Angeles and asked Chandler to have dinner with him at the Roosevelt Hotel. Chandler was then living in Arcadia, on the northeast fringe of the city. In his awkward consideration for Coxe, he had an early dinner at home before coming in so as not to burden his host with the expense of a meal. Coxe remembers Chandler's unpretentious humor and diffidence; the success generated by *The Big Sleep* had not affected him at all.

Chandler's social diffidence may also have come from the feeling of unreality that California sometimes imposes on those who are not natives. One evening while he was having dinner with Cleve Adams and his wife, they heard church bells across the valley. Mrs. Adams said how much she liked them, but Chandler said he hated them because they reminded him of England. It was not that he hated England; rather, he was momentarily saddened by his exile from it. When Alfred Knopf sent him one of Max Beerbohm's books, he replied: "I found it sad reading. It belongs to the age of taste, to which I once belonged. It is possible that like Beerbohm I was born half a century too late, and that I too belong to an age of grace. I could so easily have become everything our world has no use for. So I wrote for *Black Mask*. What a wry joke." In bad moments Chandler thought of himself as a sort of remittance man, at least in spirit, or as one of Kipling's gentlemen-rankers who feel guilty about not having made good in England: "We are dropping down the ladder rung by rung, / And the measure of our torment is the measure of our youth." Chandler should have hated England for training him for a life it could not then provide him with, but instead he blamed himself. He adored England and hated California. "We are so rootless here," he wrote. "I've lived half my life in California and made what use of it I could, but I could leave it forever without a pang."

Shortly after *The Big Sleep* was published, he wrote to George Harmon Coxe, who had just built a house in Connecticut, to ask him about the possibility of moving there. "Is there a place," he asked, "where a poor man can live? I'm sick of California and the kind of people it breeds. If after twenty years I still fail to like the place, it seems to me that the case is hopeless." Expanding on the theme, he added: "I like people with manners, grace, some social intuition, and education slightly above the *Reader's Digest* fan, people whose pride of living does not express itself in their kitchen gadgets and their automobiles. I don't like people who can't sit still for half an hour without a drink in their hands, although apart from that I should prefer an amiable drunk to Henry Ford. I like a conservative atmosphere, a sense of the past; I like everything that Americans of past generations used to go and look for in Europe, but at the same time I don't want to be bound by the rules."

When Chandler realized that his hardcover earnings from *The Big Sleep* amounted to only $2,000, he did what he could to improve the situation. His agent, Sydney Sanders, told him that the slick magazines paid far more than the pulps did, so he wrote a story, "I'll Be Waiting," which was published in the *Saturday Evening Post*. Years later Chandler described what happened: "I wrote one story for the *Saturday Evening Post* to placate my then agent, who thought I should be a slick writer. The editor liked it, but went on vacation, and his readers rejected it. The rule was then that five readers read a story and one NO knocked it out. When the editor came back, my agent took it up with him, and the editor overruled his readers. To save their faces, I suppose, they asked for a number of changes, and I, being for once in my life a nice little boy, made them. Then they published the story exactly as I had written it. It has been anthologized to death, but I still don't like it, or rather the way it is written. It is too consciously stylized. I have never written another story for the slicks, although they are much more liberal now than then. One of the *Post* editors used for years to try to persuade me to write other stories about the same character. I couldn't seem to be able to convince him that there are characters that change and grow and mature, or whatever you choose to call it, and there are characters who are complete in one performance. Sometimes I think editors can be very stupid people."

There was one real danger in writing for the slicks which Chandler recognized early. "The slicks pay good money," he wrote, "and they are very nice people, but the trouble with them is that they are very unsafe. They're never sure what they want and if they guess wrong, you are out of a job. You may go on for years getting $50,000 or even more for a serial, and then all of a sudden you find yourself out in the cold. A change in policy has destroyed your market overnight. And by that time you *may*—it's not for certain—have denatured your writing to the point where you can't get back to the thing you once did well, if without much praise or reward. But if you write books, you are not selling your stuff to editors, but to the public. It takes a long time. It's wearing, but when you have the market, you never lose it as long as you can write. Or almost never."

There is something almost physical in Chandler's distaste for the "epicene drivel" of the slicks and his refusal to become involved with the boy-meets-girl formulas and the obligatory happy endings which of necessity made the stories "artificial, untrue, and emotionally dishonest." He was not fanatical and was capable of praising individual authors who wrote for the *Saturday Evening Post* or *Collier's*, but he knew these magazines were not for him and even stopped looking at them. "There's a cheap gloss over everything that I find as sickening as bad perfume," he noted later. Eventually he became convinced that his own work was "an indirect expression of utter contempt for everything the *Post* stands for." Chandler's rejection of the slicks in 1939, when he had little money, took courage—especially since at the time he believed that the other possible source of income, Hollywood, was a "graveyard of talent."

In the meantime, he was too busy to fret about magazines he would *not* contribute to. In early May of 1939, after a visit to Erle Stanley Gardner in Temecula, and in order to escape the heat of Riverside where they had spent the winter, Chandler and Cissy took a cabin up in the hills near Big Bear Lake. At an altitude of about 7,000 feet, it is a refreshing change from Los Angeles. Today the village of Big Bear is the usual tourist mess, with the Totem Pole Art Supplies Shop and the Teddy Bear Café; but in 1939 it was a simple place in a dramatic setting, with boulders coming down to the edge of the lake, pine trees, and snow in the higher mountains.

Not long after they arrived they learned that Alfred and Blanche Knopf were visiting California, and Chandler urged them to visit the mountains, suggesting they stay at the North Shore Tavern on Lake Arrowhead, about twenty miles from Big Bear. There they met for the first time on May 13, 1939. Arrowhead is larger and more beautiful than Big Bear, with a steep rocky shoreline. In May the air is cool and clear, but the sun is warm during the day. Spring flowers mingle with the evergreens as in the lower Alps. The tavern is a simple two-story shingled building with a terrace out in front overlooking the lawn that leads down to the lake. There the Chandlers and Knopfs became acquainted and had lunch.

They discussed the possibility that *The Big Sleep* might be taken by Warner Brothers for a film but were mainly concerned about Chandler's next book. He had already written Knopf about this: "As to the next job of work for your consideration, I should like, if you approve, to try to jack it up a few more notches. It must be kept sharp, swift and racy, of course, but I think it could be a little less harsh—or do you not agree? I should like to do something which would not be automatically out for pictures and which yet would not let down whatever public I may acquire. *The Big Sleep* is very unequally written. There are scenes that are all right, but there are other scenes still much too pulpy. Insofar as I am able I want to develop an objective method—but slowly—to the point where I can carry an audience over into a genuine, dramatic, even melodramatic novel, written in a very vivid and pungent style, but not slangy or overly vernacular. I realize that this must be done cautiously and little by little, but I think it can be done. To acquire delicacy without losing power, that's the problem. But I should probably do a minimum of three mystery novels before I try anything else."

This letter reveals the seriousness of Chandler's literary ambitions and, in contrast to his defense of the detective story as literature, his desire to move gradually into "straight" fiction. His notebooks, only two of which survive, throw more light on his literary plans. Before moving to Big Bear for the summer, he wrote down this statement, which is reproduced exactly as originally typed:

Since all plans are foolish and those written down are never fulfilled, let us make a plan, this 16th day of March 1939, at Riverside, Calif.

For the rest of 1939, all of 1940, spring of 1941, and if there is no war and if there is any money, to go to England for material.

Detective novels

Law Is Where You Buy It
Based on Jade, The Man Who Liked Dogs, Bay City Blues. Theme, the corrupt alliance of police racketeers in a small California town, outwardly as fair as the dawn.
The Brashear Doubloon, a burlesque on the pulp novelette, with Walter and Henry. Some stuff from Pearls are a Nuisance but mostly new plot.
Zone of Twilight A grim witty story of the boss politician's son and the girl and the blending of the upper and underworlds. Material, Guns at Cyrano's, Nevada Gas.
If advisable, try Goldfish for material for a fourth.

Dramatic novel	*English Summer*. A short, swift, tense, gorgeously written story verging on melodrama, based on my short story. The surface theme is the American in England, the dramatic theme is the decay of the refined character and its contrast with the ingenuous honest utterly fearless and generous American of the best type.
Short-long stories *Seven From the Stars* *Seven from Nowhere* *Seven Tales from "*	A set of six or seven fantastic stories, some written, some thought of, perhaps one brand new one. Each a little different in tone and effect from the others. The ironic gem, the Bronze Door, the perfect fantastic atmosphere story The Edge of the West, the spooky story, Grandma's boy, the farcical story, the Disappearing Duke, the Allegory Ironic, the Four Gods of Bloon, The pure fairytale The Rubies of Marmelon.

The three mystery stories should be finished in the next two years, by the end of 1940. If they make enough for me to move to England and to forget mystery writing and try English Summer and the Fantastic Stories without worrying about whether these make money, I tackle them. But I must have two years' money ahead, and a sure market with the detective story when I come back to it, if I do. If English Summer is a smash hit, which it should be, properly written, written up to the hilt but not overwritten, I'm set for life. From then on I'll alternate the fantastic and the dramatic until I think of a new type. Or may do a suave detective just for the fun.

At the end of Chandler's original statement, which was typed into his notebook by his wife, Cissy added these words: "Dear Raymio, you'll have fun looking at this maybe, and seeing what useless dreams you had. Or perhaps it will not be fun." This statement, with its open reference to unfulfilled ambition, reveals the intellectual intimacy and frankness that bound the couple together, despite their difficulties. Chandler answered Cissy's note several times, scribbling in a reply whenever he looked at his plan. In September 1940 he noted: "It was not." In February 1941 he reaffirmed this with the single word: "Check." Nine months later he wrote: "Double check." In April 1942 "God help us!" Then, in his last notation, dated March 1944, he changed his mind and wrote: "Yes it was, because I had now achieved it, although not with these stories."

Chandler also made marginal notes, pointing out that the first detective story became *Farewell, My Lovely* and the second, *The High Window.* As to the third, he wrote, "Dated, I'm afraid, by events," although the theme appears marginally in the original plan for the film script *Playback.* About the fantastic stories, he noted: "And still praying I may someday do these." Chandler's plan is interesting for the way in which it reveals his high literary purpose and his desire to write in more than one style. There is little emphasis on thematic or substantive material. Chandler admired the French in this respect, describing them as "the only people I know of who think about writing as writing. The Anglo-Saxons think first of the subject matter, and second, if at all, of the quality." Similarly, Chandler was interested in the act of writing itself and in how he might experiment with different types of fiction. This is the mark of the professional. The amateur expounds on his subject, the professional says he wants to do a novella next as a change from the long novel he's just completed. Yet Chandler probably failed to realize that his plan was also influenced by personal desires. His intention to write a "dramatic" novel based on his story "English Summer" is mainly a sign of his longing to escape from California and return to the England he idealized. Had he followed this impulse, he would probably have reverted to the sentimental language of his early poetry. Chandler's plan shows how he was pulled between the languages of the two countries. Fortunately, he was able to combine the virtues of each in his work and to create a comic literature of the highest quality. He was able to do so in part because he had a clear idea of the nature of each.

Chandler's notebook contains a brief essay that he called "Notes (very brief, please) on English and American Style." It is somewhat dated, because the influences Chandler believed necessary to create a genuine American style have begun to be felt, but the conception of the piece is still valid. Here is the text:

> The merits of American style are less numerous than its defects and annoyances, but they are more powerful.
>
> It is a fluid language, like Shakespearean English, and easily takes in new words, new meanings for old words, and borrows at will and at ease from the usages of other languages, for example, the German free compounding of words and the use of noun or adjective as verb; the French simplification of grammar, the use of one, he, etc.
>
> Its overtones and undertones are not stylized into a social

conventional kind of subtlety which is in effect a class language. If they exist at all, they have a real impact.

It is more alive to clichés. Consider the appalling, because apparently unconscious, use of clichés by as good a writer as Maugham in *The Summing Up*, the deadly repetition of pet words until they almost make you scream. And the pet words are always little half-alive archaic words like jejune and umbrage and vouchsafe, none of which the average educated person could even define correctly. Its impact is sensational rather than intellectual. It expresses things experienced rather than idea.

It is a mass language only in the same sense that its baseball slang is born of baseball players. That is, it is a language which is being molded by writers to do delicate things and yet be within the grasp of superficially educated people. It is not a natural growth, much as its proletarian writers would like to think so. But compared with it, at its best English has reached the Alexandrian stage of formalism and decay.

It has Disadvantages.

It overworks its catchphrases until they not merely become meaningless playtalk, like English catchphrases, but sickening, like overworked popular songs.

Its slang, being invented by writers and palmed off on simple hoodlums and ballplayers, often has a phoney sound, even when fresh.

The language has no awareness of the continuing stream of culture. This may or may not be due to the collapse of classical education and it may or may not happen also in English. It is certainly due to a lack of the historical sense and to shoddy education, because American is an ill-at-ease language, without manner or self-control.

It has too great a fondness for the faux naïf, by which I mean the use of a style such as might be spoken by a very limited sort of mind. In the hands of a genius like Hemingway this may be effective, but only by subtly evading the terms of the contract, that is, by an artistic use of the telling detail which the speaker never would have noted. When not used by a genius it is as flat as a Rotarian speech.

The last noted item is very probably the result of the submerged but still very strong homespun revolt against English cultural superiority. "We're just as good as they are, even if we don't talk good grammar." This attitude is based on complete ignorance of the English people as a mass. Very few of them talk good grammar. Those that do probably speak more correctly than the same type of American, but the homespun Englishman uses as much bad grammar as the American, some of it being as old as Piers Ploughman, but still bad grammar. But you don't hear English professional men making elementary mistakes in the use of their own language. You do hear that constantly in America. Of course anyone who likes can put up an argument against any other person's ideas of correctness. Naturally, this is historical up to a point and contemporary up to a point. There must be some compromise, or we should all be Alexandrians or boors. But roughly and ordinarily and plainly speaking, you hear American doctors and lawyers and schoolmasters talking in such a way that it is very clear they have no real understanding of their own language, and its good or bad form. I'm not referring to the deliberate use of slang and colloquialisms; I'm referring to the pathetic attempts of such people to speak with unwonted correctness and horribly failing.

You don't hear this sort of collapse of grammar in England among the same kind of people.

It's fairly obvious that American education is a cultural flop. Americans are not a well-educated people culturally and their vocational education often has to be learned all over again after they leave school and college. On the other hand they have open quick minds and if their education has little sharp positive value, it has not the stultifying effects of a more rigid training. Such tradition as they have in the use of their language is derived from English tradition and there is just enough resentment about this to cause perverse use of ungrammaticalities—"just to show 'em."

Americans, having the most complex civilization the world has seen, still like to think of themselves as plain people. In other words, they like to think that the comic strip artist is a better draftsman than Leonardo—just because he is a comic strip artist and the comic strip is for plain people.

American style has no cadence. Without cadence a style has no harmonics. It is like a flute playing solo, an incomplete thing, very dexterous or very stupid as the case may be, but still an incomplete thing.

Since political power still dominates culture, American will dominate English for a long time to come. English, being on the defensive, is static and cannot contribute anything but a sort of waspish criticism of forms and manners. And American cannot as yet vitalize itself any more than the American gentleman can wear American tweed. It just isn't good enough. America is a land of mass production which has only just reached the concept of quality. Its style is utilitarian and essentially vulgar. The Americans are a shallow-minded people with awkwardly unstable emotions and no deep sense of style. Their language in the hands of the man in the street, a waste product probably, is as empty of deep meanings as Nazi propaganda. Why then can it produce great writing, or at any rate, writing as great as this age is likely to produce? The answer is, it can't. All the best American writing has been done by men who are, or at some time were, cosmopolitans. They found here a certain freedom of expression, a certain richness of vocabulary, a certain wideness of interest. But they had to have European taste to use the material.

Final note—out of order. The tone quality of English speech is usually overlooked. This tone quality is infinitely variable and contributes infinite meaning. The American voice is flat, toneless and tiresome. The English tone quality makes a thinner vocabulary and a more formalized use of language capable of infinite meanings. Its tones are of course read into written speech by association. This, of course, makes good English a class language, and that is its fatal defect. The English writer is a gentleman (or not a gentleman) first and a writer second.

During the early part of 1939, while still in Riverside, Chandler began thinking about his next novel, and since he intended once again to draw on previously published material, he formulated plans for what were eventually to be two different books: *The Lady in the Lake* and *Farewell, My Lovely*. The first of these was based on "Bay City Blues" (June 1938) and the recent story "The Lady in the Lake" (January 1939); the second was extracted from "Try the Girl" (January 1937) and "Mandarin's Jade" (November 1937). Since he had been able to complete *The Big Sleep* in three months, Chandler probably thought that, in accordance with his plan, he could write his next book as quickly. But the habit of "cannibalizing" delayed him. With so much material to choose from, he adopted the much slower practice of writing more than one novel at a time. Chandler kept track of his progress in a diary, and the record shows that in addition to working on novels he would occasionally start or finish a short story. The diary entries, brought to light later on for tax purposes, are confusing because of Chandler's habit of changing titles or of even using the same working title for more than one story. At any rate, on March 13 he began *The Lady in the Lake*, using as a provisional title *Law Is Where You Buy It*. Within a few days he realized that something was wrong, so he interrupted his work to finish the story "The Bronze Door." By the end of the month he had got to page fifteen of the novel and by mid-April had progressed a few more pages. It was now called *The Girl from Brunette's*. At about this point he gave up and began a new novel, tentatively called *The Girl from Florian's*, which eventually became *Farewell, My Lovely*. He was able to work consistently on this story for a month or so, but on May 22, having written 233 pages, he entered this notation in his diary: "This story is a flop. It smells to high heaven. Think I'll have to scrap it and try something new." For a few days he worked on the story that eventually became "I'll Be Waiting" and then began to check over the draft of his novel again. He went through about ninety pages before realizing it was hopeless. At this point he went back to *The Lady in the Lake*, now calling it *Goldfish*. He progressed steadily, occasionally changing the title and calling it *The Golden Anklet* or *Deep in Dark Waters* before reverting to *Law Is Where You Buy It*. Then on June 29 he made this notation in the diary: "Tragic realization that there is another dead cat under the house. More than three-quarters done and no good." Chandler estimated that he had about 55,000 useless words on paper. Once again he went back to *The Girl from Florian's*, rewriting the earlier work and moving steadily forward until he finished a rough draft on September 15. The book was now called *The Second Murderer*. "But if you think I was satisfied with this draft, you are much mistaken," he later noted, "because I rewrote the entire thing in 1940 and finally finished it, although 1940 was a pretty hard year in which to concentrate in view of what was going on in Europe. I actually finished *Farewell, My Lovely*—I mean really finished it—on April 30, 1940."

This impulsive method of working was costly and wearing, and it explains why Chandler wrote so little during his twenty years as a novelist. To him, only work that was truly felt could have quality, and this belief greatly delayed him, for with the outbreak of war he had no enthusiasm for his work. In August of 1939 he told Blanche Knopf that he needed only another 12,000 words to finish a draft of *Farewell, My Lovely*. "I know what to write," he added, "but I have momentarily mislaid the urge."

Chandler was terribly preoccupied by the war, watching Hitler move into one country after another. "The effort to keep my mind off the war," he wrote, "has reduced me to the mental age of seven." His great love for England led him to volunteer for officers' training in the Canadian army. This offer, tendered on September 29, shortly after England's declaration of war, was rejected, mainly because of his age.

With the coming of autumn and the cold weather in the mountains, Cissy and Chandler prepared to leave. Their moves were continuous if rather joyless. "There is a touch of the desert about everything in California," he wrote, "and about the minds of the people who live here.

During the years when I hated the place I couldn't get away, and now that I have grown to need the harsh smell of the sage I still feel rather out of place here." To keep going he needed the romance of the ineffable. He and Cissy had each other, but Chandler required more: "The things by which we live are the distant flashes of insect wings in a clouded sunlight."

5.

LAW
IS WHERE
YOU
BUY IT

By December of 1939 Chandler and Cissy were settled in La Jolla for the winter, once again in furnished rooms. "It must be nice to have a home," he wrote to George Harmon Coxe. "We haven't had one in so long that I look back with a touch of nostalgia to any place we have stayed in as long as six months. I don't think we shall be here long either. Too dear, too damp, too elderly, a nice place, as a visitor remarked this afternoon, for old people and their parents." He was writing, but not with much success: "I had to throw my second book away, so that leaves me with nothing to show for the last six months and possibly nothing to eat for the next six. But it also leaves the world a far far better place to live in than if I had not thrown it away." Unable to provide the Knopfs with a book for their spring list, he wrote to apologize: "I have had bad luck, bad health, and a bad disposition for a long time. I did finally get a very rough draft done but was not at all pleased with it and had to put it aside for a while in the hope of later discovering whether it was just plain lousy or whether it was a distorted point of view that made me think so. However I am a bit cheered up about it (in absentia), as my researches have convinced me that just plain lousy is the normal temperature of the detective story."

In La Jolla the weather was bad, and Chandler thought the damp-ness was giving him a rheumatic right arm. In mid-January he and Cissy moved to Monrovia, on the northern fringe of Los Angeles just below the San Gabriel Mountains, but it was only a temporary stop. "We have not yet found a place to live," he wrote, "but hope to soon and when there is a little peace in the world which knows no peace— all I ask is a quiet corner and deaf and dumb neighbors—I'll get at this thing again." Eventually they settled in nearby Arcadia, where they stayed for a number of months. For most writers, the second novel is notoriously more difficult to write than the first, and Chandler's domes-tic unrest hardly seemed auspicious for satisfactory progress. Neverthe-less, by virtue of hard work, Chandler finished what was eventually to be called *Farewell, My Lovely* in April. Two months later he was work-ing on *The High Window*. "It was not all I did during the rest of the year but it was most of what I worked at." He acknowledged that "when you have a lot of plot material lying around and when one particular set-up has a tendency to go stale, you are perhaps too much inclined to drop it and start something else." The year 1940 was not a good one for Chandler. He was ill and uncertain much of the time, and by November, as he later wrote, he "had made less real progress than I sometimes would make in a week."

Chandler also vacillated over the selection of titles for his books. He knew they were important, and in his notebooks he kept long lists of possibilities. Some of the better and funnier ones never used are *The Corpse Came in Person, A Few May Remember, The Man with the Shredded Ear, Zone of Twilight, Parting Before Danger, The Is to Was Man, All Guns Are Loaded, Return from Ruin, Lament But No Tears, Too Late to Sleep, The Cool-Off*. All are atmospheric, intended to suggest a certain quality of the book or its tone. He told Alfred Knopf that he disliked "titles like *The Strange Case of* or *The Puzzle of* or *The Mystery of* for the reason that I think they put too much emphasis on the mystery itself, and I have not the ingenuity to devise the sort of intricate and recondite puzzle the purest aficionados go for. The title might lead them to expect a type of story they are not getting." He also pointed out that Erle Stanley Gardner had virtually made a trademark of this sort of title. For *Farewell, My Lovely*, Chandler originally wanted to use another title, *The Second Murderer*, which is derived from a scene in Shakespeare's *King Richard III* in which Richard sends two comic mur-derers to kill his brother Clarence and thus clear the way to the throne. The second murderer begins to have doubts and to show signs of compunction. But when the first murderer reminds him of the money they are to get for the deed, the second murderer abruptly forgets his scruples and says, "Zounds, he dies. I had forgot the reward." Chandler obviously found this Elizabethan payoff highly appropriate to a novel so full of police corruption and bribery. Blanche Knopf thought otherwise. She searched through Shakespeare for something else, and suggested *Sweet Bells Jangle,* which she took from Ophelia's speech about the apparently mad Hamlet. Chandler countered with *Zounds, He Dies* and told Mrs. Knopf her title sounded like something out of Ethel M. Dell.

Chandler's stubbornness about titles stemmed from his belief that a title should be easy to remember and should be one that "makes itself remembered. It should convey an idea with some emotional tinge. It should be provocative but not strained. It should, if possible, have a haunting quality." Chandler admired Hemingway's titles, but thought Maugham's were pathetic: "A good title has magic, and magic is to me the most valuable ingredient in writing, and the rarest."

In the end Chandler's second choice, *Farewell, My Lovely,* was agreed upon, and the book was published in August. Advance sales of only 2,900 copies (as compared with 4,500 for *The Big Sleep*) were disappointing, and Blanche Knopf couldn't resist sending Chandler word that "the trade reaction is entirely on title." Chandler didn't take this lying down and pointed out that since Knopf had agreed to the title he was not to blame if there had been an error in business judgment. Discouraged as he was, for his loss was far greater than Knopf's, he was cheered by a complimentary review in the *Hollywood Citizen-News,* which encouraged local sales. That "a critic who confessedly does not like mystery stories and thinks they are mostly tripe should take this book seriously as a piece of writing is worth an awful lot to me," he wrote. "Because I am not innately a hack writer." It is a measure of the relationship between Chandler and the Knopfs that he felt obliged to include the last sentence.

The reviews of *Farewell, My Lovely* were highly favorable, but one can understand why Chandler was pleased by what Morton Thompson had written in the *Hollywood Citizen-News:* "I am perfectly willing to stake whatever critical reputation I possess today or may possess tomorrow on the literary future of this author. Chandler writes throughout with amazing absorption in the tasks of craftsmanship. He tries never to miss a trick. His sentences, all of them, show intense effort, constant editing, polishing, never-ending creative activity. His construction is a paradox of smoothness and abruptness of technic. He has a fine taste in story, in drama, and comedy. He employs this sense constantly and he tells his story as well as he possibly can. His book and himself are ornaments to his profession. Lord, but it is good to see honesty and pains and fine impulses again. It's been months."

One such review can make a great deal of difference to a writer, but reviews are not currency, and Chandler still had to face the problem of survival. He was discouraged about his prospects, for as he pointed out to Blanche Knopf, the book received good reviews, was well advertised, and was being bought by libraries. He had no professional knowledge of detective-story sales, but his intuition was right. "I'd like to look at a list of mysteries that have sold more than 5,000 copies in the last five years," he wrote. "I have a hunch they could be counted on the fingers of the Two-Toed Sloth." The only solution to his financial difficulties was to write a book that would be serialized in one of the slick maga-zines, but Chandler knew he was unable to write the sort of formula fiction required. "I could write a best-seller," he later wrote, "but I never have. There was always something I couldn't leave out or something I had to put in. I don't know why." In the meantime, there was plenty of room for discouragement. "If this book had sold 10,000 copies, I might have been kidded into the idea that I had a future. As it is I can't help feeling that this particular medium is about the fanciest way of wasting one's talents that I could have hit on." Yet the offhand tone of this remark suggests that Chandler had no intention of giving up. He had the lonely courage of a man doing good work who realized that *Farewell, My Lovely* was a much better book than *The Big Sleep*.

Farewell, My Lovely is an improvement because the focus of the story is more clear. In *The Big Sleep* Chandler's indignation is general-ized in a dislike for the rich, but here he concentrates on Bay City, an independent part of Los Angeles, in which the extent of corruption in California life is more vividly demonstrated. "Sure, it's a nice town," says Marlowe. "It's probably no crookeder than Los Angeles. But you can only buy a piece of a ·big city. You can buy a town this size all complete, with the original box and tissue paper." Bay City is based on Santa Monica, where Chandler lived for a time while writing the stories from which the novel is derived. It is less elegant than Beverly Hills or San Marino, a middle-class town with Spanish-style houses in stucco with wrought-iron grilles and tiled roofs built along clean, wide streets that are lined with palm trees. The commercial district is limited to a few streets, and the place has an air of universal propriety. For Chandler, Bay City was a symbol of hypocrisy: he hated the pretense of upright-ness in a place virtually owned by a few people with money. "This Grayle packs a lot of dough in his pants," says Marlowe of the million-aire in the novel. "And law is where you buy it in this town."

Chandler was continually fascinated by the ludicrous, comic-opera quality of the place. "The other day I thought of your suggestion for an article of studied insult about the Bay City (Santa Monica) police," he wrote to Charles Morton of the *Atlantic Monthly* in 1944. "A couple of D.A.'s investigators got a tip about a gambling hell in Ocean Park, a sleazy adjunct to Santa Monica. They went down there and picked up a couple of Santa Monica cops on the way, telling them they were going to kick in a box, but not telling them where it was. The cops went along with the natural reluctance of good cops to enforce the law against a paying customer, and when they found out where the place was, they mumbled brokenly: 'We'd ought to talk to Captain Brown about this before we do it, boys. Captain Brown ain't going to like this.' The D.A.'s men urged them on heartlessly forward into the chip and bone parlor; several alleged gamblers were tossed into the sneezer and the equipment seized for evidence (a truckload of it) was stored in lockers at local police headquarters. When the D.A.'s boys came back the next morning to go over it, everything had disappeared but a few handfuls of white poker chips. The locks had not been tampered with, and no trace could be found of the truck or the driver. The flatfeet shook their grizzled polls in bewilderment and the investigators went back to town to hand the Grand Jury the story. Nothing will come of it. Nothing ever does. Do you wonder I love Bay City?"

This is the moral and legal climate of the novel, and Chandler has his dumb cop Hemingway, so nicknamed by Marlowe because "he keeps saying the same thing over and over again until you begin to believe it must be good," generalize about his troubles:

"A guy can't stay honest if he wants to," Hemingway said. "That's what's the matter with this country. He gets chiselled out of his pants if he does. You gotta play the game dirty or you don't eat. A lot of bastards think all we need is ninety thousand F.B.I. men in clean collars and briefcases. Nuts. The percentage would get them just the way it does the rest of us. You know what I think? I think we gotta make this little world all over again. Now take Moral Rearmament. There you've got something. M.R.A. There you got something, baby."

"If Bay City is a sample of how it works, I'll take aspirin," I said.

This, then, is the setting for Chandler's comedy. The novel is laid out like a play and the plot proceeds through a series of dramatic scenes between characters. The story is based on the old chestnut of disguised identity, but Chandler gets away with it by using another traditional dramatic device, the love triangle, in which Marlowe is played off against the glamorous Velma Valento (alias Mrs. Grayle) and the plainer but more honest Anne Riordan. Like much of Chandler's fiction, *Farewell, My Lovely* resembles a Restoration comedy in which the plot is not so important as the picture of life portrayed through its characters and the humor produced by the jokes and situations. Marlowe also plays a role that is more customary in dramatic comedy than in fiction. He is attracted by both women in a superficial way. He leaves Anne Riordan's house, knowing that hers "would be a nice room to wear slippers in." Later, he claims that Mrs. Grayle is his type and says, "I like smooth shiny girls, hard-boiled and loaded with sin." But he always goes home to his own apartment, where there is a "homey smell, a smell of dust and tobacco smoke, the smell of a world where men live, and keep on living."

The conventions of the detective story, as used by Chandler, are very similar to those of comic drama; and in *Farewell, My Lovely*, as in most of his novels, Marlowe is like the clown in *Pagliacci* standing before the curtain to introduce the characters of his *commedia*. In this particular novel Chandler provides as wide a range of lesser characters as in *The Big Sleep*, but they are more representative. General Sternwood and his psychotic daughter Carmen, not to mention the pornographer Geiger, are all rather special types. The characters of *Farewell, My Lovely* may have ordinary biographies, but Chandler makes them all vivid and memorable and often very funny. Moose Malloy, the giant jailbird who opens the book; Jessie Florian, the alcoholic widow of a tavern keeper; the anonymous Negro manager of the Hotel Sans Souci ("Trouble, brother, is something we is just fresh out of")—all these are believable as people and are related directly to the life of Los Angeles. They are a cross-section of the city, many of them proof of the failed dream of California, Chamber of Commerce assurances to the contrary.

It is worth considering how Chandler puts across his characters. Here is a policeman: "A man named Nulty got the case, a lean-jawed sourpuss with long yellow hands which he kept folded over his kneecaps most of the time he talked. He was a detective lieutenant attached to the 77th Street Division and we talked in a bare room with two small desks against opposite walls and room to move between them, if two people didn't try it at once. Dirty brown linoleum covered the floor and the smell of old cigar butts hung in the air. Nulty's shirt was frayed and his coat sleeves had been turned in at the cuffs. He looked poor enough to be honest, but he didn't look like a man who could deal with Moose Malloy."

Here Chandler links the character to his surroundings, demonstrating his view that places get the people they deserve or at least influence those who live there. The details Chandler chooses to emphasize—the long yellow hands, the frayed cuffs, and the smell of cigars in the small room—all focus on Nulty's failure. He is one more victim of the California dream gone sour. The technique owes a lot to Dickens and serves as a reminder that despite similarities to comic drama, Chandler was writing a novel and not a play. Chandler's method is different from

Dickens' because he uses a narrator whose own characteristics are part of the scene. Marlowe's personality affects the descriptions and compromises to some degree the "objective method" Chandler believed in. Here is a description of Jessie Florian's house: "1644 West 54th Place was a dried-out brown house with a dried-out brown lawn in front of it. There was a large bare patch around a tough-looking palm tree. On the porch stood one lonely wooden rocker, and the afternoon breeze made the unpruned shoots of last year's poinsettias tap-tap against the cracked stucco wall. A line of stiff yellowish half-washed clothes jittered on a rusty wire in the side yard."

This in a sense is half-Chandler, half-Marlowe, and Chandler's skill lies in his blending of the two voices. Marlowe as a detective isn't likely to speak of a "couple of frayed lamps with once gaudy shades that were now as gay as superannuated streetwalkers"—although he might say that Mrs. Florian's "voiced dragged itself out of her throat like a sick man getting out of bed." What prevents the reader from mistrusting the voice of the narrator, or doubting its authenticity, is the liveliness of Chandler's language. It is vigorous enough to keep him amused, and again this is a stylistic trait for which Dickens was also famous.

Chandler himself enjoyed writing his fiction, and that may help explain its humor. "I am constantly tempted to burlesque the whole thing," he wrote after finishing his first novel. "I find myself kidding myself," he said after he had completed three more. "I enjoy it and find it fun," he added. The intended humor was sometimes too subtle for his readers, and he wondered: "Why is it that Americans—of all people the quickest to reverse their moods—do not see the strong element of burlesque in my kind of writing?" He was not above poking fun at himself and the way he was often equated with Marlowe:

"Yes, I am exactly like the characters in my books. I am very tough and have been known to break a Vienna roll with my bare hands. I am very handsome, have a powerful physique, and I change my shirt regularly every Monday morning. When resting between assignments I live in a French Provincial chateau on Mulholland Drive. It is a fairly small place of forty-eight rooms and fifty-nine baths. I dine off gold plate and prefer to be waited on by naked dancing girls. But of course there are times when I have to grow a beard and hole up in a Main Street flophouse, and there are other times when I am, although not by request, entertained in the drunk tank in the city jail.

"I have friends from all walks of life. Some are highly educated and some talk like Darryl Zanuck. I have fourteen telephones on my desk, including direct lines to New York, London, Paris, Rome, and Santa Rosa. My filing cabinet opens out into a very convenient portable bar, and the bartender, who lives in the bottom drawer, is a midget named

Harry Cohn. I am a heavy smoker and according to my mood I smoke tobacco, marijuana, corn silk and dried tea leaves. I do a great deal of research, especially in the apartments of tall blondes. I get my material in various ways, but my favorite procedure (sometimes known as the Jerry Wald system) consists of going through the desks of other writers after hours. I am thirty-eight years old and have been for the last twenty years. I do not regard myself as a dead shot, but I am a pretty dangerous man with a wet towel. But all in all I think my favorite weapon is a twenty-dollar bill."

After staying for about five months in Arcadia, the Chandlers moved up to the mountains above San Bernardino for the summer of 1940. They tried Fawnskin first, then took a simple but spacious cabin at Big Bear Lake. The *Black Mask* writer John Butler lived nearby, and during the summer the Ballards and Adamses came up for visits. Chandler was just beginning *The Brasher Doubloon*, which was later to be called *The High Window*, but as so often happened he was troubled by the problems of daily living and was not in a good frame of mind for work. Later in the year he told George Harmon Coxe that he and Cissy discovered they no longer liked Big Bear. "Funny thing, civilization," he observed. "It promises so much and what it delivers is mass production of shoddy merchandise and shoddy people." They therefore moved to Santa Monica, where they took a four-room apartment at 449 San Vicente Boulevard, just a few blocks from the ocean. As usual, their social life was minimal. Chandler did keep in touch with some of the writers from the Fictioneers, one of whom, Norbert Davis, lived only two houses away. Chandler's sociability was hindered by Cissy's nagging illnesses and by his own irritation at not being properly settled. They were able to get some of their furniture out of storage, but the apartment was "not somehow the kind of place to stay in." In November Alfred Knopf paid a visit, but as usual when New York publishers travel to the West Coast, it was a hurried trip.

By February of 1941 they were in a simple bungalow at 857 Iliff Street in nearby Pacific Palisades. "Good God, we have moved again," Chandler self-mockingly began a letter to Erle Stanley Gardner. "Living, if you call it that, in a big apartment house in Santa Monica, brand new and all that, I longed for your ranch. I longed for some place where I could go out at night and listen and hear the grass growing. But of course it wouldn't do for us, just the two of us, even if I had the price of a piece of virgin foothill. It's better over here, quiet and a house in a nice garden. But they are just beginning to build a house across the way. I shan't mind it as much as the good neighbors bouncing on the bed springs over at the apartment house."

During most of 1941 Chandler worked, as usual, on more than one project at a time. Two novels, *The High Window* and *The Lady in the Lake*, were being written in tandem, with occasional interruptions for a short story. It was a slow and wasteful process, but necessary for one who could not write unless he felt like it in an emotional and physical sense: "I'm always seeing little pieces by writers about how they don't ever wait for inspiration; they just sit down at their little desks every morning at eight, rain or shine, hangover and broken arm and all, and bang out their little stint. However blank their minds or dull their wits, no nonsense about inspiration from them. I offer them my admiration and take care to avoid their books.

"Me, I wait for inspiration, although I don't necessarily call it that. I believe that all writing that has any life in it is done with the solar plexus. It is hard work in the sense that it may leave you tired, even exhausted. In the sense of conscious effort it is not work at all. The important thing is that there should be a space of time, say four hours a day at least, when a professional writer doesn't do anything else but write. He doesn't have to write, and if he doesn't feel like it he shouldn't try. He can look out of the window or stand on his head or writhe on the floor, but he is not to do any other positive thing, not read, write letters, glance at magazines, or write checks. Either write or nothing. It's the same principle as keeping order in school. If you make the pupils behave, they will learn something just to keep from being bored. I find it works. Two very simple rules. A) You don't have to write. B) You can't do anything else. The rest comes of itself."

Chandler must have spent many hours looking out of the window, since it took four years for him to complete *The Lady in the Lake*, begun in April of 1939. *The High Window* took half as much time, probably because it was not a cannibalized novel. Like most intelligent people, Chandler was easily bored, and the task of working over old material and converting it into a longer work must often have seemed tedious and trivial at a time when Western civilization appeared to be falling apart. *The High Window* was at least fresh, with new characters and situations. By September of 1941 Chandler finished a draft of the book, using the title *The Brasher Doubloon*, and sent it to his agent, Sydney Sanders, in New York. It came back to him, as he later recalled, with a brutal rejection. Chandler blamed the rebuff on his own eagerness to get something into print, so he sat down at his desk to make the necessary revisions. These were completed within six months, and the manuscript was sent off on March 3, 1942. The work was completed despite yet another move, this time to one of those comical Los Angeles addresses, 12216 Shetland Lane in Brentwood Heights, just inland from Pacific Palisades. Chandler was not optimistic about the book and wrote to Blanche Knopf: "I'm afraid the book is not going to be any good to you.

No action, no likable characters, no nothing. The detective does nothing. I understand that it is being typed [by the Sanders agency], which seems something like a waste of money, and will be submitted to you, and I'm not sure that that is a good idea, but it is out of my hands. At least I felt you should be relieved of any necessity of being kind to me in a situation where kindness is probably not of any use. About all I can say by way of extenuation is that I tried my best and seemed to have to get the thing out of my system. I suppose I would have kept tinkering at it indefinitely otherwise."

Chandler's depression stemmed from his agent's view that the new novel was not in the expected mode, a predictable commercial reaction, and he added in his letter to Blanche Knopf: "The thing that rather gets me down is that when I write something that is tough and fast and full of mayhem and murder, I get panned for being tough and fast and full of mayhem and murder, and then when I try to tone down a bit and develop the mental and emotional side of a situation, I get panned for leaving out what I was panned for putting in the first time. The reader expects thus and thus of Chandler because he did it before, but when he did it before he was informed that it might have been much better if he hadn't."

Fortunately, Blanche Knopf thought *The Brasher Doubloon* "an absolutely magnificent yarn, beautifully done," but as usual balked at the title. Her reason for objecting to it surprised Chandler: "I never thought of your idea that the booksellers might pronounce Brasher as brassiere." He tried to justify the title by explaining that the coin was actually minted in New York in 1787, but agreed that what was real to an author need not be so to a bookseller. In a postscript he wrote: "How about *The High Window*? It is simple, suggestive, and points to the ultimate essential clue." The title was accepted, and like most of Chandler's, it fulfilled his definition that "a good title is the title of a successful book."

The High Window was published on August 17, 1942, and Chandler was pleased by the book's appearance. Yet, as in the past, he remonstrated against the use of his photograph on the dust jacket. Chandler hated being photographed, mainly because he was no longer young. When *Farewell, My Lovely* was in production, he asked Knopf to keep his age confidential, since he thought it bad publicity to be a middle-aged beginner. As to his appearance, he wrote that "while I am compelled by weight of opinion, some of it expert, some frankly prejudiced, to admit being one of the handsomest men of my generation, I also have to concede that this generation is now a little seedy, and I with it." The photograph produced this further observation: "I was reading in an English book the other day and noticed the remark, 'the kind of squit who has his picture on the dust cover of his book,' or something like that. I feel a good deal like that myself. It is the custom in this country, of course, but most writers are such horrible-looking people that their faces destroy something which perhaps wanted to like them. Perhaps I am oversensitive, but I have several times been so repelled by such faces that I have not been able to read the books without the faces coming between. Especially those fat crowlike middle-aged women's faces."

Knopf claimed to be disappointed by initial sales, but Chandler reminded Blanche Knopf that she had told him that "4,000 copies was the ceiling on a mystery. Either you were just saying that to comfort a broken heart or you are now repining for nothing at all." Alfred Knopf made it clear that he fully intended to continue publishing Chandler, so the firm's complaint appears to have been gratuitous. Chandler himself was relaxed about the book and recognized its faults. "*The High Window*," he said, "was not the striking and original job of work that could be promoted into anything of consequence. Some people liked it better than my other efforts, some people liked it much less. But nobody went into any screaming fits either way."

The High Window has a curious tone, for it wobbles between burlesque and an expression of anger against ruthless behavior. In the plan Chandler wrote for his future work in 1939, he originally intended the novel to be a burlesque of the sort of pulp fiction he had been writing. This element remains very strong in the book and affects the main characters. Mrs. Murdock, who is a female parody of Colonel Sternwood, is introduced in this way: "She had a lot of face and chin. She had pewter-colored hair set in a ruthless permanent, a hard beak and large moist eyes with the sympathetic expression of wet stones. There was lace at her throat, but it was the kind of throat that would have looked better in a football sweater. She wore a greyish silk dress. Her thick arms were bare and mottled. There were jet buttons in her ears. There was a low glass-topped table beside her and a bottle of port on the table. She sipped from the glass she was holding and looked at me over it and said nothing." The description is funny and would be suitable for one of the picturesque minor characters generally found in Chandler's fiction. But to give this Pasadena matron one of the main roles in the novel strains credulity. It is asking a caricature to become a fully drawn character. Chandler does the same with other major characters as well.

The burlesque element of the book is oddly mixed with the central theme: the misuse of power and the control of one person by another. Also a favorite subject with Hawthorne and James, this theme is revealed mainly through Mrs. Murdock's control over her weak son and her complaisant and neurotic secretary, Merle Davis.

Chandler felt the injustice of such a situation, having experienced it with his rich Irish uncle and his employer Joseph B. Dabney, against whom he had no protection. Jasper Murdock, whose money gave his widow her power, seems to be directly drawn from Dabney. In Marlowe's words: "I knew she was the widow of an old coot who had made a lot of money helping out the community, and got his photograph in the Pasadena paper every year on his anniversary, with the years of his birth and death underneath, and the legend: *His Life Was His Service.*" Precisely such a memorial was printed for Dabney in the *Los Angeles Times*, with a slightly different legend: "What He Gave His Monument." Dabney and his wife gave two buildings worth over half a million dollars to the California Institute of Technology in Pasadena and also donated to other charities, especially the amiably named Truelove Home of the Salvation Army.

Chandler's hatred of ruthless bullies is so great that at times *The High Window* sounds almost like a tract. There are plenty of wisecracks and funny scenes to balance the seriousness; but rarely in other books does Chandler generalize as he does, for example, in a conversation between Marlowe and two Los Angeles policemen about a case in which a rich man's son and his secretary were found dead. A coverup for the case was arranged so that the secretary was blamed for the murder of the rich boy, Cassidy. "Did you ever stop to think," says Marlowe, "that Cassidy's secretary might have had a mother or a sister or a sweetheart—or all three? That they had their pride and their faith and their love for a kid who was made out to be a drunken paranoiac because his boss's father had a hundred million dollars?"

Marlowe concludes his lecture to the police with words that explain his own role: "Until you guys own your own souls you don't own mine. Until you guys can be trusted every time and always, in all times and conditions, to seek the truth and find it and let the chips fall where they may—until that time comes, I have a right to listen to my conscience, and protect my client the best way I can. Until I'm sure you won't do him more harm than you'll do the truth good. Or before I'm hauled before somebody that can make me talk."

Chandler's anger at a world in which innocent people are made to suffer by the unscrupulous rich is expressed mainly in the story of Merle Davis, the timid secretary who has been brainwashed into believing that she pushed Mrs. Murdock's first husband out of a window because he made a pass at her. By the end of the novel Marlowe discovers a photograph that reveals Mrs. Murdock as the pusher, so he arranges to have Merle removed from the house. Ironically, Merle refuses to believe the story, for she considers that Mrs. Murdock has always been kind to her. Here Chandler's indictment of society goes deeper and shows why he was skeptical of political solutions. "You were made to think you had pushed him," Marlowe explains. "It was done with care, deliberation and the sort of quiet ruthlessness you only find in a certain kind of woman dealing with another woman. You wouldn't think of jealousy to look at Mrs. Murdock now—but if that was a motive, she had it. She had a better one—fifty thousand dollars' life insurance, in case Vannier [a blackmailer who owned the incriminating photograph] ever blew his top. You were just a scapegoat to her. If you want to come out of this pallid sub-emotional life you have been living, you have got to realize and believe what I am telling you. I know it's tough."

The seriousness of Chandler's theme shows how ambitious he was for the detective story. It may also explain why he thought he had to exaggerate the jokes and the characters in order to make the book palatable. *The High Window* has thematic unity and a pace that suggests fresh work. But it is also odd, a curious mixture of elements that seem somewhat uncomfortable together.

By the time *The High Window* was published, in the summer of 1942, the Chandlers had moved again—this time to Idyllwild, California, in the hills above Palm Springs. Shortly after that they moved to Cathedral City, the poor man's adjunct to the main resort. In quality, Cathedral City has changed little since the 1940s. The first thing you see on entering the place today is the Palm Springs Mobile Country Club—a trailer camp on Frank Sinatra Drive. Small woebegone cottages are laid out in sandy lots along A, B, C, and D streets, and also along First, Second, Third, Fourth, and Fifth streets. There are few trees, and most of the bungalows are unpainted. Chandler's living there says a lot about his bank account. He had hoped the dryness of the desert would help his sinus problem. It didn't, however, and as usual he was far from happy, though his sense of humor rescued him. "This place bores me," he wrote to Alfred Knopf. "But I've just about been talked into sticking out the mountains and the desert for another year. After that to hell with the climate, let's meet a few people. We have a one-store town here, and the meat situation would make you scream. On Wednesday morning the guy opens up at 7 a.m. and all the desert rats are there waiting for him to give out numbered tickets. Anybody who delays long enough to wash his face is automatically classed as parasitic and gets a high number, if he gets one at all. On Thursday at 10 the inhabitants bring their bronchitis and halitosis into the store and park in front of the meat counter and the numbers are coonshouted. When we, having a very late number, kick our way up to the collapsed hunk of hamburger we are greeted with a nervous smile that suggests a deacon caught with his hand in the collection plate, and we leave bearing off enough meat for the cat. This happens once a week and that is all that happens, in the way of meat.

"Of course we go to Palm Springs. If we didn't, I should not be writing this letter. I should be out in the desert trying to dig up a dead gopher. We happened on a rib roast a couple of weeks back, just walked in and said hello, and there the damn thing was. We ate for six nights running, behind drawn curtains, chewing quietly, so the neighbors wouldn't hear.

"There are a bunch of great guys in Washington, high-minded and pure, but once in a while I hunger for a touch of dirty Irish politics."

Despite Cathedral City, Chandler was beginning to earn something from the subsidiary rights he owned in *The Big Sleep* and other published novels. In April of 1943 Avon brought out *The Big Sleep* in a twenty-five-cent edition that eventually sold 300,000 copies, not including an armed services edition for which no royalties were paid. Nevertheless, his American earnings amounted to only about $1,500, not much more than what the Hamish Hamilton cheap edition produced in England with only 10,000 copies. The additional money helped, but to supplement his income Chandler wrote a few more pulp stories and began some others in a different vein. After *The Big Sleep* was published, he brought out three more stories in *Dime Detective*, some of them probably written earlier, along with the story he wrote for the *Saturday Evening Post*. Except for one further story called "No Crime in the Mountains," he did not publish any other short fiction until 1951.

Chandler realized that as a novelist he had a much wider and more literate audience than he had as a contributor to magazines. His later stories show signs of impatience with the pulp form. "Pearls Are a Nuisance" is the burlesque he intended as a basis for *The High Window*. The best of them is "The Lady in the Lake," which became one of the principal sources for the novel of the same name. "No Crime in the Mountains" seems to have been written as an exercise. The problem Chandler faced in *The Lady in the Lake*, much of which takes place in the country, is how to make an interesting character out of a taciturn country policeman with a limited vocabulary. Using Big Bear as a model, Chandler seems to have had no trouble in making his description of the cabins scattered around the edge of the lake as vivid as his portrayal of Los Angeles; but the description of character was more difficult. A comparison of the story with the novel shows the effort he made to invent mannerisms, peculiarities of appearance, and qualities of speech to make his country constable believable.

After *The High Window* was published, Chandler wrote Knopf: "I do hope the next one will be better and that one of these days I shall turn one out that will have that fresh and sudden touch that will click. Most of all perhaps, in my rather sensitive mind, I hope the day will come when I don't have to ride around on Hammett and James Cain, like an organ grinder's monkey. Hammett is all right. I give him everything. There were a lot of things he could not do, but what he did he did superbly. But James Cain—faugh! Everything he touches smells like a billygoat. He is every kind of writer I detest, a faux naif, a Proust in greasy overalls, a dirty little boy with a piece of chalk and a board fence and nobody looking. Such people are the offal of literature, not because they write about dirty things, but because they do it in a dirty way. Nothing hard and clean and cold and ventilated. A brothel with a smell of cheap scent in the front parlor and a bucket of slops at the back door. Do I, for God's sake, sound like that? Hemingway with his eternal sleeping bag got to be pretty damn tiresome, but at least Hemingway sees it all, not just the flies on the garbage can.

"Heigho. I think I'll write an English detective story, one about Superintendent Jones and the two elderly sisters in the thatched cottage, something with Latin in it and music and period furniture and a gentleman's gentleman: above all one of those books where everybody goes for nice long walks."

While finishing *The Lady in the Lake*, Chandler wrote Knopf that he was "trying to think up a good title for you to want me to change," but the book was published under that name in November of 1943. Its appearance certainly helped establish Chandler as a novelist in his own right, and his complaint against being coupled with Hammett and Cain was mainly a resentment of reviewers' laziness. The dislike of Cain goes deeper, for it reflects Chandler's romantic, even sentimental, view of the world. Cain's characters end up in sordid situations because of their overwhelming sexual passions. His stories have an inevitable downward course that always produces disaster. In this he may be a more realistic writer than Chandler, but he also lacks the idealism without which life for Chandler would be unbearable. This idealism is expressed through Marlowe. Chandler's distaste for Cain's prose is an aspect of his dislike of his moral position. Chandler exaggerates in his letter to Knopf, for there are moments of lyricism in *The Postman Always Rings Twice* and in *Serenade* where Cain tries to show what might have been, but his characters are condemned from the beginning and cannot escape their fate. His style reflects this view of the world, and what is missing is the tension that exists when people have some possibility of choice. It therefore lacks the poetry that distinguished Chandler's prose.

The Lady in the Lake had the best sales of any Chandler novel to date, but it was not a major step beyond what he had already achieved in *Farewell, My Lovely*. It lacks the sparkle of the early books, although it is better than *The High Window*. The fault probably lies in its extraordinarily long period of gestation: it's hard to maintain a feeling of spontaneity over four years. Also, the war influenced the book. Chandler has sometimes been accused of ignoring social conditions in his books, writing escapist fiction that takes no account of the realities of the Depression and the war. It is true that he did not write social realism or politically committed fiction, but as should now be evident his novels embrace the political and social realities of Southern California. *The Lady in the Lake* also brings in the war. In "No Crime in the Mountains" there is an absurd intrusion of a Japanese spy and of a Nazi who cries "Heil Hitler!" before he quite unjustifiably shoots himself instead of the narrator. But in the novel, Chandler's war references are less hysterical and therefore more realistic. The book opens with workmen digging up a rubber sidewalk for government salvage, and the war is acknowledged in casual references to characters serving in the army or about to be drafted. This is as it should be, for the war's influence was gradual and slow. As Marlowe comments when he drives up into the mountains: "The war did not seem to have done anything much to Puma Lake."

But there is also a secondary or subconscious influence on the book. When Marlowe calls on his client for the first time, everything is gray—the client's suit, the dull silver walls of the reception room, and even Adrienne Fromsett, the main girl in the story: "She wore a steel-grey business suit and under the jacket a dark blue shirt and a man's tie of lighter shade. The edges of the folded handkerchief in the breast pocket looked sharp enough to slice bread. She wore a linked bracelet and no other jewellery." *The Lady in the Lake* is a somber book because it concentrates on those who are caught up in the system of Southern California instead of those who direct it. They are the foot soldiers of society rather than the picturesque eccentrics of *The High Window* to whom the system belongs. The richest man in *The Lady in the Lake*, Derace Kingsley, is only the head of a cosmetics company. "I have a good job here," he explains when he hires Marlowe, "but a job is all it is." The novel is about all the middlemen who are forced to conform to the style and habits of a materialistic world. Everybody is under some sort of tension, even the country cop who is up for reelection and whose political slogan is "Keep Jim Patton Constable. He Is Too Old To Go To Work." As in the army, circumstances control people: no one, except Marlowe, is a free agent, and he is one only because he is not involved in the central story. What Chandler shows us is a society of men and women trying somehow to keep their lives together, but always under pressure and therefore susceptible to violence. They are monkeys in the same zoo, and for that reason *The Lady in the Lake* is less comic than

Chandler's other novels; there is no romance in the book either, no blondes for Marlowe to play with.

This novel, then, is like a morality play, a portrait of society in trouble. The police, who are entrusted with maintaining order, are attacked more vigorously than in any other Chandler book. Once again, Bay City is the setting for much of the action, along with the mountains above San Bernardino. Chandler does not attack all police, but he shows how one corrupt cop can poison an entire police force. During the course of his investigations Marlowe is threatened by the police, beaten up, arrested, and blackjacked, as well as forced to drink whiskey in order to appear drunk. He is jailed, knocked out, drenched with gin, and framed for murder—all under the orders of a single police officer, Lieutenant Degarmo, who not surprisingly also turns out to be the murderer. He gets away with what he does because nobody else cares enough to stand in his way. Some of Degarmo's fellow officers in Bay City know the truth about him and other corrupt policemen, but as one of them says, "To hell with them, I'll be in the army in two weeks."

The Lady in the Lake has its jokes and wisecracks—otherwise it wouldn't be a Marlowe book—and it maintains Chandler's standards. But perhaps more than with most writers, Chandler's work was affected by his mood, and during much of the time he spent on this book, it was not good. The war depressed him, and the solitude of his life dried him out. The interior world of his fiction, where he really lived, was affected by the experiences of his daily life—and it shows. As a comic writer, he was in the awkward position of being preoccupied by concerns that were not in the least bit comic. "The story of our time," he later wrote, "is not the war nor atomic energy but the marriage of an idealist to a gangster and how their home life and children turned out." But with the world in fact consumed by warfare and with so few people to talk to, Chandler found it difficult to maintain his comic vision. He was ripe for a change.

6.

THE
GOLDEN
GRAVEYARD

———◆———

The year 1943 was a transitional one for Chandler. He was fifty-five, and had been writing for ten years with meager rewards, but gradually his condition was beginning to improve. The long investment of time and energy had at last, during the worst year of the war, started to pay off. *The Big Sleep* was published in a paperback edition and was also reprinted by Avon with *Farewell, My Lovely* as a mystery omnibus. By the end of the following year his first four novels were in print in hardcover editions in England and America, as well as in over a dozen separate paperback reprints. His work was also beginning to be translated, first in Danish and Norwegian, then in Spanish. The tremendous outpouring of interest in Chandler had not really begun, but there were signs that it was not long off.

Chandler found it a curious pleasure to reread his work, and in thanking Alfred Knopf for the "two-bit" edition of *The Big Sleep* he observed: "I looked into it and found it both much better and much worse than I had expected—or than I remembered. I have been so belabored with tags like tough, hardboiled, etc., that it is almost a shock to discover occasional signs of almost normal sensitivity in the writing. On the other hand I sure did run the similes into the ground."

The spread of Chandler's reputation won him new admirers, among them James Sandoe, a librarian at the University of Colorado who later reviewed mystery fiction for the *New York Herald-Tribune*. After consulting Knopf, he wrote letters to a number of leading magazine and newspaper critics, pointing out Chandler's exceptional qualities as a writer. Perhaps thanks to Sandoe's letters, Chandler's books were usually reviewed as ordinary fiction rather than in separate columns devoted to brief notices of half a dozen mystery stories. The *New York Times Book Review*, for example, always treated Chandler as a serious novelist, but the editor had the perverse habit of assigning critics like John Dickson Carr and Anthony Boucher to comment on his work. Chandler feigned indifference to reviews and knew enough never to reply to one, but he was irritated by this habit of the *Times* and wrote: "Obviously people like Boucher and Carr are committed in advance to disliking me because they are well aware that I regard their kind of detective story a crashing bore. The only thing that is deadly is the assumption that the proper man to review a book is somebody who is drooling for a chance to get his knife into the writer, a snide theory of criticism, which can taste its own bile. If they don't like my opinions, why don't they sit down and refute them on the same level instead of waiting until I write something else and then take their spleen out on that? If I were offered a book by Mr. John Dickson Carr—supposing I ever reviewed books at all—would I jump at the chance because I knew I was going to dislike it and would have a field day being nasty about it? I'd say no thanks, I'm not the man for the job. I'm prejudiced. A reviewer need not perhaps be as just as Aristides, but he should at least see the good in books he may not personally care for."

Chandler's literary reputation led him to Hollywood. He was also attracted there when he realized that his income from book sales was not enough to live on. As his novels began to be sold to motion picture companies, he could see no reason why he should not be involved with the films that resulted, since they clearly needed improving. In July of 1941 he signed a contract with RKO Pictures to film *Farewell, My Lovely*. The price was $2,000, and in what Chandler later described as "a contract of almost unparalleled stupidity on the part of my New York agent" he gave virtually all other rights to RKO as well. The movie was issued under the title of *The Falcon Takes Over* and starred George Sanders. The title was an attempt to cash in on the enormous success of the film version of Dashiell Hammett's *The Maltese Falcon*, made for Warner Brothers by John Huston and starring Humphrey Bogart. In May of 1942 *The High Window* was sold to Twentieth Century-Fox for $3,500 as a second-run or B picture and was released the following January as *Time to Kill*, with Lloyd Nolan as the star. Meanwhile,

Murder, My Sweet, yet another version of *Farewell, My Lovely*, for which Chandler received no additional money, was being remade by RKO, with Edward Dmytryk as the director and Dick Powell and Claire Trevor in the lead roles.

These films were all part of a new vogue in Hollywood. Like the pulps and hard-boiled detective stories of the 1930s and 1940s, crime and murder movies grew out of Prohibition and the establishment of organized crime throughout the United States. The early gangster films —*Little Caesar, Public Enemy, Underworld*, and *Scarface*—were fictionalized accounts of actual criminals such as Al Capone, Big Jim Colosimo, Dutch Schultz, and other gangland leaders whose exploits filled the headlines. These gangster films, which introduced James Cagney, Edward G. Robinson, and other actors who portrayed toughguy crooks, were immensely popular because they appeared to reveal the private lives of hoodlums and gang leaders. But by the early 1940s it was time for a change: with the filming of Hammett's *The Maltese Falcon*, the private-eye movie came into its own.

Chandler's opportunity came in mid-1943, when he was asked to collaborate with Billy Wilder in writing the film script for James M. Cain's *Double Indemnity*. Although younger than Chandler, Wilder had had experience writing screenplays in Germany before the war, and in exile in Hollywood he had written and directed two feature films in collaboration with Charles Brackett. Wilder had discovered Cain's novelette in *Liberty* and suggested it to Joseph Sistrom, an experienced producer at Paramount who was also a detective-story enthusiast. He then consulted William Dozier, who was in charge of the studio's writers, and suggested that Chandler be approached. Dozier wired Knopf for Chandler's address and was amused and surprised to discover that he lived in Los Angeles. Invited to Paramount for a conference, Chandler, in his naïveté or his eagerness to get the job, offered to do a screen treatment for a few hundred dollars. Sistrom then phoned H. N. Swanson, one of the more important Hollywood agents, and asked him to take Chandler on and teach him how to negotiate with the studios. In the end Chandler was engaged for thirteen weeks at $750 a week, a sum of amazing magnitude for a man who had been living for a decade on a few thousand dollars a year.

At the beginning Chandler was nervous and ill at ease. Not only was he unaccustomed to working with another person; he was appalled at the idea of writing on a nine-to-five schedule in an office building. The Writers Building at Paramount was known by some as the Campus because of its cloistered courtyard; others called it the Tower of Babel because it housed so many foreign writers exiled from Europe by the war. Each room had bare walls and was furnished with plain office chairs and desks and a single upright telephone. Chandler was assigned to one of these rooms and was given a secretary, and there he began to work.

Wilder knew that Chandler was unfamiliar not only with the studio atmosphere but also with film writing, so when they met for their first conference he suggested that each of them take the text of *Double Indemnity* home over the weekend. On Monday each would come back with a sample treatment over which they could then work together. Accustomed to the unhurried pace of salaried writers, Wilder returned on Monday with a few pages from the beginning scene. Chandler, to whom Wilder had also lent a few scripts in order to give him some idea of the medium, came in with eighty pages of what looked like a final screenplay with directions about lighting and camera angles. It was a touching illustration of his anxiety to show that he was capable of professional work.

Chandler later said that his collaboration with Wilder "was an agonising experience and has probably shortened my life; but I learned from it as much about screen writing as I am capable of learning, which is not much." Chandler was originally engaged because of his ear for dialogue, but his dramatic sense was also useful for the screen version of Cain's novelette. Based on an actual murder in New York, it is a story of sexual attraction and repugnance, in which a wife plots with an insurance agent to get rid of her husband in a faked rail accident so that she can collect twice the amount of his insurance policy. The novel has a relaxed narrative pace which is appropriate to the gradual revelation of the relationship between the two principal characters; but the screenplay is divided into a series of "sequences" which project the story dramatically. It sticks close to the novel but presents the material in a series of confrontations that do not appear in the book. What is lost is the gradual deterioration of the relationship between the two plotters. This is what mainly concerned Cain, but it cannot be shown in a dramatic production that lasts only an hour and a half.

As for the dialogue, Chandler and Wilder first wanted to use as much of the original as possible, but they became aware that something was peculiar about it. It looked all right on paper, but when they got some actors to do a scene right out of the book they discovered that it sounded, as Chandler put it, like "a bad high school play. The dialogue oversaid everything and when spoken sounded quite colorless and tame." They then had a conference with Cain, who happened to be in Hollywood at the time, and in the end they realized that in the novel the illusion of naturalness was achieved mainly by typographical devices— the elimination of "he said" and "she said," the ragged right-hand margins of the page, and its cut-up look. It was written for the eye but not for the ear. They therefore had to write new dialogue that would stand up to dramatic presentation. Wilder has acknowledged that Chandler deserves most of the credit for this work.

Once the script of *Double Indemnity* was ready, Wilder immediately went into production, for during the 1940s each of the major studios made eighty or ninety movies a year, and tight schedules were essential. The film was released in April of 1944, starring Fred MacMurray, Barbara Stanwyck, and Edward G. Robinson. It received a good deal of attention, because unlike most movies of the sort the two criminals were revealed at the very beginning so that, as Wilder said at the premiere, "we can concentrate on what follows—their efforts to escape, the net closing, closing." *Life* magazine featured it as a "Movie of the Week" and it was widely reviewed and praised. Billy Wilder received most of the credit, since he also directed the film. The Paramount publicity people advertised *Double Indemnity* as "the two most important words in the Motion Picture industry since *Broken Blossoms*"—D. W. Griffith's 1919 film starring Lillian Gish. Alfred Hitchcock made a joke of this by sending Wilder a telegram: "Since *Double Indemnity*, the two most important words are Billy Wilder." In Hollywood the film made Chandler's reputation as a screen writer, and the script of *Double Indemnity* was nominated for an Academy award. It is perhaps prophetic that the one review that concentrated on Chandler was written in London by Dilys Powell of the *Sunday Times*. "Naturally Wilder himself worked on the script," she wrote; "it was another name among the credits which caught my eye." Dilys Powell then devoted nearly the whole of her review to a discussion of Chandler's fiction, which she had just discovered, equating him with Georges Simenon in quality, and praising the script of *Double Indemnity*. She noted that "Chandler's writing is at its best sharply visual, getting its effects by observed detail, the small shocking thing seen." This review was typical of the appreciation Chandler earned in England, where his work was in some ways better understood than in America.

Wilder later said that Chandler was "one of the greatest creative minds" he had encountered and claimed that he had adapted himself very quickly to the film medium; yet Chandler himself did not take easily to working in the studio. He was shy and insecure in its strange atmosphere, and he bridled at anyone who put on airs. Above all, he could not bear to be patronized. His relationship with Billy Wilder was cool and polite, with occasional rows that would require the intervention of Joseph Sistrom. Wilder later suggested that Chandler may have disliked him because he was German; more probably, the tension of the two working together made Chandler oversensitive and suspicious. One day when they were in their office, with the sun pouring through the Venetian blind onto the script, Wilder said, "Go and fix that, will you,

Ray?" At this point Chandler rose, stated that he would no longer work with Wilder, and walked out of the office. John Houseman, who was then an assistant producer at Paramount, recalls seeing a long document typed on yellow paper in which Chandler listed the indignities he was suffering from Wilder and demanded that they cease immediately. Two of them were: "Mr. Wilder was at no time to swish under Mr. Chandler's nose or to point in his direction the thin, leather-handled malacca cane which Mr. Wilder was in the habit of waving around while they worked. Mr. Wilder was not to give Mr. Chandler orders of an arbitrary or personal nature such as 'Ray, will you open that window?' or 'Ray, will you shut that door, please?' "

Joseph Sistrom was the one man at Paramount who could deal with Chandler and mediate between him and others, especially those in the executive offices, for whom, on the whole, he had no use. Sistrom was a Stanford graduate whose father, an Englishman, had worked in Hollywood before him. Frank Capra described him as having hair that was "black, bushy, and untamable; his glasses so thick they could have been cut out of inkwells." He was an intellectual with whom Chandler could talk. "I don't have to lay an egg to know how the hen does it" was one of his favorite remarks.

If Chandler was difficult with his contemporaries or his superiors in the studio, he was open and helpful to the young, and especailly to beginning writers. Meta Rosenberg, who was then an assistant to William Dozier, used to visit him in his office because she recognized from the beginning that, along with Faulkner, Hammett, O'Hara, and Fitzgerald, he was obviously above the ordinary level of film writer. He was shy and diffident, quite unlike the many Hollywood writers who try to give the impression they are in control of everything. Teet Carle, who was in charge of publicity at Paramount and who had literary ambitions of his own, would also stop by at his office. "He was incredibly friendly," Carle recalls. "I often sneaked up from my office to get close enough to him to talk." Robert Presnell, Jr., was then at Paramount writing his first screenplay and was understandably nervous about it: "Chandler was ironically sympathetic and encouraging and took time from his own work to talk to me practically any time I popped into his office looking forlorn. He said he loved interruptions more than anything—because things you do when you're supposed to be doing something else are always more fun. Digression is the spice of life. He told me to write whatever I wanted to because no one in the front office could read anyway, and even if they could, they wouldn't know a good script from a bad one." Chandler seemed clear-eyed and disenchanted about life, Presnell recalls. Chandler explained that things did not happen because of a logical plan but because everybody along the line got his cut. This of course is the theme of his fiction and the historical reality of Los Angeles.

Chandler's life at the studio did him a great deal of good. For the first time in a decade, apart from conversations with his wife and rare meetings with pulp writers, he was involved in intellectual conversations as a normal part of his daily life. He belonged to a society of fellow writers, and their company brought him out. "He loved to talk and argue about anything," Presnell recalls, "and he usually dominated, though never with arrogance—but with an ironic humor. Studios were pretty easy-going places then, and writers were gentlemen of leisure. We'd take six or eight months to write a screenplay. There was a lady named Simone, who ran the Writers Building telephone switchboard, who always had coffee and snacks available (which we all paid for) and a fridge, where there was booze. If you wanted to start your day with champagne, you could. This is where we met each morning around ten o'clock, when we came to work. It was the Club, and Chandler presided. If the conversation got going well, some of us would spend the rest of the morning at it." H. Allen Smith is another writer who remembers Chandler at Paramount. Expecting a hulking football player with Marlowe's build, he was astonished by the "mild-mannered guy of medium size with black wavy hair, horn-rimmed glasses, and a sensitive face." Chandler looked "like a poet is supposed to look." At lunch Chandler usually joined his colleagues at the writers table, which was in a small anteroom off the main commissary. There the participants would play the match game or the word game, an inventive kind of crossword puzzle traditional with Paramount writers, but mainly they just talked, with Chandler the presiding figure. Presnell claims that Chandler was the only writer he could recall from his Paramount days, "because he was so vivid, so right-on, so aware of the Human Comedy."

Chandler himself recalled these lunches with pleasure. "At the writers table at Paramount I heard some of the best wit I've heard in my life. Some of the boys are at their best when not writing. I remember Harry Tugend's wonderful crack about an actress when Tugend was trying to be a producer and hating it. He said: 'You know this is a lousy job. You got to sit and talk to that birdbrain seriously about whether or not this part is going to be good for her————career and at the same time you got to keep from being raped.' Whereat a rather innocent young man piped up: 'You mean to say she's a nymphomaniac?' Harry frowned off into the distance and sighed and said slowly, 'Well, I guess she would be, if they could get her quieted down a little.' The other was a contribution from Seton Miller, a lousy writer but a very good brain in other ways. Somebody was discussing the picture that introduced Miss Lauren Bacall to immortality, *To Have and Have Not*, and the singing she did in it. An innocent said, 'I guess they probably dubbed that song in.' Whereat Seton Miller screamed, 'For Jesus Christ sake, you damn idiot, do you think somebody actually went out and *looked* for a voice like that?' "

In manner and appearance Chandler was utterly unlike the usual flashy overdressed Hollywood type. José Ferrer, who met him once, says that he was wearing "a nondescript tweed jacket and gray flannels, seemed cheerful and pleased to meet me, which puzzled me, and was so far from the Philip Marlowe tough image that I was bewildered." At the studio, among his own kind, he was at ease and popular. But he drew a line between his working acquaintances and his private life. "Most movie people are fine to work with," he said, "but I don't like to go into their homes, don't like to listen to the same old talk—pictures and more pictures. Furthermore, I don't want their scale of living, and if you don't live as expensively as they, well, you just don't belong."

Soon after taking the Paramount job, Chandler rented an unpretentious house at 6520 Drexel Avenue, in a lower-middle-class neighborhood to the south of Hollywood near the Jewish community on Fairfax Avenue. It was the first substantial house he and Cissy had lived in for years, and at last they were able to take their furniture out of storage. Aside from that, it was ordinary, like most of the places Chandler lived in while in California. It did not reflect what he was earning at Paramount. Afterward, he admitted that he was "a bit of a stinker in Hollywood. I kept the money. No swimming pool, no stone marten coats for a floozie in an apartment, no charge accounts at Romanoff's, no parties, no ranch with riding horses, none of the trimmings at all. As a result of which I have fewer friends but a lot more money."

With his tweeds and pipe, Chandler may have looked like a professor to those at the studio, but he did not think of himself like that at all. Working with other writers made him more sociable, and this led to his drinking again. A Paramount press release on Chandler assured readers that he never drank anything stronger than tea, but he was unable to resist the genial alcoholic atmosphere of the Writers Building. Joseph Sistrom was partly to blame for this change in Chandler, for he himself was an expansive drinker, and often at the end of the day he would take Chandler to Lucey's, a famous bar and restaurant on Melrose Avenue across from the Paramount lot. Mrs. Sistrom, who was often present, recalls that Chandler had a very light head. After two or three drinks he would not exactly be drunk but fuzzy and unable to maneuver properly. The Sistroms usually drove him home, and he would have to be guided up the path to his house.

The drinking rather inevitably led to women. James Cain asserts that Chandler and Cissy were known as "Hollywood's happiest couple," but the presence of so many pretty secretaries and extras on the lot excited Chandler and reawakened his sexual interests. John Houseman blamed Chandler's Public School training for his sudden obsession with sex, but after the long period of solitude before he went to Hollywood, Chandler was all too aware of the difference between the girls at the studio and his seventy-three-year-old wife on Drexel Avenue. The atmosphere of the Writers Building did not help. William Dozier, who supervised the writers, made a point of knowing as little as possible about their private lives, so long as the scripts kept coming in on schedule. But there were rumors of parties, especially at Christmas, when the drinking began at ten or eleven in the morning, with the result that by midafternoon all sorts of liaisons were being consummated.

One of Chandler's secretaries at Paramount recalls that the loose informality of the Writers Building made Chandler aware of his lost youth. He became melancholy—Billy Wilder noted how sad he often seemed—and this mood also encouraged him to drink. He kept a bottle in the desk drawer and began to drink at three or four in the afternoon. Often he continued through the night, for in the morning he looked terrible. He would tell his young secretary how unhappy he was with a wife nearly twenty years older than himself and would explain that he had married her because she had enough money to allow him to write. When the secretary asked why he didn't divorce her if he was so miserable, Chandler said he felt obliged to Cissy and could not abandon her in her old age.

Chandler's ability to dramatize his situation and to express himself passionately led him to try to have an affair with the secretary, but nothing came of it. Like several other women who knew Chandler at this time, she did not think of him in physical terms: his skin was exceptionally white, and his pallor did not make him physically attractive to most women. Cissy was aware of what was going on, however, and was intensely jealous. Chandler was miserable, and sometimes in the middle of the night he would phone his secretary and ask her to come over. Even innocent actions had a tendency to turn sour in this tense atmosphere. At the time *Double Indemnity* was being previewed in various Los Angeles theaters, Chandler asked his secretary to accompany him to one of the showings, explaining that Cissy had already seen it and didn't want to go again. The secretary agreed and off they went. Chandler drove her back to her apartment at a decent hour and then went straight home. The next day he came into the office in a desperate state, saying that he had stayed up all night quarreling with Cissy. "You see," he explained, "I'd forgotten it was our wedding anniversary."

Although he was unsuccessful with this secretary, Chandler did have an affair with another and went off with her for some weeks.

Always he came back, however, perhaps because he disliked "the tawdry imitation of domesticity" in any prolonged relationship of this sort. Cissy and his house remained the center of his life. Chandler was also sensitive enough to know that his escapades and drinking were painful to Cissy, and he therefore tried to make up to her. Yet even here the results were sometimes unintentionally funny. Once he bought her a Lincoln sedan as a present, but it was so large that he had a hard time driving it and maneuvering it into his modest driveway. Physically, he was too small for it and seemed lost in the front seat behind the wheel.

Chandler had originally hoped that after completing *Double Indemnity* with Wilder he would be able to return to writing fiction. His Hollywood experience had made him reconsider his own work, and it is clear that he wanted to escape from detective fiction without losing its advantages. He told Alfred Knopf what he had in mind: "It is to be a story about a murder involving three men and two women, and practically nobody else. It is to take place in Bel-Air, and all these characters are wealthy people except the protagonist of the story. He is my problem. I should like to do a first-person story about Philip Marlowe. I wouldn't have to develop him very much more than I have already because he is the sort of guy who behaves according to the company he is in. But the story is not going to be a mystery, and I hope to avoid its being tagged as a mystery novel. Is this possible if I use a character who is already established in mystery fiction?"

Before he could arrange this escape from what he called "conventional mysteries" he was back at Paramount. The success of *Double Indemnity* produced an offer he could not afford to reject; he merely had to work on film scripts already under way. The first of these was *And Now Tomorrow*, based on Rachel Field's novel, on which he collaborated with Frank Partos. It was directed by Irving Pichel and the cast included Loretta Young, Alan Ladd, Susan Hayward, and Barry Fitzgerald. The second was *The Unseen*, produced by John Houseman and starring Joel McCrea and Gail Russell. Chandler wrote the screenplay with Hagar Wilde. The two films are quite different, one romantic, the other a mystery thriller. In each Chandler's task was the same—to polish the dialogue. With Billy Wilder, Chandler knew that the dialogue he wrote would remain as written, but he was angered and frustrated when the directors of these films departed from his text. Chandler had a clear idea of the function of dialogue. In his novels, for example, Marlowe's speeches are not written just for the sake of the jokes and wisecracks. They are his chief weapon. Chandler has Marlowe choose words in such a way as to throw his opponents off base so that they will reveal something they did not intend to. This is the real drama of dialogue: it is not simply a way of showing that the characters have feelings and are not deaf and dumb. But Chandler had spent a lot of time on the sets at Paramount, watching scenes being shot, and he realized that in film, unlike fiction, it was wrong to use too many words because the medium is primarily visual, not aural. "A preoccupation with words for their own sake," he wrote, "is fatal to good film making. It's not what films are for. The best scenes I ever wrote were practically monosyllabic. And the best short scene I ever wrote, by my judgment, was one in which a girl said 'uh huh' three times with three different intonations, and that's all there was to it."

Chandler's contract with Paramount expired in September of 1944, and he spent the rest of the year writing at home while his agent worked out a new agreement with the studio. By now he could afford the break, for in addition to his Paramount salary, much of which he put away in government bonds, he received $7,000 as his share of a $10,000 contract Knopf signed with Warner Brothers for the movie rights to *The Big Sleep*. Chandler was unable to write the script himself because of his prior commitment to Paramount.This year-end interruption of his link with the studio meant that once again he was working quietly at home, away from temptations. The sporadic nature of Chandler's film work helped him avoid the disastrous downward spiral that ruined his career in the oil business.

On New Year's Day of 1945 he wrote Charles Morton of the *Atlantic Monthly:* "I regret to say I have to go back to work tomorrow. The prospect makes me feel low enough to chin myself on the curbing." But the terms were satisfactory: he had a three-year contract requiring twenty-six weeks each year, with a rising salary scale beginning at $1,000 a week. In addition, he was to start out with an original screenplay of his own. "I am now doing something," he wrote, "which is not very often done in Hollywood and which I think is a lot of fun. I am writing an original screenplay—a murder mystery, but not entirely that—and if it turns out good enough, I have the right to make a book of it." His main interests were literary, and he added that for him "Hollywood is just a way-station. If it teaches me to turn out books a little faster—and I think it will—it certainly won't do me any harm. I'm probably too old and too hardened to be glamourized."

When Chandler returned to Paramount, he discovered that the studio was in a dither because its highest-paid actor, Alan Ladd, was about to be drafted into the army, and there was nothing to show for his recent months on the payroll. Since as usual Chandler had two or three pieces of unfinished work at hand, he told John Houseman that he thought one of them might be converted into a screenplay fairly quickly.

The studio was delighted. Joseph Sistrom was assigned as executive producer, and Chandler got down to work. By mid-January he was congratulating himself in a letter to Morton: "In less than two weeks I wrote an original story of 90 pages like this. All dictated and never looked at until finished. It was an experiment and for a guy subject from early childhood to plot-constipation, it was rather a revelation. Some of the stuff is good, some very much not." A week later he realized that something was wrong: "I'm afraid I am going to be in trouble for some time to come. I did a quick treatment on a story for Paramount (an original in a purely technical sense only) and they are already casting it, without a line of screenplay written. Why do I get myself in these jams?"

By now Veronica Lake had been chosen as costar, with Doris Dowling and William Bendix in the lesser roles. George Marshall, a competent if undistinguished director, was selected to make the film. Within a short time he was shooting from the unfinished script. Chandler was nervous but found the experience curiously exhilarating: "Possibly—I'm not sure—the rejuvenation of the motion picture, if and when it comes, will have to be through some such process of writing directly for the screen and almost under the camera. What you lose in finish you gain in movement: and movement is what the motion picture has been steadily losing for a long time."

As the filming proceeded, Marshall gradually caught up with the script. With fewer and fewer pages available for production, the senior executives and producers began to show signs of nervousness. At lunch in the commissary, Chandler would tease them. He would slap them cheerfully on the back and ask, "What do you think ought to happen next?" Sistrom and Houseman had confidence in Chandler, but there was gloom in the front office. One day the production head of Paramount summoned Chandler to his office and offered him a bonus of $5,000 if he finished the script in time.

Nothing could have been counted on to produce a worse reaction in Chandler. Thinking he had solved the studio's problem, the production manager, in Houseman's words, had succeeded instead "in disturbing him in three distinct and separate ways: One, his faith in himself was destroyed. By never letting Ray share my misapprehensions, I had convinced him of my confidence in his ability to finish the script on time. This sense of security was now hopelessly shattered. Two, he had been insulted. To Ray, the bonus was nothing but a bribe. To be offered a large additional sum of money for the completion of an assignment for which he had already contracted and which he had every intention of fulfilling was by his standards a degradation and dishonor. Three, he had been invited to betray a friend and fellow Public School man. The way the interview had been conducted ('behind your back') filled Ray with humiliation and rage."

Chandler was so undone that he told Houseman he could not write another word. He went home, discussed what had happened with Cissy, and returned the next morning still firm in his belief that he could not continue. The two men sat morosely in Houseman's office, and after a while Chandler spoke again. Realizing that his withdrawal put Houseman on the spot—something Public School men did not do to one another—he said that he might be able to finish the script if he wrote it while drunk. Alcohol would calm his nerves and give him the confidence to continue in the face of the mistrust and insults he had received.

Houseman was dismayed by the proposal, because Chandler was not a young man and he knew that work of this kind might endanger his health. But Chandler began to produce a series of conditions that seemed to lessen the risk. The idea was that Paramount would provide two limousines to stand by day and night outside of Chandler's house. They would fetch the doctor for Cissy, who was recovering from an operation on her foot, take the maid to do the shopping, and deliver the script to the studio. In addition, there had to be round-the-clock nurses and a doctor available to give Chandler vitamin shots, since he never ate while drinking. Further, a direct telephone line had to be installed between the house and the producer's office at Paramount, and secretaries were to be on hand at all hours for dictation, typing, and other necessities.

Houseman hesitated, since the responsibility would be his if anything went wrong; but in the end he agreed to the terms and the arrangements were made. He and Chandler went out to Perino's Restaurant, and there Chandler had three double martinis before lunch and three stingers afterward. Houseman drove him home to Drexel Avenue, and Chandler went inside to lie down on the couch. The limousines, the secretaries were all in place. For the next week or so Chandler worked intermittently. He was never out of control; he was just in another realm. Houseman recalls seeing him slumped over the dining room table, taking a nap. He wouldn't sleep for long, but would wake up and continue, glass in hand. In the evenings he would sit with Cissy and listen to the gas company's radio program of classical music that ran from eight to ten. Then he would go to his study and try a few more lines before he dozed off again. In this way, the screenplay was finished, including all the revisions thought necessary by the producer. John Houseman estimates that Chandler's recovery from this ordeal cost a good deal more than the $5,000 bonus offered by Paramount.

The effort was hardly worth it, because *The Blue Dahlia* does little to enhance Chandler's reputation. His touch is preserved in the dialogue, which is crisp and natural, but there is far too much action to allow for character development. The fault is not entirely Chandler's, whose original idea was more interesting. Fascinated by the themes of revenge and chance in murder stories, he jotted down several story ideas for films in his notebook. One is about a man who, thinking his wife had died accidentally, makes friends with her murderer. The murderer believes he is being drawn into a trap, and the tension that subsequently rises between them eventually leads to the disclosure of his guilt. The first version of *The Blue Dahlia* contains some elements of this idea. It is about two returning veterans, one of whom suffers from brain damage which makes him irresponsible. The U.S. Navy objected to the implied criticism of its medical corps and made the studio alter the story. "What the Navy Department did to the story," wrote Chandler in an ironical vein, "was a little thing like making me change the murderer and hence make a routine whodunit out of a fairly original idea. What I wrote was a story of a man who killed (executed would be a better word) his pal's wife under the stress of a great and legitimate anger, then blanked out and forgot all about it; then with perfect honesty did his best to help the pal get out of a jam, then found himself in a set of circumstances which brought about partial recall. The poor guy remembered enough to make it clear who the murderer was to others, but never realized it himself. He just did and said things he couldn't have done or said unless he was the killer; but he never knew why he did them or said them and never interpreted them."

The completed film has none of this subtlety and is, as Chandler says, a routine action thriller. Its relative flatness is due in part to the interference of the U.S. Navy, but the conditions in which Chandler wrote the script were also to blame. Some writers need drink to get them started: the Hollywood novelist Max Brand said he couldn't begin until alcohol got him "away from the world" and transported him into the world of fantasy. Other writers such as Coleridge and Rossetti, who used drugs for stimulation, held similar views. Chandler occasionally asserted that he also needed alcohol, but the results show that he never completed first-rate work while drinking. All of the pulp stories, his first six novels, and his best essays were written while he was not drinking, and while he was living a reclusive life with Cissy. The screenplays, his unfinished work, and his last novel were written while he was socially involved in the studios, having or attempting to have affairs, and drinking a great deal. His life seems to have patterned itself so that while he was most alone and thrown on his private resources, he created in his writing a vivid and convincing imaginary world; when his private life was full of incident, he wrote little and what he finished was almost a parody of his better self. At such times his social life was dramatic enough for him not to require the drama of fiction. But he was an artist, and Cissy gave him the stability that made his best work possible. There is no doubt that he understood and loved her for that, despite his occasional impulses to be free of her.

When he completed the screenplay of *The Blue Dahlia,* Chandler considered making a book out of it, as was his right according to the contract. Paramount even encouraged him, thinking it would be good publicity for the film. His agent got the *Saturday Evening Post* to agree to serialize it in six installments; but in the end Chandler decided against it, partly because he was overtired but also because, as he said, "I'm not at all sure this is my kind of book. It's all right to do something for pictures which is not your kind of story; it's quite another matter to have it published in book form."

What he really wanted to do was complete the Marlowe novel he had been working on before signing up with Paramount. But instead he agreed to work for three months on the screenplay of his own novel *The Lady in the Lake,* which had been bought by MGM. This time Paramount made no objection to his working at a rival studio, and he began there in July of 1945. He had taken the job to protect his story and keep it from being ruined by a hack writer; but from the beginning there was trouble, as Chandler himself recalled:

"I worked at MGM once in that cold storage plant they call the Thalberg Building, fourth floor. Had a nice producer, George Haight, a fine fellow. About that time some potato-brain, probably Mannix, had decided that writers would do more work if they had no couches to lie on. So there was no couch in my office. Never a man to be stopped by trifles, I got a steamer rug out of the car, spread it on the floor and lay down on that. Haight coming in for a courtesy call rushed to the phone and yelled down to the story editor (I forget the name and never met the man) that I was a horizontal writer and for Chrissake send up a couch. However, the cold storage atmosphere got to me too quick, and the coteries at the writers table in the commissary. I said I would work at home. They said Mannix had issued orders no writers to work at home. I said a man as big as Mannix ought to be allowed the privilege of changing his mind. So I worked at home, and only went over there three or four times to talk to Haight."

Chandler quickly realized that he had taken on a job that, as he said at the time, "bores me stiff." Protecting his material was one thing, but having to rewrite it from a different point of view was another. Chandler later described the sort of discussion he had with his producer, George Haight. Having read a batch of Chandler's script, Haight would say, "Can't we keep some of the book? Isn't it one of your books we bought? Isn't that why you're here?" And Chandler would reply, "I'm sick of it,

George. It's so much easier to write new stuff." This is how the conversation ended:

"For God's sake," he said, "this is supposed to be an adaptation of something we bought from you. And you keep on writing entirely different scenes. They are all right in their way, but how do I explain to the front office that a writer who was hired to do the screenplay of his own story pays almost no attention to it?"

"I guess it's just not my kind of story," I said, "or not any longer. When a writer breaks his heart to do a job and does it as well as he can, he just doesn't want to do it all over again and worse."

"But we bought the damn thing."

"Yes, but to me the point is that I am stale on it. Perhaps some other writer could do a much better job—naturally leaving out any line of dialogue that might have any possibility of making what else he did look like a dead carnation. After all, these boys are trying to exist. They are not vicious as a rule, but in order to exist when they take over a screenplay, they have to make it *their* screenplay."

"I don't like it lousy," the Producer said sadly.

"You're a producer, George. You surely must know by now that there are not twenty writers in Hollywood who can write, in the sense we are talking about."

Gradually, because of a misunderstanding between Chandler and the studio, the situation became impossible. "I assumed in the beginning," he wrote, "that a preliminary script would be all they could expect, since they take a very long time making their pictures. I found out as I began to send it in that they were regarding it as shooting script (subject to cutting) and didn't want any other writer on it. That put the heat on me and I began to get nervous. MGM never had a script in thirteen weeks since the company was organized, and here they were talking about going into production in November." In the end, when his thirteen weeks had expired, Chandler left behind an incomplete script. "I didn't finish it," Chandler admitted, "and it is probably all bitched up by now (or perhaps I bitched it up), but after that one was over I had to be hit on the head with a baseball bat to make me get out of a chair."

The script was finished by Steve Fisher, and Chandler thought it was so bad he refused to have his name associated with it. Everything about the film irritated him: when it was in production, he said he heard it was "probably the worst picture ever made," and he derided the camera-eye technique adopted by Robert Montgomery, the director and

star of the film, as being "old stuff in Hollywood. Every young writer or
director has wanted to try it. 'Let's make the camera a character'; it's
been said at every lunch table in Hollywood one time or another."
Chandler's dismissal of the film was probably caused by his realization
that he could not or at least did not finish the film himself. What made it
worse was that the film was a success and made a great deal of money.
The camera-eye technique was in fact new and had never been used
before in a full-length film. Robert Montgomery says that it involved a
special cutting technique. For the actors, it was difficult; one of them,
Lloyd Nolan, recalls that they were required to violate the first law of
film acting, which is not to look at the camera. While shooting, Montgomery would squat under the lens to remind the actors that the camera
was Marlowe, but it was difficult for them to remember not to look at
Montgomery but at the lens over his head.

After leaving MGM, Chandler took Cissy up to Big Bear Lake for a
few weeks. It was October, with warm days and cool evenings with fires
in the fireplace. "There is nothing to do and I do it," Chandler wrote.
"We go out in the woods and I chop knots out of fallen trees and break
up a few stumps of ironwood or mountain mahogany, a very hard
reddish wood that burns like coal. I try to keep work out of my head,
but can't quite do that." He was too unsettled to write much, and after
his experiences with Paramount he instructed his agent to obtain better
terms for him. The front-office people knew the strain Chandler had
undergone in writing *The Blue Dahlia* and discussed with his agent
various ways he might work for Paramount without having a "crack up."
His agent proposed that he be paid a flat fee for a film, free of the
pressure of deadlines; but Paramount suggested instead that he become
a writer-director like Billy Wilder, or even produce his own films. Despite the greater earnings these proposals would have produced, Chandler turned them down because he did not want to invest so much of his
time in Hollywood.

In January the matter had still not been resolved, so Chandler
refused to report to the studio, using the excuse that Cissy was ill with
the flu. "I no longer have a secretary," he wrote, "since I no longer have
a motion picture job. I am what is technically known as suspended. For
refusing to perform under a contract which is not a proper expression of
my standing in the motion picture business. I requested a cancellation,
but was denied that. There is no moral issue involved since the studios
have destroyed the moral basis of the contracts themselves. They tear
them up whenever it suits them. In getting rid of a writer they use a
term 'adjusting the contract,' which means paying him a few weeks'
salary under the threat of keeping him until his next option comes up,

with everyone knowing he has no assignment and that no producer on the lot wants him. This ought to work both ways.

"One of the troubles is that it seems quite impossible to convince anyone that a man would turn his back on a whopping salary whopping by the standards of normal living—for any reason but a tactical manoeuvre through which he hopes to acquire a still more whopping salary. What I want is something quite different: a freedom from date-lines and unnatural pressures, and a right to find work with those few people in Hollywood whose purpose is to make the best pictures possible within the limitations of a popular art, not merely to repeat the old and vulgar formulae. And only a little of that.

"The ethics of this industry may be judged by the fact that late last night a very important independent producer called me up and asked me to do a screenplay of one of the most advertised projects of the year, do it on the quiet, secretly, with full knowledge that it would be a violation of my contract. That meant nothing to him; it never occurred to him that he was insulting me. Perhaps, in spite of my faults, I still have a sense of honor. I may quarrel, but at least I put the point at issue down on the table in front of me. I am perfectly willing to let them examine my sleeves for hidden cards. But I don't think they really want to. They would be horrified to find them empty. They do not like to deal with honest men."

For the moment Chandler's position was strong, and he could afford the aggressive attitude he took toward the studios, which was a continuation of the toughness he had shown in the oil business. In 1945 he paid $50,000 in income taxes, which he admitted was "pretty awful for a chap who was gnawing old shoes not too many years ago." What he really wanted was to write fiction, and he was willing to work with the studios only if the terms made it worth his while. He had at last "made good" both as a writer and a money earner, and he knew it. Moreover, he had never had to be dishonest. He was a success and also a gentleman—something rare in Hollywood, to his way of thinking. Observing a group of studio executives returning from lunch at the commissary, he wrote: "I was transfixed with a sinister delight. They looked so exactly like a bunch of topflight Chicago gangsters moving in to read the death sentence on a beaten competitor. It brought home to me in a flash the strange psychological and spiritual kinship between the operations of big money business and the rackets. Same faces, same expressions, same manners. Same way of dressing and same exaggerated leisure of movement."

Chandler always kept a certain distance from what he was involved in. Meta Rosenberg remembers him at Paramount as someone who always seemed to be watching the group he was with, and himself within the group, from an authorial distance. This habit left him with few illusions. For Chandler, "the pretentiousness, the bogus enthusiasm, the constant drinking and drabbing, the incessant squabbling over money, the all-pervasive agent, the strutting of the big shots (and their usually utter incompetence to achieve anything they start out to do), the constant fear of losing all this fairy gold and being the nothing they have really never ceased to be, the snide tricks, the whole damn mess is out of this world. It is like one of these South American palace revolutions conducted by officers in comic-opera uniforms—only when the thing is over and the ragged dead men lie in rows against the wall, you suddenly know that this is not funny, this is the Roman circus, and damned near the end of a civilization."

At the same time, he was determined to get what he wanted in this marketplace. He was not half-Irish for nothing, and he took no pains to hide his feelings. About some of the MGM producers he remarked: "A lot of these boys think they are God Almighty with two pair of pants, and I unfortunately am likely enough to dispute the idea in somewhat forcible language." Elsewhere he quipped: "I don't care anything about the money, I just like to fight."

Chandler's difficulties with the studios led him to express his thoughts about Hollywood publicly. As a serious artist who hated wasting his time in a medium that debased his best efforts, he had often written about Hollywood in letters and told interviewers what he thought about screen writing. He told Irving Wallace that the screen writer was "treated like a cow, something to milk dry and send out to graze," and wrote Alfred Knopf, "I really hoped there was a way one could work in pictures and not be cynical about it. There isn't." During the months he was struggling with *The Blue Dahlia* and the screenplay of *The Lady in the Lake*, he pulled his ideas together for an article entitled "Writers in Hollywood" that was published in the *Atlantic Monthly* in November of 1945. Chandler had begun his association with the *Atlantic,* and especially with the managing editor, Charles Morton, in 1944 with his famous essay "The Simple Art of Murder," in which he criticized the deductive school of mystery writers and praised the work of Dashiell Hammett. This article irritated many detective-story fans because of its attacks on sacred cows, but it is the essential document for Chandler's own esthetic position. It also reveals him as a marvelously refreshing essayist.

The success of the essay led to an extended correspondence with Morton, who suggested subjects for further articles. Chandler was hesitant to write them for fear he might slip into "the language of intellectualism, which is a loathesome language." Eventually, however, he

agreed to Morton's suggestion that he write an essay on Hollywood
screen writers. From the beginning he had a great deal of trouble with
the piece, for although he wanted to defend and even bolster Hollywood
writers, he found that it was not easy to generalize about them "I have
no honesty about it," he informed Morton. There were some good
writers, but he had to admit that most of them were "largely overdressed, overpaid, servile and incompetent hacks." Eric Ambler has said
that Hollywood writers may be divided into two groups—those who
write novels as well as screenplays and those who write only screenplays. Most of the good scripts were written by novelists, and that is
why, to use Chandler's remark, "Good original screenplays are almost as
rare in Hollywood as virgins." Chandler dismissed the hacks altogether
and defined the better screen writer either as the entirely anonymous
technician who subordinates himself to the camera or, on the other side,
"the writer whose personal touch must be allowed to come through,
because his personal touch is what makes him a writer."

Chandler believed that the main problem lay in the way the Hollywood employment system was applied to the twenty or so writers whose
work was worth anything. The Writers Guild forced the studios to pay
salaries to their writers so that they would not be exploited. This was
fair enough, but it also corrupted writers by tempting them to work as
slowly as possible. With hacks it didn't matter, but the system made it
unlikely that artistically satisfying films would be made in Hollywood.
Having paid their writers salaries, the studios legally owned the result-
ing scripts and were free to do whatever they liked with them. Interference of this sort was ruinous for writers of any substance. It was also
psychologically bad, for without the risk and personal investment that is
generally part of all other writing, there is none of the inner urgency
necessary for decent work. "In Hollywood," Chandler wrote, "they
destroy the link between a writer and his subconscious. After that what
he does is merely a performance. His heart is somewhere else."

Most of "Writers in Hollywood" just describes the screen writer's
life, and it concludes with the unjustified assertion that the writer was
gradually becoming more important in making films. When the article
came out, Chandler thought it was being received in "frozen silence" to
judge from the lack of newspaper comment. He was also told that it had
done him harm with the Paramount producers. "Charlie Brackett, that
fading wit, said: 'Chandler's books are not good enough, nor his pictures
bad enough, to justify that article.' I wasted a little time trying to figure
out what that meant. It seems to mean that the only guy who can speak
his mind about Hollywood is either (a) a failure in Hollywood, or (b) a
celebrity somewhere else. I would reply to Mr. Brackett that if my books
had been any worse, I should not have been invited to Hollywood, and

that if they had been any better, I should not have come." Years later, noting that he had obtained his best contracts after writing about Hollywood, he said he thought many film people were underrated: "They think, many of them, what I think, but they just don't dare say it, and they are really rather grateful to anyone who does."

At the time the article came out, Chandler was still negotiating with Paramount through his Hollywood agent, H. N. Swanson. "I feel utterly alone," he wrote, "more so than when I didn't have a dime." He had also been ill with the flu, and this made him touchy. "I have developed a peculiar phobia about contracts, seem unable to function as a free man when tied up in any way." By April some progress had been made: "We are now making an armistice to be followed by a peace treaty," he wrote to Erle Stanley Gardner. "The great difficulty in dealing with a studio is that the men you deal with are in turn responsible to a New York hierarchy which has no part in making pictures, but only in exhibiting and promoting them. To them a picture is just as much a manufactured item as a can of beans. They cannot allow for the personal equation because they never meet it." Finally, toward the end of May, after refusing a number of books suggested by the studio, Chandler persuaded Paramount to buy a novel called *The Innocent Mrs. Duff* by Elizabeth Sanxay Holding. Almost immediately there were difficulties, because the producer "managed to talk all the interest out of the story, principally by the simple device of speaking of the characters as Ladd and Caulfield, etc. rather than by their fictional names." For some weeks he worked with a collaborator, but toward the end of the summer, having completed his required number of weeks in residence, he left Paramount with the screenplay unfinished. "If Paramount had had the sense to let me write my own idea of a rough screen play on Mrs. Duff," he explained to his agent, "without the interference of a producer's ideas, ambition, and eagerness to dominate a project to his own advantage, they would have got something in comparatively short time which would have shown them at a glance where the picture was. But no; they simply cannot realize that what they want from me is what I write in my own way; they think they can get that and at the same time control almost every move I make and every idea I have. It just can't be done. What I have to give them is not craftsmanship but a certain quality. If they want that, they can't get it anywhere else."

Once Chandler's contract with Paramount was concluded, Swanson arranged to have an interview with the MGM executives. "I imagine everyone ought to meet Samuel Goldwyn this side of Paradise," Chandler commented. "I've heard he feels so good when he stops." Chandler had no intention of signing on at MGM. "I will not work for dominating people like Selznick or Goldwyn," he told Swanson. "If you deprive me of the right to do my own kind of writing, there is almost nothing left."

Chandler was nearing the end of his Hollywood career and was doubtless aware of it, but 1946 was a busy year for him, and he was involved with a number of other projects. One of these was Warner Brothers' filming of *The Big Sleep*. Chandler was invited to the Warner lot to talk with William Faulkner and Leigh Brackett, the authors of the screenplay; Howard Hawks, the director; and Humphrey Bogart, who starred in the film. Chandler told the gathering that he liked the script, and especially the ending Miss Brackett had devised. When the film had to be shortened, this ending was replaced by another, written by Jules Furthman. Chandler and Hawks also talked about one of the final scenes. "At the end of the picture," he later wrote, "Bogart and Carmen were caught in Geiger's house by Eddie Mars and his lifetakers. That is Bogart (Marlowe) was trapped there and the girl came along and they let her go in. Bogart knew she was a murderess and he also knew that the first person out of that door would walk into a hail of machine-gun bullets. The girl didn't know this. Marlowe also knew that if he sent the girl out to be killed, the gang would take it on the lam, thus saving his own life for the time being. He didn't feel like playing God or saving his skin by letting Carmen leave. Neither did he feel like playing Sir Philip Sidney to save a worthless life. So he put it up to God by tossing a coin. Before he tossed the coin he prayed out loud, in a sort of way. The gist of his prayer was that he, Marlowe, had done the best he knew how and through no fault of his own was put in a position of making a decision God had no right to force him to make. He wanted that decision made by the authority who allowed all this mess to happen. If the coin came down heads, he would let the girl go. He tossed and it came down heads. The girl thought this was a kind of game to hold her there for the police. She started to leave. At the last moment, as she had her hand on the doorknob, Marlowe weakened and started for her to stop her. She laughed in his face and pulled a gun on him. Then she opened the door an inch or two and you could see she was going to shoot and was thoroughly delighted with the situation. At that moment a burst of machine-gun fire walked across the panel of the door and tore her to pieces. The gunmen outside had heard a siren in the distance and panicked and thrown a casual burst through the door just for a visiting card—without expecting to hit anyone."

Chandler's scene was not used: the movie ends quite differently, and Carmen is not present. The machine-gun burst is retained, but the victim is Mars, who is mistakenly killed by his henchmen. And that is the difference between the two media: Chandler's is a writer's scene, but it won't play.

Chandler was pleased by the final film, especially Bogart's portrayal of Marlowe. "As we say here," he wrote to Hamish Hamilton, "Bogart can be tough without a gun. Also he has a sense of humor that contains that grating undertone of contempt. Bogart is the genuine article." He disliked the convention that required giving the film a romantic twist, but he knew his objection would have no effect, since "in Hollywood you cannot make a picture which is not essentially a love story, that is to say, a story in which sex is paramount." Chandler also admired Hawks's work. Although generally contemptuous of directors, he recognized that Hawks had "the gift of atmosphere and the requisite touch of hidden sadism."

The most famous incident linking Chandler to the film of *The Big Sleep* is his reply to a telegram sent by Hawks asking who killed Owen Taylor, the Sternwood chauffeur who ends up in the family limousine under ten feet of water at the end of a pier. Chandler checked the text, thought about it, and wired back: "I don't know." Referring to the incident later on, Chandler said that Jack Warner, the head of the studio, saw the telegram, which cost seventy cents, and phoned Hawks to ask whether it was really necessary to send a telegram about such a point. Chandler commented· "That's one way to run a business."

Chandler was also involved in the actual filming of *The Blue Dahlia*, probably because the scenes were being shot before he finished the script. The experience was not pleasant, as he reported, with perhaps some exaggeration of his own role, to Hamish Hamilton: "The last picture I did there nearly killed me. The producer was in the doghouse— he has since left—and the director was a stale old hack who had been directing for thirty years without once achieving any real distinction. Obviously he never could. So there was I a mere writer and a tired one at that screaming at the front office to protect the producer and actually going on the set to direct scenes—I know nothing about directing—in order that the whole project might be saved from going down the drain. Well, it was saved."

The pressure of his work brought out Chandler's sarcastic side, as in his remarks about "Miss Moronica Lake": "The only time she's any good is when she keeps her mouth shut and looks mysterious. The moment she tries to behave as if she had a brain she falls flat on her face. The scenes we had to cut because she loused them up! And there are three godawful shots of her looking perturbed that make me want to throw my lunch over the fence." These remarks may sound extreme, but in this world of intense rivalries, jealousies, and anxieties they are actually rather mild. They also reflect Chandler's antipathy to actors. More than once he quoted approvingly the remark made by his friend, Joseph Sistrom, who said, "Of course, nobody can *really* like an actor."

The release of *The Blue Dahlia* brought Chandler considerable publicity. The studio advertisements plugged Veronica Lake and Alan Ladd, but many critics looked upon it as Chandler's film, and his name, not theirs, appeared in the headlines of the reviews. This was particularly true in England, where the art of film criticism reached a respectable level, in the work of Dilys Powell, C. A. Lejeune, and others, much earlier than it did in the United States. They knew Chandler's fiction and therefore treated his film work in that context. "I award first prize this week to Raymond Chandler, author of 'The Blue Dahlia,' " C. A. Lejeune began her review in the *Observer*. She then went on to discuss Chandler's contribution virtually to the exclusion of everyone else. In the *Sunday Times* Dilys Powell followed a similar course and pointed out that the film's main weakness was the director's failure "to bring out the quality of shady poetry which exists in Chandler's written work."

Paramount was aware of the special interest Chandler's first original screenplay was arousing, and therefore Teet Carle of the publicity department arranged a dinner in his honor at Lucey's, with a private screening to follow. George Marshall, the director, was the titular host. All the best mystery-story writers from Hollywood were invited to the party, along with Captain Thad Brown of the Los Angeles Homicide Bureau, who was known to several of them, including Chandler. The guests included Craig Rice, who was then one of the most popular detective novelists in the country, Erle Stanley Gardner, Leslie Charteris, Frank Gruber, Philip MacDonald, and Daniel Mainwaring, who wrote under the name of Geoffrey Homes. Chandler also invited some of the old *Black Mask* writers. At the dinner party the lights were suddenly extinguished, and when they were turned on again Lucey's chef was revealed stretched out on a table, apparently dead. The guests were asked to explain the murder, and at least one suggested that the man had died from food poisoning after eating one of his own meals.

Afterward *The Blue Dahlia* was shown in a projection room at Paramount. Many of the writers present, with the generosity that typifies their profession, found fault with it. Teet Carle, sitting in the back, heard three or four of them ridiculing the plot, the dialogue, and the action: "How could old Ray resort to such clap-trap?" Had they but known, Chandler was largely in agreement with them. The occasion reflected the ambivalence of Chandler's years in Hollywood—the mixture of success and failure, of pleasure and frustration that marked them.

Toward the end of the year the Mystery Writers of America awarded their highest prize, an Edgar (for Edgar Allan Poe), to *The Blue Dahlia*, and Chandler was also nominated for an Academy award for the screenplay. This success and attention could have made it relatively easy for him to get a good contract with one of the studios, but at heart

Chandler was sick of Hollywood and also fed up with Los Angeles. The house next door on Drexel Avenue contained two teenaged boys, and their noise was continuously disruptive. Physically, he was exhausted: "Can't sleep, can't eat, can't make a decision, can hardly get out of a chair." But worst of all was his feeling of isolation. "Please write," he added almost hysterically as a postscript to Charles Morton, "I haven't spoken to an educated man in a month."

He had thought of going to a clinic in La Jolla where "they take in decayed personalities and try to find out if it is any use letting them live." Instead, after leaving Paramount he visited Erle Stanley Gardner in Temecula for a couple of days. The quiet ranch life may have impressed on him the need for actually moving, for not long afterward he and Cissy went down to La Jolla, where they bought a large house overlooking the sea.

7.

THE
RELUCTANT
SUBURB

———————◆———————

La Jolla is one of those American towns from which the ugly aspects of life have been carefully excluded. There are no factories, machine shops, railway yards, advertising billboards, pool halls, graveyards, roadhouses, or miniature golf courses. The houses are large and the streets are clean, with abundant trees and shrubbery. Even the shops and banks have window boxes. La Jolla is where the rich live—many of them retired, others professional people and owners of businesses in nearby San Diego, for which, as Chandler later remarked, it was a "reluctant suburb."

When he first visited La Jolla, Chandler found the place so genteel that his "first impulse was to get out in the street at high noon and shout four-letter words." But gradually he and Cissy had come to enjoy its quiet elegance and the politeness of the inhabitants, whose lack of aggressiveness was a pleasant change from Los Angeles. The decision to move there in 1946 was to some extent Cissy's, and the house Chandler bought was a reward to her for having endured the bad times of the late 1920s and 1930s and the vagaries of Hollywood. Cissy was now seventy-six, and the place suited her. In Hollywood she was an oddity, with yellow curls that made her look like an aged Shirley Temple, but she fit right into La Jolla.

The house Chandler bought "beside the sounding sea" was sprawling and single-story. It was built on a corner lot at 6005 Camino de la Costa, which is south of the center of La Jolla, toward San Diego. The house stands on a gentle rise above street level and is built around a flagstoned courtyard containing a small fish pond, with a rock garden behind that spreads up the hill. It was, he said, "a far better home than an out-of-work pulp writer has any right to expect." The living room was large and airy, about twenty by forty feet in dimension, and at one end a large window provided a view over the ocean toward Point Loma in the distance. Chandler wrote that a "radio writer came down here to see me once and he sat down in front of this window and cried because it was so beautiful. But we live here, and the hell with it." The Chandlers furnished the room with Cissy's grand piano in a corner and bookcases and good mahogany furniture. An inside hall, glassed on the courtyard side, led to the dining room, kitchen, and maid's room on the right and to Cissy's room, a guest room, and at the end Chandler's study on the left.

The house had just been built in 1946, and the Chandlers were probably the first owners. He had some special cabinets and bookcases installed in his study, since that is where he spent much of his time. Chandler paid $40,000 for the house; today it is worth three times that amount.

At first, the house seemed to provide everything Chandler needed, and he was pleased that he had been able to give Cissy something she really wanted and liked. He had given up drink once again, and away from the studio he was free of temptations for casual liaisons, which were hard to establish in La Jolla. From previous visits Chandler knew a number of writers in La Jolla, among them Ronal Kaiser (who wrote under the name of Dale Clark), Jonathan Latimer, whom he'd met at Paramount, and Max Miller, the author of I Cover the Waterfront, who lived down the street from him. With these men he sometimes played tennis, although his eyesight was weakening. He refused to join the Beach and Tennis Club, however, because it wouldn't accept Jews as members. As in Hollywood, Chandler's social life was meager, and to some degree for the same reason—Cissy's age. Once in a while Chandler would invite the Latimers to tea, a household ritual with silver teapots and petits fours. The house was dark, with curtains drawn against the western sun, and the conversation was usually stiff. Chandler's neighbor, Max Miller, occasionally dropped in unannounced, but this usually earned him a cold reception because Chandler hated the unexpected. Jonathan Latimer recalls a similar reaction when he returned a borrowed book. Finding himself in Chandler's neighborhood, he stopped at the house and rang the bell. After a long wait, Cissy opened the door and said, "Yes?" Latimer explained that he was returning the book and wished to thank Chandler for lending it to him. Once again, Cissy said "Yes," took the book, and closed the door.

From time to time Chandler's agents or lawyers would come down from Los Angeles to see him. These visits were always businesslike. Cissy would appear briefly but then retire, and Chandler would talk with his guests. They would then leave. Chandler intended no rudeness in treating others so formally; he simply didn't know how to cope with them. With Joseph Sistrom and his wife it was different, for they were friends and would be invited to dinner. But the underlying tension and nervousness often rose to the surface. Cissy would fuss and make everyone uncomfortable, while Chandler was anxious and irritable. Once at dinner the roast was so tough Chandler couldn't cut it. Like his Irish uncle, he called in the cook and berated her. The next day the Sistroms had dinner with the Latimers and the first thing they were asked was, "How did it go?" "Awful," they answered, and then everyone laughed.

It was better when they went to a restaurant called La Plaza, a steak house with open grills run by a man called Moe Locke. Sistrom would do most of the talking and the Chandlers, no longer responsible as hosts, would be more relaxed. Once, however, the waiter came over and told Chandler that J. Edgar Hoover, who was there with his friend Clyde Tolson, wanted him to come over to his table. Chandler told the waiter to tell Hoover he could go to hell. Hoover fell into a rage, saying he would have Chandler investigated by the FBI, but Tolson eventually calmed him down.

Although Chandler's social life was almost nonexistent, he was aware of what was going on about him and commented amusingly on the "arthritic billionaires and barren old women" who lived in La Jolla. Once, in the town's public library, he was recognized by "the elderly white-haired prim-mouthed librarian," who told him she had read one of his books while she was in the hospital. "I hope it didn't make you worse," Chandler replied. "I wanted to throw it across the room, it made me so mad," she said, "but I didn't. There was something about the writing." Chandler was also enchanted by the local eccentrics: "Somewhere in this town of La Jolla there dwell a couple of gnome-like females who always dress with large pulled-down felt hats on their heads, bunchy shapeless garments under old raincoats, and carry walking sticks. They walk past our house every single day and they never walk abreast, always one several paces behind the other as if they were not on speaking terms, but were held together by some unbreakable tie. They look like something out of Grimm's Fairy Tales. One day as they passed, a real estate man who was here to size up the house happened to glance out of the window and see them. He stared open-mouthed for a couple of seconds and then said suddenly: 'What country are we in?' "

With a social life reduced to the point of seeing other people from La Jolla only once or twice a year, Chandler relied on routine to give structure to his life. After Hollywood it was delightful to be free from outside interference, but some order was necessary. Generally, Chandler would rise early and go to his study. It was small but comfortable, overlooking the garden because he disliked looking at the sea. "Too much water, too many drowned men," he remarked to an interviewer. After four or five hours at his desk he would join Cissy for lunch, served in the dining room.

Ordinarily, Chandler never did any work in the afternoon. He was not the kind to relax—to take a swim or sun himself in the patio behind the house. He was always formally dressed in jacket and tie, although there was often something askew in his appearance. Unless he had some reading to do, he would take out his Oldsmobile and go into the center of La Jolla for his errands. He would go to the post office, where his mail was kept in a box; he would then buy groceries or visit his accountant, George Peterson, or one of his lawyers, such as William Durham. He would often stop at the bookshop as well. These errands constituted his social life, or were a substitute for one. His afternoon excursions got him out of the house and exposed him to other people. He enjoyed chatting with shopkeepers, garage men, and postal clerks. He seemed to prefer their company to that of his own sort, perhaps because these encounters were brief and limited and did not impinge on him in any serious way. He enjoyed the anonymity of his life, although he occasionally complained about not being recognized. La Jolla was for years a favorite weekend resort for Hollywood actors, and the townspeople made a point of being unimpressed by celebrities. To most of his fellow citizens, Chandler was just an ordinary fellow who wrote books, probably some sort they'd never read—for, to put it at its kindest, La Jolla is not a bookish community.

By four, Chandler would be back at the house in time for tea with cakes and sandwiches on a silver tray in the living room. Tea was more Cissy's idea than Chandler's because she was a somewhat conventional person with old-fashioned tastes. In the evening the Chandlers usually had dinner at home, generally without guests, although Cissy enjoyed having her sister, Lavinia, come for extended visits. They rarely went out because, as Chandler explained, "we are badly spoiled about food and consider the better than average American restaurant not fit to eat in." Sometimes they would go to a movie, but usually they would remain at home. Cissy might play the piano or they would listen to records.

Chandler had rather ordinary tastes in music compared to Cissy and would play over and over again such popular tunes as the zither music from the film *The Third Man* or the songs from a musical comedy he enjoyed. Because of her age, Cissy would go to bed early, and Chandler would read until late at night and occasionally dictate letters. An insomniac, he rarely went to bed until well past midnight.

His companion during these late hours was always the large black Persian cat he had owned since the 1930s. She was called Taki because nobody could pronounce correctly her real name, Take, which is Japanese for "bamboo." Visitors to the Chandler household frequently noticed that the cat was treated almost like a human being and was consulted about various matters. Taki didn't "give a damn about anybody, that's why I like her," Chandler explained to an interviewer. His isolation made him invest the cat with qualities that she probably did not possess but that had a certain plausibility. Chandler admired her sense of humor and her "absolute poise, which is a rare quality in animals as well as in human beings. And she had no cruelty, which is a still rarer quality in cats." Often he wrote humorously about Taki and called her his secretary because whenever he began to write she was "usually sitting on the paper I wanted to use or the copy I wanted to revise, sometimes leaning up against the typewriter and sometimes just quietly gazing out of the window from the corner of the desk, as much as to say, 'The stuff you're doing's a waste of my time, bud.' " Chandler and Cissy were both fond of animals and invented what they called "Amuels," which are words for animals that allow the particular to stand for the general, as in Pavlova for swan or Anatole for penguin. They also used these as pet names for each other. For Chandler, Taki was a kind of substitute child, and he used her, almost always in a humorous way, as an extension of his own personality. "Our cat no more resembles the ordinary scrap-fed, put-out-at-night feline," he asserted with mock arrogance, "than Louis B. Mayer resembles a clerk in a Bronx delicatessen (or is that an unfortunate comparison?)."

The tranquillity of La Jolla allowed Chandler to complete some of the projects he had begun in Hollywood. He enjoyed the literary and intellectual world the *Atlantic* articles had allowed him to reenter. It pleased him to appear in print with Jean-Paul Sartre, Walter Lippmann, Jessamyn West, Kenneth Grahame, Jacques Barzun, and Stephen Spender, because these were the kind of intellectuals he grew up with as a young man. For the article on Hollywood he graciously yielded first place in the magazine to Albert Einstein. What added relish to Chandler's vicarious involvement in the literary world was the attention his own work was receiving. In "Who Cares Who Killed Roger Ackroyd?" Edmund Wilson's general attack on mystery writers published in the

New Yorker in 1945, he carefully excluded Chandler from unfavorable comment. "His *Farewell, My Lovely* is the only one of these books that I have read all of and read with enjoyment," Wilson wrote. "It is not simply a question here of a puzzle which has been put together but of a malaise conveyed to the reader, the horror of a hidden conspiracy which is continually turning up in the most varied and unlikely forms. To write such a novel successfully you must be able to invent character and incident and to generate atmosphere, and all this Mr. Chandler can do, although he is a long way below Graham Greene." In an article in *Harper's* for May of 1948 called "The Guilty Vicarage," W. H. Auden made a similar distinction: "Chandler is interested in writing, not detective stories, but serious studies of a criminal milieu, the Great Wrong Place, and his powerful but extremely depressing books should be read and judged, not as escape literature, but as works of art." This kind of attention naturally pleased Chandler, for it showed, as he remarked in a letter to Charles Morton, that he had succeeded in what he set out to do: "What greater prestige can a man like me (not too greatly gifted but very understanding) have than to have taken a cheap, shoddy, and utterly lost kind of writing, and have made of it something that intellectuals claw each other about?"

At the same time, he refused to be impressed by this attention—which earned him the jealousy and hatred of other mystery writers—because he thought most critics were simply illiterate. To him, *The Memoirs of Hecate County* proved that Edmund Wilson didn't know how to write, and he poked fun at the solemnity of Auden's remarks about the "critical milieu." The only useful critics were those who knew what writing was all about. When he agreed to review a novel called *The Golden Egg* by James S. Pollak for the *Atlantic*, he first gave his definition of literature as "any sort of writing at all that reaches a sufficient intensity of performance to glow with its own heat," and then regretfully pointed out that Pollak did not attain it. But the real development in Chandler is that he had grown suspicious of the kind of critical and intellectual magazines he had written for in his youth, because "they never achieve life, but only a distaste for other people's view of it. They have the intolerance of the very young and the anemia of closed rooms and too much midnight smoking." Chandler intended to set forth his own standards of critical judgment in an article for the *Atlantic* to be called "Advice to a Young Critic," but he never finished it. It is not surprising, for as he wrote to James Sandoe: "Thinking in terms of ideas destroys the power to think in terms of emotions and sensations. I have at times a futile urge to explain to whoever will listen why it is that the whole apparatus of intellectualism bores me. But you have to use the language of intellectualism to do it. Which is the bunk." Chandler was too quick and funny to wallow in generalities, and he could say more in half a paragraph about a small point of grammar than most critics could state in 3,000 words of abstractions. Thus he once wrote to Edward Weeks, the editor of the *Atlantic:* "By the way, would you convey my compliments to the purist who reads your proofs and tell him or her that I write in a sort of broken-down patois which is something like the way a Swiss waiter talks, and that when I split an infinitive, God damn it, I split it so it will stay split, and when I interrupt the velvety smoothness of my more or less literate syntax with a few sudden words of barroom vernacular, this is done with the eyes open and the mind relaxed but attentive. The method may not be perfect, but it is all I have. I think your proofreader is kindly attempting to steady me on my feet, but as much as I appreciate the solicitude, I am really able to steer a fairly clear course, provided I get both sidewalks and the street between."

This letter produced a comic sequel. Weeks showed the letter to the proofreader, a woman with the charming name of Miss Margaret Mutch, and told Chandler how amused she'd been. Perhaps it was the name; anyhow, Chandler thereupon composed "Lines to a Lady with an Unsplit Infinitive," which began:

> *Miss Margaret Mutch she raised her crutch*
> > *With a wild Bostonian cry.*
> *"Though you went to Yale, your grammar is frail,"*
> > *She snarled as she jabbed his eye.*
> *"Though you went to Princeton I never winced on*
> > *"Such a horrible relative clause!*
> *"Though you went to Harvard no decent larva'd*
> > *"Accept your syntactical flaws.*
> *"Taught not to drool at a Public School*
> > *"(With a capital P and S)*
> *"You are drooling still with your shall and will*
> > *"You're a very disgusting mess!"*

After traveling through a host of other grammatical mistakes, the poem ends:

> *She stared him down with an icy frown.*
> > *His accidence she shivered.*
> *His face was white with sudden fright,*
> > *His syntax lily-livered.*
> *"O dear Miss Mutch, leave down your crutch,"*
> > *He cried in thoughtless terror.*
> *Short shrift she gave. Above his grave:*
> > HERE LIES A PRINTER'S ERROR.

In Hollywood, with a secretary at the studio, Chandler learned how to use dictation for purposes other than business correspondence. He knew its danger and recalled the wordiness that afflicted Henry James after he took it up. But Chandler's mind was sufficiently precise, thanks to his classical education, to prevent him from rambling and to allow him to speak "prose" when he dictated. After moving to La Jolla, he corresponded with Erle Stanley Gardner and even visited Temecula to inspect Gardner's dictating equipment. Shortly afterward he bought a machine of his own on which he dictated the enormous correspondence he undertook during the ten years he lived with Cissy in La Jolla.

This correspondence arose from the reclusive life he led and from the long hours he spent alone. With Cissy in bed shortly after dinner, he had to devise some way to amuse himself. He would often read a number of books at the same time and leave them open in his study. "In that way," he explained, "when I feel dull and depressed which is too often I know I have something to read late at night when I do most of it and not that horrid blank feeling of not having anybody to talk to or listen to." At this time, he also dictated letters.

Chandler's correspondence, which was also due to a lack of stimulation in La Jolla, was a means of allowing him to converse with other people, try out his ideas, reminisce, and ruminate. Many of his letters—to Hamish Hamilton, to his agents, to Charles Morton—dealt in part with business matters, but Chandler rarely sent out a letter without some comment on writing, politics, warfare, Hollywood, or his own life in La Jolla. His correspondence with Hamilton was also a way of keeping his link with England alive, and he wrote long letters about his own youth there, his Irish relations, his schooldays at Dulwich, and his early experiences as a writer in London. These were all a sign of his continued homesickness for England.

Almost all his correspondence was with people he did not know personally. It is pathetic that a man of his accomplishment and stature felt he had to write one of his correspondents that "all of my best friends I have never met." But the correspondence allowed him a directness and openness that he probably could never have managed in personal meetings. His shyness disappeared when he sat down at his typewriter or dictating machine. He could even handle the vexing problem of modes of address by confronting it directly. Hearing that Hamish Hamilton was known to his friends as "Jamie" he wrote: "Would you mind addressing me as Ray, and will you tell me how I may most familiarly address you? I live in a world where the use of a last name is almost an insult."

Chandler's correspondence is reminiscent of some of the great letter writing of the past, but it is woefully one-sided. His correspondents are literate and intelligent, but from the evidence that survives, they were no match for Chandler. It is a pity he never kept up an exchange with anyone of his own stature, but in a sense Chandler's letters are monologues. They are like the conversation of a man sitting by a fireplace, pondering and exploring everything he could not encompass in his fiction.

They may also be thought of, when gathered together, as a writer's notebook, a record of Chandler's range and growth. In a letter to Morton he spoke of the future of fiction: "Undoubtedly, we are getting a lot of adept reportage which masquerades as fiction and will go on getting it, but essentially I believe that what is lacking is an emotional quality. Even when they deal with death, and they often do, they are not tragic. I suppose that is to be expected. An age which is incapable of poetry is incapable of any kind of literature except the cleverness of decadence. The boys can say anything, their scenes are almost tiresomely neat, they have all the facts and all the answers, but they are little men who have forgotten how to pray. As the world grows smaller, so the minds of men grow smaller, more compact, and more empty. These are the machine-minders of literature."

In another letter, answering a fiction instructor in New Jersey who wanted information useful to her students, he wrote about the importance and elusiveness of style: "In the long run, however little you talk or even think about it, the most durable thing in writing is style, and style is the most valuable investment a writer can make with his time. It pays off slowly; your agent will sneer at it, your publisher will misunderstand it, and it will take people you never heard of to convince them by slow degrees that the writer who puts his individual mark on the way he writes will always pay off. He can't do it by trying, because the kind of style I am thinking about is a projection of personality and you have to have a personality before you can project it. But granted that you have one, you can only project it on paper by thinking of something else. This is ironical in a way; it is the reason, I suppose, why in a generation of 'made' writers I still say you can't make a writer. Preoccupation with style will not produce it. No amount of editing and polishing will have any appreciable effect on the flavor of how a man writes. It is the product of the quality of his emotion and perception; it is the ability to transfer these to paper which makes him a writer, in contrast to the great number of people who have just as good emotions and just as keen perceptions, but cannot come within a googol of miles of putting them on paper."

One correspondence with a special flavor developed with James Sandoe, Chandler's admirer from the University of Colorado. As a book reviewer for the *Herald-Tribune*, Sandoe received many copies of detective stories, the best of which he sent on to Chandler. His replies constitute a running commentary on the state of detective fiction over some years, but on the whole Chandler believed that the trouble "with all these situation or plot stories is that at the end you suddenly feel as if you had been drinking city water while you thought you were drinking sparkling burgundy." Chandler was interested in Sandoe's plan to write a critical history of the detective novel, because he hoped it would bring recognition to the few mystery novelists who were real artists. He also hoped it might bridge the gap between detective fiction and "serious" literature. "Neither in this country nor in England," he wrote, "has there been any critical recognition that far more art goes into these books at their best than into any number of fat volumes of goosed history or social-significance rubbish. The psychological foundation for the immense popularity with all sorts of people of the novel about murder or crime or mystery hasn't been scratched. A few superficial and a few frivolous attempts but nothing careful and cool and leisurely. There is a lot more to this subject than most people realize, even those who are interested in it. The subject has usually been treated lightly because it seems to have been taken for granted, quite wrongly, that because murder novels are easy reading they are also light reading. They are no easier reading than *Hamlet*, *Lear* or *Macbeth*. They border on tragedy and never quite become tragic. Their form imposes a certain clarity of outline which is only found in the most accomplished 'straight' novels. And incidentally—quite incidentally, of course—a very large proportion of the surviving literature of the world has been concerned with violent death in some form. And if you have to have signficance (the demand for which is the inevitable mark of a half-baked culture), it is just possible that the tensions in a novel of murder are the simplest and yet most complete pattern of the tensions in which we live in this generation."

Chandler's letters touch a wide range of subjects, including politics, education, sports, and international affairs. His opinions are blunt, direct, skeptical, sometimes a trifle naïve or prejudiced. Politics especially puzzled him, for he could not understand why people were interested in the nonentities who governed them. Nor could he imagine why American intellectuals tended to be left wing or Communist. Did they imagine they would be better off under Stalin? Chandler lived through the era of Senator McCarthy and the House Committee on Un-American Activities, and he ridiculed them both. But he was equally impatient with the film writers known as the "Hollywood Ten" for hiding behind the Fifth Amendment to the Constitution, which bars self-incrimination: "I think the ten men who were cited had very bad legal advice. They were afraid to say they were Communists or to say they were not Communists;

therefore they tried to raise a false issue. If they had told the truth, they would have had a far better case before the courts than they have now, and they would certainly have no worse a case as regards their bosses in Hollywood." Chandler's isolation in La Jolla may have led him to express somewhat simplified opinions; at the same time, he was enough of a skeptic to believe that the evidence produced in the Alger Hiss case and in the perjury case against the Hollywood Ten was probably doctored by the government.

The workings of Chandler's mind are perhaps best revealed in a letter to a Miss Aron who, along with the rabbi of the Union Temple in Brooklyn, accused him of anti-Semitism for describing the doctor in *The High Window* as "a big burly Jew with a Hitler moustache, pop eyes, and the calmness of a glacier." Chandler's normal response when attacked was to counterattack, so he wrote that the Jews should be mature enough to demand the right to have Jewish scoundrels in fiction. "At any rate," he said, "I demand the right to call a character called Weinstein a thief without being accused of calling all Jews thieves." He explained that his fictional doctor was based on his publisher, Alfred Knopf, and finished by warning those on the lookout for anti-Semites not to worry about "those who call a Jew a Jew, who put Jewish characters in their books because there are many Jews in their lives and all interesting and all different and some noble and some rather nasty— like other people—but let them look for their enemies among the brutes (whom they can easily recognize) and among the snobs who do not speak of Jews at all.

"You are safe and more than safe with outspoken people like me," he concluded.

Having lived so long in Hollywood, where many Jews, especially emigrants from Central Europe, worked in the studios, Chandler gradually developed a theory about Jews in California and other parts of the West, which he expressed as a matter of social curiosity to his publisher in England, where Jews have a rather different position in society, as they also do, for example, in many circles in New York. "What they seem to resent," he wrote, "is the feeling that the Jew is a distinct racial type, that you can pick him out by his face, by the tone quality of his voice, and far too often by his manners. They are of all religions and no religion. When you call a man a Jew you are not thinking about his religion, but of certain personal characteristics of appearance or behaviour, and the Jews don't like that, because they know that is what you mean. They want to be like everyone else, indistinguishable from everyone else, except that they want to be Jews to themselves, and they want to be able to call non-Jews by the name of Gentiles. But even then they are not happy, because they know very well you can't insult a man by calling him a Gentile, whereas you *can* insult him by calling him a Jew. As long as this is so I don't see how you can expect the Jews not to be oversensitive, but at the same time I don't see why I should be so unnaturally considerate of this oversensitiveness as never to use the word Jew. It really seems at times that the Jews ask too much of us. They are like a man who insists upon being nameless and without an address and yet insists on being invited to all the best parties."

These remarks may offend certain Jews, but probably not those who are open-minded enough to recognize Chandler's honesty. His view may be narrow, but he does not falsify the evidence. Also, there is a certain humorous bluffness which appears when he professes gratitude for benefits received: "A couple of non-Semitic writers and myself were once discussing what a bunch of bastards they were, and one of them remarked cogently, 'Well, after all, the Jews know how to pay for what they get. If a bunch of Irish Catholics were running the motion picture business, we'd be working for fifty dollars a week.' "

In addition to his correspondence, Chandler spent a good deal of time in La Jolla writing other articles for the *Atlantic*. By 1948 he knew much more about making films than he knew when he wrote his first essay. Above all, he knew that Hollywood was primarily a "business" or an "industry" in which commercial values predominated. In such an atmosphere, Chandler wrote, the writer may have "brief enthusiasms, but they are destroyed before they can flower. People who can't write tell him how to write. He meets clever and interesting people and may even form lasting friendships, but all this is incidental to his proper business of writing. The wise screen writer is he who wears his second-best suit, artistically speaking, and doesn't take things too much to heart." Chandler even had enough detachment to see the humor of the situation, and he enjoyed recording one of the absurd "Goldwynisms" for which Samuel Goldwyn was famous: "Talking about a script deal he pounded the desk and shouted, 'I'm sick and tired of writers chiseling on producers in Hollywood. So here is the deal. You can either take it or like it.' "

Despite his skepticism, Chandler was fascinated by the possibilities of film. To underline the conflict between commercial and artistic values in the movies, he wrote an article called "Oscar Night in Hollywood," which was published in the *Atlantic* in June of 1948. His first point was that the Oscars given by the Academy of Motion Picture Arts and Sciences go only to films that are commercially successful. Why then, he asked, does anyone bother with the vulgar ballyhoo of the Academy awards? "The only answer I can think of is that the motion picture is an art. I say this with a very small voice." He had been saying it with a more forceful voice to the various directors and producers he dealt with in Hollywood, but he accomplished little. Nevertheless, he learned who the important people were in making a film. Mainly, they were the technicians—the cameraman, the lighting man, and above all the editor, who cuts and pieces the scenes together to make them appear in a natural flow. As a writer bored with the pretensions of many directors, Chandler knew that the technicians often faced impossible tasks. "The best cutter in Hollywood cannot correct a botched job of directing; he can't make scenes flow when they are shot staccato, without reference to their movement on film together. If the cutter wants to make a dissolve to cover an abrupt transition, he can't do it unless he has the film to combine for the dissolve." In Chandler's opinion, many directors also lagged behind the technical possibilities of their medium and wasted yards of film in the process. "Hitchcock, the only time I met him, gave me a lecture on this kind of waste," he wrote. "His point was that Hollywood (and England too) was full of directors who had not learned to forget about the biograph. They still thought that because a motion picture moved it interested people. In the early days of the pictures, he said, a man went to visit a woman at her home. They were old flames who had not seen each other for years. The director shot it this way. The man took a taxi, he was seen riding along in the taxi, there was a view of the street and the house, the taxi stopped, the man got out and paid, he looked at the front steps, went up the steps, rang the bell, the maid answered, he said Is Mrs. Gilhooley in? The maid said, I'll see, sir. What name shall I say? The man said: Finnegan. The maid said: This way please. Inside house, hallway, open door, maid stands at open door, man goes in, maid starts upstairs, man in living room looks around, sits down, lights a cigarette. Maid upstairs knocks on door, female voice calls Come in, she opens door. Inside maid says Mr. Finnegan to see you, m'am. Mrs. Gilhooley says wonderingly, Mr. Finnegan? Then slowly, All right, Ellen, I'll be right down. Goes to mirror, primps, enigmatic smile, starts out, shot of her descending stairs, entering living room after a slight embarrassed pause at the door. Inside living room. She enters. Finnegan stands up. They look at each other in silence. Then they smile slowly. Man, huskily: Hello, Madge. You haven't changed a bit. Mrs. Gilhooley: It's been a long time, George. A long time. *And then the scene begins.*

"*Every bit of this stuff is dead film, because every point, if there is a point, can be made inside the scene itself. The rest is just camera in love with mere movement. Cliché, flat, stale, and today meaningless.*"

In another letter Chandler described how the scene should be played: "Taxi arrives, man gets out, pays, starts up steps. Inside the house bell ringing maid coming towards door. Quick cut, fainter sound of ringing heard in bedroom upstairs, mistress at mirror, camera moves in on her face, she knows who it is, the close shot tells you how she feels about it, DISSOLVE the tea wagon is going down the hall. Cut inside room, man and woman stand close looking at each other. Will he take her in his arms, will the tea wagon get there first? Then the wonderful wonderful dialogue. SHE: Charles—it's been fifteen years. HE: Fifteen years and four days. SHE: I can hardly—(knock at door) Come in. (Tea wagon comes in) I'm sure you'd like tea. HE: Love it. SHE: It's Oolong, I grow it myself. HE: I always wondered what you did with your spare time. And so on."

Chandler sometimes wondered whether the trouble with most films was just that "they're simply no longer a novelty. The medium, the things it can do, have lost the sting. We're back where silent films were when Warner's bought the Vitaphone." But in his *Atlantic* article he was more optimistic. After commenting on the high quality of Roberto Rossellini's *Open City* and Olivier's *Henry V*, he said that the motion picture was not like literature or the theater. Rather, it was similar to music "in the sense that its finest effects can be independent of precise meaning, that its transitions can be more eloquent than its high-lit scenes, and that its dissolves and camera movements, which cannot be censored, are far more emotionally effective than its plots, which can. Not only is the motion picture an art," he continued, making the main point of his article, "but it is the one entirely new art that has been evolved on this planet for hundreds of years. It is the only art at which we of this generation have any possible chance to greatly excel."

Chandler's article was featured on the cover of the *Atlantic*. What effect it had on Hollywood is hard to know, but a year after it appeared Chandler noted: "There's a lovely fight going on about the Academy. The boys were finally shamed into giving the award more or less on the basis of merit (except the musical award, which stank) and the five major companies which have been contributing to the cost of the show have withdrawn. 'Look, fellows,' they say without saying, 'we want the Oscars to go to the best pictures all right, but we're not in business for our health. The best pictures from Hollywood, savvy.' They don't care who is best as long as it's them."

Chandler's academic interest in Hollywood was balanced by his practical involvement there, for in the spring of 1947 he signed a contract with Universal to write an original screenplay at $4,000 a week. The agreement was unusual because Chandler was guaranteed a share of the profits when the film was made, and the studio promised to accept the script unseen. William Dozier, who was then executive producer at Universal, knew Chandler from Paramount and had enough faith in his work to agree to these terms. Joseph Sistrom, then also at Universal, was assigned as the film's producer, and in due course Chandler pre-

pared a story outline. Because the plot required a border town, Chandler
wanted the story to be set in Vancouver. The move from Los Angeles
also suggests that he was bored with his usual scene. Here is the opening
of the outline:

> The crucial week in the life of a girl who decides to spend it
> in a tower suite in a hotel, under an assumed name, her identity
> thoroughly concealed with great care, to accept what comes, and
> at the end of the week to jump to her death.
>
> During this week the frustrations and tragedies of her life are
> repeated in capsule form, so that it almost appears that she brought
> her destiny with her, and that wherever she went the same sort of
> thing would happen to her.
>
> Her husband, a heel with medals on, is dead; he is supposed
> to have taken an overdose of nembutal from the effects of a pro-
> longed binge. His family who adored him don't think he took it
> at all; the police weren't sure enough to make a stink, even if the
> family wanted it, which they didn't. All *they* wanted was to see
> the last of Betty, and that went double for her. If you have the
> money and the friends, you can always cover up a suicide, and
> sometimes you can cover up a murder. The Randolphs had a legend
> to preserve; they were willing to pay to preserve it. Even to Betty.
> But that didn't cost them anything.
>
> So Betty arrives at the hotel and her name is now, let us say,
> Elizabeth Mayfield.

The immediate setting—what Chandler called the "frame" of the
picture—is the hotel, and there Betty meets Clark Brandon and Larry
Mitchell, the sons of two rivals for political control of the city. Soon
afterward the more crooked of the two ends up dead on the balcony of
Betty's room, the same balcony from which she had intended to leap.
Betty can prove her innocence only by telling her own story, but in
doing so she would almost certainly raise questions about her credibility.
When Chandler sent in this outline to his agent, Swanson, he typed out
a note to accompany it: "Swanie: I think it stinks." It's an understand-
able judgment, but the final script is a great improvement. Like *The Blue
Dahlia*, it is self-contained, but Chandler introduces a Canadian police
officer, Killaine, who acts in many ways like Marlowe. As the detective
handling the case, Killaine risks his career by believing in Betty May-
field's innocence. He is also infatuated with her, and there is a dramatic
conflict between his feelings and his duties as a police officer.

Playback is a far better script than *The Blue Dahlia*. It gradually
builds up momentum; and although it is somewhat overdone, the final

sequence—in which a Canadian coast guard cutter chases Brandon's cabin cruiser across the foggy strait that separates British Columbia from Washington State—is full of suspense.

The screenplay's weakness is that the central theme is never developed. *Playback* is about reputation, how one is tainted by association, but little is done about that. The focus is on the relationship between Betty and Killaine and on the incidents of the story.

Chandler had a hard time writing this script. Mostly he worked at home, but he also went to Los Angeles to see Joseph Sistrom. He was supposed to finish by August, but he was granted two extensions which took him into the early part of 1948. In arguing for these delays he wrote to Swanson: "I don't care anything about my reputation as a screen writer because I don't like screen writing, and never will like it. I am doing this job for the money and to establish a price and a new kind of relationship. I want to do a good job, but it is going to take me a long time because I am not very well and I don't have the steam." Swanson suggested that he stop painting a barn with an artist's camel's-hair brush. Chandler's reply was to remind him "that when I was writing for the pulps, I wrote with a camel's-hair brush, and if you don't think it paid off in the long run, look around for some of the boys who painted barns."

Chandler had difficulties in working out the details of the plot and in revealing information at the right time. "I am a good dialogue writer," he later explained, "but not a good constructionist." He was also interrupted by illness, including flu, and just as the screenplay became due, he lost his secretary. In all, it wasn't much fun. "I finished the first draft of my screenplay," he informed Hamish Hamilton, "and the way I went on anyone would think I was building a pyramid. I loathed it with a great loathing. Now I have to 'polish' it, as they say. Which means leave out half and make what is left hammier. This is a very delicate art, and about as fascinating as scraping teeth."

In the end, except for the money he received, Chandler's work was all in vain. Universal was suffering from financial difficulties and the expense of filming in Vancouver was prohibitive. Canadian weather was unpredictable, and there were no studios available for shooting indoors while waiting for the sun to come out. Universal therefore decided to write off its losses, and Chandler's script was put on the shelf.

Despite the difficulties Chandler experienced while writing *Playback*, he had time to examine closely his business relationships with publishers and agents. It was a transitional period for him, not so abrupt or definite as when he changed from businessman to writer, but he wished to consolidate his gains. By now his books had been translated into French and Swedish, and by 1950 they would be in German and

Italian as well. He needed to put his house in order for the major work
he had yet to do.

For years he had been represented by Sydney Sanders in New York
and by H. N. Swanson in Hollywood; and since 1939 his American
publisher had been Alfred Knopf. Within two years of his move to La
Jolla he changed all of these arrangements. His dissatisfaction with
Sanders had begun with the failure of his Hollywood representative,
Gerald Adams, to secure decent prices for the film rights to *The Big
Sleep* and *Farewell, My Lovely*. He had engaged Swanson as his Hollywood agent partly for just this reason. He had also argued against
Sanders' desire to have him write for the slicks. In 1946 Joseph Shaw
published *The Hard-Boiled Omnibus*, a collection of stories that had
originally appeared in *Black Mask*. Chandler was furious, because the
book contained, despite his specific wishes to the contrary, "The Man
Who Liked Dogs," which was a cannibalized story. He considered its
republication a fraud on the reader who knew *Farewell, My Lovely*.
Chandler was angry with Shaw, who was then working for Sanders, but
he put the blame on the head of the agency. "It is fundamentally his
responsibility," he wrote. "He is required to know what goes on in his
office." Combined with the discontent that had developed over the years,
it was enough to induce him to break his connection with Sanders in
November of 1946.

In a similar way, Chandler's relationship with Knopf was also
deteriorating. When Chandler read a novel called *Blonde's Requiem* by
Raymond Marshall and discovered that it was a direct plagiarism of
works by himself, Hammett, and Jonathan Latimer, he complained to
Knopf, asking him to enjoin Crown, the book's publisher, from distrib-
uting it. Knopf merely referred the matter to the firm's lawyer, who
asserted that the similarities were not sufficient to justify a charge of
plagiarism. This was the sort of thing guaranteed to enrage Chandler,
who had a highly developed sense of rectitude and who was himself
scrupulous about any accidental use of another writer's ideas. In England, at Chandler's request, Hamish Hamilton pressed charges against
Raymond Marshall, who turned out to be Rene Raymond who wrote *No
Orchids for Miss Blandish* under yet another pseudonym, James Hadley
Chase. Hamilton forced Raymond to agree to the publication of a letter
in the *Bookseller* in which the plagiarism was acknowledged and the
author promised to refrain from future acts of the same kind and agreed
to pay all legal costs. Chandler could only compare this rigorous prose-
cution of his interests to Knopf's dilatory attitude toward the matter.

Chandler also had a long-standing quarrel with Knopf over what he
considered an unjust distribution of subsidiary earnings, which were
shared equally by author and publisher. These were the early days of

mass paperback publication, but it soon became evident that contracts with traditional publishers unjustly penalized authors. As Chandler put it openly to Knopf, he did not believe that "a publisher is entitled to collect more in reprint rights than he pays out in royalties on his trade editions." On his four books from Knopf, Chandler received hardcover royalties of $9,500, while Knopf and Chandler together split the $44,000 earned by subsidiary paperback sales. This meant that Chandler's total income from the four books was $32,000, while Knopf's was $22,000, not counting the profits earned from the hardcover editions. Chandler believed it was unfair for hardcover publishers to benefit so much from a phenomenon they had done nothing to bring about and to which they contributed so little. He thought a split of 75 per cent to 25 per cent would be more just.

After leaving Sanders, Chandler engaged an English business consultant by the name of S. S. Tyler to look after his affairs and retained Swanson as his agent for both books and films. Tyler went through all of Chandler's contracts and discovered that Knopf had neglected to obtain Canadian copyright for his books, thus making them liable for pirating. Canadian copyright was essential to protect American books because the United States was not a signatory of the Berne convention, which covered international copyright matters.

Here was further cause for irritation with Knopf, but Chandler was not yet ready for a new publisher as he had no new work completed. In the meantime, he began to realize that his arrangement with Tyler and Swanson was not satisfactory. Swanson was at home in Hollywood but not in New York, while Tyler was not experienced enough in publishing to evaluate accurately the information he gathered. What he needed was a new agent to replace Sanders. Accordingly, on New Year's Day 1948, he wrote to Charles Morton asking him to recommend someone and outlining his requirements. "The best agent," he wrote, "is not necessarily the best judge of literary material. Nor is he necessarily the best-organized or largest. Though for me he would have to have a substantial position, or he could not afford the things I want. I do not expect from him a detailed organization of my affairs; agents pretend to give it, but they do not do a very good job. What I expect from an agent is tough but scrupulous trading; a wide market knowledge; a respect for the fact that it might in the long run be better business for me to do an occasional article for the *Atlantic* for a few hundreds or whatever, instead of putting the same time and energy into a short story for the *Post* at a couple of thousand. I expect an agent with an eagle eye for contracts, and a knowledge of when an expert is necessary and the ability to see that said expert does not overcharge me just because he smells fairy gold."

Chandler as a baby.   "Alfred and Raymond Chandler relaxing."

Chandler at Dulwich College.
(Courtesy of William Whiteley Ltd)

Aerial and general view
of school buildings
and playing fields.
(Courtesy of the Governors of Dulwich College)

In kilts of
the Gordon Highlanders
of Canada, 1917.

Chandler in uniform
of British Columbia Regiment
at Seaford, Sussex, 1918.

(Courtesy of Tina Whitizig)

After the war.

Pearl Eugenie
Hurlburt Chandler—Cissy.

In California after the war.

Chandler's mother,
Florence Thornton Chandler.
*(Courtesy of John W. Seifert
Photographs, Los Angeles)*

Dabney-Johnston oil wells at Signal Hill during the 1920s.
Chandler is standing at the extreme left in the second row;
Dabney is in the center of the first row, holding his hat.

OW 5¢

BLACK MASK

Tolin Drew

SPANISH BLOOD
By RAYMOND CHANDLER

Black Mask Dinner, Los Angeles, 1936.
Left to right, standing: Raymond J. Moffatt, Raymond Chandler,
Herbert Stinson, Dwight Babcock, Eric Taylor, Dashiell Hammett.
Left to right, seated: Arthur Barnes, John K. Butler,
W. T. Ballard, Howard McCoy, Norbert Davis.

Raymond J. Moffatt was not a *Black Mask* writer, but appeared at
the dinner anyhow. The signatures were written on a portion
of the table cloth which was then ripped off and sent to Joseph Shaw.

Opposite top: Chandler with Billy Wilder at Paramount studios, 1943.

Opposite bottom: Hollywood Boulevard looking east.
Grauman's Chinese theater is at the lower left; Chandler placed
Philip Marlowe's office at the crossroad of this boulevard
with Ivar Avenue at the top of the photograph.

A pictorial review of *The Big Sleep* by Milt Gross, published in *Ken* magazine, 1940.

Opposite top: Robert Montgomery and Audrey Totter in *The Lady in the Lake* (MGM, 1946).
(*Courtesy of M.G.M. Studios*)

Opposite bottom: Humphrey Bogart and Lauren Bacall in *The Big Sleep* (Warner Brothers, 1946).
(*Courtesy of Warner Brothers*)

Cissy Chandler.
*(Courtesy of John W. Seifert
Photographs, Los Angeles)*

Chandler's house at
6005 Camino de la Costa, La Jolla.

At his desk in La Jolla
with Taki, the cat.
(Courtesy of John Engstead)

Chandler, wearing gloves, with Helga Greene
in California, late 1950s.
(Courtesy of El Mirador Photo by Conrad Hug)

Morton recommended Brandt and Brandt of New York, so Chandler sent a characteristic inquiry and statement of his position to Carl Brandt, the head of the agency. "I have a mystery novel half finished. The writing is of an incomparable brilliance, but something has gone wrong with the story. An old trouble with me." He admitted his references were poor and openly acknowledged his nature: "I am not a completely amiable character any more than I am a facile and prolific writer. I do most things the hard way, and I suffer a good deal over it. There may not be a lot of mileage left in me. Five years of fighting Hollywood has not left me with many reserves of energy."

Brandt was delighted at the prospect of representing Chandler, and as he had to go to Hollywood at the end of the month, he suggested they meet. Their first discussion led to various proposals, including the possibility of publishing collections of his novelettes in England, the conversion of the *Playback* screenplay into a novel, the establishment of a radio series—to be arranged through Brandt's Hollywood representative, Ray Stark—and most important the publication of Chandler's new, unfinished novel, *The Little Sister*. The new agency agreement bolstered Chandler's morale, for he had been in the doldrums for some time, unable to do sustained work of much quality. By June 1 he sent the first half of his novel to Brandt with the following caveat: "It goes against all my principles to show it to you at this point, but I think in the circumstances you are entitled to see it if you want to." He explained that it "was all dictated to a dictaphone, an instrument which I have found very convenient for movie work, but I am not sure it is adapted to fiction writing."

From the beginning Chandler made it clear that he had no particular interest in continuing with Knopf. Aside from the small irritations over royalties and copyrights, he was dissatisfied with Knopf's sales records and advertising methods. Comparing his American sales to those in England and Sweden, Chandler believed that Knopf had somehow failed to put him across effectively. In relation to population, his Swedish sales suggested that his American sales should have been 100,000; in England, with a market only one-third as large as that of the United States, Hamish Hamilton sold as many copies as were sold in America.

Apart from these disadvantages, Chandler also noted that after ten years he hadn't "the slightest feeling of friendship or warmth" toward the Knopfs. Although he knew that Knopf was a good publisher, he thought it odd that he had no positive feelings toward the house. "It's a cold show," he concluded. "I have never been able to deal with people at arm's length."

Upon examining the sales figures, Bernice Baumgarten, Carl

Brandt's associate in charge of book publication, agreed that Knopf was not a suitable publisher for Chandler. One of her reasons for deciding on a change was her belief that Chandler should be published by a house that did not maintain a regular list of mystery novels. His work would therefore have a greater chance of being treated as serious literature.

Chandler had already thought about switching to Houghton Mifflin. He had received a personal letter from Dale Warren, publicity director of that firm, in praise of his work. For his first two letters to Chandler, Warren used his private writing paper. It was only on the third exchange, when he dictated a letter on Houghton Mifflin stationery, that Chandler realized he was a publisher. Chandler was so pleasantly surprised to find a businessman who could free himself from his commercial interests that he told Warren he was planning to leave Knopf. Initially Bernice Baumgarten had in mind another publisher, but Chandler's predisposition toward Houghton Mifflin and her belief in their capabilities led her to draw up an agreement with them for *The Little Sister*. It is perhaps accidental, but Chandler had little to do with the editorial people at Houghton Mifflin; he corresponded almost exclusively with Warren and with Hardwick Moseley, the firm's sales manager. In this way, he dealt directly with those responsible for the promotion of his work. When his last book was published, he sent a typical note to Warren: "Please don't praise the book; sell it!"

Chandler had hoped to finish *The Little Sister* shortly after he moved to La Jolla, but he had to put it off for nearly a year to write the *Playback* screenplay. "The status of my work of fiction is quo," he told Warren. He was also afraid that Hollywood had ruined his talent for fiction and was bored with Marlowe, although "for business or professional reasons I think the guy is too valuable to let die out. But I find myself spoofing more and more." Nevertheless, by July of 1948 he had nearly completed the first draft of the book. He had grown increasingly impatient with the form."I rather think that this will be my last Marlowe story," he told Hamilton, "and I'm not even yet sure that it's fit to print. I find the attitude more and more artificial. I am afraid Mr. Marlowe has developed far more than a suspicion that a man of his parts is beginning to look pretty ridiculous as a small-time private detective." In part, Chandler's impatience was caused by his awareness of his reputation. He had been the subject of articles by J. B. Priestley, Somerset Maugham, and numerous other writers and critics. As Chandler said of Marlowe: "He's getting self-conscious, trying to live up to his reputation among the quasi-intellectuals. The boy is bothered. He used to be able to spit and throw the ball hard and talk out of the corner of his mouth." Auden's critique was typically bothersome: "Here I am halfway through a Marlowe story and having a little fun (until I got stuck) and along comes this fellow Auden and tells me I am interested in writing serious studies of a criminal milieu. So now I look at everything I put down and say to myself, Remember, old boy, this has to be a serious study of a criminal milieu."

As he continued into August, he felt worse about the book. He was full of doubts and wrote that "there is nothing in it but style and dialogue and characters. The plot creaks like a broken shutter in an October wind." A week later he continued his complaint: "The story has weaknesses. It is episodic and the emphasis shifts from character to character and it is, as a mystery, overcomplicated, but as a story of people very simple. It has no violence in it at all; all the violence is off stage. If it has menace and suspense, they are in the writing. I think some of it is beautifully written, and my reactions to it are most unreliable. I write a scene and I read it over and I think it stinks. Three days later (having done nothing in between but stew) I reread it and think it is great. So there you are. You can't bank on me. I may be all washed up." To this letter he added a postscript: "It contains the nicest whore I ever didn't meet."

He finally finished the book in September, and since he had no secretary, he took the risk of sending his only copy by registered mail to Bernice Baumgarten with the request that it be retyped in New York. When this was done, copies were sent to Hamish Hamilton, who immediately put the book into production, while Carl Brandt tried to place it serially in the United States. He succeeded in selling it to *Cosmopolitan* magazine for $10,000, which was a substantial sum, although Chandler found the abridgement "quite loathesome," adding: "They leave out everything that gives the story any kind of quality—that was to be expected—but they have actually inserted stuff that I did not write, which makes me look ignorant. (Of course I am ignorant, but I try to hide it.)"

The appearance of galleys from London once again depressed him. "My God, what a writer suffers with proofs," he wrote. "By the time he has got the damn book written he hates it. And then proofs—oh my God." His fresh doubts derived from his recognition of the mismarriage of his talents with his material. In a frank piece of self-analysis he wrote: "If a man writes as well as I do (let's face it honestly) he creates a schism between the melodramatic exaggeration of his story and the way he writes about it." To bridge the gap between the detective story and the literacy his style represented, he invested *The Little Sister* with an extra dose of characterization, wit, and description.

The result is an overripe book. It contains many familiar Chandler features, but there is no organic development beyond what he had written before. The "little sister," Orfamay Quest, is an extension of

Merle Davis, the terrified secretary in *The High Window*. But, unlike
Merle, Orfamay is a part of a family that includes a confidence trickster
who tries to blackmail his other sister, a rising movie star, who in turn is
a friend of a prostitute and a racketeer. These relationships give Chandler an opportunity to write about the interlocking levels of Hollywood
society, although *The Little Sister* is in no sense a real Hollywood novel.
Chandler often spoke of writing such a book but he did not think
himself capable of it. The problem was how to deal simultaneously with
the public absurdity of Hollywood and the private lives of the characters. While reading Nathanael West's *The Day of the Locust*, he remarked that it didn't "appear to be a Hollywood novel at all, so far as
I've gone, merely a novel about some people in Hollywood, which is an
entirely different matter." He admired Scott Fitzgerald's *The Last
Tycoon* with reservations. He thought Monroe Stahr, the hero of the
novel, was "magnificent when he sticks to the business of dealing with
pictures and the people he has to use to make them; the instant his
personal life as a love-hungry and exhausted man enters the picture, he
becomes just another guy with too much money and nowhere to go."
The problem was that "you cannot make a close-up and a long shot in
the same 'take' "; nor, conversely, can you show "the poignant humanity
and the icy heartlessness of this magnificent but childish colossus, the
movie business, in terms of a hot-pants actress, an egomaniac director, a
snide executive, four frantic secretaries, and a sweet young thing in an
open Cadillac." The one writer he thought capable of writing a Hollywood novel was James Gould Cozzens, Bernice Baumgarten's husband,
who Chandler believed had "the very rare faculty of picking up and
rationalizing a complicated background rather quickly."

The Little Sister shows the results of Chandler's dispiriting years in
Hollywood, but most of the scenes that deal with the movies are just
decorative. There is a scene in an agent's office where the waiting room
is filled with out-of-work actors. It is funny in the way it shows everyone's pretensions, but it is also a sad revelation of the empty lives
involved. Another scene at a film studio opens with the head of the
studio sitting in a courtyard with his three boxer dogs. He engages
Marlowe in a conversation and tells him: "The motion picture business
is the only business in the world in which you can make all the mistakes
there are and still make money." All you need, he claims, are 1,500
theaters around the country. Marlowe then moves to a set where the
actors spend their time stealing scenes from one another. At the lunch
break one of them comments: "We're all bitches. Some smile more than
others, that's all. Show business. There's something cheap about it.
There was a time when actors went in at the back door. Most of them
still should." These scenes read as though Chandler were trying to

avenge himself for all the irritations he had endured while working in Hollywood. The agent, for example, walks up and down in his office with a Malacca cane, a habit of Billy Wilder's that annoyed Chandler when the two worked together at Paramount Marlowe comments. "It could only happen in Hollywood that an apparently sane man could walk up and down inside the house with a Piccadilly stroll and a monkey stick in his hand." Hollywood's bitchiness seems also to have embraced Chandler.

The main trouble with these scenes is that they have little to do with the story. They are included because Chandler is trying to expand Marlowe's consciousness, but they don't come across as a necessary part of the novel. The seams show. Chandler also uses descriptive passages to establish Marlowe's mental state. One chapter opens with Marlowe driving along Sunset Boulevard and commenting on the hot rods driving in and out of the traffic and the "sleazy hamburger joints that look like palaces under the colors." Gradually Marlowe becomes depressed by the restless emptiness of everything, the lack of human communication, the indifference and the ugliness. Years later Chandler wrote that the scene was "an attempt to find out whether purely through the tone of the description I could render a state of mind." Much of the passage is objective, but some of it is mannered: "California, the department store state. The most of everything and the best of nothing."

The Little Sister contains many efforts to broaden Chandler's subject matter and give a greater feel of the city. Driving across Los Angeles, Marlowe stops at a roadside restaurant, where he parodies the owner's mentality: "Bad but quick. Feed 'em and throw 'em out. Lots of business. We can't bother with you sitting over your second cup of coffee, mister. You're using money space." Later he drives as far north as Oxnard and returns along the sea: "On the right the great solid Pacific trudging into shore like a scrub-woman going home. No moon, no fuss, hardly a sound of the surf. No smell. None of the harsh wild smell of the sea. A California ocean." The whole landscape is affected by what people have done to it: "I smelled Los Angeles before I got to it. It smelled stale and old like a living room that had been closed too long. But the colored lights fooled you. The lights were wonderful. There ought to be a monument to the man who invented neon lights. Fifteen stories high, solid marble. There's a boy who really made something out of nothing."

To give an authentic feeling to his portrayal of the police world, Chandler used some notes he had made early in 1945 while gathering material for *The Blue Dahlia*. This was almost the only research he ever did as a writer. He met Captain Thad Brown, the head of the Los Angeles Homicide Bureau, who showed him what little there was to see of his department at police headquarters. Here are Chandler's notes: "The Los Angeles Police Department, Homicide Bureau, occupies two rooms on the Main Street level of the City Hall. These rooms are roughly fifteen feet square and have brown linoleum on the floor. The outer room contains a walnut table, a few wooden chairs, three or four telephones and about fourteen plainclothes dicks in Hart Schaffner and Marx business suits, all six feet tall or better, all with their hats on, all tough. Their toughness is a very deep thing. It is not a matter of being rude to people or acting hard-boiled. It is a solid ingrained toughness. It is possible for these men to be very pleasant or very unpleasant almost without change of expression. They stand around, smoke, talk, telephone and as the occasion requires, walk through an open door in a pebbled glass partition without any formality into the room of the Captain in charge of the Homicide Bureau. He has a flat-top business desk and two telephones on a shelf to his right. There is no equipment of any kind on his table. He has a hard wooden swivel chair without even a cushion or a felt pad. His desk is in one corner of the room (nearest the open communicating door) and at another desk level with his sits a girl secretary. She has a telephone and a typewriter. She is middle-aged, has faded orange-colored hair, pays no attention to anybody and seems to be principally engaged in making out reports of investigations. These are made out single-spaced on letter size paper. The remaining furnishings of this office consist of a couple of green metal filing cabinets and one straight wooden chair without arms. This is absolutely positively all."

Chandler used this information for accuracy in *The Blue Dahlia,* but when it came time to write *The Little Sister* he not only borrowed from these notes, including the orange-haired secretary, but put them to use as part of a set piece that the head of the bureau, Christy French, delivers: "It's like this with us, baby. We're coppers and everybody hates our guts. And as if we didn't have enough trouble, we have to have you. As if we didn't get pushed around enough by the boys in the corner offices, the City Hall gang, the day chief, the night chief, the chamber of commerce, His Honor the Mayor in his panelled office four times as big as the three lousy rooms the whole homicide staff has to work out of. As if we didn't have to handle one hundred and fourteen homicides last year out of three rooms that don't have enough chairs for the whole duty squad to sit down in at once. We spend our lives turning over dirty underwear and sniffing rotten teeth. We go up dark stairways to get a gun punk with a skinful of hop and sometimes we don't get all the way up, and our wives wait dinner that night and all the other nights. We don't come home any more. And nights we do come home, we come home so goddam tired we can't eat or sleep or read the lies the papers print about us So we lie awake in the dark in a cheap house on a cheap street and listen to the drunks down the block having fun. And just about the time we drop off the phone rings and we get up and start all over again. Nothing we do is right, not ever. Not once. If we get a confession, we beat it out of the guy, they say, and some shyster calls us Gestapo in court and sneers at us when we muddle our grammar. If we make a mistake they put us back in uniform on Skid Row and we spend the nice cool summer evenings picking drunks out of the gutter and being yelled at by whores and taking knives away from grease-balls in zoot suits. But all that ain't enough to make us entirely happy. We got to have you."

This somewhat unrealistic speech is Chandler's way of adding a further dimension to his work. He wanted to give a psychological explanation of police behavior, because, as Marlowe states elsewhere, "civilization had no meaning for them. All they saw of it was the failure, the dirt, the dregs, the aberrations and the disgust."

Aside from these sociological passages, there are many in which Marlowe and the other characters just trade wisecracks. The self-consciousness of these exchanges is revealed in Chandler's notebooks where he listed humorous similes for future use—such as "as exclusive as a mail box," "as lonely as a lighthouse," "as much sex appeal as a turtle," and "as systematic as a whore." Whenever he used one of these in the novel, he marked the intitials "L.S." against it in the notebook. The habit suggests that he was more tired than usual when he wrote this book.

All of these devices, especially the effort to deepen character and lend meaning to the landscape, were attempts at giving his work greater weight. Although they are extraneous to the story, they were useful as experiments, and they eventually led to more integrated work in *The Long Goodbye*. In the meantime, Chandler sensed what was wrong: "I feel that in *The Little Sister*, or a good part of it, I rather lost touch with what my kind of writing is all about and went off on a tangent, playing with the wisecrack and witty remark. The tension should come first." Elsewhere he remarked: "The plot didn't have enough lift or imagination and there was too much writing around the edges, too much decoration." What caused this, apart from weariness? When he sent the manuscript to the publisher, he referred to it as 75,000 words of "ill-written and ill-constructed nose-thumbing." He expressed further doubts by saying that it was "a mite fruity for the carriage trade and a little too literate for the Democrats, besides having only six murders in it. But I have not ripened into manhood. My five years in the salt mines left me a typical case of arrested development, and the more I stay away from the picture business, the better I like it." For financial reasons, he was not able to do so entirely, and the threat of having to resume work on screenplays made it difficult for him to write sustained fiction of high quality. He knew this and it annoyed him. For this reason, the best explanation for the shortcomings of *The Little Sister* is found in a remark he made to Sandoe: "It's the only book of mine I have actively disliked. It was written in a bad mood and I think that comes through."

8.
NO
THIRD
ACT

The weeks following book publication are always hard on a writer. He worries about things he usually never thinks about—reviews, sales, publicity. He may enjoy the attention he receives, but inevitably there are disappointments as well. Advance sales for *The Little Sister* were under 10,000 copies, which was less than hoped for, but Houghton Mifflin reported interest in paperback publication and spoke of the possibility of an auction for these rights. In the end the novel sold 16,000 copies in the American trade edition, which was better than any of Chandler's other books had done, but it was well below English sales. Hamish Hamilton had published the book a few months earlier and sold 26,000 copies, although earnings were smaller because of a lower sales price. In all, Chandler received $10,000 for hardcover sales, not a bad return in itself, but woefully inadequate in terms of the time he devoted to it.

The book was widely reviewed, for it was Chandler's first in six years, and as the reviewer in *Time* pointed out, the thousands of readers who belonged to the Chandler "cult" had been waiting for it a long time. Anthony Boucher of the *New York Times Book Review* attacked it for, of all things, "its scathing hatred of the human race." But a more typical reaction was *Newsweek*'s decision to run a general article on mystery writing in America, with Chandler as the central figure. Most American critics were disappointed that *The Little Sister* did not go beyond where Chandler left off with *The Lady in the Lake;* but in England J. B. Priestley, among others, tried to place Chandler in the wider context of contemporary American fiction: "To read him is like cutting into an over-ripe melon and discovering that it has a rare astringent flavour. He reduces the bright California scene to an empty despair, dead bottles and a heap of cigarette butts under the meaningless neon lights, much more adroitly than Aldous Huxley and the rest can do; and suggests, to my mind, almost better than anybody else the failure of a life that is somehow short of a dimension, with everybody either wistfully wondering what is wrong or taking savage short cuts to nowhere." This sort of reaction typifies the English view of Chandler. He had created a world that was more free and formless, more exciting, and also more depressing than anything yet come to England. And it was his care for the human race, not his hatred of it, that inspired the vision he presented.

Chandler was too experienced to be affected by reviews, although he resented some of them because they struck a note that came close to his own preoccupations. "The American reviews that I have seen or heard of are generally favourable," he wrote to Hamilton. "*Time* said I was in danger of becoming a talented hack. That's not an unpleasant fate in times like these. The *Atlantic* man reviewed the book at considerable length on the announced basis that he felt about mysteries about as Edmund Wilson did. I do not grudge reviewers their sad amusements, but there is something rather comical in a man's starting to review a book by saying he doesn't like the kind of book it is and then proceeding to deprecate it in a nice way for not being something it never pretended to be. He made one good point, though: that my 'virtues are merely diversions thrown in to entertain and amuse. They are embellishments; they are not intrinsic elements that transform the genre.' Rather, it is a good point to the extent that it makes plain in simple language what I have suspected for a long time: that the better you write a mystery, the more clearly you demonstrate that the mystery is not really worth writing. The best mystery writers are those whose perceptiveness does not outrange their material." In another letter he extended this notion by saying he had no objections to some adverse comments on his book made by the English critic Desmond MacCarthy: "I thought he had a good point too that a man reading a mystery doesn't want his attention distracted by good writing."

Here Chandler's defense mechanism is evident: he pretends his book is being criticized because it is too good. But he knew the faults of

The Little Sister and had described them long before any reviewer wrote a word. What upset him was the doubt these reviews created that he would be able to do what he wanted to do with the mystery story. "I am very uneasy in mind," he wrote to Hamilton. "I seem to have lost ambition and have no ideas any more. I don't really want to do anything, or rather one part of me does and the other doesn't. One of the penalties of even a mild success is an indifference to it, and the effort to do something that will attract interest and praise is really something it is a pity to lose. I read these profound discussions, say in the *Partisan Review*, about art, what is it, literature, what is it, and the good life and liberalism and what is the definitive position of Rilke or Kafka, and the scrap about Ezra Pound getting the Bollingen award, and it all seems so meaningless to me. Who cares? Too many men have been dead too long for it to matter what any of these people do or don't do. What does a man work for? Money? Yes, but in a purely negative way. Without some money nothing else is possible, but once you have the money (and I don't mean a fortune, just a few thousand quid a year) you don't sit and count it and gloat over it. Everything you attain removes a reason for wanting to attain anything. Do I wish to be a great writer? Do I wish to win the Nobel Prize? Not if it takes much hard work. What the hell, they give the Nobel Prize to too many second-raters for me to get excited about it. Besides, I'd have to go to Sweden and dress up and make a speech. Is the Nobel Prize worth all that? Hell, no. Or I read in some book like Haycraft's *Art of the Mystery Story* various so-called critical articles on the detective novel—and what second-rate stuff it all is! The whole business is on a plane of diminished values; there is a constant haste to deprecate the mystery story as literature for fear the writer of the piece should be assumed to think it is important writing. This conditioned approach might well be the result of the decay of the classics, a sort of intellectual insularity which has no historical perspective. People are always suggesting to writers of my sort, 'You write so well why don't you attempt a serious novel?' By which they mean Marquand or Betty Smith. They would probably be insulted if one suggested that the aesthetic gap, if any, between a good mystery and the best serious novel of the last ten years is hardly measurable on any scale that could measure the gap between the serious novel and any representative piece of Attic writing of the Fourth Century B.C., any ode of Pindar or Horace or Sappho, any Chorus of Sophocles, and so on. You cannot have art without a public taste and you cannot have a public taste without a sense of style and quality through the social structure. Curiously enough this sense of style seems to have very little to do with refinement or even with humanity. It can exist in a savage and dirty age, but it cannot exist in the age of Milton Berle, Mary Margaret McBride, the Book of the Month Club, the Hearst press and the Coca-cola machine. You can't produce art by trying, by setting up exacting standards, by talking about critical minutiae, by the Flaubert method. It is produced with great ease, in an almost offhand manner, and without self-consciousness. You can't write just because you have read all the books."

The weakest part of this rambling argument is the sentence in which Chandler asserts that by serious fiction most people mean Marquand and Betty Smith. His omission of such writers as Hemingway, Fitzgerald, and Faulkner is curious and can only be explained by the coincidence that during the 1940s, when the country was preoccupied by the war, there was little new work from the best American authors. Chandler admired the fiction of such younger writers as James Gould Cozzens and Eudora Welty, but they were not yet setting standards. Moreover, it was perfectly natural for him to compare himself to John Marquand, whose most popular books were published during that decade and whose reputation was then very high. Marquand was a Boston author and a natural subject for discussion with Dale Warren and Charles Morton; he was also a client of Carl Brandt's and well known to Bernice Baumgarten. In one letter to her Chandler remarked of Marquand that "a man has no right to write that well and in the end say so little. He writes the perfect Victorian novel, sad but not too sad, romantic in an epicene sort of way, beautiful detailed observation and the total effect of a steel engraving with no color at all. I guess God made Boston on a wet Sunday."

Again and again Chandler reverted to the comparison of the detective story with the "straight" novel. It became almost an obsession, revealing his own discontent, his worry that he would not be able to bridge the gap between them. He spoke of Dorothy Sayers' apparent attempt to do so, but claimed that "she didn't really make it, because the novel of manners she aimed at was in itself too slight a thing to be important. It was the substitution of one popular trivial kind of writing for another." Chandler's own attempt lay ahead of him and was to occupy his best efforts for some years, but in the meantime all he could do was express a hope: "I am not satisfied that the thing can't be done nor that sometime, somewhere, perhaps not now nor by me, a novel cannot be written which, ostensibly a mystery and keeping the spice of mystery, will actually be a novel of character and atmosphere with an overtone of violence and fear." Chandler refused to be apologetic about what he had written so far: "If people call my book just another mystery I can't help it, but by God I'm not going to do the calling myself."

Chandler's discontent reached its height when *The Little Sister* was published. He was harassed by annoyances and interruptions and veered impulsively from one project to another. He was also distressed by domestic problems. "It is a nice house, one of the nicest in La Jolla," he explained to Carl Brandt, "but it seems impossible to get any competent help here. Also, apart from that, the house is too expensive. Disregarding the investment and the taxes we find that in La Jolla everything costs too much, every service is overpriced, everybody is on the chisel. Once the place was worth it. But we don't have the same seclusion any more." Chandler also found that he was spending far too much time tending to ledgers and income tax data: "I am cutting my own throat by using up my time and energies doing things that have nothing to do with writing."

In addition to his financial and literary difficulties, he was worried about Cissy's chronic illnesses and his own physical disorders. He suffered from bronchitis, sore throats, and skin allergies. One of these, angioneurotic edema, was a rash that spread over his chest and neck. It was so irritating that Chandler could bear it only by taking morphine. He also suffered from a skin allergy on his hands that made his fingers split. He took X-ray treatments and had his fingers bandaged when he typed. Later, when they healed, he was told not to touch carbon or newsprint and to wear gloves while reading. He said he felt "like a fading beauty of the stage." As if these weren't troubles enough, by the end of 1949 he came down with shingles. "I seem to be crumbling slowly," he remarked. These medical problems continued to bother him for years and were inevitably accompanied by psychological side effects. "The news from here is rotten," he wrote to Dale Warren. "Nervous, tired, discouraged, sick of the chauffeur-and-Cadillac atmosphere, bored to hell with the endless struggle to get help, disgusted with my lack of prescience in not seeing that this kind of life is unsuited to my temperament."

In a later complaint against La Jolla, Chandler wrote: "I seem to be of the temperament that needs the stimulation of a larger place. I just go slack and indifferent without that stimulation." He had nobody to talk to, but what was worse, the vitality of city life, which he records so colorfully in his fiction, was wholly absent from the quiet streets of La Jolla. To escape, Chandler made extensive plans for travel. For four years he intended to visit England; but each time the pressure of work, illness, or inertia produced delays, and the Chandlers did not actually go to England until the autumn of 1952. In the meantime, they traveled within California. When they were first in La Jolla, they often visited Erle Stanley Gardner. Trained as a lawyer, Gardner was, like Chandler, part businessman and part writer. Chandler was always astonished by the bulk of Gardner's work: in Temecula he had a ranch with three secretaries to handle his affairs and was therefore able to devote all his time to writing. Chandler was too nervous and cautious to do this; as a writer, he was also too irregular and fastidious. "I know him well and like him," Chandler wrote of Gardner. "He is a terrible talker, just wears you out, but he is not a dull talker. He just talks too loud and too much. Years of yapping into a dictaphone machine have destroyed the quality of his voice, which now has all the delicate chiaroscuro of a French taxi horn. His production methods amaze me (he can write a whole book in a week or ten days easily) and once in a while he does something pretty good."

Chandler also escaped from La Jolla by taking business trips to Los Angeles; for pleasure, he and Cissy preferred the desert, usually Palm Springs, where the dry climate would cure his bronchitis or her cough. They must have made a strange couple in a resort hotel, a pair of introverts twenty years out of style who just wanted to be left alone. In the autumn of 1951 they visited a hotel near Santa Barbara. "I don't know if you have ever been to a dude ranch," he wrote to Hamilton. "I had never been to one before. This one is called the Alisal, which in Spanish means a grove of sycamores, according to the publicity. It is situated in an inland valley, the Santa Ynez Valley just north of Santa Barbara, and is almost as dry as the desert, very hot in the daytime, very cool in the mornings, in the evenings and at night. I should think it must be pretty awful in the summer. We found the place both very amusing and intensely boring, expensive, badly run but nicely laid out with the usual swimming pool, tennis courts, etc. The kind of place where the people who work in the office wear riding boots, where the lady guests appear for breakfast in levis riveted with copper, for lunch in jodhpurs with gaudy shirts and scarfs and in the evening either in cocktail gowns or in more jodhpurs and more gaudy shirts and scarfs. The ideal scarf seems to be very narrow, not much wider than a boot lace, and run through a ring in front and then hangs down on one side of the shirt. I didn't ask why; I didn't get to know anybody well enough. The men also wear gaudy shirts, which they change constantly for other patterns, all except the real horsemen, who wear rather heavy wool or nylon and wool shirts with long sleeves, yoked in the back, the kind of thing that can only be bought in a horsy town. I imagine the place is a lot of fun for the right sort of people, the people who go riding in the morning, swimming or tennising in the afternoon, then have two or three drinks at the bar, and by the time they arrive for dinner are able to be quite enthusiastic over the rather inferior and much too greasy cooking. For us who were rather tired and out of sorts and consequently much too finicky, the place was a trial. But it was fun to see a whole army of quail stroll unconcernedly past the bungalows in the evening and to see birds that looked like jackdaws, which we never see anywhere else, not even in the mountains." There Chandler sat in tweeds and a tie, reading C. S. Forester's Horatio Hornblower trilogy and finding it dull stuff. He probably didn't know that Forester had also gone to Dulwich, and wouldn't have cared. And with him was Cissy, now eighty years old, in frocks and costumes designed to disguise that fact.

Although he could sound like a grumpy old man, Chandler also had a streak of enthusiasm in his character which made him enjoy the quirks and oddities of life. Going to a dude ranch was in itself a sign of his youthfulness. This part of his character became more evident in the last years of his life, and it was his way of thumbing his nose at advancing old age. When it came time to buy a new car, Chandler sought the advice of Charles Morton, who knew all about them, and at his suggestion began to examine Triumph and Jaguar sports cars. Cissy herself nearly gave him a Jaguar, but it turned out to be uncomfortable. Chandler reported the final decision to Morton: "Gave up fussing with automobiles and my wife gave me a 98 Olds, which is plenty good enough for anything I could pick up along the sidewalk."

Chandler's vitality was mainly expressed in his work, for the world of the imagination was where he could let himself go, unshackled by the restraints of real life. But occasionally, like a small boy doing something forbidden, he would find something that delighted him. After driving up to San Francisco and back, he sent an exuberant note to Carl Brandt: "The thing I love about S.F. is its go to hell attitude. The narrow streets are lined with NO PARKING AT ANY TIME signs and also lined with parked automobiles which look as if they had been there all day. For the first time in my life I saw a lady traffic cop, a real cop too, complete with nickel star and whistle. I saw one other cop. He was driving around with a piece of chalk on the end of a long stick and about once a block he took a swipe at some rear tire, just to keep his hand in. The taxi drivers are wonderful too. They obey no laws but those of gravity and we even had one who passes street cars on the left, an offense for which you would probably get ninety days in Los Angeles."

In order to produce income for living in La Jolla, Chandler spent a great deal of time trying to arrange for a radio show and later a television program to be based on his work. Since it would be a serial, the idea was to have Philip Marlowe as the central character and invent new episodes and stories about him. Radio shows based on Dashiell Hammett's Sam Spade and Erle Stanley Gardner's Perry Mason had already been produced in this fashion. Chandler made negotiations difficult because he insisted on the right to approve the script. He believed that Marlowe was an important commercial property and did not want to have this character ineptly introduced to the wide audience of radio listeners. "My idea about the Philip Marlowe series is that it would have to live on its dialogue," he wrote. "There just isn't anything else to distinguish it from any show of the type that the usual hacks could think up. The plots of these shows don't matter; they're just an excuse for people to go places and say things, but the things they say are all-important. The dialogue has to have sparkle."

In 1947 Chandler's Hollywood agent at the time, H. N. Swanson, sold a Marlowe program to the National Broadcasting Company as a summer replacement for the Bob Hope show. Van Heflin was selected to play the role of Marlowe, and Milton Geiger wrote the script. Chandler was so nervous about its success that he asked Erle Stanley Gardner to listen to it. Gardner told him he thought the program was better than most others of the kind, but he was bothered by the first-person narration. A week later he explained what he meant: "I listened to the Marlowe program last night and found it rather difficult to follow. It was so crisp, so fast moving, that I couldn't relax and keep up with it. I had to strain my attention to keep the program from going off and leaving me.

"I felt as though I had listened to a mystery book which had been compressed into a thirty-minute dramatization." The critic John Crosby agreed, for he noted that "if plots get any more abbreviated, they'll be doing 'War and Peace' on a fifteen-minute show and have time left over for the commercial."

Chandler seems to have understood what went wrong with the program, but he did not insist on script approval, saying, "There's not much I can do about it either way." In a letter to Gardner he complained: "I gave up trying to tell them what I thought was wrong. I think the show was badly written and not too well acted and that it never solved the main problem of a show like this; which is to create a form and style that will ride without plot. You can't always have a good story."

The show was not renewed for the fall season because MGM wouldn't let Van Heflin continue. Chandler did nothing about reviving it until he changed his literary agent and found himself represented by Ray Stark, Brandt's Hollywood specialist. He went to Los Angeles to consult Stark, and the trip awakened his old mixed feelings about the place. "These Hollywood people are fantastic when you have been away for a while," he wrote. "In their presence any calm sensible remark sounds faked. Their conversation is a mess of shopworn superlatives interrupted by four telephone calls to the sentence." He got on well with Stark and reported that "everybody in his bagnio is nice." Chandler made it clear to Stark that he was primarily concerned with the quality of the script, which he considered the key to the show's success. "I would rather have an expensive writer and cheap actors than a name star and a cheap writer." The point, he explained, was that "Philip Marlowe is supposed to have a unique quality and he is all I have to sell."

Chandler was sufficiently concerned about the matter to write out a series of suggestions to be passed on to whoever wrote the series. The problem with a first-person character, he said, was that he tended to dominate and become offensive. "To avoid that you must not always give him the punch line or the exit line. Not even often. Let the other characters have the toppers. Leave him without a gag. A devastating crack loses a lot of its force when it doesn't provoke any answer, when the other man just rides with the punch. Then you have to top it yourself or give ground." Chandler said that Marlowe's wisecracks "should be jerked out of him emotionally" rather than be self-conscious and that "any effect of gloating" should be avoided.

Stark succeeded in selling "The Adventures of Philip Marlowe" to the Columbia Broadcasting Company in September of 1948 at a weekly rate of $250, to be increased to $400 should the program find a commercial sponsor. Gerald Mohr was chosen to play Marlowe and Mel Dinelli was selected as the writer, although he soon withdrew in favor of a team of writers, Gene Levitt and Bob Mitchell, who together wrote 101 shows, enough for two years of the program. After the first three or four programs Chandler did not insist on checking the scripts. Most of them deal with blackmail and duplicity. In "The Jade Teardrop," according to the authors' notes, "a person innocent of a major crime cannot go to the police lest he reveal the record of a minor crime which he is living down." Another in the series, "The Torch Carriers," is almost a parody of Chandler: "A guy loves a girl so much he jeopardizes his life to remove her body from a crashed car lest she be found dead in the company of a killer whom she loved."

The program did well and earned a good listener rating, the highest of those sustained by the network. Chandler was satisfied with the program, although he would sometimes pretend otherwise, as when he remarked: "The character (let us keep this a secret or they might stop paying me) has about as much relation to Marlowe as I have to Winnie the Pooh."

After *The Little Sister* was published, Stark arranged for a single live television broadcast of the story. He had already tried to put the Marlowe series on television as well. CBS made a pilot film but was unable to find a sponsor for it, although the radio program continued as before. Chandler was always involved in these negotiations. Although he admired Stark's energy, he had doubts about him when the radio series was sold to Century Artists, a packaging company in which Stark had an interest, rather than directly to one of the networks. He was also too tough a Hollywood negotiator to believe that because television was new he should charge lower prices for his work, as Stark suggested he do. "You can't sell a property for a cheap price to cheap people and expect it to be used for anything but a cheap purpose," he explained. "The real question is, does that matter? I rather think it does, some-how."

Chandler was contemptuous of television: he thought it lacked good camera work, good directing, and good scripts. Like everybody else, he was also offended by the commercials; he used a "blabb-off," a device that cut off the sound during the advertisements, but it didn't help much. "I've spent a little time lately looking at television for the first time," he wrote in 1950, "and my opinion is that the people who look at television for any length of time and with any regularity have not ceased to read. They never began. It's a great deal like the chimpanzee who played the violin. He didn't play it in tune; he didn't play anything recognizable as a melody; he didn't hold the bow right; he didn't finger correctly. But, Jesus, wasn't it wonderful that he could play the violin at all."

After two years the radio show was dropped. At this point Chandler was engaged in a quarrel with Warner Brothers, which also involved Stark. The negotiations went badly, and on December 1 Chandler wrote to Carl Brandt to say that he no longer wished to be represented by Ray Stark and that he intended to return to Swanson. Chandler changed agents mainly because of personality conflicts. About Swanson he wrote: "You can reach out and touch him. He's substantial. He's there. Stark is like a flickering light reflected on a wall. That is how he affects me. I am not questioning his abilities, nor am I suggesting that there is anything he should have done for me that he has not done in the way of disposing of anything I wrote or getting me better terms. My position quite simply is that I like Swanie, that I have known him for a long time, that I know where I am with him."

Swanson went to work, and by July of 1951 "The Adventures of Philip Marlowe" was back on the air, with Gerald Mohr playing the leading role as before. Chandler also wanted a television show, for the money, but he doubted he would ever get one, given his standards and the kind of people who controlled the medium: "It was bad enough to have the sub-human hucksters controlling radio, but television does something to you which radio never did. It prevents you from forming any kind of mental picture and forces you to look at a caricature instead. There's no escape." Chandler believed that television was in the hands of people who did B pictures in the early days and who controlled radio: "The writing, I suppose, is no worse than it was in lots of radio shows, but by being more intrusive it *seems* worse. If you have spent fifteen years building up a character, a fairly complicated character, you can't deliver him to the sort of people that do these shows. I don't think the plots are terribly important. But I think the actor and the dialogue are very important—so much so that if I were offered a television show (which I have not been) I would have to demand approval of the actor playing Philip Marlowe and also script approval. I simply can't afford to have this character murdered by a bunch of yucks. A voice like Gerald Mohr's gave you a personality which you could fill out according to your fancy. But television shoves the whole thing right down your throat. And if the actor says one flat, stupid, trashy line, it sticks out like a lighthouse in a storm."

When CBS canceled the Marlowe radio show in October, Chandler began to think that a packaging corporation like Ray Stark's Century Artists was perhaps necessary after all to keep a show on the air. The networks wanted too many options. "The idea of tying a man up for ten years and then feeding him dog biscuits strikes me as a little thick," he grumbled to Edgar Carter, Swanson's associate. With a touch of sour grapes he added: "Perhaps the show was too good, perhaps not enough people were slugged or knifed or shot. There are a half dozen shows of this type on the air, it seems to me, which have been on for years and have been sponsored and are solid, and not one of them worth listening to."

Certainly Chandler did not do as well with radio and television as some of his contemporaries did. His years of tough dealing with the Hollywood studios may have made him too difficult for the networks and agents who were packaging shows of this kind. He was willing to be stubborn, even if it meant no show. By the mid-1950s he was out in the cold. As one of the originators of the genre, he had the disagreeable experience of realizing that his imitators had taken over the radio and television market.

Nevertheless, Chandler was always involved with projects, most of them incidental to his life as a writer. When *The Little Sister* was published in 1949, he received a number of proposals, and his reaction to them reveal much about his inner life and sense of himself. Prior to publication day, Houghton Mifflin was approached by the Doubleday Mystery Guild with an offer of $5,000 for distributing *The Little Sister* to its membership. The proposal struck Chandler as all wrong, as he wrote to Hardwick Moseley: "I am against this thing—hard against it. In most respects it is a very bad thing for a writer to get in touch with real money, but it does help with decisions of this sort. $2,500 [Chandler's share] just isn't important enough to me; not worth any kind of sacrifice, and possible danger to a reputation that, after all, has grown up against all the rules." Chandler did not wish to be associated with mystery writers: he wanted to be known as a writer, without any modifying adjective.

Another proposal astonished him even more: "I don't know what's happening to the writing racket in this country. I get an offer of $1,200 a year for the use of my name on the title of a new mystery magazine. *Raymond Chandler's Mystery Magazine.* I have nothing to do with the magazine, no control over the contents and no contact whatever with the editorial policy. They are not even faintly aware that the offer is an insult and that for a writer to trade on his reputation without putting something in the pot is not permissible." Like most writers, Chandler was of two minds about publicity. He wanted his books to be read; he wanted to be known. At the same time, he was repelled by the vulgarity associated with publicity, the blatant selling of oneself. He knew that other writers did things he would not do: "They go on autographing tours as a matter of course, they talk at book fairs, they are very occasionally photographed as Men of Distinction holding a glass of blended whiskey that I should be almost afraid to pour down the drains, for fear of corroding the metal. I don't want to be revoltingly old-school-tie, but it does seem to me that a line has to be drawn, and I am even willing to argue that you can rule out ethics and you would still, if you had any vision, have to draw that line as a matter of policy. But such is the brutalization of commercial ethics in this country that no one can feel anything more delicate than the velvet touch of a soft buck."

At the same time, he coöperated fully when *Newsweek* approached him and let him understand that he was being considered for a cover story to coincide with the publication of *The Little Sister. Time* had interviewed him with the same intention in 1943, but the article was never published. In July of 1949 he was visited by a *Newsweek* reporter and photographed, but all that was published was an article on mystery fiction in which he was featured. There was no cover photograph. Chandler felt demeaned and with his customary openness expressed his feelings to his agent: "So you give them everything they want, talking yourself silly and exhausting yourself with posing for God knows how many pictures, get reproductions of older pictures made for them, and in the end not only do they not give you anything they promised, but they don't even review the book at all. They absolutely ignore it. What hurts here is the sense of guilt unrewarded, like the pickpocket who gets the empty wallet. When you let yourself be persuaded into a deal like that you know in your heart that it stinks, but you are just corrupt enough to gloss it over in the hope that it will build up the sales. Then you get left and the sense of humiliation is not pleasant. There is no halfway about publicity. You either take it where and when you get it, in any form, however vulgar, or you stick to your instincts and say, 'I am not interested in personal publicity of any kind, any time, any place, for any purpose.'" It was a momentary conviction, for Chandler was human enough to allow himself to be interviewed often in later years.

In 1949 Chandler was also invited to join the American branch of the PEN Club, an international association of writers. He told Bernice Baumgarten he didn't know what to do about it: "They evidently consider the invitation a great honor, and I just don't give a damn. If they knew what a bastard I was, they probably wouldn't want me. Their board of directors contains the names of some people whom I regard as blithering idiots, but not all, and I couldn't very well say that anyhow." Later he brought up the subject again, explaining that he wasn't "in the least attracted, but I don't know why. Once a cad, always a cad."

After Chandler was signed up by Houghton Mifflin, he was occasionally visited by an extraordinary character by the name of Harrison Leussler, the firm's West Coast trade salesman. Leussler was nicknamed "Sheriff" because of his Western airs and was an inexhaustible conversationalist: "He has some good stories and is not by any means a bore, but, brother, how can he keep it up? I was as limp as a deflowered virgin after he left." On another occasion Chandler reacted more vigorously: "We had him here to dinner and by 9:30 he had me so exhausted that I went and put my pyjamas on—a hint which would be considered rather too broad in the best society (if there is any) but it was just right for him. Anything less pointed would have missed him by a yard and I didn't quite feel like holding up a card with large letters on it saying: FOR CHRIST'S SAKE STOP TALKING AND GO HOME!"

Leussler was a great admirer of Chandler's work and suggested to Hardwick Moseley, the sales manager, that Houghton Mifflin publish a selection of Chandler's *Black Mask* and *Dime Detective* stories. Since recommendations from the sales staff naturally carry weight, the project was soon under consideration. Several collections of Chandler's stories had already been published in paperback. *Five Murderers* and *Five Sinister Characters* were brought out by Avon in 1944 and 1945, with *Finger Man* following in 1946. In the same year, World Publishing Company published *Spanish Blood* and *Red Wind*. Several of these were also published in translation in France, Italy, and Argentina.

Houghton Mifflin was enthusiastic about a hardcover collection, but Chandler answered the formal proposal written by the editor-in-chief, Paul Brooks, in a typically casual manner. "I quite agree with your remark that under ordinary circumstances a publisher who suggests a volume of short stories ought to have his head examined," he said, adding archly, "Have you had this done?" He observed that "you probably realize that I am going to have to revise and edit this trash.

There are crudities here and there which I can no longer tolerate." He pressed Brooks on one point: "You say some of them I will doubtless want to omit. Or in other words they stink. Which? I doubt if I'm the best judge." He argued against using his *Atlantic* article "The Simple Art of Murder" as an introduction because the stories did not live up to its promise, so the essay was published as an appendix. Chandler wrote a brief new preface, which first appeared in the *Saturday Review of Literature*, and the collection as a whole was entitled *The Simple Art of Murder*. In March of 1950 Chandler learned that Hamish Hamilton was also interested in publishing the stories, so he immediately urged Hamilton to do nothing against his better judgment. Hamilton persisted, however, and brought out a similar edition, although it contained fewer stories.

The book was well reviewed, and advance sales in America were 5,400 copies, which was considered more than satisfactory for a book of this kind. Publication in hardcover of the early stories, most of them written in his apprenticeship as a writer, was proof of Chandler's growing stature as a writer.

They also introduced an ethical problem, which Chandler had been aware of when he complained about Joseph Shaw's inclusion of a cannibalized story in his anthology. When some of the stories from *The Simple Art of Murder* were reissued in paperback in 1952, Chandler received a complaining letter from E. Howard Hunt of the American embassy in Mexico (later famous for his role in the Watergate scandals in Washington during the Nixon administration), accusing Chandler of self-plagiarism. Chandler replied that no plagiarism was involved since he owned the copyright and was legally entitled to use his work as he wished. He justified their publication further by asserting that the stories were unknown to a whole generation that had grown up in ignorance of *Black Mask*. He concluded with this mildly sardonic remark: "I think my principal reason for writing this letter is that in all these years you are the only person who has ever raised this objection, that is to say, the only person other than myself."

While engaged in these and other projects, Chandler was also writing articles—one more about Hollywood, and another about publishing. Most of the material about movies was similar to what had already been published, and that is probably why the *Atlantic*, for which the piece was intended, rejected it. This manuscript has disappeared, but another called "A Qualified Farewell" has survived. It was first intended for the *Screen Writer*, the journal of the Writers Guild, but Chandler withdrew it when there was a change of editors. Although it is repetitive of earlier articles, it is a good demonstration of Chandler's stylistic methods as an essayist. The sentences are aphoristic, and they contain unusual or suprising images and similes. "You have to have passion," he wrote. "Technique alone is just an embroidered pot-holder." As for the screen writer's hopes, "You go in with dreams and you come out with the Parent-Teachers Association." Chandler's analysis is cogent, but what you remember are the images, as in this passage: "What Hollywood seems to want is a writer who is ready to commit suicide in every story conference. What it actually gets is the fellow who screams like a stallion in heat and then cuts his throat with a banana. The scream demonstrates the artistic purity of his soul and he can eat the banana while somebody is answering a telephone call about some other picture."

Another subject that fascinated Chandler was publishing. He was always very outspoken in his dealings with publishers and agents. Carl Brandt said of him: "It's never of much use to argue with Chandler. You've got to let him work it out himself." As a former businessman, Chandler imagined that he was more astute in financial matters than most writers were, but his commercial sense sometimes created more problems than it solved. Used to dealing with oil men, he found the American publisher secretive and aloof: "The minute you try to talk business with him, he takes the attitude that he is a gentleman and a scholar, and the moment you try to approach him on the level of his moral integrity he starts to talk business." He was genuinely puzzled by this apparent schizophrenia and wrote openly about it to Paul Brooks at Houghton Mifflin: "Yours is a strange business. I don't know how you maintain the balance between a sense of what is worth printing and the economic necessity of publishing junk that will sell. Does it need a compartmented mind or just a mild touch of cynicism? What shelter is there for your soul?"

On the whole Chandler had amiable relationships with his publishers and agents, but he had no compunctions about making sarcastic remarks, especially about agents. "The idiotic thing about agents," he said, "is that nobody likes them, nobody wants them, and they don't really do their jobs in all sorts of ways. Yet everybody is afraid to offend them, including publishers and editors of considerable power and prestige."

Finally, he decided to pull together his feelings about agents in an article that was published in the *Atlantic* under the memorable title "Ten Per Cent of Your Life." What most influenced his writing this piece was his memory of working with Ray Stark in Hollywood. He had already warned Carl Brandt of the dangers inherent in the new kind of incorporated agency then being established which was really a talent trust with a variety of clients—writers, actors, producers, directors. In the *Atlantic* article Chandler dealt briefly with the traditional literary agency and then turned to the situation in Hollywood. "This brings me, not too eagerly," he began, "to the orchid of the profession—the Hollywood agent—a sharper, shrewder, and a good deal less scrupulous practitioner. Here is a guy who really makes with the personality. He dresses well and drives a Cadillac—or someone drives it for him. He has an estate in Beverly Hills or Bel-Air. He has been known to own a yacht, and by yacht I don't mean a cabin cruiser. On the surface he has a good deal of charm, because he needs it in his business. Underneath he has a heart as big as an olive pit." The crux of Chandler's argument is that the extraordinary profits to be made in Hollywood brought in an unscrupulous type of individual whose only interest was a fast buck: "The law allowed him to incorporate, which, in my opinion was a fatal mistake. It destroyed all semblance of the professional attitude and the professional responsibility to the individual client." The consequence, even in the early 1950s, was that the clients, whether writers, directors, or actors, "became the raw material of a speculative business. He [the agent] wasn't working for you. You were working for him."

The essay, when published, did not attract much attention: it was too specialized. Bernice Baumgarten claimed that she "squirmed" when she read it, and Chandler suggested she write a reply, but she didn't. Writing the article may have cleared the air for Chandler, but it solved no problems. If having an agent was bad, not having one was worse.

The title Chandler chose for his unpublished Hollywood article "A Qualified Farewell" was appropriate, for even as he wrote it he was reading the galleys of forthcoming novels sent him by Stark to see if any seemed suitable for the screen. Generally he returned them without comment, but in explaining his lack of interest in one that had been bought by MGM, he added that "Goldwyn would be a dangerous type for me to have anything to do with. He would probably scream at me and I should probably call him Goldfish [his real name] and walk out. Why start so perilous an adventure?"

It was not until 1950 that he finally agreed to do a film script of Patricia Highsmith's *Strangers on a Train*, which was to be directed by Alfred Hitchcock for Warner Brothers. "Why am I doing it?" he asked rhetorically. "Partly because I thought I might like Hitch, which I do, and partly because one gets tired of saying no, and someday I might want to say yes and not get asked."

Chandler was also interested in the theme of hidden guilt that lies at the heart of Patricia Highsmith's novel. Two strangers meet on a train. One of them, a rising architect called Guy Haines, would be happier if his wife were out of the way so that he could pursue his career and remarry; the other, Charles Bruno, a drunken and psychotic mother's boy, wishes his father were dead so he could inherit the family fortune. The two men have lunch on the train and each tells the other his story. Bruno then suggests they swap murders: Guy would kill Bruno's father, and Bruno would kill Guy's wife. Neither would be caught because there was no motive to link the murderer to his victim. Guy is horrified and dismisses Bruno as a lunatic. But Bruno kills Guy's wife. The rest of the novel is devoted to Bruno's attempts to blackmail Guy into fulfilling his side of the "bargain." It is a silly story because it is unbelievable. It is interesting only as a psychological study of an individual under pressure.

Hitchcock knew that the novel had to be tightened up for screen treatment. He and Whitfield Cook, who had just written *Stage Fright* for him, turned Guy into a prominent tennis player, since tennis is cinematic and contains an element of suspense. The father of the girl Guy wants to marry is made a senator instead of a millionaire in order to create a sharper contrast between Bruno's anarchic actions and the laws of society. Finally, the setting of the film is limited to Forest Hills and Washington instead of being spread all over the country, as in the novel.

These changes had all been made by the time Chandler signed a contract with Warner Brothers in early July to complete the script. His salary was to be $2,500 a week, with a five-week guarantee. Chandler's contract allowed him to work at home, so Hitchcock drove down to La Jolla for story conferences. Chandler hated "these god-awful jabber sessions which seem to be an inevitable although painful part of the picture business." Although he wouldn't work at the studio, he also disliked Hitchcock's intrusion into his house and became sarcastic and disagreeable. One day, while waiting at the front door of the house for Hitchcock to get out of his limousine, Chandler remarked to his secretary: "Look at that fat bastard trying to get out of his car!" The secretary warned him that he could be heard. "What do I care?" replied Chandler. Hitchcock also found the meetings a strain and later recalled: "We'd sit together and I would say, 'Why not do it this way?' and he'd answer, 'Well, if you can puzzle it out, what do you need me for?'"

Despite these difficulties, Chandler finished a first treatment by July 18. Aside from transforming an introspective novel into a script suitable for filming, he had to face the question of plausibility. He did not think that the audience would believe Guy capable of committing a murder, so he changed the script in a fundamental way. Guy pretends that he will murder Bruno's father, but he really plans to tell him that his son is psychotic and in need of medical attention.

The scene in which Guy tells Bruno that he will fulfill his "promise" to kill his father of necessity caused him the most trouble, as he noted in the course of writing his second treatment:

I nearly went crazy myself trying to block out this scene. I hate to say how many times I did it. It's darn near impossible to write, because consider what you have to put over:

1) A perfectly decent young man (Guy) agrees to murder a man he doesn't know, has never seen, in order to keep a maniac from giving himself away and from tormenting the nice young man.

2) From a character point of view, the audience will not believe the nice young man is going to kill anybody, or has any idea of killing anybody.

3) Nevertheless, the nice young man has to convince Bruno and a reasonable percentage of the audience that what he is about to do is logical and inevitable. This conviction may not outlast the scene, but it has to be there, or else what the hell are the boys talking about?

4) All through this scene (supposing it can be written this way) we are flirting with the ludicrous. If it is not written and played exactly right, it will be absurd. The reason for this is that the situation actually is ludicrous in its essence, and this can only be overcome by developing a sort of superficial menace, which really has nothing to do with the business at hand.

5) Or am I still crazy?

Chandler's solution is to have Bruno do most of the talking. His remarks are disjointed, ranging from fury to self-pity, and this hint of madness gives the scene the "menace" Chandler referred to. As for Guy, he mainly asks questions and nods his head in agreement or gives noncommittal grunts of "Uh huh." It is a clever piece of writing but fundamentally specious for the reasons Chandler cited.

Whenever Chandler sent a few pages of script to Hitchcock, he would also write a letter emphasizing the need for verisimilitude and logical exposition. He was convinced that Patricia Highsmith had not much bothered herself about these concerns. But the problem he faced also led him to consider the fundamental differences between fiction and screen writing:

The question I should really like to have answered, although I don't expect an answer to it in this lifetime, is why in the course of nailing the frame of a film together so much energy and thought are invariably expended, and have to be expended, in exactly this sort of contest between a superficial reasonableness and a fundamental idiocy. Why do film stories always have to have this element of the grotesque? Whose fault is it? Is it anybody's fault? Or is it something inseparable from the making of motion pictures? Is it the price you pay for trying to make a dream look as if it really happened. I think possibly it is.

When you read a story, you accept its implausibilities and extravagances because they are no more fantastic than the conventions of the medium itself. But when you look at real people, moving against a real background, and hear them speaking real words, your imagination is anaesthetised. You accept what you see and hear, but you do not complement it from the resources of your imagination. The motion picture is like a picture of a lady in a half-piece bathing suit. If she wore a few more clothes, you might be intrigued. If she wore no clothes at all, you might be shocked. But the way it is, you are occupied with noticing that her knees are too bony and her toe-nails too large. The modern film tries too hard to be real. Its techniques of illusion are so perfect that it requires no contribution from the audience but a mouthful of popcorn.

The more real you make Guy and Bruno, the more unreal you make their relationship, the more it stands in need of rationalisation and justification. You would like to ignore this and pass on, but you can't. You have to face it, because you have deliberately brought the audience to the point of realising that what this story is about is the horror of an absurdity become real—an absurdity (please notice because this is very important) which falls just short of being impossible. If you wrote a story about a man who woke up in the morning with three arms, your story would be about what happened to him as a result of this extra arm. You would not have to justify his having it. That would be the premise. But the premise of this story is not that a nice young man might in certain circumstances murder a total stranger just to appease a lunatic. That is the end result. The premise is that if you shake hands with a maniac, you may have sold your soul to the devil.

The trap posed by this central unlikelihood is never evaded, and in the final script Chandler simply walks around it and in place of probability presents picturesque scenes. The low quality of Chandler's shooting script may be due to the uncertainties he felt about his work. Chandler was known as a dialogue writer, but the dialogue of this script is simply embarrassing. Everything is overstated and blatant. Relationships between people are so blunt as to make the script a caricature of human behavior. Many of the minor parts are satisfactory, but the major scenes are absurd. It is curious, but the faults may be due to Chandler's having to work from another writer's model: it is always easier to write dialogue for characters you have invented yourself. You know how they speak. Moreover, in his fiction Chandler's dialogue depends a good deal on the surrounding narrative and descriptive prose. Naked, in a screenplay, it is less convincing.

When Hitchcock received Chandler's final script, he was unhappy with it: "The work he did was no good and I ended up with Czenzi Ormonde, a woman writer, who was one of Ben Hecht's assistants." But if Chandler seemed to be using a hammer and nail where a thumbtack would do, the script from which Hitchcock shot the film read as though it had been written by people wielding pickaxes and sledgehammers. Where in Chandler's script Guy's original reaction to Bruno's proposal is left vague, in the film he says: "Of course I agree; I agree with *all* your theories." After talking to his estranged wife early in the story, he remarks in Chandler's words: "I felt like breaking her cute little neck." In the film this is changed to "I'd like to break her foul, useless little neck. I said I could strangle her." There is then an immediate cut to Bruno's hands being manicured by his mother.

Hitchcock had no illusions about what he had created. "As I see it," he said, "the flaws of *Strangers on a Train* were the ineffectiveness of the two main actors and the weakness of the final script. If the dialogue had been better, we'd have had stronger characterizations. The great problem of this sort of picture, you see, is that your main characters sometimes tend to become mere figures."

Whether different behavior by Hitchcock or Chandler could have improved matters is impossible to know. Certainly the atmosphere in which they worked gave little opportunity for cordiality, and by mid-August their relationship had begun to deteriorate. One day, after lunching with Hitchcock in La Jolla, Chandler came down with food poisoning. Not wishing to work, he told Stark that Warner Brothers should take him off salary. As a result, he received a letter from Finlay McDermid, the head of the story department, expressing "my own and the Studio's deep appreciation of your integrity." The next day Warner's legal department sent one of those needlessly grating notices which stated that "due to your physical incapacity preventing you from rendering services for us we elect to exercise the right in said contract granted to us to suspend said contract as to the payment of compensation payable to you thereunder during the aforesaid period." Chandler took no offense, letting this pass as a typical piece of Hollywood legalism, but he wrote Stark about another matter that concerned him: "Hitchcock seems to be a very considerate and polite man, but he is full of little suggestions and ideas, which have a cramping effect on a writer's initiative. You are in a position of a fighter who can't get set because he is continuously being kept off balance by short jabs. I don't complain about this at all. Hitchcock is a rather special kind of director. He is always ready to sacrifice dramatic logic (insofar as it exists) for the sake of a camera effect or a mood effect. He is aware of this and accepts the handicap. He knows that in almost all his pictures there is some point where the story ceases to make any sense whatever and becomes a chase, but he doesn't mind. This is very hard on a writer, especially on a writer who has any ideas of his own, because the writer not only has to make sense out of the foolish plot, if he can, but he has to do that and at the same time do it in such a way that any kind of camera shot or background shot that comes into Hitchcock's mind can be incorporated into it."

Because Hitchcock was so hard to work with, Chandler wanted Stark to arrange a lump-sum payment for his work instead of a salary. The pressure would be reduced if he could work at his own pace. He was also disturbed when he heard that his script was being given to members of Hitchcock's staff for further work. "What this adds up to is that I have no assurance, to put it rather bluntly, that anything much more is happening to me than that my brain is being picked for whatever may be in it, and that someone else or a couple of someone elses are at work behind the scenes, casting the stuff into a screen play form the way he wants it."

Stark was unable to change the contract, and Chandler continued on as before—only under greater pressure because he was suddenly told that the script had to be finished before the end of September so that Hitchcock could start shooting outdoor scenes in Washington before the leaves turned. On the evening of September 26 Chandler sent off the final pages of the script. The next morning Western Union telephoned to notify him of a telegram from Stark saying that Warner Brothers had taken him off salary. He thought this fast work, but when he received the actual telegram he realized he had been suspended the day before and that he had worked an extra day for nothing. Chandler became indignant and sent off letters to his agent and lawyer demanding to be paid for the extra day and also for the week for which he had voluntarily waived salary. He also wrote Finlay McDermid a letter expressing some of his resentment toward Hitchcock: "Are you aware that this screenplay was written without one single consultation with Mr. Hitchcock after the writing of the [final] screenplay began? Not even a phone call. Not one word of criticism or appreciation. Silence. Blank silence then and since. You are much too clever a man to believe that any writer will do his best in conditions like this. There are always things that need to be discussed. There are always places where a writer goes wrong, not being himself a master of the camera. There are always difficult little points which require the meeting of minds, the accommodation of points of view. I had none of this. I find it rather strange. I find it rather ruthless. I find it almost incomparably rude."

By now Chandler was very angry, and when he learned that he had worked the extra day because Stark's office had failed to pass on Warners' message in time, he decided to get rid of Stark as his agent. He had earlier written that "the thing about agents that really annoys me is not that they make mistakes, but that they never admit them." He therefore concluded his letter to Stark's agency with these words: "Some explanation should have been made. There is no reason why I should put up with this sort of treatment, and no reason why I should have to deal with an agency which regards it as so much a matter of routine that it doesn't even have to be explained."

The affair had now blown up to a considerable degree, with Chandler the main sufferer. Ray Stark told him that Warners had kept him on only at the agency's insistence, and this, while angering him further, also seemed to justify his earlier doubts about Hitchcock. "Either he loathes the script or he is mad about something," he wrote. "Even in Hollywood, where a producer loves you to death until the end of the job and can't recognize you on the street the next day, this is carrying things pretty far."

He was further humiliated when he received the final script as rewritten by Czenzi Ormonde, with a request that he respond to the studio's proposal that screen credits be shared. Chandler naturally disliked the final script and even wrote Hitchcock a letter about it, which he never sent. He had anticipated the question of attribution in a letter to his agency. "My dilemma," he said, "is that I ought to refuse credit in connection with such a poor job, but for professional reasons and for the record, and because I haven't had a screen credit for several years, I may have to take whatever credit I'm entitled to. A very sickening situation."

In the end he agreed to one extra day's pay from Warner Brothers and settled for a shared credit. He explained away his troubles by attributing them to an initial error of judgment. "The fallacy of this operation," he wrote, "was my being involved in it at all, because it is obvious to me now, and must have been obvious to many people long since, that a Hitchcock picture has to be all Hitchcock. A script which shows any signs of a positive style must be obliterated or changed until it is quite innocuous, even if that means making it quite silly. What Hitchcock does with his camera, his actors and his stage business is quite all right. I haven't a thing against it. And I'm not going to suggest that he would do better if he had a little more sense of dramatic plausibility, because maybe he wouldn't do better. Maybe he'd do worse. Stark seemed to enjoy suggesting that my script was bad. But it wasn't bad. It was far better than what they finished with. It just had too much Chandler in it and not enough Hitchcock "

Apart from the obvious attempt at self-justification, this letter reveals the basic trouble with the collaboration. Chandler and Hitchcock were in many ways alike. Both believed in spontaneity and freshness, in characters and settings rather than in strictness of plot. As Chandler wanted to engender an emotional reaction through his writing, so Hitchcock was mainly after mood or feeling in his films. Yet working together was impossible, for they were unable to blend their emotional intentions in a finished work. They began to criticize each other for faults which, in fact, they shared. Chandler, who generally cared nothing for plots, worried about Hitchcock violating the narrative logic of his script. Hitchcock, with the same impulses, couldn't get Chandler to create plausible characters.

Chandler seems to have been the more volatile of the two, perhaps because he was always alone. Having complained about the need for story conferences with Hitchcock, he later objected to not having any. These veerings of temperament, generally expressed in a superficially calm and even lawyerly way in his correspondence, were natural for a writer who invested a great deal of feeling in whatever he did or said. They were the source of his strength as a novelist, allowing him to make imaginative leaps into the minds of his characters. But they were a nuisance when it came down to a cooperative venture like making a movie.

Predictably, Chandler had a low opinion of the finished film. "The picture has no guts, no plausibility, no characters and no dialogue," he wrote after seeing it. "But of course it's Hitchcock, and a Hitchcock picture always does have something." The film's popularity embittered him. "I don't know why it's a success," he mused in a letter to Hamish Hamilton, "perhaps because Hitchcock succeeded in removing almost every trace of my writing from it." Clearly he was disappointed that his venture with Hitchcock had turned out so badly. He took it hard, for the film's success was a sign of a certain failure in himself, and he knew it. All he could do was pretend to ignore it and adopt a superior attitude.

There were compensations that came mainly from other work he was doing, for every day Chandler wrote something, regardless of the commercial results. One story from this period is called "A Couple of Writers." It is about a married couple, both of them marginal writers, who torture each other with and about their failures. Their whole life is infested with writing: the wife, who is a playwright, talks like a character in a novel; the husband, a novelist, speaks lines from some imaginary play. He's a drunk; she's a bitch. She tries to run away but comes back, knowing there's no other life for her or for him. He just drinks. By the time Chandler wrote this story, he had a clear idea of himself as a writer and knew what he could and could not do. Hollywood helped make him aware of his strengths and weaknesses, although it never inhibited him. "I'm awfully sorry for writers," Chandler remarked at about the time he was writing this story. "They try so hard, they are so damn vulnerable, and they look so silly when they overextend themselves. I should be grateful that I went through the arty and intellectual phase so young and grew out of it so completely that it always seems a little juvenile in others, whatever their ages."

"A Couple of Writers" is about the sort of people Chandler knew in the 1930s, when he was writing for the pulps. "I've known a number of these not-quite writers," Chandler remarked when he sent the story to Carl Brandt. "No doubt you have also. I know one who sold a short story (most of which, incidentally, I had written for him) to that semi-slick MacFadden publication that Fulton Oursler used to edit—I forget the name of it. Some cheap outfit bought the picture rights for five hundred bucks and made a very bad B picture with Sally Rand in it. This fellow thereupon got drunk and went around snooting all his writer friends because they were working for the pulps. A couple of years later he sold a short story to a pulp magazine, and I think that is the total of his contribution to literature in a commercial sense. To hear this fellow and his wife discussing and analysing stories was a revelation in how much it is possible to know about technique without being able to use any. If you have enough talent, you can get by after a fashion without guts; and if you have enough guts, you can also get by, after a fashion again, without talent. But you certainly can't get by without either. These not-quite writers are very tragic people and the more intelligent they are, the more tragic, because the step they can't take seems to them such a very small step, which in fact it is. And every successful or fairly successful writer knows, or should know, by what a narrow margin he himself was able to take that step. But if you can't take it, you can't. That's all there is to it."

Chandler knew that he had written "a completely useless uncommercial story" but he decided to "annoy Carl Brandt with it" in the hope that it could be placed. For nearly a year Brandt sent the story around, but rarely to magazines likely to publish it. In the end it was never accepted. Chandler was disappointed and told Bernice Baumgarten that "if a thing as well written and penetrating and at the same time as lightly handled as that cannot find a home, why go on trying?" She answered that the magazines had found it depressing and suggested a happy ending, to which he sent the only possible reply: "How the hell would you put a happy ending on that story? What is 'happy'?" But the ending wasn't what was wrong. The trouble is you don't care enough for the characters to worry about what happens to them. They are in a trap they have created for themselves and have no alternatives. It is sad, but not moving, and this robs the story of a vital dimension.

After he stopped working on the Hitchcock film for Warner Brothers, Chandler wrote to Brandt about his literary plans: "From now on I am going to write what I want to write as I want to write it. Some of it may flop. There are always going to be people who will say I have lost the pace I had once, that I take too long to say things now, and don't care enough about tight active plots. But I'm not writing for those people now. I'm writing for the people who understand about writing as an art and are more able to separate what a man does with words and ideas from what he thinks about Truman or the United Nations (I have a low opinion of both). If I feel like writing a fast tough story, I'll write it, but not because there is a market for it and because I've done it before. If I feel like writing a poetic or ironic fantasy, I'll write that. You have to get some fun out of this job and you can't get it by filling orders."

From the beginning of his writing days in London, Chandler was attracted to a type of story he called fantastic: "Every man, I suppose, has some sort of secret place in his heart where he keeps the impracticable but cherished notions. Mine, or one of them, is the fantastic story—not science fiction—a quite realistic story, usually, which has as its premise an impossible thing, but is otherwise quite natural." Chandler was interested in the psychological consequences of a fantastic occurrence: "If a man should wake up in the morning and find that he was nine inches high, I wouldn't be interested in how he got that way but in what he was going to do about it."

In the plan Chandler made for his future writing in 1939, he included a volume of fantastic stories. Aside from those he wrote and published, he sketched out several others, or at least worked them out in his mind. "My own favorites are The Edge of the West (probably a bad title here, since it refers to the Welsh Marches, not our West) and The Disappearing Duke. The first was about a man, secretary to some idiotic organization called the Fairylore Society, who got into fairyland through an old house in the West of England and disappeared. A friend followed his trail, found the house, no one in it but an old butler who served him a delicious dinner, after which he (the man, not the butler) strolled out into the moonlight and when he looked back the house had vanished. Soon after he found himself in fairyland, but the fairies wouldn't have him. Not the type. They sent him back.

"The other one is about a 'rising young novelist,' rather a dated phrase, I suppose, who was invited to tea by a duchess and fell in love with her. His father was a magician, and by prodigious incantations he caused the duchess' husband to become invisible. This was very annoying to the duke. When he finally managed to get into his own house there was a perfectly absurd conversation between him and the duchess along the lines of: 'For heaven's sake, don't let the servants know.' I forget how the thing ended because I haven't looked at it in years. I only mention these to give you an idea of what sort of thing I mean by the fantastic story."

The opening of this second story still exists, but it was probably never finished, because after the intrusion of the first piece of fantasy it is difficult to know what to do next. "The trouble with fantastic fiction as a general rule," Chandler wrote, "is the same trouble that afflicts Hungarian playwrights—no third act." Two of his stories—"The Bronze Door," published in 1939, and "Professor Bingo's Stuff," which came out in 1951—solve the problem to some degree. The first is about a man who buys an antique door and installs it in his house. People who pass through it disappear, enabling the protagonist to get rid of his enemies easily. The second is about a man who can make himself disappear by taking a pinch of snuff. This enables him to murder his wife's lover. In both of these stories the fantastic element that is meant to solve the protagonist's problems backfires in the end. In "The Bronze Door" the protagonist makes himself disappear; in "Professor Bingo's Snuff" he confesses to the murder.

These stories are not important as fiction, but they throw light on a curious aspect of Chandler's mind. They are both wish-fulfillment stories and products of a romantic temperament. Yet they also show that the wishes can never come true. "The Bronze Door" is set in the London Chandler knew as a young man and is intended as a spoof of the English detective story. It is also almost a parable of his life as a professional writer. Chandler seems to have realized that he could never have developed in the world he imagined he loved, but he was able to flourish in one he detested. The parallel may be extended, for in each of these stories a marriage is dissolved. There is no justification for linking this to Chandler's discontent with Cissy; rather it suggests that the freedom that is supposed to come from a dissolved marriage might prove to be a trap. In fact his marriage gave him the freedom and confidence to do his best work.

By the early 1950s Chandler had become so well known among serious writers that he not only was reviewed by them but exchanged letters with them. He was also visited. One of the first to come was J. B. Priestley, who had only recently reviewed *The Little Sister* for the *New Statesman*, calling it a successful attempt "to turn a cheap, popular

formula into something much better." When Chandler received a telegram from Priestley asking to be met at 3:30 at the Tijuana airport,
where he was arriving on a flight from Guadalajara, Chandler was
irritated and upset. "I wish to God people would let one know things a
little *in advance*," he wrote to his secretary. But Priestley was coming at
Hamish Hamilton's suggestion, so Chandler put himself out and drove
down to Tijuana—"a damned long unpleasant drive, if there ever was
one"—and booked him into a hotel in La Jolla because Cissy was ill.
Later on Chandler reported: "He is a likable, genial guy; fortunately a
great talker, so about all I had to do with him last night was click my
tongue against my teeth. He was not entirely satisfied with my company,
for which I do not at all blame him, and suggested gently as I departed
from him late last night at the door of his hotel that tonight possibly we
might meet some of the fellows. So this morning I burst into tears and
threw myself at the feet of Jonathan Latimer, who knows everybody and
likes everybody (whereas I am just the opposite); so tonight I am going
to take him over to Latimer's house where will be gathered a reasonable
selection of what passes for intelligent humanity in our city."

Chandler's nervousness was self-engendered, for Priestley remembered his first evening with him as a pleasant occasion. "He was rather
surprising," he recalled. "He was rather shy, rather a ruminative kind of
man, biting at a pipe. More English in type than American. Indeed, I
think I described him in print as looking rather like a boffin in an Ealing
comedy. He had a good deal of dry humour, but I wouldn't say that he
was a witty talker. We got on very well, at least I hope we did." They
talked generally rather than autobiographically, except about Hollywood, for which they had a mutual distaste. Chandler's library especially impressed Priestley: "He had an enormous number of books there.
They were a very good collection of books, and they were not books
kept for show—he'd obviously read them."

What bothered Chandler most about Priestley's visit was the
patronizing tone he expected to be subjected to. A part of Chandler's
endless debate with himself over the serious novel versus detective
fiction was that any encounter with an intellectual equal put him on the
defensive. Priestley had already gone on record as his admirer, but
Chandler wasn't satisfied: "He likes my books, says he smiling politely
in order to get the subject out of the way and forget it, then he wishes I
would write something without murders in it. Now isn't that a typical
attitude? You slam murder mysteries à la Edmund Wilson, because they
are usually written, you say, by people who can't write well. And the
moment you find someone who you are willing to admit can write well,
you tell him he should not be writing murder mysteries. Meantime, have
you read any good trash lately?"

On the second evening Chandler took Priestley for drinks to Latimer's house, where a number of the guests were Hollywood writers. Afterward he took the whole group out to dinner. For a reformed drinker, it must have been a bizarre evening: "When Priestley was here I threw a party for him at the Marine Room, the guests being mostly Annie Oakleys invited by Jack Latimer and his wife, people I had never seen before and don't care if I never see again. I think I had about eight Scotches that night, which was well below the average of the participants, but this was purely self-protection on my part. If I hadn't had them, I would probably have wanted to call the cops to throw the bastards out."

Chandler may have been relieved when Priestley left, but there is no doubt that the visit stimulated him. "He plays the part of the blunt-spoken Yorkshireman very well," Chandler wrote. "He was very pleasant to me and went out of his way to be complimentary. He is rugged, energetic, versatile, and in a way very professional; that is, everything that comes his way will be material and most of the material will be used rather quickly and superficially. His social philosophy is a little too rigid for my taste and a little too much conditioned by the fact that he finds it impossible to see much good in anyone who has made a lot of money (except by writing of course), anyone who has a public school accent or a military bearing, anyone in short who has speech or mannerisms above the level of the lower middle class. I think this must be a great handicap to him, because in his world a gentleman of property is automatically a villain. That's a rather limiting viewpoint."

Other English novelists also found merit in Chandler's work. One of these was Somerset Maugham, whom he never met but corresponded with as a result of an untypical action of his own. In a letter to Hamish Hamilton Chandler inserted this remark: "Incidentally, if I knew Maugham, which I fear I never shall, I should ask him for an inscribed copy of *Ashenden*. I've never asked a writer for an inscribed copy and as a matter of fact I attach very little value to such things. (I wouldn't mind having the prompt copy of *Hamlet*). And I suppose it declares my own limitations of taste to pick *Ashenden*. But I'm a bit of a connoisseur of melodramatic effects, and *Ashenden* is so far ahead of any other spy story ever written, while his novels, the rest of them, and as good as they are, do not outclass the field."

Hamilton arranged for the inscription and sent the book to Chandler. Its arrival prompted a letter from Chandler that explains his feeling of kinship with Maugham as a man: "I have a feeling that fundamentally he is a pretty sad man, pretty lonely. His description of his seventieth birthday is pretty grim. I should guess that all in all he has had a lonely life; that his declared attitude of not caring much emotionally about people is a defence mechanism, that he lacks the kind of surface warmth that attracts people, and at the same time is such a wise man that he knows however superficial and accidental most friendships are, life is a pretty gloomy affair without them. I don't mean that he has no friends; I don't know enough about him to say anything like that. I get my feeling from his writing, and that is all. In a conventional sense he probably has many friends. But I don't think they build much of a fire against the darkness for him. He's a lonely old eagle."

Chandler might as well have been describing himself. He also admired Maugham's skills as a writer, while recognizing, as Maugham himself did, what his limitations were: "I don't suppose any writer was ever more completely the professional. He has an accurate and fearless appraisal of his own gifts, the greatest of which is not literary at all but is rather the neat and inexorable perception of character and motive which belongs to the great judge or the great diplomat. He has no magic and very little gusto. His style, which has been greatly praised, seems to be no more than a good competent mandarin English which often only narrowly eludes dullness. He can convey the setting for emotion but very little of the emotion itself. His plots are cool and deadly and his timing is absolutely flawless. As a technician he is far ahead of the good second-raters like Galsworthy and Bennett and J. P. Marquand. He never makes you catch your breath or lose your head, because he never loses his. I doubt that he ever wrote a line which seemed fresh from creation, and many lesser writers have. But he will outlast them all with ease, because he is without folly or silliness. He would have made a great Roman."

The correspondence between Maugham and Chandler which followed the inscription led to Chandler's lending Maugham material on detective fiction for an article he was writing entitled "The Decline and Fall of the Detective Story," which has been preserved in Maugham's book of essays *The Vagrant Wood*. This long article begins with the old-fashioned tale of detection and ends with contemporary work, including an appraisal of Chandler and Hammett. Maugham quotes Chandler's essay "The Simple Art of Murder" and then praises the two writers for their accuracy of observation and realism. For Maugham, "Raymond Chandler is the more accomplished. Sometimes Hammett's story is so complicated that you are not a trifle confused: Raymond Chandler maintains an unswerving line. His pace is swifter. He deals with a more varied assortment of persons. He has a greater sense of probability and his motivation is more plausible. Both write a nervous, colloquial English racy of the American soil. Raymond Chandler's dialogue seems to me better than Hammett's. He has an admirable aptitude for that typical product of the quick American mind, the wisecrack, and his sardonic

humour has an engaging spontaneity." With all this, Maugham nevertheless thought the detective story had come to an end because no
original talent had since come forth: there were only imitators, more
brutal, more slangy, more sexy. Maugham therefore concluded his essay
with a stunning remark: "I do not see who can succeed Raymond
Chandler."

One might suppose that Chandler would have been pleased by this
praise, but he was too much a professional engaged with his subject to
be disconcerted by agreeable comments. He simply disagreed with
Maugham's thesis that the detective story was dead. "I'm going to write
him a long letter one of these days," Chandler said, "and take up the
argument with him. I may even write an article in reply if anybody
wants to print it. I should have valued his references to Philip Marlowe
even more if he had remembered to spell Marlowe's name correctly."
Here is the touch of acid in a man who was so nervous about being
patronized that he could not accept praise either.

Another visitor to La Jolla, shortly following on Priestley, was S. J.
Perelman. The two men had originally met in Hollywood during the
1940s, and afterward Perelman published a parody of Chandler entitled
"Farewell, My Lovely Appetizer" in the *New Yorker*. In 1951 Perelman
returned to California and he and Chandler met in La Jolla. Evidently he
liked the place, and Chandler suggested that the Perelman family settle
in nearby Rancho Santa Fe. After Perelman left, Chandler made in-
quiries about houses and schools and sent this information on to Perelman. He said he could not vouch for the academic standing of the
available school and added: "I have one relative, fortunately distant,
who graduated from the Fairfax high school in Los Angeles while still
struggling with the alphabet." Perelman responded from Key West in
part as follows: "I'm seated in an all-plastic motel overlooking another
all-plastic motel which in turn overlooks the Gulf Stream, but there is no
man in America (or for that matter the world) but yourself who could
convey the grisly charm of the establishment. It's roughly three in the
afternoon, sun beating down in a fury, and no sound but the occasional
flapping of the laundry on the line outside and the occasional flush of
the toilet in the next cubicle as the obviously clandestine lovers who
sneaked in an hour ago punctuate their ecstasies. Hurray for progress
and a cheap, hygienic rassle." After apologizing for the delay in answering Chandler's letter, Perelman described his recent experiences in Miami
Beach: "I'd spent the four or five days prior [to going to Key West]
rubbering at Miami Beach and points immediately north, and a depressing sight it is too. There are 97 blocks of skyscraper hotels fringing
Miami Beach, all with piss-elegant names like the Lord Tarleton and the
Sherry-Frontenac. I actually had a cocktail (you see what I have to

subject myself to for copy) in the Peekaboo Room of the Broadripple Hotel, a conjunction of syllables I wouldn't have believed had I been told about it. When you reflect that within the past two months I have been in Las Vegas, Miami Beach, and am returning to Las Vegas for another treatment when I leave here, I think you will admit that I earn a hard dollar." Thanking Chandler for the information about Rancho Santa Fe and also about a dictating machine, Perelman added that as to the latter, he was "saving up for a lush secretary something about 5'7" with a capacious bosom who'd be willing to sit on my lap and keep my mind off sex. It's very much on that theme at the moment, since this room I'm in has one large double bed, one single, and one folding cot in the closet. It seems pitiful to me that all this potential trysting space should go begging. And begging it will go if the missies I've seen around here the last two days are any sample. They all wear pince-nez, speak with the Florida drawl commonly recognized as only second to the New Jersey accent for pure horror, and simper. It's a melancholy prospect, and I'll thank you to feel some compassion."

To this Chandler replied as best he could, suggesting that Perelman "shouldn't give the stuff away like that when you can sell it, unless of course your letters are just rough notes for articles." As for Rancho Santa Fe, Chandler explained that in their passionate effort to keep the place simple the landowners had eliminated nearly all the amenities and that there was only one store. He also thought that plumbers and electricians and carpenters were probably so scarce "that one would find the aristocratic hauteur of their manners even more trying than the union scale for tramping dirt into the best carpets." Nevertheless, he recommended it as a good place to bring up children, "not that I regard that as one of the essential occupations."

It's a pity for Chandler's sake that Perelman did not move to California, because he would have supplied Chandler the stimulus and friendship he lacked in La Jolla. He had liked Perelman immediately: "There is one hell of a nice guy, easy going, unassuming and without vanity." Compared to some who spend half their time emphasizing their importance, Perelman "doesn't give it two minutes. Did I say two minutes? He doesn't give it ten seconds. He acts as though he didn't care, and I don't think it's an act." For his part, Perelman had a high opinion of Chandler. "I more than liked his work," he later wrote; "in my belief, he was the major social historian of Los Angeles, along with Nathanael West, and I reread him very often with admiration and laughter."

Chandler had by now reached a crucial point in his development. He had accomplished a great deal but had not quite attained the level of achievement he believed he was capable of. The five years that had passed since he left Hollywood had not given him what he hoped for. He had been able to finish a novel but knew its limitations. His articles and stories were interesting but not important. Living in La Jolla had forced him to go back to writing movie scripts again. He got the money, but otherwise the experience was a disaster, a throwback to the Hollywood he had escaped from, and a drain on his psychic energies.

He was now in his early sixties, and time was running out. He still had what in some ways was his best work ahead of him, but to bring it out he had to work in even more difficult circumstances than those of the five years just past.

9.
THE
LONG
GOODBYE

———◆———

Ironically, Chandler's freedom to work at home instead of in a studio or office may have been one of the reasons why he wrote so little. Somehow he had to get involved in everything about him, even if he complained all the time about being distracted from his work. He was extraordinarily thorough and liked to be businesslike, organized, and prepared for any eventuality. He never ran out of anything, whether gasoline or office supplies. He was the kind of man who ordered everything by the case, and he had eighteen pairs of shoes. These habits indicate a nervous imagination that made it possible to conceive novels; they also betray an anxiety that made it hard to write them.

Partly because of Cissy's age, Chandler was involved in all the domestic arrangements of the house. He may have been a good office manager in Los Angeles during the 1920s, but he did not know how to treat servants. Instead of telling the cleaning woman and cook what he wanted, he would criticize them for not doing what he expected. Rather than tell the gardener to plant the azaleas in the shade he would say, after they were all in place, "Don't you know anything about gardening? You can't put azaleas in the sun." Chandler did not see the fault as his, but his own account of the problem is revealing. "The domestic situation here is impossible," he wrote in 1954. "In going on 8 years we must have had 60 or 70 people. Few of them lasted more than three or four days of increasing discouragement. Few of them were clean. We have had four good cooks. One lasted about six weeks and was obviously (in the end) only working to pick up some extra money around Christmas time. One was a fine German woman but she turned neurotic, had several accidents, set her room on fire and decided the job was a jinx. One was a superb cook but a thoroughly nasty personality. The fourth we still have and have had for years, off and on, but she has a litle girl, an arthritic husband, and we never feel safe with her."

The real trouble, especially at the beginning, was that he was too shy to be able to treat people naturally. One visitor noted that "he is nervous and jittery and walks with a loping, disjointed walk. He is ill at ease when talking to strangers and rarely looks at the person he is addressing." Chandler had a sarcastic side and used it to express the aggressions his shyness created. He would make offhand comments that were meant to be funny but weren't entirely so. Of children he said: "I don't like the little bastards. I like to hear the patter of little feet going away from me, especially about two houses away." Sometimes he would get into a situation that was too much for him and he would be outrageously rude. Once, while *The Blue Dahlia* was being filmed at Paramount, Chandler invited some of his friends from the oil days to come out to the studio for lunch. While they were eating at the commissary, an old man came up to the table and told Chandler that he admired his work so much he wanted to shake him by the hand. Chandler, embarrassed, replied, "I never shake hands." The old man stood there for a moment, not knowing what to say or do, and then he walked away. As he did, Chandler said in a voice loud enough to be heard at the neighboring tables, "Who's that old bastard? Imagine coming around here and making a nuisance of himself!" Chandler's friends were speechless, but there was an explanation. Chandler did not customarily shake hands because his skin allergy made it painful; besides, he considered it an overdone American habit. But taken off guard, he was unable to be gracious, as he always was with people he knew.

When he first settled in La Jolla, Chandler felt ridiculous having a private secretary, but at the beginning the amount of work he had to do justified it. After trying several others, he engaged Mrs. Juanita Messick, who worked for him for about four years starting in 1950. Her presence was a stabilizing influence. Chandler converted two of the three bedrooms into the work section of the house. The second bedroom, next to Cissy's, became the office and there all the files were kept. The end room containing a single bed where Chandler slept also was his study. There he had a small wooden desk for his own work. Screenplays and letters he was willing to dictate, but his own fiction was different. Every day, from nine to twelve or one o'clock, Chandler typed out his fiction. He used half-sheets of yellow paper to reduce the amount of retyping necessary in case of mistakes. He worked rapidly, for the typing was the last stage of a procedure that took many hours of preliminary work. Often the night before he would work out in his head what he wanted to say, so that when he sat down to type it came spontaneously and fresh onto the page. Chandler said that the first draft was merely the material from which the story would be drawn, and he rarely fiddled with it, changing a sentence or phrase here or there. Instead, he rewrote the entire book, or passages of it, again and again. In this way he kept the language as alive as he could. When at last he had a book he thought he could stand by, he would give his stack of yellow half-pages to Mrs. Messick to be retyped on full sheets, eight inches by eleven. After this, there would rarely be any substantive revision. When the final copy was ready, it was sent to the publisher. Only at this stage, with the book in its final form, would he discuss it with Cissy or anyone else. He needed to keep his mind pure as he went along, unaffected by the ideas or suggestions of others.

After the morning's work, Chandler and Mrs. Messick would join Cissy for lunch. The conversation was usually about books, of which the house was full. Cissy was a more selective reader than Chandler, who would read anything from detective novels (to keep his hand in) to books on international affairs, religion, and philosophy. Hamish Hamilton gave him the choice of his list, and Chandler would ask for new English and American novels as well as books on history and politics. He was interested in books on language but avoided literary history and criticism. He described his literary taste by saying: "I am at home with the avant garde magazines and with the rough tough vernacular. The company I really cannot get along with is the pseudo-literate pretentiousness of, let us say, the *Saturday Review of Literature*. That sums up everything I despise in our culture, including the out-at-elbows professors mewling maliciously at everyone who has the brains and guts to make a dime."

In the afternoons Mrs. Messick would continue typing or filing. Under his direction, she prepared an elaborate file of all his works and kept reports of royalty statements and subsidiary earnings, including translations. Chandler also used what he called a Tickler File, a device for keeping track of delinquent publishers. Subsidiary earnings were generally paid by the hardcover publisher who shared in them. This file was intended to make sure that all earnings due were reported on the royalty statements and paid. There was also the usual business correspondence—about the translation of *Farewell, My Lovely* and its serial publication in *La Stampa* of Turin, about possibly doing a screenplay of Daniel Fuchs's *The Long Green* for Twentieth Century-Fox, about the award of a prize by *Ellery Queen's Mystery Magazine* for being "one of the ten best active mystery writers."

Chandler was aware that Mrs. Messick might feel awkward working at his house since she would not necessarily know where her responsibilities ended and Cissy's began. "You don't have to be so damn polite," he told her. If she was bored, he said, she should simply say, "Well, I'm going out for a while." Or "I'm going to San Diego this afternoon, and if you don't like it, to hell with you."

Earlier he had had a secretary with "a sort of officy personality" that had bothered him, so he went out of his way to tell Juanita Messick what his situation was: "This is not a factory. As you have probably realized by now, my greatest problem in life is to do any work. More and more, as the years go by, I am distracted and irritated by gardeners, plumbers, electricians, carpenters, insurance men, and all the types that you have to have to do things for you, and that a man who is really a business man (which I am not) should be able to take in stride and then put out of his mind. To me, each of these things is an operation. I get tired much more easily than I used to. Unfortunately I have a rather pugnacious temperament and I lack the stamina that ought to go with it to make it effective. I was once a main eventer, but I'm strictly a four-round prelim boy now. So the more of this stuff you can accustom yourself to handle, the more happy I shall be and the more productive my life would be. It costs a lot of money to live in La Jolla; it costs a lot of money to live the way we live, although I don't think we live extravagantly. And I can't make that money wrangling with technicians. I don't know why the hell I write so many letters, and I don't know why the hell when I do write letters, I have to write such long letters. I guess my mind is just too active for my own good. I have too much in me that never gets a chance to get said. It's probably not worth saying, but then that doesn't help me to realize that."

The problem of having a secretary bothered him so much that he dictated a statement called "Advice to a Secretary" to another woman who worked for him. In it he explained: "Nobody knows everything. It is unlikely that you would know as much about the handling of language as the professional writer; even if you knew it in theory, that is in a textbook sense, you would be a generation behind any competent practicing writer." Chandler's natural egalitarianism and lack of pretense made things worse. He called others by their first names and wanted them to call him "Ray." "I dislike the employer-employee relationship," he wrote. "I dislike the knowledge that because I can pay somebody to do some work, I can therefore stop paying them to do it. I hate to have power over people; I love to have power over my own mind and do not have nearly enough of it." Chandler believed it was important to act and speak openly: "Assert your personal rights at all times. You are a human being. You will not always feel well. You will be tired and want to lie down. Say so. Do it. You will get nervous; you will want to go out for a while. Say so, and do it. If you get to work late, don't apologize; just give a simple explanation of why, even if it is a silly explanation. You may have had a flat tire. You may have overslept. You may have been drunk. We are both just people."

Perhaps aware that he was exaggerating the problem, Chandler wrote a parody of his statement, calling it "Advice to an Employer." It contains such suggestions as "Never be at loss for a word. If you are, just look natural and the disagreeable aura will suffice. It is improper for an employer to answer the phone. Always let the help do it: especially if she has gone to the terlet. In this case just yell: 'Miss Whoosis, is that THE PHONE?' *Always* mess up the files. This makes sure the secretary can be blamed if *you* have lost something."

Chandler dictated all these messages to his secretaries, a practice which suggests that he had some difficulty in talking to them directly. But in fact, once he knew them he was easygoing and casual, and his notes were often intended as jokes, as in this one sent to Juanita Messick before Easter: "Office will be closed Thursday and Friday. On Friday you should go to church for three hours. On Thursday you will have to be guided by your conscience, if any. Leona [the cook] won't be here from Wednesday night until the following Monday, but she doesn't get paid this time. Some damn nonsense about the child getting married. I suppose the nuns have told her she is to become the bride of Christ. Do Catholics get confirmed at the age of 8? I thought you had to have some idea what it was all about."

At the end of the day, toward five o'clock, the secretary would join Chandler and Cissy for tea, and Taki the cat would always be present. At the end of Juanita Messick's first year as Chandler's secretary, Taki died, which made their Christmas a very unhappy one. Taki had become, he wrote weeks afterward, "so much a part of our lives that even now we dread to come into the silent empty house after being out at night." After tea Cissy would suggest a drink, and Chandler would bring in a decanter of sherry for his wife and secretary. He never took anything himself, and Mrs. Messick assumed he had never been a drinker. Liquor was kept in the house for others, but Chandler had mastered his desire for it.

At the end of his article of qualified farewell to Hollywood, Chandler had written: "I am a writer, and there comes a time when that which I write has to belong to me, has to be written alone and in silence, with no one looking over my shoulder, no one telling me a better way to write it. It doesn't have to be great writing, it doesn't even have to be terribly good. It just has to be mine." He had left Hollywood just for this purpose, and after the publication of *The Little Sister* he began a new novel. Despite the delays, interruptions, and domestic problems that filled his life, he completed 50,000 words of this book by the end of 1951. He was unsure of its quality: "Somewhere along the line I shall either wake up with a horrible gray feeling, which is the subconscious telling you that you have shot a blank, or else a comparatively warm glow, which is the same subconscious telling you that you have at least achieved passing marks."

The book was called *Summer in Idle Valley*, although it was finally published as *The Long Goodbye*. It is hard to imagine worse psychological conditions than those endured by Chandler as he wrote this book. Cissy was almost constantly ill, and there were many times when his worry about her health threatened to undermine his confidence in his own work. In a revealing letter to Hamilton, he expressed some of these feelings:

"I do hope to have a book in 1952, I hope very hard. But dammit I have a great deal of trouble getting on with it. The old zest is not there. I am worn down by worry over my wife, and that is why I am writing this myself and keeping no copy. We have a big house, rather hard to take care of, and the help situation is damn near hopeless. For months after we lost our last cook, Cissy wore herself out trying to get someone, to endure what we got, to give up and start again. We cannot live here without help. Cissy can do very little; she has lost a lot of ground in the last two years. She is a superb cook herself and we are both pretty much over-fastidious, but we can't help it. I have thought that the sensible thing might be to get a small house and do for ourselves, but I am afraid she is no longer even capable of that. When I get into work I am already tired and dispirited. I wake in the night with dreadful thoughts. Cissy has a constant cough which can only be kept down by drugs and the drugs destroy her vitality. It is not TB nor is it anything cancerous, but I am afraid it is chronic and may get worse instead of better. She has no strength and being of a buoyant disposition and a hard fighter, she fights herself to the point of exhaustion. I dread, and I am sure she does, although we try not to talk about it, a slow decline into invalidism. And what happens then I frankly do not know. There are people who enjoy being invalids, being unable to do anything, but not she. She hates hospitals, she hates nurses, and she does not greatly love doctors. In bad moods, which are not too infrequent, I feel the icy touch of despair. It is no mood in which to produce writing with any lift and vitality.

"You say nice things about what I write and I know you mean

them, but I have never felt important as a writer. In every generation there are incomplete writers, people who never seem to get much of themselves down on paper, men whose accomplishment seems always rather incidental. Often, but not always, they have begun too late and have an overdeveloped critical sense. Sometimes they just lack the necessary ruthlessness and think other people's lives as important as their own, other people's happiness more essential than the expression of their own personalities, if any. I guess maybe I belong in there. I have enough material success to see through it, and not enough sense of destiny to feel that what I do matters a great deal.

"Don't think I worry about money, because I don't. There are always ways to make money if you really need it. I rather envy people who think art and literature worth any sacrifice, but I don't seem to feel that way. My salute to posterity is a thumb to the end of the nose and the fingers outspread. Publishers read too many critics, in the course of business, naturally. And just who are the critics after all? People of small accomplishment, mostly, whose dignity in life depends on the perpetuating of a set of artificial values conceived by other critics who were also people of small accomplishment. My standards are too high for me to admire the successful hacks very much, and too unorthodox for me to care what the pundits say. Well, all this matters nothing, except that a writer to be happy should be a good second-rater, not a starved genius like Laforgue. Not a sad lonely man like Heine, not a lunatic like Dostoievsky. He should definitely not be a mystery writer with a touch of magic and a bad feeling about plots."

In this mood Chandler attempted his most ambitious work and tried to take the mystery story into a realm where it had never been carried before. In a peculiar sense, the distractions of his daily life prevented him from being self-conscious about making his new novel better than *The Little Sister:* he had time only to write the book as best he could. He rarely mentioned the book while he was writing it; but finally, in May of 1952, he sent what he hoped was the completed novel to Brandt and Brandt. He told Hamilton he would soon be receiving a copy and observed that it was a little longer than *The Little Sister*, but he didn't care: "I was not writing for speed. I'm bored stiff with the edge of the chair stuff, and much prefer in these times the flat-on-the-back-on-a-comfortable-couch-with-pipe kind of thing. Add tall cool drink if you can spare it. Anyhow, it's out of my system and the hell with it." To Bernice Baumgarten he explained his intentions more fully: "I wrote this as I wanted to because I can do that now. I don't care whether the mystery was fairly obvious, but I cared about the people, about this strange corrupt world we live in, and how any man who tries to be honest looks in the end either sentimental or plain foolish. Enough of that. There are more practical reasons. You write in a style that has been imitated, even plagiarized, to the point where you begin to look as if you were imitating your imitators. So you have to go where they can't follow you."

When the book arrived, both Carl Brandt and Bernice Baumgarten read it, and Brandt wrote a three-page note outlining his reactions to it. He liked the book but was bothered by a number of small points which, in bulk, constitute the major part of his memorandum. Two days later Bernice Baumgarten wrote a letter to Chandler in which she virtually repeated what Brandt had said. The main objection was that Marlowe had become Christlike and a sentimentalist. "We feel that Marlowe would suspect his own softness all the way through and deride it and himself constantly," she noted. Then followed about a dozen lesser objections. Carl Brandt must have realized that the tone was wrong because he added a postscript: "All this goes for me too—but on reading the clear copy of the letter, I realize we haven't underlined as we would like, how much we admire the book."

The letter should have been rewritten, but it wasn't, and when Chandler received it he was deeply troubled. He asked Juanita Messick for her comments and she gave him her support. Chandler then sent off a telegram to New York asking that the typescript be returned for revision. When she sent the manuscript off, Bernice Baumgarten enclosed a note saying: "I hope our letter didn't upset you."

In the meantime, Chandler wrote to explain his telegram, and his letter is friendly but slightly acid. "It may be that I am no good any more," he said about the sentimentalizing of Marlowe. "God knows, I've had enough worry to drive me off the beam. Being old-fashioned enough to be deeply in love with my wife after twenty-eight years of marriage I feel the possibility that I have let emotion enter my life in a manner not suitable to the marts of commerce, as the cliché has it. Of course there is also the possibility—faint as it is, I admit—that you could be a little wrong." Chandler was relying on his instincts: "Curiously enough I seem to have far fewer doubts about this story than I had about *The Little Sister*."

Two weeks later he wrote directly to Carl Brandt to report on his progress: "I am doing a good deal of revising on my book, especially towards the end, which I think I shall change. But I probably do not have the same confidence that I had before I received Bernice's remarks. Some of the things she said are matters which I would automatically have taken care of on revision. Some seem to me quite without point. As to the character of Marlowe, I may be all wrong but I was trying to write the book the way I wanted to write it and not the way somebody else thinks I ought to write it. The irony of a writer's career—I suppose most writers are confronted with it in some form—is that he may write a couple of books which pass with little notice at the time of their publication, and then as time goes by they slowly build up a reputation and in the end are used as yardsticks by which to measure his later work, sometimes by the very people who were quite unable to discern any merit in the early performance at the time. A writer of my type should never show unfinished work to anyone. He should wait until he is sure that he has what he wanted, or as near to it as he is capable of producing."

Bernice Baumgarten then wrote to say how distressed she was to learn that she had upset him. Chandler replied that there was no need to apologize. "One never knows what sort of impact a letter will make," he said, "since one never knows the mood or very much the circumstances in which it will be read. Complete tact requires more knowledge than is given us." He then explained the difficulties he had in revising: "My kind of writing demands a certain amount of dash and high spirits—the word is gusto, a quality lacking in modern writing—and you could not know the bitter struggle I have had this past year even to achieve enough cheerfulness to live on, much less to put into a book. So let's face it: I didn't get it into the book. I didn't have it to give."

Chandler's revision of the novel was interrupted by a trip to England, but subconsciously he was moving toward a break with Brandt. When he returned to New York, he didn't even phone the agency. Carl Brandt must have known the end was in sight when he wrote: "I feel very sad that you didn't have an opportunity of getting in touch with us so that we might have had time together." Within five weeks he received a telegram from Chandler: "I herewith terminate my agency account with you. Please acknowledge." The break was inevitable, for as with the rupture with Knopf, it had actually taken place six months earlier when Bernice Baumgarten sent her ill-advised letter. The episode shows how extraordinarily delicate an agency relationship is. It requires the mixture of two antagonistic elements—business acumen and artistic judgment. Unfortunately, no one at Brandt and Brandt knew how strongly Chandler felt that the moment he "tries to influence a writer in his work, the agent just makes a nuisance of himself." Yet Chandler would not have undertaken the revisions, which were necessary, had he not received the letter. The trouble was that his nervous mechanism could not accommodate his personal irritation and his artistic honesty at the same time.

Chandler's method of revision is revealed in two hundred yellow half-sheets of typescript containing passages of the book that were omitted or rewritten. The drafts are all written out fresh, without reference to earlier versions. Sometimes the same phrase reappears, but each scene has its own unity and energy, and there is no literal imitation. The new passages are like grafts on a living organism, and each has its vitality. The passages are all well written: it is not a matter of substituting an awkward or confused scene with something better. Instead, each is just a different way of telling the story. Sometimes extraneous material is cut out, but Chandler is mainly concerned with emphasis, and this is a matter of rhythm.

There are three versions of the last paragraphs which show how Chandler dealt with the problem of sentimentality. The scene describes the way in which Terry Lennox leaves Marlowe's office, and it is emotionally charged because the friendship that once existed between the two men is one of the important themes of the book. This is the first version:

"He turned away and went out. I watched the door close and listened to his steps going away. After a little while, I couldn't hear them but I kept on listening.

"Don't ask me why. I couldn't tell you."

This version fails because it is flat. Chandler rewrote it in pen, which was unusual for him:

"He turned and went out. I watched the door close and listened to his steps going away. Then I couldn't hear them, but I kept on listening anyway. As if he might come back and talk me out of it, as if I hoped he would.

"But he didn't."

This reveals the emotional state, but it is sentimental; the last sentence is like a catch in the throat. The final version reads:

"He turned and walked across the floor and out. I watched the door close. I listened to his steps going away down the imitation marble corridor. After a while they got faint, then they got silent. I kept on listening anyway. What for? Did I want him to stop suddenly and turn and come back and talk me out of the way I felt? Well, he didn't. That was the last I saw of him.

"I never saw any of them again—except the cops. No way has yet been invented to say goodbye to them."

This is comparatively prolix, but is understated. The details of the setting, such as the imitation marble corridor, take on some of the emotional burden. The change is basically tonal, and the Marlowe portrayed here is consistent with the character as established earlier in the book. It is also less abrupt as an ending, more appropriate than the others for a book of this length. In general, Chandler's revisions make the episodes more dramatic and give them deeper texture, so that the reader is brought more fully into the minds and feelings of his characters.

There is no doubt that Chandler intended to put all of himself into *The Long Goodbye*. He knew it was his last chance to do so. What he most wished to express may be discovered in part by considering a book called *Mr. Bowling Buys a Newspaper* by Donald Henderson, which was published in 1944. This is an ordinary mystery story with no special literary distinction. But for Chandler, it was a kind of marvel. He never tired of recommending it to others, and he gave away dozens of copies to friends and acquaintances. Its attraction for Chandler is quite obvious: it is a clear projection of how he saw himself. It is the story of a man with a Public School education who somehow never made anything of his life. In order finally to make some mark in the world, he commits a series of murders that are almost impossible to solve because they are apparently motiveless.

This is the outline of the novel, but the real theme of the book is that Mr. Bowling's failure is due to the absence of love in his life. Again and again, Henderson makes this point; as when Bowling recalls being sent away to school as a boy: "He needed love. It was no good sneering at it, it just showed your bally ignorance." A few pages later: "He was hungry for love, spiritual love, and loving God didn't seem quite adequate, you wanted long, feminine, golden hair to stroke." Bowling marries, but the relationship with his wife is a failure. He then has an affair with a maid, and the results are the same. Later in the novel comes this comment: "For some reason or other, he thought, his life-handicap was to be deprived of love, and by love he meant real and mutual love, not pyjamas and a bed."

Bowling's failures seem very like those Chandler endured. Instead of becoming a composer as he wanted to do, he takes a job as a salesman. He lives in a shabby neighborhood and remembers his youth with increasing bitterness. He has not lived up to what it promised, including a romance with a childhood sweetheart that was never consummated. Perhaps the most telling passage occurs toward the end of the book, when Mr. Bowling is being interrogated by the police for the murders he committed: "The superintendent mentioned, coldly, the name of Mr. Bowling's old school: it seemed to Mr. Bowling the hardest blow of all. He had been plucked out of that school, and its much-lauded advantages, and thrown into—what? Into a world at its rawest, and its most changing, a world which had less room for a gentleman than ever, unless he had money and powerful connections; and it did seem to Mr. Bowling that this was hard."

There can be little doubt that Chandler read these lines with feeling. It was Dulwich and Los Angeles, and the girl with the cornflower-blue eyes he had left behind in an England he could not support himself in. Even Mr. Bowling's desperate decision to commit murder has a parallel

in Chandler's suicidal impulses. Yet it would be foolish to overdraw the
parallel. Chandler was not a failure like Mr. Bowling; he was world
famous as the best detective novelist of his time, and his marriage to
Cissy was a mature and deep relationship. But the theme of *Mr. Bowling
Buys a Newspaper*—the need for love and friendship—is the very one
Chandler developed in *The Long Goodbye*.

The exploration of this theme required fundamental changes in the
character of Marlowe, who, in accordance with the formula of detective
fiction, always remained apart from the other characters and never
became emotionally involved with any of them. He was just a catalyst,
the character who pulled aside the curtain so that the comedy could
begin. But by the time he began *The Long Goodbye* Chandler wanted to
move on to a different level of treatment. He was no longer satisfied
with a comic view of the world. The skies had darkened and now, like
Canio in *Pagliacci*, he was saying *"La commedia è finita."* As his vision
became more personal, his work grew more novelistic, less like a play
than before. This meant that Marlowe became his most important character. In *The Long Goodbye* Marlowe is a man of feeling who is no
longer hesitant about becoming involved with the other characters. He is
the device Chandler uses in trying to move the detective story into the
mainstream of traditional fiction.

It is no coincidence that while writing the first part of this novel he
answered a total stranger with a five-page letter nearly 2,500 words long
in which he describes the details of Marlowe's life. Throughout Chandler
adopts the facetious pretext that Marlowe is a living person, saying for
example, "Marlowe has never spoken of his parents, and apparently he
has no living relatives." Chandler describes Marlowe's birthplace in
Santa Rosa, California, his university education in Oregon, his early
employment as an insurance investigator, and a later job in the office of
the district attorney of Los Angeles County. He describes his physical
appearance, states that the actor who would best represent him is Cary
Grant, and deals with various details of his life such as the kind of
matches he uses and his dislike of sweet drinks. He discusses his literary
taste and preference for certain films, the kind of guns he owns. Marlowe's apartment "contains a living room which you enter directly from
the hallway, and opposite it are French windows opening on an orna-
mental balcony, which is just something to look at, certainly not anything to sit out on. Against the right-hand wall as you stand in the
doorway is a davenport. In the left-hand wall, nearest the hallway of the
apartment house, there is a door that leads to an interior hall. Beyond
that, against the left-hand wall, there is this oak dropleaf desk, an easy
chair, etc.; beyond that, an archway entrance to the dinette and
kitchen." And so the description continues, covering every aspect of

Marlowe's life and character. What is astonishing is the degree to which Marlowe became a real person to Chandler. The mass of details suggest that he was more deeply involved with his character than he had been in the earlier books.

Marlowe was not an extension of Chandler, although they had certain characteristics in common. They were both lonely men, isolated in the nonsociety of California, and they held individualistic moral positions that were at odds with the standards of most of the people they associated with. Chandler would sometimes say, when the character of Marlowe was being offered for radio or television adaptation, "I am Marlowe," but this was to emphasize the need to preserve his unique quality. In other respects—Chandler's intellectualism, Marlowe's physical toughness—they were quite different.

It used to be thought that artistic creativity was the result of an unconscious impulse. For example, some have asserted that art is regressive, an attempt to create a vision of what the world should have been like. Other explanations of creativity have included the notion that the artist is schizophrenic and that art is a sign of ego gratification. Sometimes this last theory has been applied to Chandler, with the suggestion that Marlowe is what Chandler would like to have been—a big strong tough guy who has a way with blondes. The principal drawback to these theories is that they are concerned only with the unconscious. They ignore the conscious intellectual effort that goes into artistic creation. Juvenile fantasies cannot stand up to the rigorous intellectual activity that art requires.

A literary character, especially if he is the hero or central character of a book, will almost certainly have something to do with the author's own experience and with his unconscious. To some degree he may well be modeled on the author, or even the author's inflated idea of himself; but once he starts to talk and act, once he enters the world of fiction in which he lives, he develops his own characteristics. His behavior is affected by the people he meets in the story and by what happens to him. This is what artistic creation is all about: it is not faintly disguised reality; it is the creation of something entirely new. That is why it is so dangerous, a threat to society and even a criticism of nature, as Claude Lévi-Strauss has shown.

Chandler knew what he was doing: he had consciously created a character suitable for his first five books; now he wanted to move in a new direction with *The Long Goodbye*. His state of mind gave him the impulse and he drew on himself, but the writing was under control.

Although it is cast in the form of a detective novel in which Marlowe eventually reveals the murderer of two of the characters, *The Long Goodbye* is really about the nature of friendship, its uses and abuses, and about the qualities of love. The first five chapters of the novel deal with Marlowe's friendship with Terry Lennox, whom he occasionally meets for a drink at the end of the day. Lennox is married to the daughter of a multimillionaire, Harlan Potter, whom he describes as "a cold-hearted son of a bitch. All Victorian dignity on the outside. Inside he's as ruthless as a Gestapo thug." Terry calls his wife, Sylvia, a tramp, but he admits that he himself is less than satisfactory in bed. Marlowe is only slightly acquainted with Lennox, but he admires his curious dignity, his politeness, the code of honor he lives by despite the messiness of his life.

The description of Marlowe's relationship with Lennox is intended to reveal Marlowe's attitude toward other people. Where no one else will help Lennox, Marlowe does. Once he takes him home after Sylvia abandons him at a nightclub; he takes him home again to keep him from being arrested for vagrancy. But friendship also produces complications. As *The Long Goodbye* gets underway, Sylvia Lennox is found murdered, and under pressure from her father, and a bribe, Terry agrees to take the blame for the murder. He disappears into Mexico and is reported dead. The case is officially closed, and the Potter name is cleared.

In the meantime, Marlowe meets the famous novelist Roger Wade and his beautiful wife, Eileen. They are neighbors of Terry Lennox's, and Wade has paid visits to Sylvia in the past. He is a terrible drunkard and half suspects that he may have killed her himself and then blanked out. Before long, Wade is found dead. Marlowe learns that his wife, Eileen, was formerly married to Lennox. She killed Sylvia out of jealousy, and then killed Wade because he talked too much and was unreliable. At the end of the book, when Lennox reappears, Marlowe refuses to have anything to do with him, calling him a "moral defeatist." His complaisance has produced an unnecessary murder. Friendship, Marlowe learns, doesn't amount to much compared with self-protection. Marlowe is especially bitter about Wade's death, which was arranged to suit the convenience of Harlan Potter and Eileen. "He was of no real importance, of course," says Marlowe. "Just a human being with blood and a brain and emotions. He knew what happened too and he tried pretty hard to live with it. He wrote books. You may have heard of him."

Marlowe's cynicism is now almost complete, but he admits that he has been hurt and expresses his feelings. "You bought a lot of me, Terry," he says. "For a smile and a nod and a wave of the hand and a few quiet drinks in a quiet bar here and there. It was nice while it lasted. So long, amigo. I won't say goodbye. I said it to you when it meant something. I said it when it was sad and lonely and final." The lonely Marlowe needs friendship, but he's not going to get it. He knows too much about it, how tenuous it is, how much a matter of convenience.

The world is a jungle, as in Conrad's *Heart of Darkness*, and the only people who keep it going are the policemen on the corner, with whom Chandler closes the book.

Chandler's own sense of loneliness in California, where he had no relatives or longstanding friendships, also influenced the way he described Roger Wade. It is usually a bad sign when a novelist starts talking about writing in one of his books, but the point Chandler makes justifies it. In the society portrayed in *The Long Goodbye*, Wade, the most creative character in the book, is literally destroyed by the forces that move about him: he is murdered to preserve a lie. Wade has published a dozen novels, but he doesn't care about them. He is drunk most of the time, mainly because of a feeling of self-disgust that poisons everything around him, including his relationship with Eileen. He knows that he and Eileen are playing a game, and that the game is destroying them. Late one night he drunkenly types out several pages of mixed self-pity and honesty which reveal underneath the wreckage of a romantic dream. This is the heart of what he writes: "Better call someone quick before the pink things crawl on my face. Better call, call, call. Call Sioux City Sue. Hello, Operator, give me Long Distance. Hello, Long Distance, get me Sioux City Sue. What's her number? No have number, just name, Operator. You'll find her walking along Tenth Street, on the shady side, under tall corn trees with their spreading ears."

But there is an even more telling statement earlier in Wade's message. "Come on, Wade, let's get up and go places," he writes. "Places where we haven't ever been and aren't ever going back to when we have been." This grammatical confusion is derived from the vision Chandler himself expressed in his early poem "Nocturne from Nowhere" about the girl with cornflower-blue eyes:

> *Let me go back*
> *Into that soft and gorgeous future*
> *Which is not past,*
> *Never having happened*

This is the essential fact about Wade and, by extension, Chandler and Marlowe. Nothing has ever really happened, although in some faraway youth there was a romantic sense or feeling, like the play of light on spring cherry trees or the sight of an incredibly beautiful girl across the aisle on a bus. As with the figures on Keats's Grecian urn, the dream is never fulfilled, and if it had been, it would have faded. But it persists for Wade as an irritant and as a symbol of limitation.

Marlowe admires Wade for attempting to speak this truth. He tells Eileen: "Your husband is a guy who can take a long hard look at himself

and see what is there. It's not a very common gift. Most people go
through life using up half their energy trying to protect a dignity they
never had." But for Wade, dignity is not even an issue. He knows why
he drinks and what other people say about it: "If I had a ten-year-old
kid, which God forbid, the brat would be asking me, 'What are you
running away from when you get drunk, Daddy?' " He is running away
from the vision of the girl in Sioux City who walks along the shady side
of the street and makes everything else meaningless. "I've written
twelve best sellers," says Wade, "and if I ever finish that stack of
magoozlum on the desk there I may possibly have written thirteen. And
not a damn one of them worth the powder to blow it to hell. I have a
lovely home in a highly restricted residential neighborhood that belongs
to a highly restricted multimillionaire. I have a lovely wife who loves me
and a lovely publisher who loves me and I love me best of all. I'm an
egotistical son of a bitch, a literary prostitute or pimp—choose your
own word—and an all-round heel. So what can you do for me?"

If Wade's vision destroys him, Chandler knew that the coin had
another side. You have to leave some things behind in order to achieve
something else. His skill as a writer rests on his ability to express both
the romance of an impossible world and the quality of a possible one,
and more important the light that each casts on the other. Marlowe
sympathizes with Wade because his own attitude toward women is
romantic. The convention of the detective story, which kept him free of
involvement with women, helped preserve this attitude; but in *The Long
Goodbye* Chandler tries to have Marlowe face up to women as women.
Yet even here there is a curious ambiguity or contradiction that reflects
Chandler's own attitude toward sex and his experience with Cissy. Later
in his life he wrote: "I have written practically nothing about his
[Marlowe's] sex life because I thought it was his own business, but I did
in my last book break down a little. It is impossible to think that such a
man would not have a sex life, but so many writers of this sort of story
have made it too blatant and too vulgar." Marlowe's approach, he
explained, was based on "a certain obscure technique which depends
almost entirely on making a woman feel you respect her." This approach
is in itself romantic, for Chandler shifts to himself and says, "I suppose
that a man who was married for almost 31 years to a woman he adored
becomes in a sense a lover of all women, and is forever seeking, even
though he does not know it, for something he has lost. You can never
cheapen a woman. No man of my sort thinks of her exactly as she
thinks of herself. After all, her body is to her a familiar thing; but to
some it is always a sort of shrine." He referred to his own marriage in a
similar way: "Ferocious romantics of my sort never make do with
anything. They demand the impossible and on very rare occasions they

achieve it, much to their surprise. I was one of those, one of the perhaps two per cent, who are blessed with a marriage which is forever a courtship. I never proposed marriage formally to anyone. My wife and I just seemed to melt into each other's hearts without the need for words."

This is the romantic side of Chandler, which was as vivid to him as its opposite. He was a man of strong contradictory impulses. "I am both sensual and idealistic," he said. Once when criticizing Erle Stanley Gardner's use of sexual imagery to titillate the reader, he wrote: "Sex cannot be dealt with in this three-cushion style. You have to face it squarely or leave it alone. Anything else is a little nauseating." The harshness of his expression may be a clue to the kind of life he was living with Cissy. Chandler knew that she was no longer or perhaps never had been one of the golden blondes with strawberry complexions that appear in his books. He had lost out there, as his early infidelities and drunkenness proved. The relationship with Cissy was deep, but it didn't touch certain portions of his being. With Cissy now eighty and racked with illness, Chandler, like Marlowe, also went to bed alone. Chandler had enough self-control to give up drinking for extended periods during his life, and during his last years with Cissy in La Jolla he probably also gave up sex. It would be an exaggeration to say that he was alternatively attracted and repelled by sex, but there is certainly strong feeling in the way he has Marlowe reject the advances of the psychotic young girl, Carmen Sternwood, in *The Big Sleep*. When Marlowe finds Carmen coyly waiting for him in his bed, he orders her out abruptly. He then opens the windows and fumigates the apartment: "I went back to bed and looked down at. it. The imprint of her head was still in the pillow, of her small corrupt body still on the sheets.

"I put my empty glass down and tore the bed to pieces savagely."

For a man having an attitude toward women that Chandler described as natural for "any vigorous and healthy man who does not happen to be married," this is an extraordinarily violent reaction. It would appear that somehow Carmen was a threat to the kind of compromise with life, to the self-imposed limitations, that Chandler made Marlowe agree to in order to function at all.

In the letter that prompted Chandler's long description of Marlowe, the writer mentioned a theory expressed by Gershon Legman in *Love and Death* (1949) that Marlowe was homosexual. Chandler replied that "you can certainly dismiss the remarks of Mr. G. Legman, since Mr. Legman seems to me to belong to that rather numerous class of American neurotics which cannot conceive of a close friendship between a couple of men as other than homosexual." Similar assertions have been made about Chandler himself without any evidence to support them other than Chandler's outspoken dislike of homosexuals. This is pre-

sumed to have masked a hidden attraction. On the other hand, there is a
great deal of evidence to prove Chandler's heterosexuality.

In *The Long Goodbye* Chandler immediately gets Marlowe involved
with women. The first is Eileen Wade, who is blonde with telltale eyes of
cornflower blue. Early in the novel he kisses her, but she is not pleased.
"That was wrong," she says. "You're too nice a person." Later on she
attempts to seduce him. They are in her bedroom and after they kiss, she
tells him to carry her to the bed. "I did that. Putting my arms around her
I touched bare skin, soft skin, soft yielding flesh. I lifted her and carried
her the few steps to the bed and lowered her. She kept her arms around
my neck. She was making some kind of whistling noise in her throat.
Then she thrashed around and moaned. I was as erotic as a stallion. I
was losing control. You don't get that sort of invitation from that sort of
woman very often anywhere."

They are interrupted by the houseboy, and the spell is broken.
Eileen remains on the bed and continues making sounds, but now
Marlowe hears them as just "weird noises." He goes downstairs, drinks
most of a bottle of Scotch, and passes out on the couch. The passage is
curious for its language, for the way in which the seductive and repel-
lent aspects of sex are placed side by side. It represents both attraction
and revulsion. The scene is not as violent as the destruction of the bed in
The Big Sleep, but it is a powerful study of the nature of control.
Marlowe is as frightened of his own being as he is of the situation. He
sees himself as a stallion, and the strength of his passion thrills and
disgusts him at the same time.

The plot prevents the relationship between Marlowe and Eileen
from developing, but Marlowe is soon attracted to Linda Loring, Harlan
Potter's other daughter, who is married to a dreadful prig whom she
soon discards. The principal encounter between the two comes at the
end of the novel and shows how Chandler was once more trying to move
into new territory. Linda arrives at Marlowe's place with an overnight
bag. They are both tired and overwrought, and the bag gets them off to
a bad start. Marlowe starts to take it into the bedroom, and Linda
accuses him of jumping to conclusions. "The hell with the overnight
bag!" Marlowe then says. "Mention it again and I'll throw the damn
thing down the front stairs. I asked you to have a drink. I'm going out
to the kitchen to get the drink. That's all. I hadn't the least idea of
getting you drunk. You don't want to go to bed with me. I understand
perfectly. No reason why you should." Linda tells him there's no need to
lose his temper, and Marlowe retorts, "That's just another gambit. I
know fifty of them and I hate them all. They're all phoney and they all
have a sort of leer at the edges."

Chandler renders Marlowe's nervous aggressiveness convincingly, and after they've calmed down and made love, he has Linda suggest they get married. But Marlowe knows it's just a sort of game with her, and that she doesn't really love him. She knows it too and cries on his shoulder. The next day she leaves, and the episode is closed. But Marlowe has been touched far more than in any of the other novels. This time he goes into the bedroom and pulls the bed apart in order to remake it. "There was a long dark hair on one of the pillows. There was a lump of lead at the pit of my stomach."

From the beginning of the book it is obvious that Chandler intended *The Long Goodbye* to be his major effort as a novelist. It has an expansiveness his other books lack. It is not as crisp and fast-paced as *Farewell, My Lovely*, but here Chandler wanted to do something different. He enriches *The Long Goodbye* with comments of all sorts about the society in which Marlowe lives. These are made far more relevant to the story itself than they were in *The Little Sister*. Early in the book Marlowe is questioned by the police and then put in jail under suspicion of being an "accessory" to the crime. This curious booking has no legal status, and the Los Angeles police have to release their suspects after the third day so as not to violate habeas corpus. It is nevertheless unpleasant, and Chandler uses the occasion to describe what it's like to be in jail, the impersonality, the boredom. Also, when a lawyer is sent to make plans for Marlowe's release, an arrangement he rejects, the two men discuss a number of illegal police maneuvers. These comments on society are a natural part of the story and are not obtrusive. There is only one extraneous chapter, and that is one in which Chandler describes a typical day in Marlowe's life. The phone calls and visitors have nothing to do with the central plot, but the writing is amusing enough to let Chandler get away with it. Sometimes the interjections don't quite come off, as when Chandler includes a long commentary on blondes. Here he seems to be trying to fill in all the interstices, to make this novel the definitive Chandler. Appreciation of such passages is largely a matter of taste. The best are those which combine Marlowe and the world he lives in. Here is the opening of a chapter set in an hotel in Beverly Hills:

"At eleven o'clock I was sitting in the third booth on the right-hand side as you go in from the dining room. I had my back against the wall and I could see anyone who came in or went out. It was a clear morning, no smog, no high fog even, and the sun dazzled the surface of the swimming pool which began just outside the plate-glass wall of the bar and stretched to the far end of the dining room. A girl in a white sharkskin suit and a luscious figure was climbing the ladder to the high board. I watched the band of white that showed between the tan of her thighs and the suit. I watched it carnally. Then she was out of sight, cut off by the deep overhang of the roof. A moment later I saw her flash down in a one and a half. Spray came high enough to catch the sun and make rainbows that were almost as pretty as the girl. Then she came up the ladder and unstrapped her white helmet and shook her bleach job loose. She wobbled her bottom over to a small white table and sat down beside a lumberjack in white drill pants and dark glasses and a tan so evenly dark that he couldn't have been anything but the hired man around the pool. He reached over and patted her thigh. She opened a mouth like a firebucket and laughed. That terminated my interest in her. I couldn't hear the laugh but the hole in her face when she unzipped her teeth was all I needed."

Without saying anything about life in Beverly Hills, this says everything.

The vision of Southern California Chandler presents in *The Long Goodbye* is bleak. One evening before he goes to sleep Marlowe stands at the window of his apartment and looks out over the city. He listens to the noise from the streets below and can see the glare of light in the sky. Now and again he hears the wail of a siren from a police car or fire engine, and this is what he thinks: "Twenty-four hours a day somebody is running, somebody else is trying to catch him. Out there in the night of a thousand crimes people were dying, being maimed, cut by flying glass, crushed against steering wheels or under heavy tires. People were being beaten, robbed, strangled, raped, and murdered. People were hungry, sick, bored, desperate with loneliness or remorse or fear, angry, cruel, feverish, shaken by sobs. A city no worse than others, a city rich and vigorous and full of pride, a city lost and beaten and full of emptiness." What can a man do in so ambiguous a world? Marlowe's answer is romantic: he has his self-respect, which allows him to tell a cop to go to hell, and he has learned enough to believe that friendship and love have little chance against greed. He is still the hero Chandler defined in "The Simple Art of Murder"—the man who "goes down these mean streets" and who "is not himself mean, who is neither tarnished nor afraid."

This would appear to be a sentimental position, because it puts Marlowe on a higher plane than any of the other characters. "I don't mind Marlowe being a sentimentalist," Chandler wrote, "because he always has been. His toughness has always been more or less a surface bluff." What this does to *The Long Goodbye* as Chandler's bid for the complete novel depends rather on the definition of novel that is used. In most serious European fiction the central character knows more at the end of the novel than he does at the beginning. His humanity has been put to a test against the norms of society. He may fail or succeed, accept or reject what experience teaches him, but he knows what the issues are. He is without illusions, although like Don Quixote he may know that illusions are necessary for survival. Emma Bovary, Anna Karenina, Charles Gould in *Nostromo*, Molly Bloom in *Ulysses*, Christopher Tietjens in *Parade's End*, all do battle with a code of behavior. Whether they free themselves from it or are defeated by it, they no longer adhere to it at the end. They become themselves.

This same impulse is found in American fiction; but in the less highly developed, relatively formless society of the United States, the heroes of fiction react differently. Some nineteenth-century heroes like Natty Bumppo, Huckleberry Finn, and Melville's various wanderers just run away and take refuge in the wilderness. With the closing of the frontier, later fictional heroes lack this option. They are forced to assume a more ambivalent attitude toward the world they live in. They know what power and money are and fight battles over them, but in order to keep civilization alive at all, they tend to hold on to some sort of code of behavior. In this sense, American fiction is less mature than European.

Judgment of *The Long Goodbye* depends on the standards that are being applied. Certainly Marlowe does not attain the degree of understanding and liberation achieved by the great heroes of European fiction. But he is not unlike the heroes and heroines of Hemingway, Faulkner, Steinbeck, and Dreiser. These fictional men and women are divided individuals who are trying to come to terms with their surroundings. In order to give themselves some stability, they evolve patterns of behavior that permit them to cope. Their lives may be tragic, spoiled by the very codes they live by or fail to live by, but they have little option to do otherwise. Chandler seems to have had a clear idea of the effect of his nationality on Marlowe, for he wrote in his notebook: "To me Marlowe is the American mind; a heavy portion of rugged realism, a dash of good hard vulgarity, a strong overtone of strident wit, an equally strong undertone of pure sentimentalism, an ocean of slang, and an utterly unexpected range of sensitivity."

In the company of the writers mentioned above and with such a character, *The Long Goodbye* has stature. Chandler engages Marlowe in new experiences and reveals sides of him that were formerly hidden. He has a friendship with Terry Lennox and a brief affair with Linda Loring. At the end there is just a blank, a void that has to be filled with something, even a code of behavior that sounds sentimental; but that is the nature of America as Chandler saw it.

There is another side of the matter that is worth considering. Chandler had the vision of a complete novelist, but for financial reasons he took up a kind of writing that limited him. At the same time, the detective novel released creative powers in him that would never have come out had he tried the so-called straight novel. This is a curious paradox which also casts light on *The Long Goodbye*. It can be explained partly by considering Chandler's position in California. Unlike James, Joyce, or Conrad, who were all in exile from worlds they detested, Chandler was in exile from a world he thought he loved. Instead of his adored England, he lived in a place where values seemed to shift with the tides. No wonder he clung to the code of the Public School gentleman and applied it to his fictional hero as well.

Chandler's comic vision also requires a balance of sentimentalism to make it palatable. A great satirist such as Swift, whose chief weapon was wit, was able to present a view of the world that was all of a piece, without any softening around the edges. But for such writers as Dickens and Mark Twain, who relied heavily on feeling, the horror of what they saw in the world around them was unbearable. Out of sympathy with their characters they softened reality by introducing humor. This was not so much a conscious policy as the result of a change of mood natural in writers of this kind. Also, comedy and sentiment naturally go hand in hand, as we know from the tradition of the *commedia dell'arte* and the sad clown, made most famous in our time by Charlie Chaplin. Chandler does not belong to either extreme: his comic vision is not so broad as Dickens', nor is his satire as bitter as Swift's. He is somewhere in between, an intellectual who was also a man of feeling. For that reason his character Marlowe is both a wit and a sentimentalist.

With all this, the pleasure of *The Long Goodbye* does not lie in its ideas but in the writing. Earlier, Chandler had explored a point that is relevant to his achievement in this book: "There is a great difference (to me at least) between a tragic ending and a miserably unhappy ending. You cannot write tragedy on the level of the suburban novel; you just get misery without the purging of high emotions. And naturally the quality of the emotions is a matter of projection, how it is done, what the total effect of style is. It's not a matter of dealing with heroic-sized people."

In *The Long Goodbye* Chandler was trying to stretch his muscles, to do something different because he wanted a change. Nevertheless, he was always alarmed by a new task. "No matter what he may have done in the past," he said of the writer, "what he is trying to do now makes him a boy again, however much skill in routine technical things he may have acquired, nothing will help him now but passion and humility." At the same time, Chandler knew what he had, or he wouldn't have been in the profession. He knew himself well enough to quote without false modesty what his English publisher thought of him: "To Jamie Hamilton I am not just a tough writer; I am the best there is in my line and the best there has ever been; I am tough only incidentally; substantially I am an original stylist with a very daring kind of imagination."

But what finally made *The Long Goodbye* work was Chandler's attitude toward writing. It flows through and colors all of his prose. He had to spend hours over errands in La Jolla, had to tend a desperately sick wife and then sit up late at night because he had insomnia. But to make up for all of this there was the pleasure of sitting down at his typewriter in the morning. He had heard of a writer who said he hated to write, and this attitude so astonished Chandler that he wrote a letter to Hamish Hamilton which perhaps better than anything else explains the achievement of *The Long Goodbye*: "But a writer who hates the actual writing, who gets no joy out of the creation of magic by words, to me is simply not a writer at all. The actual writing is what you live for. The rest is something you have to get through in order to arrive at the point. How can you hate the actual writing? What is there to hate about it? You might as well say that a man likes to chop wood or clean house and hates the sunshine or the night breeze or the nodding of flowers or the dew on the grass or the songs of birds. How can you hate the magic which makes a paragraph or a sentence or a line of dialogue or a description something in the nature of a new creation?"

10.
NOCTURNE

———◆———

Often after the end of World War II Chandler made plans to go to England. It had been nearly forty years since he lived there, and the passing time had converted him into an Anglophile. California also helped make him feel this way. "I still regard myself as an exile and want to come back," he told Hamish Hamilton in 1946. He liked English books and magazines and preserved such English traits as remained in his behavior without, however, being mannered or affected. He was especially impressed by English manners. He liked to illustrate their perfection by retelling a story told by the American critic Logan Pearsall Smith about how "by devious ways he secured an invitation to a country home which had a very old library he wished to search; how the old gentleman, his host, would wander around and occasionally peer in at the library windows while Smith was browsing; how he never entered the room; how Smith sat at meat with the family day after day and none ever enquired of him what he sought in the library; and how he departed leaving them as ignorant as when he came, a tribute to his breeding that only a wise man could have thought of."

Chandler's correspondence with Hamish Hamilton, the food parcels he sent to Hamilton and other members of his staff during and after the

war, kept him close to England, and in his nostalgia he virtually pictured
it as the new Jerusalem. Planning a trip in 1949, he wrote to Hamilton:
"I do not come to England as a visiting author, God forbid, but as a man
who loved England when his heart was young and has never loved in the
same way since, nor ever shall." He then recounted an anecdote to
illustrate his feelings. It was about a little hotel in Luxembourg. "The
atmosphere was cheerful, people from all the countries of Europe, almost, were there, having their ease. At two tables were English people,
only two. At one sat an elderly couple formerly well-to-do, now not so
well-to-do. At the other a demobbed tank officer with his mother. On all
the tables in the hotel dining room but these two were bottles of wine.
This is a true story. The English could not afford wine. Those who had
never surrendered drank water in order that those who had surrendered
might drink wine."

Despite this glowing vision, Chandler was dismayed by details.
"What gets me about going to England," he complained to Carl Brandt,
"is the awful mess of red tape, the reservations, the deadlines, the not
knowing where to go. (Certainly not the Dorchester, one might as well
stay at that stinkhole the Beverly Hills Hotel.)" In 1949 he wanted to
make a film in England, but Ray Stark was unable to make the arrangements, so he planned to pay his own way. He peppered Hamilton with
questions: "What clothes do I need of a special kind, if any? Do I need a
dinner jacket etc.?" The 1949 trip was finally canceled because of ill
health, and it was not until 1952, after many false starts, that Chandler
and Cissy actually set off for England. Originally, they planned to go on
one of the Cunard Line ships, but then he found out about direct
sailings from Los Angeles to London via the Panama Canal. This would
eliminate the need to stop and change in New York: "The only point of
an ocean journey is that you can't get off the boat, that you slowly and
horribly accustom yourself to a distasteful routine, and that after a
while you are surprised to find that it is not very distasteful at all. But
you certainly do not want the damn thing changed until you arrive at
your destination."

Living a reclusive life, Chandler knew nothing whatever about
travel arrangements. At the same time, he was anxious to have every
detail settled in advance so there would be no last-minute snags. This
meant an extensive correspondence with Roger Machell of Hamish
Hamilton about hotel accommodations in London and frequent phone
calls and letters to the travel agent about bookings. Even passports were
a strain. It is typical of Chandler's relationship to Cissy that they
obtained one passport between them, and the photograph shows as
drawn and haggard a couple as could be imagined. Chandler even
ordered food packages, including tins of ham and tea and three bottles

each of whiskey and gin, to be sent to himself at the hotel in London. Some of these were intended as gifts for his English correspondents, but he was taking no chances. He also made out a new will.

At length, Chandler and Cissy embarked on a Swedish motorship, the *Guyana* of the Johnson Line, on August 20. The ship sailed from Los Angeles via the canal and made stops at various Caribbean islands, for it was a combination freight and passenger vessel. The passage took about three weeks, and Chandler found the ship immaculate, noting that it was always being painted. "In fact I did very little but eat, read a lot of paper-back books and sleep," he wrote to a former school friend. The trip was not a complete success, however, because thinking only of tweeds for England, Cissy had neglected to bring any light clothes for the passage through Panama and the tropics; so they were forced to sit inside, where there was air conditioning.

They arrived at the Tilbury docks in the Thames toward the end of the first week in September. Roger Machell met them and drove them up to the West End, where they put up at the Connaught Hotel in Carlos Place, halfway between Berkeley and Grosvenor squares. Cissy was not well and that made Chandler worry about details. They were always nervous when not on home ground, and the strangeness of London troubled them. Shortly after they arrived, Cissy hurt her foot getting into a taxi. It was a bad bruise, but she tried not to fuss about it. Then they were invited to dinner by Hamish Hamilton and his wife. Hamilton casually mentioned that Chandler might wear a dinner jacket, and Chandler became greatly upset because he hadn't brought one. Hamilton immediately agreed that the evening should be informal, but then Cissy began to fear that she did not have a sufficiently elegant gown for the occasion. She and Chandler spent all afternoon traipsing up and down Bond Street, looking for something suitable, but nothing would do. An hour before the dinner was due to begin, Chandler rang up to say they couldn't come. Distressed at the potential loss of his guest of honor, Hamilton suggested that he come alone, but by now Chandler's nerves were so on edge that he refused decisively, saying that it was outrageous to think he would abandon his wife. So the dinner party took place without the Chandlers.

Hamilton already had misgivings about seeing Chandler in England: "I rather dreaded meeting Ray in London after a pen-palship of so many years. I'd heard from those who knew him that he was difficult, and unlike the friendly image I had built up in my mind. Fortunately all went well. He looked fiercer than I had expected, with his thin-lipped mouth, and habit of frowning and jutting out his lower lip, but one soon realised that these were mannerisms. The only trouble was that he was a bit lonely in London at first, and I unfortunately didn't have much spare time to talk and drink as he would have liked."

More successful was a dinner party arranged by the film critic Dilys Powell and her husband, Leonard Russell, the literary editor of the *Sunday Times*. The guests included Val Gielgud from the BBC and Nicolas Bentley, whose father's book, *Trent's Last Case*, Chandler had demolished in "The Simple Art of Murder." Dilys Powell has described the evening herself: "He came to dinner with his wife, with Cissy, who was a great deal older than he was. She was sweet, quiet, fluffy, and at her advanced age still fluffily blonde. He was obviously very proud of her. But we did find him at the beginning a little bit difficult and edgy. One felt that he felt he was being high-hatted in a way, and goodness knows, we were all really lying on the ground for him to walk over us, because we admired him so much. I remember at the end of the dinner, because it was in a way, a rather too formal party, I struggled to catch the eye of the chief woman guest who was Cissy, his wife. I couldn't catch it, and Ray, who was sitting next to me, suddenly rose to his feet and cried out. 'Cissy,' he said, 'you are about to behold one of the ancient English ceremonials.' He obviously thought the whole thing a stupendous joke. He was also extremely exasperated at having the women taken away from the men after dinner. He really thought very little of this."

Another occasion was a lunch given by J. B. Priestley in his flat in Albany, just off Piccadilly. Priestley had not seen much of Cissy in California because she had been ill at the time of his visit, so at the lunch, as he recalled, "I got an entirely wrong impression of her simply because I didn't know her real age, and she seemed to be a rather affected woman in her early sixties, quite pleasant and good conversation and so on, whereas of course as I learned afterwards, long afterwards, she was in point of fact at that time about eighty, and so a very gallant eighty indeed."

Fortunately, the visit was not all parties. Chandler was especially eager to meet some of the men in Hamish Hamilton's warehouse who packed up the books he frequently received from the firm. One of these was Arthur Vincent, known as "Vince," who was somewhat awed, as were the others, by Chandler's visit. Authors generally know only the editorial side of a publishing house, but Chandler was an exception. Soon he was getting on famously and went off with the warehousemen to a pub, where he was reintroduced to the game of darts. Arthur Vincent asked him, "Here, Ray, how the devil did you think of a bloke like Marlowe? Are you writing your perishing life?" Chandler replied, "Good heavens, Vince, no. I wish I had the pluck."

Another friend was Frank Francis, proprietor of the Piccadilly Bookshop, from whom Chandler later ordered many books. Francis later recalled the first of many visits: "He was short, very unassuming and very quiet, gentle. He introduced himself to me and then sat down, and after having got used to the idea that this was *the* Chandler we settled down for long conversations. I discovered that if Mr. Chandler liked you he insisted on being called by his Christian name, which was Ray, and if I addressed him as Mr. Chandler he really got furious. He used to sit down and watch and listen to people as they bought the odd book. And my shop being rather small, most of my customers I knew extremely well, and after they'd gone out he used to pass comment and I discovered he was a very keen observer and most accurate in judging a person's character."

Chandler and Francis would occasionally go to a pub, when Chandler would never consider ordering anything stronger than beer. He enjoyed being lionized and was grateful for the attention he received. On an English Sunday "gloomy enough for a crossing of the Styx," he sent a note to Paul Brooks of Houghton Mifflin saying: "In England I am an author. In the USA just a mystery writer. Can't tell you why." In America Chandler was well enough known to be invited to teach at the Harvard summer school, but he was not really a celebrity in either the United States or England. Nevertheless, he was certainly well known in English literary and intellectual circles. In 1949 Alistair Cooke had devoted one of his broadcasts from America to the hard-boiled school of detective fiction and ended it by prophesying that Chandler would "be remembered when lots of what we now regard as our literary giants are buried in the school books." In London Chandler was interviewed by the press, and although his nervousness sometimes made him a difficult subject, Cyril Ray noted in the *Sunday Times* that "only the young in heart could wear such a necktie."

The attention Chandler received also made him conscious that nobody was interested in Cissy. He became defensive and proud, and he resented any implication that there was something peculiar about his marriage. Yet some of his irritability undoubtedly stemmed from his concern for her and recognition of her special problems. Like many American tourists, they had predictable reactions: they thought the bar of the Connaught was as cold as an icebox; they found the food inedible, even at good hotels; prices they considered high and the goods offered, shoddy.

Chandler was nevertheless able to see one of his old Dulwich friends, William Townend, who came up to London for lunch; he also paid a visit to the Public Schools Club, of which he was an overseas member, just to have a look around. He was then sent a bill for a guinea,

which prompted a strong letter of complaint addressed to the secretary.
His meeting with Townend made him conscious of the difference between postwar England and the country he had known as a young man.
On the whole, he found it "a much more amiable and attractive place"
than he remembered. "The present generation of English people impressed
me very well," he wrote. "There is a touch of aggressiveness about the
working classes and the non-Public School types which I think is something new and which I personally do not find at all unpleasant, since it is
even more emphatic in this country. And the real Public School types, or
many of them, with their bird-like chirpings are becoming a little ridiculous, I thought." Eric Partridge, whom Chandler also met at this time,
having corresponded with him on the use of slang and the vernacular,
remembered that he spoke seriously about the future of society and that
he seemed well instructed in political and economic questions.

Before returning to America, Chandler had to be vaccinated, and
the reaction was so strong that he had to spend several days in bed.
Then, on his last day in London, he had to endure being photographed
for Hamish Hamilton's publicity department by a "Russian-Armenian
lady in the smock and the Apache style coiffeur." But these discomforts
were made up for by the unalloyed pleasure of meeting Roger Machell,
who more than his other new friends and acquaintances seemed to live
up to Chandler's idea of the English gentleman, the larger-than-life
figure he had been thinking about over the years. For Chandler, Machell
was "a cheerful, rather pudgy, light-hearted character with a droll sense
of humor and the sort of off-hand good manners which you rarely find
except in a genuine aristocrat. He is a great grandnephew of Queen
Victoria, he is the grandson of Prince Hohenlöhe, and his mother, Lady
Something or Other Machell, lives in St. James's Palace. Just why, I
don't know, because none of this information came from Machell himself. He was badly wounded in the war and made a joke about it. He
seemed to think it was characteristic that he should have been wounded
while telephoning London from a French pub. A bomb dropped on it and
blew a piece of a wall through his chest. It just missed killing him, but
he seems to show no ill effects now. He said he got a commission as a
major in some guards regiment, but he didn't know how, probably pure
luck or someone made a bad mistake. When he reported one morning to
a barracks in London in uniform he found them in the act of changing
the guard. He said he didn't know whether he was supposed to salute
the guard or if the guard was supposed to salute him, so he just sat in
his car outside until it was all over. He has the sort of humorous self-
deprecating manner which by sheer magic of personality is never overdone or posey or artificial. He lives handsomely in chambers in the old
Albany, drives a ramshackle old car, mixes perfectly awful Martinis in a

two-quart water pitcher (two of them would knock you out for a week) and took us on a wonderful tour of London, including the East End bombed-out district, making all the time such comments as 'Well, let's run down and take a look at the Tower, supposing I can find it' and 'Over there is St. Paul's or something of that sort.' He had us in giggles the whole time, yet he is in no sense of the word an intentional comedian. I claim that a man who can get away with this sort of thing and be perfectly natural about it is a bit of a genius."

Chandler's return to California via New York was an uninterrupted vexation, and his letters describing it reveal him at his most petulant, complaining about everything. "I didn't like the *Mauretania*," he wrote to Hamilton. "It wasn't a ship at all. It was just a damned floating hotel." The Cunard officials infuriated him by losing a suitcase he had placed in the hold and then producing it, after an hour and a half, without explanation. Cissy had to stand on the pier all this time, while Chandler fumed up and down in search of the case, and when no one took responsibility for the delay or apologized, he fired off an indignant letter to the company offices in London. Fortunately, the customs officials let them through without asking them to open their luggage.

In New York the Chandlers stayed for some days at the Hampshire House, which they also disliked. Ralph Barrow, an old friend who was formerly a lawyer in Los Angeles, came down to visit them from Old Chatham, New York. Dale Warren of Houghton Mifflin also arrived from Boston and had dinner with the Chandlers and two lunches afterward. They had never met, despite their lengthy correspondence, and Warren found the conversation an uphill struggle. There were silences that had to be filled. Chandler's shyness and irritability contributed to the awkwardness, and on returning to California he wrote Warren, attributing his own unsociability to a "subconscious reluctance to have anything to do with New York taxi drivers. Those that don't whine or bluster want to make a travelogue out of a ten-block ride." As for New York itself, it struck him as "a dirty, lawless, rude, hard-boiled place. It makes even Los Angeles seem fairly civilized."

The Chandlers returned to California by train, and the three-day journey was another nightmare. Cissy developed an infection on her bruised ankle, which Chandler ascribed to harsh train towels insufficiently rinsed of the detergents with which they were washed. Juanita Messick and her husband met the Chandlers at the station and took them home for dinner. She noted he was less an Anglophile than he had been before the trip. The illness and exhaustion forced them to ask Lavinia Brown, "Cissy's unfortunate sister," as Chandler described her, to come back and help straighten out their affairs, even though she had been living in the house during their absence.

After an interval to catch his breath, Chandler wrote to his friends in England to thank them for their many kindnesses. In his letter to Hamilton he summed up what the trip had meant to him: "Well, Jamie, let's face it. We loved London and we had a lovely time there. What little inconveniences we happened to have suffered were all due to our own inexperience and probably would not happen again. All your people were wonderful to me. It was really extremely touching. I am just not used to being treated with that much consideration. There are things I regret, such as losing several days over my vaccination, such as not going to any of the picture galleries, such as only seeing one rather poor play, such as not having dinner in your home. I spent too much time talking about myself, which I don't enjoy, and too little time listening to other people talk about themselves, which I do enjoy. I missed seeing something of the English countryside. And childish as it may sound, I missed very much not having hired a Rolls Royce and a driver for a day and driven to Oxford or Cambridge or some place like that. But all in all there was a hell of a lot I did not miss, and all of it good. And for that you above all others are to be thanked."

Chandler's gloom continued into the winter. He was worried about his revisions of *The Long Goodbye* and his wife's illness. As to the first, he told Hamilton: "It has always been clear to me that if the good Lord had intended me to be an important writer, he would not have allowed me to waste twenty of my years in offices. There are things about writing that I love, but it is a lonely and ungrateful profession and personally I'd much rather have been a barrister or even an actor." But for the moment Chandler was mainly troubled by Cissy's illness. Within a month of their return she had to enter a hospital. On her return Chandler wrote Hamilton that "she is pretty shattered and is still in bed. Very weak, very white, very frail. I have tried to work on the book and have made a little progress, but it's difficult to concentrate for any length of time and it's difficult to get enough sleep. Be as patient with me as you can."

Christmas celebrations were abandoned. Cissy's suffering brought out Chandler's gentle and sentimental side, which he expressed, for example, in the concluding words of a Christmas letter to Leonard Russell: "So may I now wish you and Dilys Powell whatever in this sad world remains of peace and happiness, such as red sunsets, the smell of roses after a summer rain, soft carpets in quiet rooms, firelight, and old friends."

Cissy's illness had been developing for some time, although no one seemed to know exactly what it was, probably some form of emphysema. Before the trip to England, she had been under treatment by a specialist in San Diego who operated a clinic. There she was X-rayed, examined, and given shots intended to reduce her suffering. Cissy loathed going to the clinic, so Chandler, who was always considerate, always with her when she was examined, suggested that Dr. Helming, their ordinary physician, give her treatments in La Jolla under the specialist's guidance. "For diagnostic purposes a clinic and a clinic specialist may be admirable," he wrote, "but what you get otherwise is a hard-boiled efficiency, a sense of hurry so marked that you practically have to grab your doctor by the sleeve in order to ask him a question. There is no warmth, no personal touch, no consideration, no feeling for the patient as an individual; or if there is such a feeling, it is not expressed."

Chandler probably knew that Cissy was incurably ill. She was in her eighties and there was no way to stop the ravages of her disease. "I have a sick wife who is not getting any better," he noted. All he could hope for was something that might reduce her pain. In the meantime, Chandler was himself constantly ill with one thing or another. "I am a worn, tired man," he wrote in a memo to his secretary. "I have lost my appetite and I have lost so much weight that I've had to punch two fresh holes in my belts. My clothes don't fit me any more." In response to an inquiry from Hardwick Moseley, he half snarled: "I'm sick as a dog, thank you, with one of these lousy virus infections the doctors have invented to cover up their ignorance."

Despite all these difficulties, Chandler had too strong a sense of humor to take the world entirely seriously. He sent memos to Juanita Messick about various things, one of them about the instructions that accompanied a new meat grill he had bought. "What drivel sales people do talk! Take cigarette advertising. Every favorite brand is milder and less irritating than every other. The ideal cigarette has no taste at all. Therefore why smoke? What we need for broiling is a non-spattering steak, a steak containing no grease, fat, or other injurious ingredients, and incidentally, no flavor. What we need is a steakless steak broiled on a heatless broiler in a non-existent stove and eaten by a toothless ghost."

Some of the cheerfulness was artificially induced. When Chandler returned to La Jolla in 1952, he announced that he had learned how to drink on the *Mauretania*. He had discovered the gimlet, a cocktail made with gin and Rose's lime juice. In the evenings before dinner Chandler and his wife would have a single gimlet and that would be all. It was the first time he had done any drinking in his own house for six years. Gradually, as Cissy grew weaker and the situation became more obvious, Chandler began to increase the amount he took. He told Juanita Messick that he would drink some champagne, just enough to blot out the pain of realizing that his wife's condition was fatal, but not enough to get drunk. She said she doubted he could do it, but for a considerable length of time he drank his way slowly through case after case of Mumm's champagne.

What really kept him going, however, was his work. His correspondence with Hamish Hamilton and Roger Machell reveals him in generally good spirits. He chaffed Machell about an interview of himself that had been arranged for publicity during his stay in London. As usual, he criticized the photograph. "The hands are obviously those of a strangler," he noted. "The physical description of Chandler is unrecognizable by anyone who knows him. He calls me small. What is his standard? I have hardly ever weighed less than twelve stone—is that small in England? I have often weighed almost 13 stone. Attired for the street I am an inch short of six feet. My nose is not sharp but blunt, the result of trying to tackle a man as he was kicking the ball. For an English nose it would hardly even be called prominent. Wispy hair like steel wool? Nuts. It is limp. Walks with a forward-leaning lope, huh? Chandler cantered gaily into the cocktail lounge, rapidly consumed three double gimlets and fell flat on his kisser, his steel wool hair curling gracefully against the pattern of the carpet. No wonder this man Forster thinks me observant. By his standards anyone who noticed how many walls the room had would be observant."

But the best thing was that his revisions were going well. On May 11, 1953, he told Hamilton that he was four-fifths of the way through his correction of *The Long Goodbye*, explaining that it was almost entirely new writing because of his inability to edit: "If it isn't right, I always have to start all over and rewrite it. It seems easier to me; it isn't easier I know, it just seems easier. Every now and again I get stuck on a chapter, and then I wonder why. But there's always a reason, and I have to wait for the reason to come to me." At the end of May he said the final script would be ready by mid-July, and he was good to his word. Certain minor corrections were necessary, adjustments in spelling and usage. Some of these are amusing. Chandler answered a query from Roger Machell that "bastardly bastard" was correct. "Perhaps I am thinking of a song which begins: 'A bastardly bastard from Bastardville.' Dastardly would be impermissible. It is what we call a two-dollar word and Marlowe would only use it tongue-in-cheek. It conveys a suggestion of pomposity, of Senatorial pseudo-dignity. I mean, to us it does that." In an effort to save time, Houghton Mifflin set the American edition of the book from Hamish Hamilton galleys, but when Chandler received the proofs, he was distressed to discover a number of errors: "What gets me down is the little things, the verbal carelessnesses, the unnecessary tautologies, the things said that had in mind some development that didn't work out. They make me look bad. You would probably answer that such things don't matter, that no one notices them. And in that I believe, or would believe, if you said so, that you were entirely wrong. People do notice. I do, why wouldn't others?"

Earlier, Hamilton had complained about the length of the book— 130,000 words—which he suggested might require a higher price. Chandler couldn't believe it was so long but conceded that it did come to 112,000. In defense he penned this characteristic reply: "A writer whose effects depend so much on by-play, whose concern with the action of a story is far less than his concern with the effect of it on his characters, a writer whose conviction it is that the best way to comment on large things is to comment on small things—such a writer (and I am now beginning to sound like a speech before the House) cannot be condensed to one third of his length without making him ridiculous. The story would be like a Caesar salad with no anchovies, no parmesan cheese and no garlic croutons. Or don't you have Caesar salad over there?"

At the end of 1953 The Long Goodbye was published in England, with a first printing of 25,000 copies, and received generally favorable notices. Chandler was especially pleased to be reviewed by Leonard Russell in the Sunday Times as a novelist and not merely as a detective-story writer and believed it was the first time this had ever happened to him. But he was also reviewed by detective fiction experts from whose genre he was trying to escape. "Maurice Richardson in the Observer annoyed me very much," he wrote of that paper's regular crime novel reviewer. "I was almost weak enough to write to him, but that is a losing game." In the United States, where the book was published in late March of 1954 with sales of about 15,000 copies, the reception was also favorable, although not up to Chandler's own conception of the book as a definite step forward. The reviewer for Time was aware that the book "crossed the border between good mystery and good novel," but the New Yorker snidely observed that a work which appeared to be about "nymphomania in exalted circles as much as anything else, hardly seems worth all the bother." Chandler was quite reconciled to the possibility of bad notices: "It is always a misfortune to be taken seriously in a field of writing where quality is not expected nor desired. The highbrows find it hard enough to forgive popularity, even moderate popularity such as mine, but popularity plus pretentions to any kind of literary distinction—that is too, too much. How they must have suffered over Maugham!"

Chandler was pleased and distracted by the attention and praise he received, but he was not blind to the realities of the world he lived in. During the week of his American publication, he passed on this bit of Californiana to Hardwick Moseley in Boston: "A family on the street behind us has a black French poodle, small, toy size, I guess. The animal is taking piano lessons, $35 a month. As of now he can play Peter, Peter Pumpkin eater, not technically very exacting, but one has to begin, n'est-ce pas? Little steps for little feet. Later on one hopes he'll make his debut in Carnegie Hall. The people can afford it and that's all it takes. It's nice to have ambitious neighbors, and to live in a milieu where money is spent on Art, not just on Cadillacs, Jaguars and colored butlers."

But beneath the surface good humor there was incurable trouble. Toward the end of 1953, with *The Long Goodbye* finished and no other large projects in the offing, Chandler wrote a long memorandum to Juanita Messick suggesting that he no longer needed a full-time secretary. Fortunately, she had come to the same conclusion and planned to become a teacher, so there were no hard feelings. In the course of his memorandum he spoke of Cissy's health: "Her heart seems to be getting more and more tired. She gets completely out of breath at the slightest exertion. That shows she's not taking in enough oxygen. I am pretty pessimistic, and I think I shall have to look for another doctor, because Helming is pessimistic too, although he tries to be kind. The mere fact that he is pessimistic and shows it is bad."

A month later Cissy was substantially worse: "It is 3.40 a.m. and if I sound a little goofy, I've had a hard night and I'm pretty tired. But for some reason I don't feel sleepy—just got a headache. Cissy has been very sick, and that is why I am awake at 3.40 a.m. The doctor only left about half an hour ago. The medicine she takes for her cough is very constipating, and from time to time she gets in bad trouble. This time she got in such bad trouble she was in agony."

In the early part of 1954 Chandler received a letter from James Fox, a younger mystery novelist he had known for some time who wished to dedicate one of his books to him. Shortly afterwards, they met for dinner in La Jolla, and Fox, who knew Europe well, suggested that the Chandlers move to the French Riviera, where they might find a suitable house and live at a favorable rate of exchange on a dollar income. Chandler was interested but he realized that Cissy's condition made it impossible: "One goes to a place in an adventurous spirit, takes what comes, and gradually finds out how to manage. But you can't do that when you have with you someone who must be protected from every possible kind of effort. For instance a short time ago we had some people here for a few hours. We liked them and my wife enjoyed having them. While they were here she seemed to be doing fine. But after they left she coughed for four hours. It wasn't anyone's fault; she didn't even know she was exhausting herself. She liked it. Just the same, four hours of coughing was the price of such an innocent evening." The situation made him feel trapped, and more and more he resented La Jolla. "The whole of California is very much what someone said of Switzerland: un beau pays mal habité."

Then, in May, Chandler received a different report: "My wife has just got through with a lung specialist in San Diego who came to the conclusion that there was nothing the matter with her lungs, that she did not have bronchitis or any abnormal amount of scar tissue and that her cough was probably a heart condition." Chandler presumed the diagnosis was honest since it cost the doctor a patient, but it meant starting all over again, visiting the Scripps Clinic in La Jolla and perhaps even a specialist in Los Angeles. "God, what a runaround these croakers give you!" he wrote. "One inch of professional protocol means more to them than a mile of human life. If they don't know what's the matter with you, they will go to any lengths to prevent your finding out, and they will pass you from hand to hand with bright smiles until you die of old age or exhaustion." Through much of the summer Cissy was extremely ill, taken in and out of hospitals, and Chandler could not resist an ironic comment about a doctor who could not diagnose her illness: "Perhaps she doesn't have a cough. Perhaps we are both just imagining it." Her last days are best described by Chandler himself. "You probably realized when we were in London that Cissy was in rather frail health," he wrote to Hamilton. "When we got back she looked and felt better than she had in a couple of years, but it didn't last. She had an obscure and rather rare ailment I am told called fibrosis of the lungs. I don't think they know very much about it or what causes it. It's a slow hardening of the lung tissue, starting at the bottom of the lungs and progressing upwards. The part that is fibrosed returns no oxygen to the blood, which of course puts more strain on the heart and the breathing." Chandler described the doctors they consulted for two years, the treatments they tried: cortisone injections, ACTH, even African snakeroot. Cissy was in and out of hospitals, there were nurses at all times, and her sister, Vinnie, came to stay. By December 7, 1954, Chandler knew she was dying: "In the middle of the night she suddenly appeared in my room in her pyjamas looking like a ghost, having evaded the nurse somehow. We got her back in bed and she tried it once more, but this time the nurse was watching. At three a.m. on the morning of December 8th her temperature was so low that the nurse got frightened and called the doctor, and once more the ambulance came and took her off to the hospital. She couldn't sleep and I knew it took a lot of stuff to put her under, so I would take her sleeping pills and she would tie them in the corner of her handkerchief so that she could swallow them surreptitiously when the nurse was out of the room. She was in an oxygen tent all the time, but she kept pulling it away so that she could hold my

hand. She was quite vague in her mind about some things, but almost
too desperately clear about others. Once she asked me where we lived,
what town we lived in, and then asked me to describe the house. She
didn't seem to know what it looked like. Then she would turn her head
away and when I was no longer in her line of vision, she seemed to
forget all about me. Whenever I went to see her she would reach her
handkerchief out under the edge of the oxygen tent for me to give her
the sleeping pills. I began to be worried about this and confessed to the
doctor, and he said she was getting much stronger medicine than any
sleeping pills. On the 11th when I went to see her I had none and she
reached out under the edge of the oxygen tent with the handkerchief,
and when I had nothing to give her she turned her head away and said,
'Is this the way you wanted it?' About noon that day the doctor called
me up and said I had better come over and talk to her as it might be the
last chance I would have. When I got there he was trying to find veins in
her feet to inject demerol. What an irony that I should have written
about demerol in my last book! He managed to get her asleep, but she
was wide awake again that night. That is she seemed to be wide awake,
but I'm not even sure that she knew me. She went to sleep again while I
was there. A little after noon on December 12th, which was a Sunday,
the nurse called up and said she was very low, which is about as drastic
a statement as a nurse ever makes. Vinnie's son was here then with
Vinnie, and he drove me over to the hospital at fifty miles an hour,
breaking all the traffic regulations, which I told him to ignore as the La
Jolla cops were friends of mine. When I got there they had taken the
oxygen tent away and she was lying with her eyes half open. Another
doctor had his stethoscope over her heart and was listening. After a
while he stepped back and nodded. I closed her eyes and kissed her and
went away.

"Of course in a sense I had said goodbye to her long ago. In fact,
many times during the past two years in the middle of the night I had
realized that it was only a question of time until I lost her. But that is
not the same thing as having it happen. Saying goodbye to your loved
one in your mind is not the same thing as closing her eyes and knowing
they will never open again. But I was glad that she died. To think of this
proud, fearless bird caged in a room in some rotten sanitarium for the
rest of her days was such an unbearable thought that I could hardly face
it at all. I didn't really break until after the funeral, partly because I was
in shock and partly because I had to hold her sister together. I am
sleeping in her room. I thought I couldn't face that, and then I thought
that if the room were empty it would just be haunted, and every time I
went past the door I would have the horrors, and the only thing was for
me to come in here and fill it up with my junk and make it look the kind

of mess I'm used to living in. It was the right decision. Her clothes are all around me, but they are in closets or hidden away in drawers. I have a couple of very old friends staying with me, and they are patient and kind beyond any expectation. But the horrors are all mine just the same. For thirty years, ten months and four days, she was the light of my life, my whole ambition. Anything else I did was just the fire for her to warm her hands at. That is all there is to say."

This letter was written in the first week of January 1955. It illustrates Chandler's extraordinary ability to touch the nerve, to say what is never said, by leaving out none of the important details. In the meantime, he had to cope. Not knowing what to do about the funeral, he consulted Juanita Messick, who suggested a service in one of the small chapels of St. James's Episcopal Church. She recommended a chapel because the Chandlers knew so few people in La Jolla. Chandler agreed but insisted that the funeral be held in the main church. It was a trying and gruesome occasion, and in order to get through it, Chandler took a great deal to drink. Cissy's coffin—open and surrounded by hundreds of flowers—was placed in the nave of the church. About eight people were present. Vinnie and her son were there, as were Juanita Messick and Jonathan Latimer. Stuart Palmer, another friend, drove down from Hollywood with James Fox. Somehow, they got through the service, and afterward Cissy's body was taken off in a hearse. It was cremated, and her ashes were placed in a vault in the Cyprus View Mausoleum in San Diego.

Chandler did not go to the mausoleum because he was too drunk; also, for him, it was all over. In this way he snapped his fingers at death. "I am one of those who do not believe in personal immortality, since I see no need for it," he later wrote. "God probably finds something to preserve, but what I don't know. He might find even in me, a sensual, sardonic, cynical man, some essence worth preserving, but I don't think it is anything I could recognize. So much of us is external, environmental, caused by our experiences here on earth, so little of us is pure and undiluted."

But at the moment there was just emptiness. After the funeral the small group went to Chandler's house and drank a lot. All Chandler wanted was to blot out reality. It was an Irish wake, except that it lacked catharsis: the drink didn't get them through the experience; it just numbed them. Chandler tried to give Stuart Palmer the cat he had bought to replace Taki. It was just another sign of his loss and melancholy.

In due course Vinnie left, and he was joined for a time by his former "business manager," S. Stapleton Tyler, and his wife. Chandler's emotional mechanism allowed him to appear quite resilient and he could even talk about his condition with some objectivity. When the Tylers left, Vinnie came back to keep him company. "I try not to think too much about Cissy," he wrote to Hamilton. "Late at night when people have gone to bed and the house is still and it is difficult to read I hear light steps rustling on the carpet and I see a gentle smile hovering at the edge of the lamplight and I hear a voice calling me by a pet name. Then I go to the pantry and mix a stiff brandy and soda and try to think of something else." He got out some of his poetry but found it too sad to read, especially at night. During the day he also recognized its quality, which he termed "Grade B Georgian." He spent a good deal of time making plans to return to England. But he had bad moments as well, which he described to Roger Machell: "For instance I sit up half the night playing records when I have the blues and can't get drunk enough to feel better. My nights are pretty awful. And they don't get any better. I've been alone since Saturday morning when Vinnie went home. Alone except for Mabel the Marble, my Pennsylvania Dutch cook and house-keeper. She has a lot of fine qualities, but she is not much company.

"Tomorrow is or would have been our thirty-first wedding anniver-sary. I'm going to fill the house with red roses and have a friend in to drink champagne, which we always did. A useless and probably foolish gesture because my lost love is so utterly lost and I have no belief in any after life. But just the same I shall do it. All us tough guys are hopeless sentimentalists."

The sentimentalism alternated with fits of depression and self-pity. He withdrew more and more, staying in Cissy's room and hardly ever leaving it. He was drinking heavily, whiskey this time. Vinnie returned to stay with him, but it didn't do much good. Only two days before planning his anniversary celebration he phoned his friend Bruce Weston, a captain on the La Jolla police force, to tell him that if he didn't come quickly, he would find a corpse on the floor. It was the third time he had made the threat since Cissy's death. Once he even phoned Roger Machell in London, but when he got through he fell into a silence punctuated by the operator's annoyed instructions: "Speak up, Cali-fornia. You're through to London now. Speak up, California."

Then on the afternoon of February 22, a fortnight after the abor-tive anniversary celebration, he phoned Bruce Weston once again, say-ing that he intended to shoot himself. While he was on the phone, Juanita Messick came into the house and overheard part of what he was saying. When he finished, he asked whether she had heard the conversa-tion. She told him she had and that he was being silly. She persuaded him to put on his dressing gown and go into the living room to watch some television while she went to the kitchen to make some coffee. While there, she saw a police car coming down the hill, so she opened the back door and signaled that it was all right. She then went back to the living room and found it empty. Then to the bedroom, and the dressing room that led to the bathroom. No Chandler. Then she heard a shot. At this point she ran to the front door to catch the police before they left. Then another shot went off

A very tender rookie cop entered the house and with considerable trepidation opened the bathroom door. There was Chandler standing in the tub with the shower curtain drawn around him. He had a .38 revolver in his hand and looked rather shamefaced. There was a bullet hole in the ceiling. The police put him in bed, and then the sergeant decided that he had to be sent to the psychiatric ward of the county hospital. The committal form was completed, and Chandler, still in his pajamas and dressing gown, was led down the front stairs to the police car. He was still quite drunk, though now looking rather jaunty and pleased with himself as he was driven off in the back seat of the car. The official report stated that he was dazed and incoherent, unresponsive to questions by the police.

Chandler's own account of the episode differs only in detail: "I couldn't for the life of me tell you whether I really intended to go through with it or whether my subconscious was putting on a cheap dramatic performance. The first shot went off without my intending it to. I had never fired the gun and the trigger pull was so light that I barely touched it to get my hand in position when off she went and the bullet ricocheted around the tile walls of the shower and went up through the ceiling. It could just as easily have ricochoted into my stomach. The charge seemed to me to be very weak. This was borne out when the second shot (the business) didn't fire at all. The cartridges were about five years old and in this climate I guess the charge had decomposed. At that point I blacked out. The police officer who came in then told me later that I was sitting on the floor of the shower trying to get the gun into my mouth, and then when he asked me to give him the gun I just laughed and handed it to him. I haven't the slightest recollection of this. And I don't know whether or not it is an emotional defect that I have absolutely no sense of guilt or embarrassment at meeting people in La Jolla who all knew what had happened. It was on the radio here, on the wire services, in papers all over the country, and I had letters from all over the place, some kind and sympathetic, some scolding, some silly beyond belief."

The extraordinary press reception may have been gratifying later on, but in the meantime Chandler was in the county hospital. Fortunately, Neil Morgan, a young friend who was a newspaperman on the *San Diego Tribune*, had a hunch that Chandler needed help, and on the way to work the next morning he stopped at the hospital and found

Chandler there, looking very miserable and ashamed. Asked how he felt, he answered, "I feel like a bath and some decent coffee." Morgan arranged for his release on the proviso that he be committed to a private sanitarium under the care of a doctor. He then took him to a hospital in Chula Vista, near the Mexican border below San Diego, which was noted for drying out patients who drank too much. Chandler found it somewhat more difficult to get out of this place. "I stuck it for six days," he later wrote, "and then I got the feeling I was being strung along with half-promises. At this point I announced that I was going to discharge myself. Upheaval. This simply wasn't done. All right, I said, Tell me the law that keeps me here. There wasn't any and he [the clinic psychiatrist] knew it. So finally he conceded that I could leave any time I wished but would I come to his office and talk to him. I said I would, not because I expected any good from it, but because it would make his case record look better, and in addition, if he was perfectly frank with me, I might be able to help him."

This account has a touch of bravado that doesn't ring true, but Chandler had little patience for what he called "psychiatric claptrap" and portrayed psychiatric hospitals in his novels with little respect. He phoned Neil Morgan to ask him to fetch him, and when he left, as he later wrote, "the head nurse kissed me and said I was the politest, the most considerate and cooperative and most resilient patient they had ever had there, and God help any doctor who tried to make me do anything I wasn't convinced I ought to do." When he reached home, he somewhat rashly invited Morgan in for a drink and then telephoned the real estate agent to say that he would sell the house to the first buyer that came along.

The death of Chandler's wife and his own attempted suicide were among the most emotionally depleting events of his life. He had struggled to complete his most ambitious book, knowing all the time that his wife was dying "by half-inches." Then she died and he was completely alone. His life was empty in every respect, and the future seemed completely without purpose. For a long time he was inconsolable, drifting along from day to day on the edge of despair. "I have received much sympathy and kindness and many letters," he wrote Leonard Russell, "but yours is somehow unique in that it speaks of the beauty that is lost rather than condoling with the comparatively useless life that continues on. She was everything you say and more. She was the beat of my heart for thirty years. She was the music heard faintly at the edge of sound. It was my great and now useless regret that I never wrote anything really worth her attention, no book that I could dedicate to her. I planned it, I thought of it, but I never wrote it. Perhaps I couldn't have written it."

Within a few weeks Chandler managed to sell the house overlook-

ing the sea at Camino de la Costa. It was not easy: "Yesterday I finished
the rather agonizing business of getting the furniture out of my house
and closing it for the new buyer. When I walked through the empty
rooms checking the windows and so on I felt a little like the last man on
a dead world." His furniture was put into storage, while his books went
into boxes and were placed in the garage of Mrs. Marge Suman, the
person in his accountant's office who actually looked after his affairs. It
was typical that a man without friends among fellow writers was helped
by the ordinary people of La Jolla who had no artistic pretensions and
who were most generous in time of need.

During these last days in La Jolla he stayed at the Del Charro
Motel, which is simple and agreeable, and then took the train to Chicago, with the intention of continuing on to see his friend Ralph Barrow
in Old Chatham, New York, before sailing to England. In Chicago he
was met by Vincent Starrett, the journalist, and had lunch with him and
his wife. Chandler was still wobbly; his fingers were splitting again,
requiring him to wear gloves, and when he reached Old Chatham he
began to be affected by sinus problems. Nevertheless, he was in good
spirits. "The weather up until today has been lousy and I loved it," he
reported to Hardwick Moseley. "After the endless calm of Southern
California what a joy to slither through snow and feel a biting wind."
He was also impressed by his host's establishment. "Around here they
have estates," he wrote Neil Morgan. "This one is over a hundred acres
of overgrown farmland. The last owner was a rich woman who didn't
farm and in the twenty years she lived here trees grew all over hell. We
have brooks and waterfalls and frozen pools and snow. I am up to my
eyebrows in Early American, Cape Cod, Georgian, Revolutionary, Dutch
and what looks to me like Mint Julep. At any rate it has the wide
pillared porches.

"I don't know how long I will last. Yesterday we went into
Chatham (there are about six Chathams, so be very careful with the
OLD) to get the laundry from the laundromat. The man carried it out to
the car, and seeing that I was somewhat old and feeble, said: 'Thank
you, Mr. Barrow.' I said (always too fast with the answer): 'Oh, I'm not
Mr. Barrow. I'm just her lover.' He didn't turn a hair, but wait until the
local postmistress gets the lowdown. They will either drag me behind a
chariot or shoot me with an arbalest."

His sinus continued to bother him, so he went to New York for
treatment. He first stayed at the Waldorf and was enraged by its prices.
"This town is the clip joint of the universe," he wrote to Roger Machell,
explaining that he'd had to pay three dollars for a pot of coffee in his
room. Alone again, he began to drink. Soon he was in the New York

Hospital for a series of sinus tests and also for drying-out purposes. On his release he moved to the Grosvenor Hotel at 35 Fifth Avenue, which he much preferred to the impersonal grandeur of the large hotels uptown. Waiting around for the *Mauratania* to sail got on his nerves, for aside from Dorothy Gardiner, the secretary of the Mystery Writers of America and only an acquaintance, he really had no friends. He was now a world celebrity with his books translated into a dozen languages including Japanese, but there was nobody he knew well enough in New York to phone up.

It was a melancholic moment, for returning to England meant having to start a new life alone. He had survived two crises but was still shaky. So much of his life was now over that he needed courage even to consider the future. Often he despaired. Drinking alone in the Grosvenor, he phoned Ralph Barrow and Juanita Messick to tell them he was going to jump out of his hotel window. Somehow, they kept him talking until someone from the hotel went up to his room and put him to bed.

The next day he would be all right, for such crises always cleared the air. He even began to like New York. It was still a tough town, "but it has magic as well," he wrote to a friend in California. He tried to cheer himself up with the prospect of finishing a new book, *Playback*. Fortunately, with an income that ranged from about $15,000 to $25,000 a year—all royalties and subsidiary income from books already written—he was well off. In his will he even made a provision to set up a prize for the best detective novel of the year, under the supervision of Hamish Hamilton and Ralph Barrow.

So he fluctuated in mood during this struggle for survival before sailing to England. He was torn by what was happening to him, but he also wanted to record what he loved in a fitting way. A month after Cissy's death, Chandler wrote a poem called "Requiem" which captures a different mood and reflects a certain strength that helped him ward off despair:

> *There is a moment after death when the face is beautiful*
> *When the soft tired eyes are closed and the pain is over,*
> *And the long, long innocence of love comes gently in*
> *For a moment more in quiet to hover.*
>
> *There is a moment after death, yet hardly a moment*
> *When the bright clothes hang in the scented closet*
> *And the lost dream fades and slowly fades,*
> *When the silver bottles and the glass, and the empty mirror,*
> *And the three long hairs in a brush and a folded kerchief,*

And the fresh made bed and the fresh, plump pillows
On which no head will lie
Are all that is left of the long wild dream.

But there are always the letters.

I hold them in my hand, tied with green ribbon
Neatly and firmly by the soft, strong fingers of love.
The letters will not die.
They will wait and wait for the stranger to come and read them.
He will come slowly out of the mists of time and change,
He will come slowly, diffidently, down the years,
He will cut the ribbon and spread the letters apart,
And carefully, carefully read them page by page.

And the long, long innocence of love will come softly in
Like a butterfly through an open window in summer,
For a moment more in quiet to hover.
But the stranger will never know. The dream will be over.
The stranger will be I.

11.
ONCE
IN
A WHILE
FOREVER

————◆————

On April 12, 1955, occupying a single First-Class cabin on the *Maure-tania*, Chandler sailed for Southampton. It was a brave gesture for a man who detested loneliness yet found it difficult to be at ease with strangers. So much depends on chance in a transatlantic crossing: it can be invigorating or wearisome, depending on the weather and one's table companions. Fortunately, Chandler was seated with Jessica Tyndale, the American representative of the English banking firm of Guinness Mahon. She was a capable and understanding woman, and an agreeable companion, someone he could look after and spoil a little, as he always enjoyed doing. The trip was unremarkable for Chandler except that while on board he received word that he had been awarded an Edgar by the Mystery Writers of America, who had judged *The Long Goodbye* as the best mystery novel of the year. To celebrate, he gave a little party for his table mates. Later, from London, he sent a characteristic cable: "Naturally, I am deeply appreciative of the Edgar as the climax of a fairly long and shady career which has, at least, proved to me that the best of our work, however slighted at first, will be read, enjoyed, and even in extreme cases, be critically acclaimed long after most of the so-called 'important' books have become one with ten-year-old telephone directories. I love you all and, as we say in London, 'Thank you so very much.' "

Arriving at Southampton on April 19, he was already in the role he played off and on for the rest of his life. Roger Machell had offered to pick him up at the ship, but Chandler sent him a mysterious-sounding telegram: "Don't meet. Have woman with much luggage." He made going up to London on the boat train a kind of adventure; he looked after Jessica Tyndale's comforts and needs and was a solicitous companion and guide. But when he arrived at the Connaught, which he liked, his mood began to change. He recalled being there three years before with Cissy and he told a reporter from the *Daily Sketch* that there he and Cissy had spent "the happiest week of our lives after the war. But I don't sleep more than four hours a night. Often not at all. There are ghosts. Memories that keep me awake. I get up and dress, wander round the old haunts. Trying to recall our wonderful time together. Remembering. Life has lost something."

In going to London, Chandler hoped he would find a new life, but once he got there, he felt so lonely he didn't care what happened to him. He began to slip and to numb his sensibilities with drink. Yet he never kept his misery to himself. Perhaps he was aware of the therapeutic value of talk for those suffering from loss, for he was extraordinarily open, even with newspaper reporters he had never met before. Patrick Doncaster interviewed him for the *Daily Mirror*, although the piece was never published because of a newspaper strike. They talked about Hollywood girls, and then Doncaster changed the subject:

" 'Mrs. Chandler,' I said gently.

"He put down his gimlet, a gin and lime drink you associate with pukka sahibs and outposts of Empire rather than a Hollywood thriller writer whose chief character swigs Scotch.

" 'What about Mrs. Chandler?' he said edgily. 'She's dead. Died last year.' He looked away across the bar. He twitched a little, jumpy. Then something choked in his throat.

" 'I've not got over it yet,' he said quietly. And a big tear rolled down his cheek."

Ian Fleming, who met him later, remembered that "he was very nice to me and said he liked my first book, *Casino Royale*, but he really didn't want to talk about anything much except the loss of his wife, about which he expressed himself with a nakedness that embarrassed me while endearing him to me. He showed me a photograph of her—a good-looking woman sitting in the sun somewhere."

Driven to despair by his solitude, Chandler repeatedly threatened suicide. In hopes of lessening his unhappiness, Hamish Hamilton and his wife, Yvonne, gave a luncheon party in his honor. There he met a number of literary people who, as usual, made him feel ill at ease. One of the guests, Natasha Spender, Stephen Spender's wife, who is thought by her friends to be a warm and compassionate person, saw that he was having a miserable time and, in hopes of cheering him up, invited him for dinner the following week. This was the beginning of an extended friendship between the two as well as an introduction to the Spenders' circle of acquaintances. At the time, Stephen Spender was editor of *Encounter*, and he knew many writers in London. To the dinner party they gave for Chandler at their house in St. John's Wood the Spenders invited a number of young people who might amuse him. One of these, Jocelyn Rickards, recalls that she and Chandler hit it off immediately because of their mutual distaste for pretentious literary conversations.

At first, the attention Chandler received rather bewildered him, and he wrote a country-boy letter to Hamish Hamilton about the Spenders' party: "The whole thing last night was rather weird. Natasha Spender is a charming and devoted hostess and served up a magnificent meal and everybody got tight. They poured it on me a little too thick, I imagine." In his confusion Chandler admitted, "I never got the names straightened out except for a little dark girl with a very affected voice (to my ears only perhaps) who wrote her name in my pocket diary, invited herself to lunch and made it fairly clear that she was open to almost any kind of proposition. A man drove me back and she cuddled up to me and said that she had been living with him for the past 12 years, but had stopped sleeping with him five years ago. I haven't the faintest idea what this is all about, but I couldn't keep her from coming to lunch." Chandler also spoke of "Sonia somebody" who said that "I was the darling of the British intellectuals and all the poets raved about me and that Edith Sitwell sat up in bed (probably looking like Henry the IVth, Part 3) and read my stuff with passion. They said that Connolly had written a piece about me which was considered a classic. The funny part of it was that they seemed quite sincere. I tried to explain to them that I was just a beat-up pulp writer and that in the USA I ranked slightly above a mulatto."

The Sonia referred to, Sonia Orwell, recalls that the dinner was a jolly affair with lots of laughter. The guests all admired Chandler extravagantly and also considered him very picturesque. If he couldn't understand them, they found his American accent and slang very colorful. It was an additional attraction, like his dapper clothes—the somewhat light-colored California suits that he wore with yellow gloves—which appealed to their English love of eccentricity.

Gradually he began to change. A curious side effect of a feeling of loss can be a sense of heightened potential, and given a pretty girl with no axe to grind, Chandler came into his own. He himself uttered the jokes and wisecracks that formerly appeared only in his books. No longer having to be defensive about Cissy or himself, he became increasingly extroverted. Dilys Powell recalls that one evening after rising from the table at a dinner party in her house, he suddenly flung his arms around her and cried out, "Well, when do we get down to the serious necking?" He enjoyed being lionized and gradually began to relax. "You go to luncheon with eight people and next day five of them invite you to a dinner party," he wrote. "So dine, drink and drab is about all you do." Even his appearance had changed. The thin pipe-smoking recluse of earlier years had filled out, and in good form he looked like a very distinguished man of affairs, a silver-haired celebrity with style.

When he was in a good mood, he was gay and jolly. He especially enjoyed taking his "girl friends" to lunch. They were all thirty years or so younger than himself, and it helped his ego to be seen with a pretty girl in a good restaurant. He found out which the best ones were—the White Tower, Boulestin's, the Café Royal, the Connaught and the Ritz—and he visited them often enough to be known and recognized, which he enjoyed. At several he even opened an account. Sometimes he would be so witty in restaurants that people at neighboring tables would stop talking just to listen to him crack jokes. Helga Greene, who was the daughter of the chairman of the Guinness Mahon bank, and who first met Chandler through Jessica Tyndale, said that "he was the best company in the world, and he got the best out of you. Other friends have told me they didn't know they could be so witty as when they were with him. He was so stimulating, and he had himself such an immense amount of charm."

But as always with Chandler, there was another side that had to be expressed and as Natasha Spender says, "he alternated quite wildly between exuberance and depression." The girls he took to lunch did not simply go for their own pleasure. They knew that at heart he was sad and suffering. They therefore formed what Nastasha Spender called a "shuttle service" to make sure he was not neglected. The idea was, as Jocelyn Rickards recalls, "to keep him socially engaged as he was such an old gentleman that he would never dream of standing one up for lunch because death seemed preferable." Natasha Spender hoped that their attention would "see him through to a point where he would want to go on living" and "reverse the process of slowly killing himself with drink." One member of this group, Alison Hooper, recalls that they would "take turns to keep him company at crucial hours—such as mealtimes when the idea was to get him to eat at least something, since like many alcoholics he tended to starve. There was a lunch hour patrol, a drinks-and-dinner shift—even on occasions a dawn watch." If he was drinking a lot, he could be very trying, and at first his friends didn't know what to do with him. Chandler had a way of getting under people's skins; when he formed a friendship, he intended it to be a two-way affair, and was therefore often demanding. Alison Hooper remembers him as "a lost soul who drew out a Nannie-response from women through his helplessness even when it was tinged with his own particular brand of sardonic humour." Often when he was overtired and depressed he would telephone his friends in the middle of the night and ask them to come and see him. If they objected, he would become querulous and provoking and say something like, "Then you don't care what happens to me?" or "Is that all our friendship means to you?" Remembering his generosity and gaiety in better times, they would come to his side.

The strain became intolerable, but the more he got to know his "girl friends" the better they learned how to cope with what several have called his "emotional blackmail." Once Jocelyn Rickards visited him on an afternoon and found him lounging about in bed with a bottle of Ballantine's whiskey. She was irritated at finding him in this state and scolded him, telling him he was a hopeless case. She said she wouldn't have anything more to do with him and then slammed out of the room and went home. Shortly afterward, for she lived nearby, the phone rang, and there was Chandler. "No one has ever spoken to me like that in all my life," he said plaintively. "More's the pity," she answered. "Then you wouldn't be where you are now." There was a pause and Chandler said, "I know I'm bad, but you know it's 'tiny steps for tiny feet.'" She laughed and the tension evaporated. Almost always Chandler knew what he was doing and had the frankness to admit it.

The strain of so much activity took its toll on Chandler. Unused to a social life in California, he began to fall apart. He drank too much and became forgetful and irritable. J. B. Priestley invited him for dinner as guest of honor, and he never showed up. When chided about it, he replied: "In a situation like this all one can do is grovel, if one feels guilty or not." He said he had not understood that "the party was arranged around me. It just never occurred to me at all that way." To discourage further invitations, he added: "I'm dull at parties now as I drink nothing but water and soda. My liver started turning me yellow." At about the same time, he was also invited to a dinner in his honor by Eric Ambler and his wife, with the other guests including Noel Coward and Somerset Maugham. Once again, Chandler failed to appear. He invited Ambler to lunch in order to apologize and explained that he was unreliable in engagements of this sort. The inevitable result was that he was invited to fewer and fewer parties. Chandler the celebrity ceased to be someone to celebrate. The problem arose through a combination of nerves and drink. Knowing he had to meet prominent people, he would try to calm his anxiety by having a couple of whiskeys. By the time he was supposed to be at the party, he was no longer capable of going to it. He was much better at spur-of-the-moment affairs, which he could accept without the initial terror. His mistrust of intellectual conversation and fear of being patronized were also to blame. But Chandler's child-like helplessness, always worsened by drinking, was mainly due to his loneliness and grief. What made him suffer most was his occasional clear-eyed awareness that he was betraying his own code of gentlemanly behavior. This increased his despair.

From time to time he would try to pull himself together. At the insistence of his friends, he consulted doctors and underwent hospital tests. He tried to stop drinking but, as Natasha Spender recalls, the cures "he always undertook with courage—sometimes very dramatised courage" were usually short-lived. He ignored the advice of his physicians and they, in turn, refused to offer further treatment.

Fortunately for his sanity, Chandler was distracted by his public life. He was frequently interviewed by the press and found, as he wrote the detective novelist Hillary Waugh, that he was regarded not as a mere mystery writer "but as an American novelist of some importance. People —well-bred English people—come to me in this rather exclusive hotel and thank me for the pleasure my books have given them. I don't think somehow we shall ever reach that status in America." He had become friendly with Ian Fleming, since they were both somewhat out of the highbrow literary swim, and he reviewed Fleming's latest novel, *Moonraker*, for the *Sunday Times*. He was delighted when the *Daily Express* ran a public opinion poll to find out who the most popular authors, movie stars, artists and entertainers were, according to highbrow, middlebrow and lowbrow tastes. "Marilyn Monroe and I," he wrote with obvious pleasure, "were the only ones that made all three brows."

During the summer of 1955 Chandler also became involved in a heated public controversy. He wrote a letter to the *Evening Standard*, protesting the imminent hanging of Ruth Ellis, a condemned murderess. There was no doubt she was guilty, but Chandler's Galahad instincts were offended by "the idea that a highly civilised people should put a rope around the neck of Ruth Ellis and drop her through a trap and break her neck." He did not quarrel with the official court judgment, but the "medieval savagery of the law" struck him as being obscene. The letter was published at a time of considerable public outcry over capital punishment, and many other prominent persons, including Members of Parliament, wrote in support of Chandler's position. But it was all to no purpose, and the unfortunately named Dr. Charity Taylor, governor of

Holloway Prison, carried out the sentence and Ruth Ellis was hanged in July.

Within a month of his arrival in England, Chandler was thrown out of the Connaught for having a woman in his room, and after this humiliation he moved to the Ritz. But the transient nature of hotel life didn't suit him. With the help of Helga Greene and Alison Hooper, he obtained a flat at 116 Eaton Square. It was across the way from Jocelyn Rickards and a few hundred yards from Ian Fleming. Helga Greene, who also lived around the corner, was divorced and had just started a literary agency. Learning that Chandler had no representative, she was eager to get him on her list.

The move to Eaton Square did not fundamentally change his life, but he enjoyed the settled feeling of having a flat and was pleased with the elegance of the long square with its gardens and the colonnaded doorways of the houses facing the street. Yet even here Chandler could find drama. Coming home one night, as he told his friends, he was knocked on his head and had his money stolen. No one believed his story, although it was admired as an ingenious way to explain a bruise that had probably been caused by falling down while drinking. Chandler enjoyed such stories: sometimes he would persist and even elaborate on them; he was also capable of admitting they were fantasies if contradicted.

"I don't think you would recognise me if you saw me now," he wrote to Neil Morgan shortly after the move. "I have become so damned refined that at times I loathe myself. Mostly I run around with the St. John's Wood–Chelsea literary-artistic crowd, and perhaps they are a little special. Of course I know some cockneys too, but the people I do run around with have expressions of their own which need translating. For instance: 'I simply adore her' means 'I'd stick a knife in her back if she had a back.' 'They are absolutely and utterly precious' means 'What rubbish, but that woman never did have any taste.' 'I'd rather care for that' means 'Give it to me quick.' And 'I'm simply impossibly in love with him' means 'He has enough money to pay for the drinks.'

"It has been a wonderful spring, the squares flaming with the most gorgeous tulips three and even four feet high. Kew Gardens is a paradise of green and color, rhododendrons, azaleas, amaryllis, flowering trees of every kind. It catches you by the throat after the hard dusty green of California. The shops are beautifully dressed and full of all kinds of wonderful things. Harrods is easily the finest department store in the world. Nothing in New York or Los Angeles can equal it.

"But the women! If they ever had buck teeth I don't see them now. I've seen glamour girls at parties that would stun Hollywood. And they are so damned honest they won't even let you pay their taxi fares. If you know them well enough you can give them the money privately, but you can't give it to the driver. If you want them to go to bed with you, you have to say 'please' five times. They expect to be treated as ladies. They are perfectly willing to sleep with you if they like you and if you treat them with deference, because in a country where women outnumber men so excessively that is almost inevitable, but they don't want to be treated as easy lays. They want you to work up to it slowly and fastidiously, and I certainly think they're right."

After his wife's death, Chandler's sexual life underwent a change. In the last years in La Jolla, his physical urges were buried under an avalanche of other concerns. Cissy's death destroyed a sense of security, but it also made him feel that he had sexual opportunities such as he had not enjoyed in years. By the time he arrived in England, he had only his own inhibitions to deal with. In an interview for the *Daily Express*, while commenting on Marlowe's relationship to Linda Loring in *The Long Goodbye*, he said that "the affair he had, I'd like myself." Doubtless his drinking interfered with his prowess and he was ill so often that sex was simply not an issue. Nevertheless, he appreciated the benefits of English life: "In the artistic society of London about one man in three is a homosexual, which is very hard on the ladies but not at all hard on me."

For Chandler, England in the 1950s was a good country to live in because it was free of the puritanical attitudes toward sex that pervaded America. Chandler was aware of a kind of parallel change in himself when he noted that "I smoked a pipe from morning to night when my wife was alive and I loved it. I used to drink a great deal of tea, and my wife loved that, just as she loved to see me smoking a pipe." After her death Chandler never smoked a pipe, although he continued to drink tea. What he wanted was a new relationship to replace the old that would give him intense feelings in both a physical and domestic form.

England seemed to offer everything and yet nothing. He had his "girl friends" but no single one to cherish. Also, he suffered from realizing how often he fell below his ideal of gentlemanly behavior. This made him try to make up for it in other ways. Always generous, he gave presents to those who had been kind to him. He sent bunches of roses, sprays of orchids, jewelry, silk stockings by the dozen and even money to those he liked. His giving probably helped him believe in his own usefulness: instead of feeling suicidal and purposeless, he began to think of himself as someone necessary to those in need. The role he adopted required a certain amount of fantasizing, because he had to invent for his "girl friends" pathetic circumstances requiring his attention. According to Natasha Spender, "in his mind, we all became characters in a

Raymond Chandler novel." He created for himself the sort of problem he formerly had Marlowe solve in the books. Chandler's self-deception was a sign of his illness, for as his novels show, he had a clear eye for the realities of life. But he was also a romantic, and this side of his nature now became dominant in his life.

Naturally, he could not be a Galahad for everyone, so he became increasingly concerned for Natasha Spender. He seems to have imagined, for example, that she was a failure as a musician. "This is not true," she writes, "I was at that time conducting quite a successful career as a concert pianist." For him, she was nevertheless a lady in distress. Meanwhile she appears to have been unaware of the role she was playing in his imagination. "Of course it was touching of him to worry," she writes, "but *we* were all worried about him."

The friendship was at once deluded and heroic. On one occasion Natasha Spender had to give a concert with an orchestra in Bournemouth but did not mention it to Chandler because she thought he was too ill to go. He found out about it, however, and getting out of his sick bed, he put on full evening dress and hired a car to go down to Bournemouth and drive her home afterwards. The mayor and town officials had arranged a reception and supper at one of the spa hotels, and there Chandler appeared, looking like a ghost. He was quite drunk, and when he approached the table all he said was, "I've come to take you home!" He was persuaded to sit down and then at the end of the supper, he and Natasha Spender went out to the Rolls Royce whose back seat was filled with flowers and ice buckets full of champagne. They set off for London, stopping from time to time to drink the champagne. On the way down, Chandler had become friendly with the driver and so insisted that he drink some champagne as well. As they drove through the night, Chandler unexpectedly grew more and more sober. At one point, in the midst of his extraordinary gesture of the car and the flowers and the champagne, he turned to Natasha Spender and said, "I know what you are all doing for me, and I thank you for it, but the truth is I really want to die." He spoke without any touch of self-pity.

When he wanted to, Chandler could see himself clearly. He balanced his sentimentalism with a cold, unsparing eye. More than once he told the story of "the fellow who wanted to take his bride to see the little lake near Saint Cloud with the swans on it that he remembered so vividly from a childhood in France. It was to be one of the highlights of their honeymoon. When they arrived there and established the location—no lake, no swans. There never had been a lake there and there never had been any swans."

During the summer of 1955 Chandler continued to see Natasha

Spender and often took her to lunch at his favorite restaurants Then he discovered she was ill. Since Chandler was also recuperating from a hospital cure they decided, with Stephen Spender's approval, to go to Italy together for a rest and change. They stayed at a small hotel on the side of Lake Garda and visited Venice and Verona as well. To keep him occupied so that he would not start drinking again, Natasha Spender took him sightseeing, but Chandler wasn't much of a tourist and showed little interest in ruins and buildings. "I preferred to sit at the Caffè Dante in Verona and drink Caffè gela con latte, which is iced coffee with frozen cream."

By the end of September Chandler's English residential permit expired, so he returned to New York on the *Queen Elizabeth*. He was upset at having to leave, and his drinking had made him weak and unstable. He described his fellow First-Class passengers as "a lot of fat American businessmen and a few English equally repulsive. The usual frightfully overdressed women with a different fur every night, a sprinkling of likeable people one didn't have any reason for approaching." He was withdrawn and grumpy. "I sit in a corner alone with my back protected on both sides. I once said good morning to a passenger, but it was an accident—I was thinking of something else."

What made the trip exceptionally trying was that Chandler was still on a cure, and crossing the Atlantic without drinking is no pleasure. The only humorous moment on the trip Chandler invented for the person who had sent him a dozen roses for his cabin: "I wore one in my buttonhole and was almost immediately accosted by a charming old gentleman." After docking in New York Chandler went to stay with the Barrows in Old Chatham. The months in England had heightened his sensibilities and now, like many returning Americans, he found his native country crude and disagreeable. The weather was so cold he told Roger Machell: "I feel like one of those poor guys the Nazis used to put in ice baths to see how much the human organism could stand. I have to melt my whiskers before I can shave." He went to a horse show and found it graceless. The male riders "looked chunked and unlithe." Their coats were "too damned red" and to Chandler "it all seemed like a nouveau riche attempt to do something that wasn't in the blood." It is clear he was not enjoying himself: "I miss everybody very much—even the people I didn't like."

After leaving Old Chatham, he returned to New York for a cocktail party given in his honor by the Mystery Writers of America. By November 3 he was back in La Jolla, staying at the Del Charro and smoking Craven A cigarettes out of nostalgia for London. "Am I comfortable?" he asked Helga Greene. "No. Am I happy? No. Am I weak, depressed, no good, and of no social value to the community? Yes.

Outside my room is an illuminated swimming pool. Phooey on it!"
Meanwhile, he had been worried by unfavorable reports about Natasha
Spender's health. He decided therefore to return to England and booked
a flight via Scandinavian Airlines. Just before leaving, he wrote a charming note to his friend Neil Morgan, who was about to get married. It
reflects the jauntiness he must have felt at the prospect of returning to
London:

> On the eve of my departure into regions where Eskimos starve
> and the polar bears wear mittens and goloshes and are still dis-
> satisfied (Anybody ever see a polar bear that really liked anybody?),
> and on the eve of your dive into marriage with a lovely girl—I'm not
> sure dive was the word I wanted—may I wish for you the kind of
> magic that Maeterlinck's donkey could hear; the roses opening,
> the grass growing and the day after tomorrow coming. May I
> wish for you the kind of magic vision that birds have, such as on
> a morning after rain seeing a worm make love to its other end.
> (This joke was stolen from me and somehow finally got to Groucho).
> May I wish for you the knowledge (I'm getting a little heavy-handed
> here) that Marriages do not Take Place, they are made by hand;
> that there is always a moment of discipline involved, that however
> perfect the honeymoon, the time will come, however brief it is,
> when you will wish she would fall downstairs and break a leg. That
> goes for her too. But the mood will pass, if you give it time. Here
> are a few words of sound advice. I know.
>
> 1. Ride her on a short rein and never let her think she is riding
> you.
> 2. If the coffee is lousy, don't say so, just throw it on the floor.
> 3. Don't let her change the arrangement of the furniture more
> than once a year.
> 4. Don't have any joint bank accounts unless she puts in the
> money.
> 5. In case of a quarrel, remember it is always your fault.
> 6. Keep her away from antique shops.
> 7. Never praise her girl friends very much.
> 8. Above all never forget that a marriage is in one way very
> much like a newspaper. It has to be made fresh every damn day
> of every damn year.

On a Friday night in late November Chandler flew from San Diego
to Los Angeles, and from there over the North Pole to Denmark, where
the following morning he changed to a BEA flight to London. Arduous
as flying was, Chandler preferred it to the long days at sea. On his

arrival at the Connaught, he found that Natasha Spender had to undergo an operation. After consulting Stephen Spender, he immediately suggested a trip to Madrid and Tangier to help build up her strength. The Spenders thought the rest would benefit Chandler as well, for as usual, he was drinking too much. Once underway, Chandler found himself talking several languages at once: "The Spaniards are stupid and unwilling to learn," he noted with some querulousness. "French gets you anywhere, English and Italian mostly just draw blank looks. German they never heard of. The Arabs are far brainier than the Spaniards, but you get tired of them, there are so many." Chandler was never an enthusiastic tourist.

From Tangier they went up into the mountains: "Chauen is wonderful for climate—it's about the only place in Europe or North Africa where you can be sure of being able to sunbathe in the middle of the day. It's about the same elevation as Big Bear, but flowery and green and a new hotel stands on the edge of a drop into a lovely valley." But except for a trip to Tetuán, they spent most of their time in Tangier, which Chandler found charming—"clean, well-policed, with a climate even better than California's." He was especially impressed that because it was an international city, Tangier had no income tax. Once or twice they visited the Honourable David Herbert, a younger brother of the Earl of Pembroke, who lived in the hills behind the city. "He is very witty and amusing," Chandler wrote, "and has those extraordinary manners which don't exist anywhere but in real English bluebloods. That is, he seems to have no manners at all or none that show. He said that when his grandfather died in the night he was quite small and knew nothing about it until the next morning when their nanny came into the nursery and said to the children: 'Good morning, my Lord. Good morning, my Lady. Good morning, Master David.' Whereupon David burst into tears because he was the only one of the three who hadn't stepped up a rank."

After a fortnight's rest they returned to London, where Natasha Spender successfully underwent her operation. Meanwhile, Chandler's chronic drinking, abetted by his concern for Natasha Spender and his own continuing depression, brought on a fresh relapse. One night shortly before Christmas, the hotel doctor was summoned after midnight, and Chandler was taken by ambulance to the London Clinic. After a fortnight of tests and relative quiet, he was released, and it was announced that he had a form of malaria. "All my vomiting fits, chills, fever, forty-eight hour flu, etc. were explained," Chandler wrote. His case was relatively mild, he said, but the disease was a nuisance "because in between the attacks you feel perfectly or almost perfectly all right; hence you don't link them up. You think each one has a separate cause."

Chandler's recuperative powers were given a boost by his belief in the usefulness of his help to Natasha Spender. His ebullience poured over into a general appreciation of London, even in January, when it is dark by four in the afternoon. "I walked all the way up Bond Street to Oxford and then along to Tottenham Court Road, and then I took the tube back to Green Park, a slight step from the Ritz," he wrote to James Fox. "Strange, but I had never been in a tube since I was a young man in London. Only once have I been in a bus. But it's just damn silly to go everywhere in a taxi as I have been doing, especially in a city with such a magnificent transport system. It cost me tuppence to get here from Tottenham Court Road and Oxford Street. It would have cost with tip about five bob in a taxi."

Chandler's experiment with the London Underground coincided with a realization that he should live more economically than before. With the guidance of the Spenders, he took a small flat in a house at 49 Carlton Hill in St. John's Wood, N.W.8. The house was just off the Abbey Road and only a few hundred yards from the Spenders in Loudoun Road. To those who know London well and have a car, St. John's Wood is quiet and charming. But aside from being near the Spenders, it was wholly unsuitable for Chandler. He hated his "beastly flat" and thought that the place had "no class." The Spender family, including the children, brought him meals and sat up with him at bad times, but Chandler's health remained poor. He knew the real cause, however, for at the time he wrote that "all that is really wrong with me is that I have no home, and no one to care for in a home, if I had one."

His yearning for a center to his life and his deluded hope that Natasha Spender might share it with him became increasingly frustrating. She would remind him of her devotion as a wife and mother, but Chandler would dismiss her views as so much humbug. Mrs. Spender writes that "it made him feel very anxious and 'threatened' if he realised that there was opposition to his own rigid and idiosyncratic moral code, which was then energetically used to destroy the realities of other people's, with accusation of 'sham,' 'hypocrisy,' 'snobbery' or whatever." She believes that his loneliness and fear of being deserted made him test the devotion of others by acting in a difficult manner. "You once called me a 'passionate moralist' and it was a happy phrase, because that is what I think I am," he later wrote to another friend. "I am scrupulous in my own code, but I don't give a damn about bourgeois hypocritical morality." This stance was convenient, for Mrs. Spender remembers that he was quite capable of exploiting her own arguments and saying, with an air of triumph, that since she believed in Christian charity, she was therefore committed to looking after him. Chandler's hectoring was just part of his nature, but he was also capable of being completely disarming: when Natasha Spender told him she thought that most people acquire their neuroses during their childhood, he answered: "I don't know about that. I pick mine up as I go along." He was not an easy person to argue with.

Beneath it all, Chandler was imprisoned by a passion that made him impatient of anything but a complete relationship. He dreamed of a romantic fulfillment, union with the girl with the cornflower blue eyes. All along—and this was his torture—he knew it could never happen. Nevertheless, it remained the central vision of his life.

Inevitably, the situation in Carlton Hill deteriorated. Chandler's hopes and fantasies collided with Stephen and Natasha Spender's view of their relationship. He reacted violently against his earlier willingness to be thought of as one of the family.

In time he began to detest the sort of dinner party he had formerly enjoyed. "London is wonderful up to a point," he wrote, "but I get very tired of the bitchy women who are all darling, darling, darling when they meet you, but have an assortment of little knives for your back." Homosexuals were often invited to the parties he attended, and then Chandler would bristle, looking at them with the "ugly, Hapsburg lip grimaces" that Ian Fleming described. "My reaction to them may be uncharitable," Chandler admitted; "they just make me sick. I can't help it." On another occasion he explained his dislike of homosexuality on the ground that it was a reminder of "our own normal vices" which in their own way "fill us at times with the same sort of revulsion." But what troubled him most was his own behavior. "Dissimulation is too difficult and too wearing," he wrote. "That fine adjustment of behavior which permits one to be in the same room with the woman you adore, others being present, and to be neither too affectionate and familiar nor too quiet and remote to avoid the other, is just too subtle a decorum for me."

Chandler was often so ill and out of control that his social involvements and discussions of morality were wholly unreal. Gradually he acknowledged the uselessness of his infatuation. "I'll never forget," he later wrote about Natasha Spender, "her devotion to me when I needed it most, and she will never know that when I got drunk in London, especially in Carlton Hill, it wasn't because I wanted to get drunk, but because I knew I was in a hopeless situation, and just didn't give a damn what I did, if only I could for a little while forget how hopeless it was."

This painful state was ended when Chandler was once again forced to leave the country. He had already overstayed the legal amount of time allowed him in England for 1955, and was to pay heavily for it in taxes, but he could not afford a similar financial blow in 1956. He therefore flew from London to New York on May 11 via BOAC. This was the time when sleeping berths were still provided, and Chandler got one, although he said it was meant for a midget. Then there was the usual horror of customs. "God, what barbarians," he observed. "Surely no country in this world can be more distressing to get into." Jessica Tyndale met him with a car at the airport and took him to the Grosvenor Hotel. "I could hardly wait to close the door before ordering a bottle of Scotch and some ice," he wrote.

It was an ominous sign. His experiences in England and his rude return to America had taken a great deal out of him. Although he probably did not realize it, he was in a decline that before long was to prove irreversible, despite moments of relative stability. In New York he saw a good deal of Jessica Tyndale and her husband, although he was bored with talk about politics and kept wishing he were back in London. "I tried not to talk about England," he wrote, "although I wanted to. One can get to be an awful bore that way." He then went up to Old Chatham to visit the Barrows, but as he noted, "after the alert, lively minds of the English people I know, they seemed torpid." Hardwick Moseley from Houghton Mifflin was also present with his wife. Chandler drank a great deal and began to resent the "ingrown, self-sufficient life" of the Barrows, which he himself lacked. He refused to eat anything and sat for much of the day in a stupor. Finally, he fell downstairs, and it was decided he would have to leave. The Moseleys drove him to New York and left him with Jessica Tyndale. Two days later he was taken by ambulance to New York Hospital. He was so ill he was given blood transfusions for sixteen hours. The diagnosis of malaria was abandoned. "What was the matter with me—and has been for a long time—was a total mental, physical and emotional exhaustion masked by my drinking enough whiskey to keep me on my feet, and then a severe malnutrition," he wrote to Neil Morgan. The hospital put him on a high-protein diet, and by the fifth day he was well. "I felt happy, absolutely happy, for the first time since my wife died. All the rest has been play-acting. This was genuine and the mood has not changed." He explained what had happened in greater detail to Helga Greene: "It was as though some Authority had looked down on me and decided: 'This man has had enough, endured enough, failed enough, but always loved too much. He is not going to have any more trouble. He is not even going to have to fight.' A strange, almost mystical experience and not at all in my line."

Once out of the hospital he went to the Grosvenor for a few days of further recuperation: "I haven't a damn thing to do but write letters, read, take a taxi or bus uptown and potter about a bit, or just go for a walk through the Village, which always fascinates me with its quaint houses, little culs-de-sac, iron railings painted in odd colors, innumerable hidden restaurants, and the people themselves, the way they dress and the look they have of belonging to another world from uptown New York." He visited Brentano's and had lunch with his French editor, Marcel Duhamel of Gallimard, who happened to be in town.

By mid-June he was in La Jolla at the Del Charro and within a short time took an apartment at 6925 Neptune Place. Not far from his former house, it was on the beach overlooking the Pacific and was one of a set of apartments arranged around a courtyard. There were two bedrooms, but its main attraction was a storeroom where he could put his papers when he was away. He took some of his furniture out of storage and tried to make a selection from his library. "Dear God," he wrote, "what on earth shall I do with books that overflowed a large house? I guess you have to be ruthless with possessions."

Chandler was still bored and homesick for London. "I'm not anti-American," he said, "but there just isn't any life here for people like me." The worst thing was dining out alone. "Four days a week I have someone to go with, but the other three are hell." He went to a few parties, but they were no help. "I am already sick to death of skins like burnt orange and smiles like gashes. I am sick of people who never put a glass down and cocktails where no one (but me) can sit down. Alas, not all my country is hopelessly vulgar, but this part of it certainly is."

All too soon he was back again at the same Chula Vista clinic Neil Morgan had taken him to in 1955. He was difficult about going, but Juanita Messick persuaded him that it was necessary and drove him there. He insisted on having a bottle with him in the car and was furious when he discovered he couldn't take it into the sanitarium. By mid-July he was released and took a trip to San Francisco to visit Louise Landis Loughner, a woman who had written him a charming letter after he had attempted suicide. Chandler kept a box full of fan letters from women, and when he discovered Mrs. Loughner's telephone number, he got in touch with her. Once again, he found himself involved with a woman he imagined to be in trouble, but he was not strong enough to be an effective Galahad. He suffered yet another bout of drinking and this time went to a hospital in Pasadena. After his release he continued to see Mrs. Loughner, and in October he told his lawyer that he wished to change his will in her favor because he intended to marry her. The foundation for this marriage seems to have been singularly feeble, however, for after a weekend together in November, it was all over. "I can't stand quarrels," Chandler explained. "I don't quarrel myself; they say it takes two. It doesn't. I'm very sorry and very lonely, but I know the same sort of thing would happen periodically."

Chandler's break with Mrs. Loughner only briefly preceded Natasha Spender's arrival in America. On a tour with concerts in Boston and Washington, she accepted Chandler's invitation to visit him. They agreed to meet in Arizona, and presumably as a joke, they went to Chandler, which is outside of Phoenix, where they stayed for some time at the Hotel San Marcos. When she first arrived, Mrs. Spender seemed to Chandler to be tired and jumpy, while she, in turn, was worried by his continued drinking. The desert air was healing for them both, however, and Chandler reported that she was "quite insatiable as a sightseer" and said that he had "driven all over Arizona with her, mountains, desert and every other damn thing." By December 20 they were in Palm Springs and stayed there through Christmas. Early in January Chandler went to Los Angeles, where Natasha Spender was staying with old friends of hers, Professor and Mrs. Edward Hooker of the University of California. They all dined together twice, and on one occasion, the other guests were Gerald Heard and Christopher Isherwood. Chandler wrote that he liked Isherwood and felt at ease with him, but Isherwood's memory is that the occasion was tense because of Chandler's dislike of homosexuals. Chandler said he was amused by Gerald Heard, although he disliked his tendency to pontificate: "Americans generally seem to be quite content to be lectured at for a whole evening. I resent it, no matter how clever the talk is." Natasha Spender sometimes chided Chandler for being rude, but he didn't think that being blunt was reprehensible: "I think people are extremely rude when they carry on a very private and intimate conversation (I call it 'the Derek-Peter-Nigel routine') which excludes another guest who may also, and it has happened to me, be the guest of honor. You cannot interrupt these people, because they constantly interrupt one another and someone is always talking." Unfortunately a few days after the party Professor Hooker suddenly died, so Chandler invited Mrs. Hooker to Palm Springs for a few days' rest after the memorial service.

On January 26, 1957, Natasha Spender left for Los Angeles in order to see Mrs. Hooker and Isherwood again before going to New York. Chandler was disappointed that she wouldn't spend her remaining days in California with him, but on her last night in Palm Springs he took her to an elegant restaurant and made a great fuss over the occasion. Natasha Spender's visit to California had revived his old desires, but by now he realized that his hopes were groundless, and that there had never been a question of a close relationship with her. Nevertheless, he acknowledged once again his indebtedness and wrote: "I do absolutely feel that I owe her an enormous gratitude for making life bearable to me again."

He was sad and bitter by turns. Feeling that he was "still the out-sider, always available, never essential," he tried to work out his position. Even while acknowledging that Natasha Spender's help was altruistic—"you would have done the same for anyone in deep trouble," he wrote—he still felt disillusioned. "London for me will be forever haunted by a lost love. But I think it was never a true love. I was just bedazzled by something happening to me so suddenly, when I had more or less given up the idea of anything ever happening to me except an eternity of sor-row." But Chandler still felt impelled to make a gesture. In June, he there-fore asked his London solicitor, Michael Gilbert, to deliver to Natasha Spender what he said was "in the nature of a farewell letter to her." It did not make him happy, but it cleared his mind: "Most people adapt themselves to the situations life has imposed on them. I happen to be the eternal rebel. Perhaps it is the Irish blood in me. At any rate, impossible as I can be, my soul is my own, and I keep it clean."

During the first years after Cissy's death, Chandler tried to keep working, but he had neither the conviction nor the tranquillity to com-plete anything substantial. His stay in England had made him conscious of the differences between British and American English, and he wanted to write something with an English setting. He was particularly keen to do a play. In order to test his ear for English dialogue, he wrote a series of short sketches which were all episodes in what he called "A Routine to Shock the Neighbors"—a title that derives from what Natasha Spender calls his "virtuoso improvisations at luncheons at the Con-naught" which did indeed titillate those at neighboring tables. Chandler also called them "Pornographic Sketches," since several of them dealt with sex. He would send them around to various of his friends such as Dilys Powell and Helga Greene and ask them to tell him where he had gone wrong. Here is the opening of one called "Faster, Slower, Neither," whose theme is self-evident:

> "Well, really, much as one hates to interrupt at a time like this, isn't the tempo—well, one might possibly say a bit adagio?"
>
> "I'm most frightfully sorry. I didn't know you had to catch a train. Do you rather want it presto agitato?"
>
> "Darling, it's not that at all. Well—how does one usually ex-press it?"
>
> "Usually one doesn't. My mistake, of course. Terribly sorry again. I had the notion that as it was such a beastly rainy afternoon, one might possibly spend a few quiet hours—"
>
> "Darling, I simply adore that too. But do they have to be as quiet as this?"

"By quiet, I suppose you mean slow."

"Darling, isn't that slightly a crude word at this time? I meant only that one could spend the hours delightfully—but would they have to be devoted to one performance? Theatres have matinees, occasionally, I'm told."

"I have been so very stupid. Please try to forgive me. (Pause.) Could that be in the slightest degree better, or—or—?"

"Oh, much better darling. I'm afraid—oh, couldn't you please an occasional pause rather spices the—"

"Conversation, I expect you were about to say. I gather you mean presto ma non agitato?"

"Exactly, darling, and you are so understanding. And darling, and—oh—oh—darling!"

"Yes, darling?"

"Oh—darling—darling—darling—please don't speak!"

"Not a word."

"Oh, darling, darling, DARLING—please don't speak."

"I'm not. You're doing all the talking." [and so on]

By the beginning of 1957 Chandler was feeling well enough to ask Hardwick Moseley for books about playwriting because he specifically wanted to write for the English stage. "There are about 40 active theatres there," he explained, "and they don't have to be sold out six months in advance in order to give a play a chance." He also wanted to write an English novel, "not as a tour de force, but as a writer perfectly at home with the nuances of British English and yet ambitious to make it come a little more alive." He wanted to make use of his "pornographic sketches" in a substantial work. "If you think we and the upper-middle and upper-class English speak the same language, you couldn't be more wrong," he said.

By chance, in a box put away in his storeroom, Chandler found a story he has written twenty years earlier. It was the story he had mentioned in his literary plan of 1939 as the draft of a book he would write after becoming established as a mystery novelist. It was called "English Summer" and he decided to work it over in the hope that it might become the basis for a novel or play. It is about an American who thinks he is in love with a refined and apparently sexless English lady who is married to a hopeless drunk. The American visits them in the country, and one day while out on a walk he meets and is soon seduced by a woman with a voracious sexual appetite. When he gets back, he finds that the apparently frigid lady has killed her husband in order to make herself available to the American, and she lets him know it, counting on his natural chivalry to protect her. The American has no illusions, but he doesn't think he can desert her. "He has, according to his code and mine," Chandler explained, "incurred an obligation, and we Americans are a sentimental and romantic sort of people, often wrong of course, but when we have that feeling we are willing to destroy ourselves rather than let someone down."

Chandler's own comments are enough to show the limitations of the story, but whatever his intentions the original draft reads like a spoof of the Gothic tale. The situation is absurdly melodramatic, with the golden-haired girl sitting with a tea tray in her flower garden being compared to the black-haired seductress who rides a stallion called Romeo and lives in a half-ruined castle on an island. The story has a serious theme, suggesting that men will always be exploited, whether the predatory female is gentle and well mannered or violent and passionate, but it doesn't hold up as literature. Nevertheless, it shows how Chandler really felt about what happened to him after Cissy's death. He never expanded the story into a novel or play because he probably realized that it was impossibly exaggerated.

In the meantime, he planned to resurrect the novel that was based on his screenplay called *Playback*. He had written about half of it in 1953 but put it aside to finish *The Long Goodbye*. For a long time he couldn't summon up the spirit to go on. "I don't know how many times I have taken the Marlowe story out and looked at it and put it away again with a sigh, knowing all too well that my heart was too sad to let me capture the mood of gusto and impudence which is essential to that sort of writing. Perhaps you can help me out of it," he wrote to Helga Greene. By now Chandler had overcome his initial dislike of mixing business and personal friendships and had engaged Helga Greene as his literary agent. She naturally encouraged him in his work. Her support was essential, because after Natasha Spender's departure he fell into a depression and began drinking once again. By mid-August he was in the sanitarium, this time with a broken wrist as well as the need to be dried out. He discussed his drinking with his physician, Dr. Whitelaw Birss, who told him that he was "one of the most highly-strung and emotional people he ever met, that alcohol can never give me any real relaxation because my mind operates mostly on the subconscious level, which alcohol can't reach, while it merely irritates the emotions it can reach."

His nervousness was a product of the anxiety that had obsessed him ever since his wife's death. It arose from a frustrated sex drive—a masculine impulse—that lies at the heart of romanticism. With some bravura he wrote to Michael Gilbert, "Thank God I can still copulate like a man of thirty." But his life had become a series of unfulfilled quests. "I haven't had a woman since ages ago," he wrote Helga Greene in 1957. "Perhaps, as the years dump their refuse on me, the time will come when I don't need one. It hasn't come yet and it makes me pretty damn nervous at times." Not long afterwards, he took up the theme again: "Surely you understand that the older I get, the more desperately I long for the presence of someone I love, to hold her and touch her and fondle her and that nothing else is any good at all. No number of letters, however loving, can add up to one long clinging kiss." Yet there was the inevitable other side: "I am no boudoir mechanic. There are men who can live like that, who can take the occasional sexual gratification, stolen from another man as a rule but not always, and be smugly content. Just as there are men who can keep mistresses in snug little flats. But to me there is always a whorish flavour about this sort of life. What a man wants and needs, and surely a woman too, is the feeling of a loving presence in a home, the intangible and ineffable sense that a life is shared."

On his release from the nursing home, Chandler was still depressed, almost totally without hope for an improvement in his condition. "Something in me has died or gone to sleep for a while," he wrote to Helga Greene. "I hope the latter. It has nothing to do with you. I have just been hurt too bloody much, but I'll get over it. I don't blame anyone or anything, except myself. But when I think what I was when Cissy died and what I am now, much more than three years has happened to me. Is this too introspective? You're damn right it is. In fact, it is disgustingly morbid. But I'm sure I'll snap out of it, and welcome you with open arms."

Alarmed by his condition, even though she was ill herself, Helga Greene had by this time promised to visit him during the late autumn. Her arrival worked like a tonic. Originally, he had promised Houghton Mifflin that he would complete the book by April 1, 1958, but with Helga Greene at hand, work went on much more rapidly than expected. In early December he wrote Hamish Hamilton that the book was "now going very well, mostly due to Helga's stimulating influence. She was with me in La Jolla from Nov. 11th to the 20th and then we came to Palm Springs for the warmth and sunshine, and she left for New York on the 28th. She has a terrific intelligence. One day at lunch and for about an hour afterwards we spitballed the idea and plot and motivation and characters and sets of an entire play. (In case you don't know the meaning of this slang term, it means free improvisation. The idea is not to care how silly your suggestions may be, because in the end something useful will almost always emerge.'"

Helga Greene's influence strengthened his own determination, and he finished *Playback* by the end of December, three months ahead of schedule. "By getting up at 6 a.m. and working ten hours straight with no food but coffee and Scotch I finished the Marlowe book," he wrote to

Paul Brooks at Houghton Mifflin. "Haven't gone over it yet but I think it will stand up."

Helga Greene had cheered Chandler up enormously, and her spirit began to pervade his whole life: "With Helga around I feel as though I could write anything—sonnets, love poems, idiocies, plays, novels, even cookbooks. What on earth happened between this rather cool, aloof woman and me? Something very strange." When they first met in London and she brought him flowers and fresh eggs after a weekend in the country, he found her "very cold," but in California she seemed utterly different. "She is so easy to get along with," he wrote, "and while she was here in Palm Springs she was so even tempered and unexacting and such fun to talk to and dance with." Chandler evidently wanted to place Helga Greene on a pedestal. He pictured her as a badly hurt and lonely woman who was too shy to speak of the sufferings that afflicted her after her divorce from Hugh Greene. But the image wouldn't stick: she just wasn't as pathetic as he made her out to be. She was a very energetic and efficient literary agent, the mother of two sons whose upbringing engrossed her and, as the daughter of a rich banker, hardly in need of financial support. She wasn't someone he could help very much. Her great value to Chandler was that she was far more honest and considerate than a number of the women he became involved with. Chandler knew this instinctively, but as his life gradually unwound, like a ball of string losing its shape, he became increasingly unreliable in his relationships. He was mistrustful and skittish, as older people often are, both wanting and not wanting to be looked after. Despite this instability, Chandler recognized Helga Greene's qualities for what they were and came more and more to realize that she had only his best interests at heart.

Playback was published in 1958 with somewhat disappointing sales of 9,000 copies in America. Except for the central character who has to live with a dangerous secret, it is quite different from the screenplay. Universal-International Pictures threatened to sue Chandler for giving the novel the same title as the script, but his lawyer pointed out that there was no "negative covenant" involved, since the media of film and literature were not competitive. Universal did not accept the argument, but neither did they sue, so the matter was dropped.

The use of Marlowe in the novel made it necessary to change the setting from Vancouver, and this created a problem for Chandler. "I have lost Los Angeles as a locale," he wrote. "It is no longer the part of me it once was, although I was the first to write about it in a realistic way. It was hot and dry when I first went there, with tropical rains in winter, and sunshine at least nine-tenths of the year. Now it is humid, hot, sticky, and when the smog comes down into the bowl between mountains which is Los Angeles, it is damn near intolerable." La Jolla was finally chosen as the setting, under the name of Esmeralda.

Playback is not nearly so good as *The Long Goodbye*; it is, in fact, the weakest of Chandler's novels. But it has a surprising amount of gusto and vitality. It is funny and touching and always readable—only one doesn't care about the characters as much as in the early books. The book also reflects disconcerting changes in the author's attitude. When Chandler realized he needed information about the local police, he asked a reporter, Pliny Castanian, to arrange a visit to the San Diego jail. Chandler was so impressed by the efficiency and good manners of the police officers he met that in the novel he pictured them as polite civil servants, totally unlike the sleazy, half-crooked cops he portrayed in Los Angeles and Bay City. There is also much more sex in the novel than in the earlier books. By chapter five Marlowe is having intercourse with the girl he is supposed to be protecting; by chapter thirteen he is in bed with his employer's secretary, and the scene has no integral part in the story; at the end the phone rings, and it's Linda Loring in Paris, saying she wants to marry him, and he agrees.

These changes made many readers think that Chandler had gone soft. *Newsweek* even ran a special news item on the change in the hard-boiled dick, which Chandler acknowledged by saying: "I thought it was time Marlowe was given something worth having, some love of his own. You see, there's a lot of him in me, his loneliness." *Playback* is full of autobiographical echoes, and the ending mirrors his own wishes. Yet there is much that is vigorous. The scene in which a drug addict hangs himself in a privy shows that Chandler knew what was going on behind the elegant façade of contemporary life. Despite the book's overt sentimentalism, it is the product of a youthful mind.

For Chandler, the main thing was that the book was written at all. Eight years earlier, when Hemingway published *Across the River and into the Trees*, Chandler was irritated by the way the critics attacked it. He knew it was not a masterpiece; it was a book written by a sick man who didn't know whether he was going to get better, and as Chandler said, "he put down on paper in a rather cursory way how that made him feel to the things he had most valued." Most of the "primping second-guessers who call themselves critics" wouldn't have had the guts to write the book, said Chandler. "That's the difference between a champ and a knife thrower. The champ may have lost his stuff temporarily or permanently, he can't be sure. But when he can no longer throw his hard high one, he throws his heart instead. He throws something. He just doesn't walk off the mound and weep." And neither did Chandler.

Meanwhile he learned from his London solicitor, Michael Gilbert, that he was being charged with English taxes for overextending his stay in London during 1955. The authorities still considered him a British subject because of his naturalization prior to working for the Admiralty in 1907. Chandler had never bothered to renounce his British nationality, and during World War II he allowed himself to be registered as an alien in California. The nuisance was minimal and he was proud to be associated with England during those years. Eventually, however, he grew tired of the ambiguity and the refusal of the immigration authorities to admit that he was an American because of his birth; so he went to court in Los Angeles to sue the Attorney General of the United States for the return of his citizenship. The scene in court was absurd because the presiding judge did not want to take jurisdiction. A number of decisions denying American citizenship to Japanese-Americans had been successfully appealed, to the embarrassment of lower-court judges, and Chandler's did not want to become involved in a similar situation. Counsel for both sides spent two hours trying to assure the judge that he was competent. "The judge was finally persuaded to take jurisdiction and to sign a decree and findings of fact in my favor," Chandler wrote. "Then, damn it all, the three members of the local U.S.D.A.'s staff came over and shook hands with me and said they had felt all along that my case was good, but that they had to take orders from their superiors in Washington. I thought this a rather fine gesture."

This decree settled matters in the United States, but in England Chandler was still caught up in a bureaucratic mill. When he arrived in 1955 with an American passport, he tried to register as an alien. "The Home Office people didn't know where I should do it, you didn't know," he reminded Gilbert, "and the chap in Piccadilly Place didn't think I had to register. Then I got this stern letter from the Commissioner ordering me to do such and such and report immediately to the Aliens Registration Office, and when I got there, they wouldn't look at my passport photographs or the five shillings I had been ordered to bring. They gave me the V.I.P. treatment, all smiles and courtesy. The next time I had to report, I got the refugee treatment. Not from the same people, however. All very polite, but very searching, and no damned nonsense."

The mess in which Chandler became embroiled was so complicated that he was advised not to return to England in the spring of 1957, as he had planned to do. He became involved in an immense correspondence with Michael Gilbert, Helga Greene as his agent, and two firms of accountants who were supposed to prepare information to convince British authorities that Chandler's extended stay had been unintentional, caused in part by his own illness, rather than solely out of concern for Natasha Spender. Chandler expended a great deal of energy on the matter, for he enjoyed legal entanglements and fancied that he had a lawyer's mind. After a year of consultations, he was required to pay £646 to the Inland Revenue, not to mention the fees due those he had employed in the case.

As he completed the final text of *Playback* in Palm Springs, Chandler was sufficiently encouraged to be thinking about his next book. This was inspired by Marlowe's decision to marry Linda Loring. Chandler claimed that Helga Greene's cousin, Maurice Guinness, talked him into the idea of marrying off Marlowe. Chandler believed he should marry someone quite out of his ordinary style of life, a "woman with a lot of money who wants to live a rather smart expensive life," and the point was that "there would be a struggle of personalities and ideas of life which would make a good sub-plot." He conceived of the story as "a running fight interspersed with amorous interludes. Marlowe, a poor but sincere man, in spite of his tendency to crack wise, will hate Linda's style of living, he will hate the house she has rented for the season in Palm Springs, an over-decorated job of which I have an exact description. He will detest the bunch of freeloaders who are about all you can find for party guests. She on her side will never understand why he insists on sticking to a dangerous and poorly paid profession. I think they will only completely agree in bed."

"Poodle Springs" was the name Chandler adopted for Palm Springs, "because every third elegant creature you see has at least one poodle." Linda Loring's house was to be modeled on one owned by Mrs. Jessie Baumgardner, an acquaintance. It had some unusual features. "The front wall, for example," he wrote, "is made of Japanese glass with butterflies in between the two sections. Every room has a door to the outside and a glass wall. There is an interior glass-walled patio which has an almost full-sized palm tree in it, a lot of tropical shrubs, and some pieces of desert rock which probably cost somebody nothing but some petrol, and probably cost her $200 a rock." When he returned to La Jolla, he found another house that he considered more suitable to Linda Loring's character because of its "offhand elegance and virtuosity which was once fairly usual in England among the upper classes. The people who live in it are clearly rich, but their enormous drawing room, or living room as we call it, escapes the air of having been done by an expensive decorator. It is full of things which I feel sure are priceless but are treated in the most casual way. It has space and warmth. You sit in the room and you know that everything in it cost the earth, and you feel perfectly comfortable and at ease." Chandler wrote the first few chapters of a novel set in this place, but it was never finished.

The outburst of literary activity inspired by Helga Greene's visit had required the help of a secretary to replace Juanita Messick. Chandler placed a blind advertisement in a local paper which was answered by a telegram that caught his fancy. The person who sent it, Chandler soon realized, was "not by temperament the type to make an efficient secretary." But he hired her anyway, because she was a woman in need, and Chandler was the eternal Galahad. She was an Australian whom I shall call Anne Jameson and had two children; she needed a job because after fourteen years of marriage she was separating from her husband. She was also a woman with literary ambitions. After engaging Chandler's interest, she told him about a book she wanted to write exposing medical malpractices. She wanted him to collaborate with her, and Chandler wrote enthusiastically about the proposal to Paul Brooks at Houghton Mifflin. When the idea was rejected, he was disappointed, but he must have returned to his literary senses enough to know that such a book was not in his line and would interrupt his proper work as a novelist. Meanwhile, Mrs. Jameson began to suggest that he go to Australia, telling him, as he reported, "that Australia had never been understood and that as literary material it is practically untouched." Lacking any true source of inspiration, he added that a "new locale might stimulate me, perhaps."

But Anne Jameson did not limit herself to literary projects. She told Chandler all about her rather messy divorce proceedings. Feeling sorry for her and for the two children, Chandler invited them to Palm Springs. One evening after dinner he told her that as she had to look after the two children, he planned to go and dance with some of the ladies he had seen at the hotel. She agreed, and after the headwaiter arranged introductions to a pair of women who "did look like ladies," he spent a decorous evening with them. It was a curiously old-fashioned and lonely episode which had its origin in his own and Cissy's habit of going out to dance halls where the custom was, as Chandler said, to dance "in silence and dignity." When Chandler returned to his hotel, he was accused by Mrs. Jameson of consorting with call girls, and on the following day she took the children back to La Jolla. Meanwhile, Chandler continued in his new habit. "I have become quite nutty about dancing," he admitted to Helga Greene. One night he picked up a waitress from a restaurant called the Doll House, and he behaved with such exceptional courtesy and correctness, even to the point of sending her a bunch of roses the next day, that the poor girl broke down and wept.

When he returned to La Jolla there was work to do, so he resumed his employment of Mrs. Jameson. By now he had become quite fond of the children. But he was soon caught up in the drama of Mrs. Jameson's relationship with her husband. She asked Chandler to have Christmas dinner with herself, the children, and even Mr. Jameson, despite the divorce. The idea appalled Chandler, but to oblige he agreed and "exerted all the charm I possess, which is probably not much, to be nice to him." Afterward he took them all on a long drive which ended in a row, with Chandler telling Mr. Jameson he wouldn't speak to him any more. Undoubtedly, Mrs. Jameson was undergoing a considerable strain, but Chandler allowed himself to be drawn into her troubles far more than was wise. "The Jameson family has taken a lot out of me in many ways," he reported to Helga Greene, "but of course they had to have someone to turn to, or they were lost. But I'd like to think Anne could get back her courage—she has plenty of it deep down—because I want to devote my life to you and to work and not be forever tormented by the problems of someone else." Yet his own impulsiveness and instability were partly at fault. He made Mrs. Jameson his heir and allowed her to wear the ring he had given Cissy. No wonder she thought she could pour out her troubles to him.

The arrival of 1958 meant that Chandler was free to return to England again, and in mid-February he flew to New York and stayed at the Beekman Tower Hotel in order to be near Jessica Tyndale. One day, suddenly feeling that he had deserted the Jamesons, he phoned them and invited them to fly to New York, with the intention of going on to join him afterwards in England. In a flurry of activity, Chandler booked passages for the Jamesons on a Cunard liner while he flew on to London to plan for their arrival there. From the airport he went directly to Helga Greene's country house at Clandon in Surrey for the weekend and then took a room for himself at the Ritz. The pressure and worry about arrangements for the Jamesons made him drink about a bottle of whiskey a day, but Helga Greene made sure he ate regularly, and he was able to make the few revisions she thought necessary before *Playback* was sent to Hamish Hamilton.

The Jamesons arrived in early March and stayed for ten days in Helga Greene's house before moving to a small apartment she had taken for Chandler at 8 Swan Walk in Chelsea. Opposite the Botanical Garden and close by the Royal Hospital, it was a quiet, restful place. But for the Jamesons, abruptly thrust into an alien world, it was difficult. Chandler was unable to cope with their problems, which included housekeeping and an abrupt change in temperature, and he couldn't give them as much time as they were used to receiving in La Jolla. Chandler had agreed to accompany the Jamesons to Australia, but now that he was back in London he lost interest in going anywhere else. Nevertheless, he booked passage for all of them on the *Orcades* of the Orient Line for a May sailing. Meanwhile, without the full-time attention he hoped for from Helga Greene, who had her agency to run and who declined his offers of marriage, he began phoning up some of his old "girl friends" from earlier visits. He was caught up in a whirl of women, and was in the middle hardly knowing where to turn, except to the bottle.

Also, he was the returned celebrity. Chandler was always "good copy" because what he said was so unexpected and disarming. Americans rarely defend their country abroad by writing letters to the editor, but when René MacColl attacked the United States in the *Daily Express*, Chandler replied with a defense. The episode created a great deal of heat, and afterwards the *Express* received many letters from its readers. In the spring of 1958, with *Playback* forthcoming, Chandler was again in the news. He had his photograph taken by Douglas Glass for "The Portrait Gallery," then published every weekend by the *Sunday Times*. He was also interviewed and asked to appear on radio and television.

One episode, which might have been fruitful, came to nothing. Chandler and Helga Greene had been planning a trip to Tangier to get some sun, and one day they had lunch at Boulestin's with Ian Fleming, with whom Chandler maintained a chaffing friendship. Fleming told them it was raining in Tangier and suggested instead that they go to Capri, stopping on the way to interview Lucky Luciano, who had been repatriated to Naples by the United States. The idea of America's most famous crime writer interviewing America's most famous crook seemed appealing. The *Sunday Times* agreed to pay expenses and fees, and Chandler wrote a polite letter to Signor Luciano Lucania proposing a meeting. Luciano replied by telegram: "Don't come on my account. Have nothing to say." But plans had now been made and Chandler and Helga Greene flew off, ready to take their chances. Henry Thody, the Rome correspondent of the *Sunday Times*, made the arrangements, and eventually Luciano came to the Hotel Royal, where Chandler was staying. They talked for some time and got on well together, Luciano later calling Chandler a "swell guy." It must have been an unusual experience for Luciano to be treated so charitably. The article Chandler wrote was called "My Friend Luco" and it defends the famous racketeer as a scapegoat. "Luco is my friend," it concludes. "He was considerate to me far beyond any need on his part. Nothing can give him back his life or his freedom. The job done on him was too thorough. He is not poor. He lives in a comfortable part of Naples. He has a modest car and a man to drive it. He wouldn't dare to drive himself for fear that some accident might give the police another chance to charge him with some crime. He has a modest business. But all this is not a life—it is only a façade of a life. Perhaps it will never be more.

"For some reason—I don't know why—he trusted me. I have not betrayed him. That may be some small consolation to him. To a man who has suffered so much even a small consolation may be important. I hope so."

The piece was not printed on the grounds of possible legal action, but aside from Chandler's obvious identification of himself with his subject, it just isn't very good. Instead of giving a vivid portrait of

Luciano, it is full of generalizations about American politics and crime. It is a tired and querulous essay, reflecting his mood at the time.

After the interview, he and Helga Greene had originally planned to go to Capri or Ischia for a fortnight or so to work on a proposed play. But at the hotel Chandler began drinking quantities of Italian vodka. "Helga and I are having a bit of a row," he wrote. "She says I organise too much and I say the same of her." Shortly after the interview Chandler returned to London, where he was met by Natasha Spender with whom he remained on friendly terms despite his earlier letter to her. He planned to go to Australia but then changed his mind. He had never been keen about it, but in order to avoid having to decide, he drank so much it became impossible for him to sail.

By the first week of May he was in a nursing home at 31 Queen's Gate, and there he remained until he was well enough to return to the now available flat at 8 Swan Walk. The immediate pressure was off, although he felt guilty about not being with the Jamesons, especially when letters began to arrive full of complaints and expressions of misery. Helga Greene was also away on a trip with Richard Crossman and his wife, and that meant he was on his own. For once it seemed to have a salutary effect.

Thanks mainly to the presence of a male nurse, Don Santry, Chandler began to establish a certain routine. His life during the summer of 1958 was quietly social and moderately sober. He liked to take a hired car on shopping expeditions to Harrods for clothes or gifts or to Berry Bros. & Rudd for whiskey and wines, and he enjoyed being driven to Boodle's, the Athenaeum, or the Garrick for lunch. In the evenings he generally dined at Boulestin's or the Connaught, although he also liked the less fashionable restaurants of Kensington and Chelsea, among them the much-lamented La Speranza. He spent a lot, but his basic expenses were not high. His flat cost him sixty pounds a month, with another twenty pounds for telephone calls.

Chandler was best at lunch, especially if he had mangaged to eat some sort of breakfast. He would often meet Nicolas Bentley or his solicitor, Michael Gilbert, at the Garrick, of which he had been a member since 1955, thanks to the efforts of Eric Ambler and Roger Machell. Michael Gilbert recalled that he once ordered tripe à la mode de Caen, which probably hadn't been made there in years. When at last it came, Chandler took one look at it and told the waiter: "It looks as if it's been fifteen days in an open boat. Take it away and give it a Christian burial." Gilbert is convinced he ordered the dish simply to make the wisecrack.

During the summer of 1958 Chandler stayed in close touch with Gilbert, whom he'd asked to establish, for tax purposes, a company called Philip Marlowe Ltd. in the Bahamas. The idea was that Chandler's earnings would be paid into the company, which in turn would pay Chandler a salary. The establishment of this tax dodge was immensely complicated, and as usual with legal matters it required the involvement of a great many people. There is a huge pile of correspondence regarding the matter, but it was all to no purpose, since Chandler did not live to benefit from it.

With his male friends Chandler was not quite the extroverted wit he had been with his "girl friends" in 1955; also he had aged. His conversation was quiet and he never dominated the talk. He had a genuinely modest sense of himself. Aside from meeting writers like Eric Partridge and Nicolas Bentley at his club, he also kept in touch with "Vince" and the other warehousemen from Hamish Hamilton. He enjoyed playing darts with them, and after a while they prepared a special dartboard for him which, as Hamilton recalled, had "the titles of his books on one side, and a number of very promising-looking blondes on the other." Vincent later observed that Chandler "sort of knew about darts but not much," and remembered that when they gave him the special board, "what he said about those darts was nobody's business. He didn't hit the board, so we suggested he throw the board at the darts, and he thought that was a wonderful idea." When he stayed at the Ritz, Chandler had the board hung up on his wall, where it certainly must have raised many an eyebrow.

Toward the end of the day Maurice Guinness, Helga Greene's cousin, would occasionally stop in to see him on his way home from work. Chandler was always what he called a "horizontal man," who preferred lying down to sitting up. He loved to lie on a couch or bed, looking like a beached porpoise. When Guinness paid his visits, Chandler would mix them drinks, and the two of them would lie down on the bed, side by side, and converse. Then Guinness would go home.

Generally speaking, he kept busy. Julian Symons, for whom he prepared a list of his favorite mystery novels for a newspaper article, remembers seeing him at Helga Greene's, reclining rather grandly like a pasha on her couch, while she tried surreptitiously to water his whiskey. Ian Fleming arranged for a talk with Chandler on the BBC. By the time the taping session began, Chandler was quite drunk, so Fleming had to direct the conversation from one subject to another. It is the only recording that has been preserved of Chandler's voice, American in tone but English in diction and enunciation. Terence Tiller also asked him to read some poetry for the BBC, and with his usual modesty Chandler read poems by Jon Silkin, Cecil Day Lewis, Stephen Spender, W. H. Auden, and Louis MacNeice. The only poem of his own that he read was "Song Without Music," an elegy for Cissy. Inevitably, Chandler's reputation had begun to precede him. Before his appearance on a television show called "Late Extra," the producer warned everyone that Chandler might turn up drunk and made emergency arrangements in case his condition was too bad. In the end, the producer passed out before the show began, while Chandler appeared cold sober.

Aside from a review of a Fleming novel for the *Sunday Times*, the only writing Chandler completed in 1958 was a preface to Frank Norman's book, *Bang to Rights*. Norman was something of a literary marvel, a young man of twenty-seven who had spent most of his life in institutions, including prisons. Finally, he decided to go straight and wrote a fresh and authentic account of his life in prison. Stephen Spender published a portion of the book in *Encounter* and told Chandler about it. He and Natasha Spender then invited Chandler to meet Norman for lunch at the Café Royal. Chandler, dapper with gloves and cane, was excited by the prospect of meeting what he imagined was a hardened criminal, but Norman's manner and humor disarmed him. Chandler then offered to write a preface for *Bang to Rights*. Norman was delighted, although at the time he really didn't know who Chandler was and had to be put right by his publisher. The preface is enthusiastic and warm. "There is no damned literary nonsense about his writing," said Chandler. "The situation is there, the people are there and you are there with them; and this is a rare thing."

Chandler was generous to young writers whenever possible because he knew their terror himself. As late as 1957 he wrote: "I always feel like a beginner when I start a new job." He was also completely free of petty jealousy. "Any decent writer who thinks of himself occasionally as an artist would far rather be forgotten so that someone better might be remembered," he said. His confidence and dedication molded his feelings: "Any man who can write a page of living prose adds something to our life, and the man who can, as I can, is surely the last to resent someone who can do it even better. An artist cannot deny art, nor would he want to. If you believe in an ideal, you don't own it—it owns you."

But as the summer wore on, Chandler's condition worsened. He was not doing any serious work, not even pretending to write his play or the *Cook Book for Idiots* that he and Helga Greene planned to collaborate on. He was also depressed by the flood of gloomy letters that arrived from Australia. There were no jobs, there was no money. Chandler gave Anne Jameson the English rights to *Playback*, and Helga Greene bought them back for £2,000 so that she could have the cash. Chandler sent additional amounts. Mrs. Jameson wanted him to fly to Sydney, but he refused, saying he was nearly broke, having given her "practically all the loose money I had." Shortly afterward her unpaid bills started to arrive from California. "This is no time to depress you," he wrote, "but I am sure you know that since February 1957 I have never for one moment been free of some sort of worry about you, at times too poignant, at others almost unbearable. Financially I have taken quite a beating. Because the Nassau company is not yet functioning, I even had to borrow money to send you that $1,000. But what is more disastrous than that is that the constant worry is undermining my ability to write, so that I can't replace money as I should. It is much harder for you than for me, but it is hard on me also."

With the time for his departure from England approaching, he became increasingly depressed and indecisive about where to go. Then Anne Jameson telephoned from Australia to say that Mr. Jameson had died and that she wished to return to California. Chandler agreed to return as well, with the understanding that his nurse, Don Santry, would accompany him. They left in mid-August on a polar flight from London to Los Angeles. It was a nightmare of delayed luggage, bad food, and unexpected stops at Winnipeg and San Francisco. La Jolla was suffering from a heat spell, and Chandler hated the La Jollan Hotel, where he was staying; he said, with reason, that it was about to be converted to a Methodist old people's home.

Chandler was by now a rather weary Galahad. "Anne's children were frantic at seeing me again and I love them," he wrote to Helga Greene, "but my home is in Europe. For some reason, perhaps you, I have grown away from the American attitude to life. Americans are kindly and generous people, vital and energetic, but no cachet. I'd rather have decadence with style, if I have to have it, rather than crudeness. And the accents! My God, I never realised how bad they were. Yet everyone here has welcomed me with enthusiasm. I'm an ungrateful dog, I suppose." He spent his time helping Mrs. Jameson find a house for herself and her children, a matter of some urgency with school soon starting. "It's not much use going into the Jameson mess on paper, but it is a mess," he wrote to Helga Greene. "I do think I owe a duty to Anne and her children—a self-imposed duty—but frankly I think I also owe some duty to myself, and I find the atmosphere of confused emotionalism very far from what I need to do any productive work."

He hated being back and felt trapped: "I feel lost and worn out and involved in a situation which makes demands on me, although it is really none of my business." A few days later he reiterated his despair: "I simply cannot devote all my thoughts to the troubles of the Jameson family if I am ever to write anything. It is not that I am not fond of them, but they seem unable to do anything without involving me."

He was again drinking heavily and in due course was in the hospital. Once more his resilience brought him around, however, and he was discharged. He rented a small cottage belonging to a Mrs. Margaret

Murray at 024 Prospect Street, near the center of La Jolla. In addition to a small study just inside the front door, there was a living room with a glassed-in dining room beyond, both with a view over the sea below. With flowers in the garden it was charming, and Mrs. Murray was an agreeable landlady, always bringing him fruit and other small presents. Here, with Don Santry in attendance, Chandler set himself up. When feeling well, his routine was to get up at about four or five in the morning, make himself some tea, and write. Breakfast he would take in the late morning and then do errands and have lunch. During the rest of the day he did little but read and see people. After an early dinner he would usually be in bed by nine.

He was working on "The Pencil," the first Marlowe short story he had written in twenty years. It was based on murders carried out by an organized crime syndicate. "The basic idea is too damned serious to be witty about," he wrote. "That has a tendency to cramp me. Yet it is a rather good idea and has never been done to my knowledge." The story is not convincing because of the improbability of Marlowe's identifying the two "hit men," the anonymous out-of-town murderers who kill their man and vanish. It has the gusto if not the magic of early Chandler but is infused with his own preoccupations. "The women you get and the women you don't get—they live in different worlds," Marlowe broods. "I don't sneer at either world. I live in both myself."

Aside from "The Pencil," Chandler was not doing much serious work. He arranged for a Philip Marlowe television program, which was written by E. Jack Neuman and starred Philip Carey. Hamish Hamilton was interested in publishing a collection of Chandler's letters, but the work of sorting them out and editing them required a different temperament from Chandler's. He had a clear idea of their quality, for when Hamilton first made the proposal Chandler said he was "staggered to think I could be so brilliant for no money." But he disliked the emphasis on himself; as early as 1949 he wrote: "If I wrote a non-fiction book, it would probably turn out to be the autobiography of a split personality."

This did not mean that Chandler did not write. Every morning he would sit at his desk, for however much he drank the night before, he was clearheaded in the morning and did not suffer from hangovers. At Neil Morgan's request, he wrote a few columns for the *San Diego Tribune*. Some of these were old articles which he edited, but there was also an amusing sketch about Anne Jameson's cat and dog, a pair of columns on the San Diego police, and a rather maudlin piece on sex. He lacked the strength to do any real creative work, but he was too much a writer ever to stop. "I live for syntax," he said. He kept his machine oiled mainly by writing letters. Fascinated by the uses to which language could be put, he explained his own obsession with words by writing: "I have more love for our superb language than I could ever possibly express."

Meanwhile, the domestic arrangements were getting worse. In early October he wrote of Anne Jameson: "My taking her on as a secretary and paying her $50 a week was almost pure charity, as she is not worth it to me and has done practically nothing in the past two weeks except move and do some unpacking." He asked Helga Greene to visit him, but she was unable to do so and suggested that Mrs. Kay West go in her place. She had been a neighbor of Chandler's at Swan Walk and had done secretarial work for him during the previous summer. At first Chandler demurred, but with the departure of Don Santry to England he agreed, and she came over. He did not want to live alone in his cottage.

Kay West's arrival marked the beginning of the end. Chandler had earlier written to Helga Greene: "Can a man not be genuinely in love with two women—especially a man who expects nothing but the privilege of loving them?" It was the attitude of a man who desperately wanted to hold on to life and who refused to accept the realities of old age. Chandler was furious when he had to have a tooth removed. He was incontinent and would ring up a friend and say, half-shamed, half-enraged, "I've wet my bed!" He was like a moth that persisted in flapping its wings against a window pane. He was disappointed that his dreams had not come true; but faced with the emptiness of his life, the realization that there was nothing left, he refused to be resigned or philosophical. Instead, he relied on his feelings and impulses, his own sense of blunt honesty; and the result was chaos. Like a king with a court, he surrounded himself with other people, but no monarch was ever less stable than he.

Chandler was delighted with Mrs. West's company and wrote to Helga Greene that "Kay is buzzing around all over the place, washing dishes, making beds, doing the breakfast, washing my military brushes, and mending, taking letters, doing everything. She is so damned energetic that she makes me feel lazy." She and Chandler played darts, which he enjoyed, and began cooking meals together, which also pleased him. A few days later he reported: "I have worked her into cooking three meals a day, washing all the dishes, and keeping the house tidy. She also goes shopping for food and so on with me. We have two of those nylon bags and we each carry a load home. You know I gave Anne my car."

Meanwhile, there was a good deal of drinking, and Chandler's doctor again ordered him taken to the hospital. Chandler was angry about going, but when he got out he told Helga Greene that "Kay has been unbelievably kind and I think Dr. Birss sent me to the hospital more for Kay's sake than mine. I have let her do the meals, the washing-up, the housework and on top of that expected some secretarial work from her. It was really a bit too much."

From the beginning Mrs. Jameson was upset by Kay West's arrival, especially when Chandler told Michael Gilbert to make Kay West the beneficiary of his will. There were constant phone calls, sometimes with no one on the line, and this upset Chandler. He kept a whiskey always ready by his bed, and if he was suddenly disturbed, he would start drinking and then go on to more. At nine o'clock on the morning he returned from his drying-out session at the hospital, he was met by Mrs. Jameson, who said, "Let's have a drink to celebrate!"

It was too much for Kay West, who went to the hospital herself for a rest. Chandler was confused and angered by this development. Meanwhile, the drama was being reported by all parties to Helga Greene, who was also ill in the London Clinic. Most of the letters contain accusations by one member of Chandler's entourage against another. Helga Greene resisted becoming involved because she hoped Chandler might work out an arrangement with Mrs. Jameson and her children that would give him companionship and a peaceful life. But he never made a proposal or, if he did, he never acted on it. He just drank.

Finally, on February 2, 1959, Helga Greene flew to La Jolla. Finding Chandler very ill, she called the doctor, and once more he was sent to the La Jolla Convalescent Hospital. Chandler probably knew he was dying, for most of his last letters are about wills. A week earlier he had told Michael Gilbert to make Anne Jameson his heir instead of Kay West. He said the doctor told him he couldn't live more than four or five months. "He's a liar," Chandler remarked; "I'll live forever."

Chandler remained a week in the nursing home and was quite frail when released, although within a few days he was able to go into La Jolla with Helga Greene. He wanted to buy a ring, because in the hospital she had finally agreed to his marriage proposal. She realized that the situation in La Jolla was bad and that the confusion he created around him was killing him. Helga Greene hoped that the marriage would add years to his life and give him happiness. If they could settle in London as a married couple, he might have the tranquillity he needed to work. He had begun to regret marrying Marlowe off and wanted to convert the "Poodle Springs" piece into a short story and then start a new Marlowe novel. As a token of his own commitment to the marriage, Chandler wrote out a new will, changing the beneficiary from Anne Jameson to Helga Greene.

In hopes of getting Chandler away from the confused atmosphere of La Jolla, Helga Greene convinced him to go to New York to accept the presidency of the Mystery Writers of America, to which office he had just been elected. They packed up the house, and Leon Johnston, the new housekeeper, threw away all of Chandler's and Cissy's private note-books. The rest of his possessions were put in storage. Anne Jameson was upset by Chandler's imminent departure, although she knew noth-ing of the change in his will. Others were sad, especially his landlady, Mrs. Murray, who always called him "Pappy." Chandler wrote a little testimonial in her guestbook which ended: "I should like to take you in my arms and carry you to the distant place to which my destiny makes me go. I can't do that. I can only say what I have said and may God bless you wherever you are and whatever you do."

Chandler's hopes of a happy life with a woman he had long courted offered a respite from his worries, and he looked forward to returning to London, where a house had been procured for them at 86 Elm Park Road in Chelsea. In early March he and Helga Greene left for New York. They stayed at the Beaux Arts Hotel on East 44th Street, where Jessica Tyndale was also living. The weather was rainy, cold, and blustery, but they emerged from the hotel for a few social occasions, including a dinner with Hillary Waugh and Dorothy Gardiner of the Mystery Writers of America. There was a question about whether he would be able to attend the MWA party given in his honor, but he managed to go, leaning on his cane. There was a little ceremony, and Chandler made a charming speech that revealed the continuing vitality of his humor: "I should thank you from the bottom of my heart for your great kindness in inviting me here. I not only should but I do. But I feel a certain embarrassment before you for two reasons. I now know that the ballot was sent to me, but I never saw it. It was apparently filed before I saw it, possibly in my file headed Don't Bother Me Now, File Later. So when I received a telegram from Catherine Barth telling me I had been elected president against enormous opposition I was stunned. Not by the oppo-sition, of course; I am an opposition man myself. But I was lulled into a false security by being told that I really didn't have to do anything, the executive vice-president did all the work. How he does it and still finds time and energy to be a writer I don't know. I have on rare occasions—quite rare—got up at four or five in the morning and pounded the typewriter for ten hours straight without food, but not without whisky. Of course I often had to throw the stuff away—I don't mean the whisky—but it was a nice try if no cigar.

"The second cause of my embarrassment is that before I had the remotest idea of being your president I had made very firm plans to go to England for quite a long time. What I shall accomplish there I don't know. I may go out when it isn't raining and I may possibly contrive a closer liaison between the Crime Writers Association and the MWA."

He then concluded by introducing Helga Greene as his English agent and spoke of the advantages that had subsequently accrued to him. Finally, he said: "I thank you all again for your great kindness to me, and I am sure you will be relieved to know that, however much love I may have inside me, I have no more words that need be said."

The weather continued to get on everybody's nerves, but Chandler was anxious to meet Helga Greene's father, H. S. H. Guinness, who happened to be in America on business. Chandler was conventional enough to want to make a formal request for his daughter's hand. They dined, and Mr. Guinness apparently seemed distressed that his daughter should be marrying a man who was almost exactly his own age. Chandler thought he was being snubbed, as he later explained in a letter to Helga Greene: "It seems very strange to me that your father should have turned so completely against me, when you said I behaved beautifully the night he had us to dinner. I know he thought I was a bit old—but he is a bit old himself. Someone must have told him things to my discredit for him to refuse to see me. Of course many things could be said to my discredit, but he would have no knowledge of them unless they were told him."

Chandler was hurt by the refusal of Mr. Guinness to accept his unnecessary request that he be welcomed as a son-in-law. Helga Greene, who was in her forties, had no intention of being bound by her father's will. But by now, Chandler's mood was altered. As in the meantime he was receiving pathetic letters from Anne Jameson describing the various problems she and her family had fallen into during his absence, Chandler decided to return to California instead of going to London. The cold he had picked up from the bad weather in New York made La Jolla seem agreeable, at least for the moment. He went back to the same cottage Mrs. Murray had not yet let to anyone else—and then took ill again from heavy drinking. On March 23 he was sent to the La Jolla Convalescent Hospital with pneumonia caught from being neglected in his cottage. Two days later he was transferred by ambulance to the Scripps Clinic. He died there at 3:50 in the afternoon of March 26, 1959.

It was a sad, faceless sort of death for a man who had so enriched literature with his wit and perception. The newspapers published long and appreciative obituaries. The *Times* of London observed that "his name will certainly go down among the dozen or so mystery writers who were also innovators and stylists; who, working the common vein of crime fiction, mined the gold of literature." American papers followed the same line, noting his appeal to intellectuals as well as to ordinary readers. The *Los Angeles Times* ran a special editorial on him, stating that "Chandler had made the private eye a national glamour figure."

Meanwhile, Anne Jameson telephoned Michael Gilbert in London, and he told her about the new will. She later filed suit against Helga

Greene, charging that she had exerted undue influence to make Chandler change the beneficiary. In the trial that ensued, her lawyer was forced to withdraw the challenge and the judge dismissed the charge "with prejudice," which meant that Mrs. Jameson was forbidden to reopen the matter in the future. The estate was valued at $60,000 plus whatever future earnings might accrue through ownership of the copyrights. Helga Greene, just returned to England, was too ill to fly back for the funeral, and Chandler lay alone in the undertaker's parlor, reaping the neglect his indecisiveness had earned him.

Four days after he died Chandler was buried in a small plot in Mount Hope Cemetery in San Diego. The day of the funeral was a bank holiday in England, so Helga Greene and Roger Machell couldn't even send flowers. Chandler's accountant, George Peterson, acted on behalf of Helga Greene, and the former rector of St. James's Episcopal Church in La Jolla conducted the funeral service as he had done for Cissy, although somehow no one thought to have Chandler buried with his wife's remains or to have him cremated as he wished.

It was a clear, bright Monday when the Anglican service was read over Chandler's coffin before it was lowered into the ground. Seventeen people were present. These included representatives of the Mystery Writers of America; Ned Guymon, a celebrated collector of detective stories; and the scattered acquaintances Chandler had in La Jolla. Like so many strong individualists able to afford it, he was looked after mainly by his servants and employees. In its obscurity and impersonality, his burial was complementary to his birth. Chandler rose from the blank anonymity of America and seemed to be returning to it in the end. In between, he had led a tortured and lonely life only temporarily relieved by moments of happiness and given meaning by his stubborn adherence to the highest standards of art. This above all has made his name survive the grave.

Chandler was a naturally gifted and fluent writer, but for nearly fifty years he was unable to find a medium that suited him. He endured continuing disappointments and frustrations and, already sensitive, he became withdrawn and introverted. When at last he began to write stories for the pulps and published his own novels, he pulled together the opposed aspects of his nature and created something extraordinarily vital and original. Chandler tended to deprecate his own importance as a writer, but he had a clear idea of what he had achieved, and he knew that his writing held him together. Asked whether he ever read his own work when it was published, he answered: "Yes, and at very great risk of being called an egotistical twerp, I find it damn hard to put down. Even me, that knows all about it. There must be some magic in writing after all, but I take no credit for it. It just happens, like red hair. But I find it rather humiliating to pick up a book of my own to glance at something and then find myself twenty minutes later still reading it as if someone else had written it."

His double vision—half-English, half-American—enabled him to see the world he lived in with exceptional insight. His vision of America has become increasingly fulfilled, although twenty-five years ago few people could have imagined the relevance of his work today. He was a prophet of modern America; out of the European literary tradition he wrote about a world that both repelled and delighted him. He did not generalize or theorize. Rather, he trusted his impulses, and like Chaucer or Dickens he wrote about the people, places, and things he saw with scorn and also with love. This has made him one of the most important writers of his time, as well as one of the most delightful.

CHANDLER'S PUBLICATIONS

This list is not intended to be inclusive. Its purpose is simply to give a brief survey of Chandler's important published work. The list contains only Chandler's published novels as brought out in England and America, and a record of the publication of his stories and articles from 1933 to his death in 1959. It does not include any of the material written by Chandler as a young man in England because it does little credit to him. Nor does the list mention the many collections of Chandler's stories both in paperback and hard cover, the omnibus publication of his novels, the paperback editions of his novels, nor any of the many translations of his work. Nor does it contain reviews, letters to the editor, or other ephemeral material. Readers wishing a more complete list should consult Matthew J. Bruccoli, *Raymond Chandler, a Checklist*, Kent State University Press, 1968. This volume does not include translations, but a large collection of these is available in the Department of Special Collections in the Research Library of the University of California at Los Angeles.

BOOKS

(the publishers are listed in the order of appearance of each book)

The Big Sleep. New York: Alfred A. Knopf, 1939; London: Hamish Hamilton, 1939.

Farewell, My Lovely. New York: Alfred A. Knopf, 1940; London: Hamish Hamilton, 1940.

The High Window. New York: Alfred A. Knopf, 1942; London: Hamish Hamilton, 1943.

The Lady in the Lake. New York: Alfred A. Knopf, 1943; London: Hamish Hamilton, 1944.

The Little Sister. London: Hamish Hamilton, 1949; Boston: Houghton Mifflin, 1949.

The Long Goodbye. London: Hamish Hamilton, 1953; Boston: Houghton Mifflin, 1954.

Playback. London: Hamish Hamilton, 1958; Boston: Houghton Mifflin, 1958.

STORIES

"Blackmailers Don't Shoot." *Black Mask,* December 1933.

"Smart-Aleck Kill." *Black Mask,* July 1934.

"Finger Man." *Black Mask,* October 1934.

"Killer in the Rain." *Black Mask,* January 1935.

"Nevada Gas." *Black Mask,* June 1935.

"Spanish Blood." *Black Mask,* November 1935.

"Guns at Cyrano's." *Black Mask,* January 1936.

"The Man Who Liked Dogs." *Black Mask,* March 1936.

"Noon Street Nemesis" (republished as "Pick-up on Noon Street"). *Detective Fiction Weekly,* May 30, 1936.

"Goldfish." *Black Mask,* June 1936.

"The Curtain." *Black Mask,* September 1936.

"Try the Girl." *Black Mask,* January 1937.

"Mandarin's Jade." *Dime Detective Magazine,* November 1937.

"Red Wind." *Dime Detective Magazine,* January 1938.

"The King in Yellow." *Dime Detective Magazine,* March 1938.

"Bay City Blues." *Dime Detective Magazine,* June 1938.

"The Lady in the Lake." *Dime Detective Magazine,* January 1939.

"Pearls Are a Nuisance." *Dime Detective Magazine,* April 1939.

"Trouble Is My Business." *Dime Detective Magazine,* August 1939.

"I'll Be Waiting." *Saturday Evening Post,* October 14, 1939.

"The Bronze Door." *Unknown,* November 1939.

"No Crime in the Mountains." *Detective Story,* September 1941.

"Professor Bingo's Snuff." *Park East*, June–August 1951; *Go*, June–July 1951.

"Marlowe Takes on the Syndicate." *London Daily Mail*, April 6–10, 1959, also published as "Wrong Pidgeon," *Manhunt*, February 1961. Reprinted as "The Pencil."

ARTICLES

"The Simple Art of Murder." *Atlantic Monthly*, December 1944.

"Writers in Hollywood." *Atlantic Monthly*, November 1945.

"Oscar Night in Hollywood." *Atlantic Monthly*, March 1948.

"The Simple Art of Murder." *Saturday Review of Literature*, April 15, 1950.

"Ten Per Cent of Your Life." *Atlantic Monthly*, February 1952.

NOTES

Every book is different, and therefore each one imposes special problems on a writer wishing to give a clear indication of his sources. In general, I have followed orthodox and commonsense methods in this book, but the state of Chandler's papers and his popularity as an author require an introductory statement.

Virtually all of Chandler's novels and stories are in print in a variety of editions throughout the English-speaking world and in translations elsewhere. Ordinarily, it is the custom to cite quotations of printed work from the first hardcover editions published. Chandler first editions are now so rare and inaccessible, however, that I have decided instead to give chapter or section reference when quoting from a novel or story, rather than refer to the page of a particular edition. Chandler's work lends itself to the procedure, since his chapters and sections in stories are generally short. The reader will suffer a slight inconvenience in checking a source, but it is improbable that he or she would have had the volume from which a page reference might have been made.

When quoting from a manuscript or notebook, I have given as complete bibliographical information as I can. The letters create a more complicated problem, which requires mention of the various collections of Chandler papers.

The largest of these is owned by Mrs. Helga Greene, Chandler's heir and executrix. They include, in addition to manuscripts of published and unpublished works, screenplays, photographs, notebooks, original letters, carbon copies of letters, and photostats of his extensive correspondence. This collection is referred to in the notes as "RC files." The next largest collection is found in the Department of Special Collections in the Research Library of the

University of California in Los Angeles. Chandler gave certain of his own papers to this library as well as a nearly complete collection of his printed work, including books and magazines in English and other languages. Other large but limited collections include Chandler's correspondence with his English publisher, Hamish Hamilton; his American publishers, Houghton Mifflin and Knopf; his agent, Brandt and Brandt; and his editor at the *Atlantic Monthly*, Charles Morton.

The letters in these and other smaller collections fall into different categories, as follows: original letters as signed and sent by Chandler, drafts of letters later typed by a secretary and presumably sent by Chandler, photostats of letters, carbon copies of letters, and transcripts of letters. Most of these transcripts are found in the library at UCLA, where they were deposited by Dorothy Gardiner after completing her share of the work in coediting *Raymond Chandler Speaking*. Unfortunately, many of the transcripts, which were made before the day of easy and cheap photo reproduction, contain errors and omissions and are therefore not reliable.

Because copies of Chandler's correspondence have been preserved in all of these forms, I have always tried to quote from the most reliable text available. Whenever possible, I have used the original signed letter or a photostat of it, or else a carbon or draft; only when these are not available have I used the transcripts. I have provided this note to explain any differences in text between the quotations cited here and those found in the volume *Raymond Chandler Speaking*.

For the sake of readability, I have not cluttered up the text with numbered notes. Instead, I have listed the notes in the back of the book alongside the number of the pages on which the quotations appear. The notes are listed in the same sequence as quotations appear on the page in the text.

The notes refer only to written documents and not to verbally reported remarks, even if they appear within quotation marks. The source of these remarks and of all other information on which each chapter is based is provided in a general note for each chapter. As stated in the introduction, I have not indicated omissions in works and letters quoted. I have not changed the order of sentences, however, and the material omitted is always irrelevant to the matter under discussion.

CHAPTER 1. NEBRASKA TO DULWICH

Information about Chandler's family and their background comes in part from such published books as Albert Cook Myers, *Immigration of Irish Quakers into Pennsylvania 1682–1750* (1902), and J. P. Prendergast, *The Cromwellian Settlement of Ireland* (1922). The Raymond Chandler files owned by Mrs. Helga Greene also contain letters from relatives and a family tree prepared in 1960 with the help of professional genealogists in Ireland. Information concerning Maurice Chandler at the University of Pennsylvania comes from F. J. Dallett, archivist of the university. The Very Reverend Howard Lee Wilson, dean of St. Matthew's Cathedral in Laramie, Wyoming, also provided information about the marriage of Chandler's parents.

Mr. Austin Hall, the librarian of Dulwich College, and Mr. T. E. Priest, secretary of the Alleyn Club, gave me information about Chandler's years at Dulwich. Several published books were also useful: the *Dulwich Year Book*, an annual compilation of information about the school; W. R. M. Leake and others, *Gilkes and Dulwich* (1938); A. H. Gilkes, *A Day at Dulwich* (1905); William Young, *History of Dulwich College* (1889); and various catalogs and records preserved at the school, including *Extracts of Minutes of the Governors*. Sir Alwyne Ogden and Sir P. G. Wodehouse, both contemporaries of Chandler at Dulwich, also provided information.

For Chandler's brief time in the Admiralty, I received help from the Information Office of the Admiralty, and from the Civil Service Commission in Basingstoke.

Details about Chandler's career in journalism were discovered from reading the files of the *Westminster Gazette* and the *Academy* for the period of Chandler's association with these papers. J. A. Spender's *Life, Journalism, and Politics* (1927) was also useful.

Page
1   RC to Michael Gilbert, July 25, 1957.
1   Jon Manchip White to the writer, September 25, 1974.
1   RC to Edgar Carter, June 3, 1957.
2   RC to Hamish Hamilton, January 24, 1949.
2   RC to Dale Warren, March 14, 1951.
2   RC to Alfred Knopf, July 16, 1953.
3   Stanley Kunitz, ed., *Twentieth Century Authors, First Supplement* (1955), entry for RC.
3   RC to Charles Morton, November 20, 1944.
4   RC to Morton, January 1, 1945.
4   RC to Hamilton, November 10, 1950.
4   RC to Leroy Wright, March 31, 1957.
4   *Twentieth Century Authors, First Supplement.*
5   RC to Hamilton, July 15, 1954.
6   *Ibid.*
6   RC to Blanche Knopf, June 14, 1940.
6   RC to Morton, January 1, 1945.
6   RC to Blanche Knopf, June 14, 1940.
7   RC to Hamilton, January 11, 1950.
8   RC to Hamilton, December 11, 1950.
8   RC to Hamilton, December 20, 1949.
8   RC in interview with René MacColl, *Daily Express*, April 25, 1955.
9   Quoted in W. R. M. Leake and others, *Gilkes and Dulwich*, n.d., p. xix.
9   A. H. Gilkes, *A Day at Dulwich*, 1905, p. 58. *Ibid.*, p. xxv.
10 P. G. Wodehouse to the writer, September 18, 1974.
10 RC to Hamilton, November 10, 1950.
10 *Ibid.*
10 RC to Warren, April 20, 1949 (including Priestley comment).
10 *Ibid.*
10 John Houseman, "Lost Fortnight," *Harper's Magazine*, August 1965, p. 61.
11 RC to Helga Greene, April 28, 1957.
11 *Ibid.*
12 RC to Hamilton, July 15, 1954.
12 Autobiographical statement. RC files.
    Although Chandler referred to the name of his pension as Narjollet, it

Page

is probable he meant Marjollet. The "M" and "N" keys are side-by-side on·the typewriter. The Marjollet family was well known as owners of pensions and hotels in Paris, whereas the Narjollet family are Burgundian in origin and only in recent years have any of them lived in Paris. The address of Chandler's pension was also the site of the Café Vachette, a meeting-place for students and also frequented by Verlaine, Moréas, Barrès, and others.

13 RC to Hamilton, December 11, 1950.
13 RC to Greene, July 13, 1956.
13 RC to Hamilton, December 11, 1950.
14 RC to Wesley Hartley, November 11, 1950; quoted in *Raymond Chandler Speaking* (1962), p. 21.
14 RC to Michael Gilbert, March 25, 1957.
14 RC to Wright, March 31, 1957.
15 *Ibid.*
15 RC to Hamilton, December 11, 1950.
15 RC to Wright, March 31, 1957.
15 *Twentieth Century Authors, First Supplement.*
16 Matthew Bruccoli, ed., *Chandler Before Marlowe* (1973), pp. 3–4.
17 Quoted in interview with MacColl, *Daily Express*, April 25, 1955.
17 RC to Hamilton, April 22, 1949.
17 RC to Hamilton, December 11, 1950.
17 *Ibid.*
17 *Ibid.*
18 *Ibid.* Chandler's memory may have been playing tricks on him. Vizetelly and Company under Ernest Vizetelly were prosecuted for publishing Zola and the company collapsed. In the end, however, Vizetelly succeeded in publishing most of Zola in English.
18 Richard Middleton, *Academy*, August 12, 1911, p. 210.
18 RC to Hamilton, December 11, 1950.
19 *Academy*, August 19, 1911, p. 250.
19 RC to Hamilton, April 9, 1949.
19 *Ibid.*
19 *Chandler Before Marlowe*, p. 57.
19 *Ibid.*, p. 67.
19 *Ibid.*, p. 70.
20 RC to Hamilton, December 11, 1950.
20 *Ibid.*
20 Autobiographical statement. RC files.
20 *Chandler Before Marlowe*, p. 71.
22 RC, "Nocturne from Nowhere." RC files.
22 Autobiographical statement. RC files.
22 RC to Wright, March 31, 1957.
23 RC to Gilbert, July 25, 1958.

CHAPTER 2.   THE RETURN TO AMERICA

Information about Chandler's early years in California comes primarily from Dr. Paul Lloyd, the son of Warren Lloyd, whose family gave a warm welcome to Chandler when he arrived in Los Angeles. Research in various newspaper files, telephone directories, and commercial and civic directories produced corroborating material. Mrs. Ruth A. Cutten, a close friend of Warren Lloyd's daughter, Estelle, also supplied valuable help.

Chandler's war experiences are documented by letters and photostats of official records provided by the Public Archives of Canada, the Department of Veterans Affairs in Ottawa, Colonel J. G. Boulet and his staff in the Information Service of the Department of National Defence in Ottawa, and the Air Historical Branch (RAF) of the Ministry of Defence in London. Important background sources included such printed books as G. W. L. Nicholson, *Canadian Expeditionary Force 1914–1919* (1962); Harwood Steele, *The Canadians in France 1915–1918* (1920); George Nasmith, *Canada's Sons and Britain in the World War* (1919); and J. F. B. Livesey, *Canada's Hundred Days* (1919).

Apart from the correspondence referred to below, my account of Chandler's postwar banking career is based on information received from the Administrator of National Banks in Washington, the archivist of the Bank of Montreal, and Miss Pamela Döerr of Barclays Bank in San Francisco.

Information about Chandler's wife, Cissy, comes mainly from the Raymond Chandler files and from Miss Kathrine Sorley Walker of the Helga Greene Literary Agency. Further information was obtained from various public records.

My account of Chandler's life in the oil business is based on material gathered from several of his former colleagues and friends from that period of his life. Mr. and Mrs. Milton Philleo, Mr. and Mrs. Ernest Dolley, Messrs. John Abrams and Theodore Malquist, and Dr. Lloyd all provided invaluable information, which was corroborated by readings of a more general nature about the oil business in Los Angeles and material taken from various industry directories and from the files of the *Los Angeles Times*.

Page
25   RC to Hamish Hamilton, December 11, 1950.
25   Stanley Kunitz, ed., *Twentieth Century Authors, First Supplement* (1955), entry for RC.
25   RC to Charles Morton, January 15, 1945.
25   RC to Hamilton, November 10, 1950.
26   Autobiographical statement. RC files.
26   RC to Hamilton, November 10, 1950.
26   Typescript of "To-morrow." RC files.
27   RC to Eric Partridge, January 30, 1952.
27   Autobiographical statement. RC files.
28   RC to Alex Barris, April 16, 1949.
29   RC to Deirdre Gartrell, March 2, 1957.
29   RC to Gartrell, July 25, 1957.
30   RC, "Trench Raid." Raymond Chandler Collection, UCLA.
30   George Nasmith, *Canada's Sons and Britain in the World War* (1919), p. 470.
30   RC to Bert Lea, December 30, 1948.
31   RC to Roger Machell, July 11, 1954.
31   *Twentieth Century Authors, First Supplement.*
31   *Ibid.*

Page
33 RC to Jessica Tyndale, January 18, 1957.
36 RC to Helga Greene, May 5, 1957.
36 *Ibid.*
36 John Abrams to the writer, July 6, 1974.
37 RC to Greene, May 5, 1957.
39 Abrams to the writer, July 6, 1974.
40 *Ibid.*
40 RC to Howard C. Heyn, press cutting; newspaper unknown. RC files.
40 RC to Hamilton, July 15, 1954.
40 RC to Cyril Ray, interview, *Sunday Times*, September 21, 1952.

CHAPTER 3.   BLACK MASK

For general information about pulp magazines in the United States I have read Frank Gruber, *The Pulp Jungle* (1967); Ron Goulart, *Cheap Thrills, An Informal History of the Pulp Magazines* (1972); and Philip Durham, "The Black Mask School," in *Tough Guy Writers of the Thirties*, edited by David Madden (1968). I have also received individual help from a number of the original contributors to *Black Mask*, notably W. T. Ballard, George Harmon Coxe, Dwight Babcock, and Prentice Winchell. Mrs. Erle Stanley Gardner, Mr. Joseph Shaw, Jr., and Mrs. H. M. Shaw have also helped in various ways. Mr. Keith Deutsch, who has revived *Black Mask*, has been especially helpful in a number of ways, including lending me copies of his file of this magazine. Other sources of information are acknowledged in the notes that follow.

42 RC, untitled typescript for "Short Story Writing 52AB." RC files.
42 *Ibid.*, p. 5. RC files.
43 RC, "Strong Waters" typescript, second version of "Beer in the Sergeant Major's Hat," p. 1. RC files.
43 RC to Charles Morton, January 15, 1945.
43 RC to George Harmon Coxe, April 9, 1939.
43 RC to Hamish Hamilton, November 10, 1950.
44 RC to James Howard, March 26, 1957.
44 RC to Hamilton, November 10, 1950.
44 RC to Coxe, April 9, 1939.
44 RC to Morton, October 28, 1947.
44 Frank Gruber, *The Pulp Jungle* (1967), p. 40.
45 *New Yorker*, February 15, 1936, p. 12.
45 H. L. Mencken to Theodore Dreiser, February 11, 1919, in *Letters of H. L. Mencken* (1961), p. 142.
45 Mencken to Ernest Boyd, April 3, 1920, in *Letters of H. L. Mencken*, p. 180.
45 H. L. Mencken, "Autobiographical Notes 1925," quoted in *Menckeniana*, Fall 1971, p. 1 (note).
45 Mencken to Fielding Hudson Garrison, December 31, 1920 in *Letters of H. L. Mencken*, p. 216.
45 Joseph Shaw, ed., *The Hard-Boiled Omnibus* (1952), p. vi.
46 *Ibid.*, p. viii.

Page
46 Joseph Shaw, "Greed, Crime, and Politics," *Black Mask*, March 1931, p. 9.

46 *Ibid.*

46 Joseph Shaw, "Here's Looking at You," *Black Mask*, April 1933, p. 7.

47 RC to Morton, November 20, 1944.

47 RC to H. R. Harwood, July 2, 1951.

47 G. K. Chesterton, "A Defence of Detective Stories" (1902); reprinted in Howard Haycraft, *The Art of the Mystery Story* (1946), p. 4.

47 RC, "The Simple Art of Murder," *Atlantic Monthly*, December 1944; reprinted in RC's book *The Simple Art of Murder* (1950) and in *The Second Chandler Omnibus* (1962).

48 RC, dedication of paperback book *Five Murders* to Joseph Shaw; reprinted in *The Boys in the Black Mask* (1961), p. 3. Exhibition Catalog, UCLA.

48 RC, "The Simple Art of Murder" (1944).

48 RC to Cleve Adams, September 4, 1948.

48 RC, letter to *The Fortnightly Intruder* (Los Angeles), July 1, 1937, p. 10. UCLA.

48 Quoted in Irving Wallace, "Murder for Money" typescript, p. 14; an interview with Chandler finally published, in a shortened version, by *Pageant* magazine in July 1946. Custody of FM.

48 RC, "The Simple Art of Murder" (1944).

49 RC to Erle Stanley Gardner, May 5, 1939.

49 RC to Howard, March 26, 1957.

49 RC to Alex Barris, March 18, 1949.

49 RC to Morton, December 18, 1944.

49 Lester Dent to Philip Durham, October 27, 1958. UCLA.

50 *Ibid.*

50 *Ibid.*

50 RC to James Sandoe, October 17, 1946.

50 RC to Coxe, April 9, 1939.

50 Wallace, "Murder for Money" typescript, p. 12.

50 Joseph Shaw to Frederick Nebel, January 25, 1946.

50 Joseph Shaw, note on Chandler (unused preface for *The Hard-Boiled Omnibus*). Shaw Collection, UCLA.

50 RC, "The Simple Art of Murder." Reference is to an entirely different article of the same name, published originally in the *Saturday Review of Literature* (New York), April 15, 1950, and subsequtenly used as the introduction to *The Simple Art of Murder*.

50 RC to Alfred Knopf, January 12, 1946.

51 RC to Barris, April 16, 1949.

51 RC to Cleve Adams, September 3, 1948.

51 RC, "The Simple Art of Murder" (1950).

51 RC to Cyril Ray, interview, *Sunday Times*, September 21, 1952.

51 RC to Frederick Lewis Allen, May 7, 1948.

51 RC to Paul Brooks, July 19, 1949.

52 RC, "Blackmailers Don't Shoot," Part 1, first paragraph.

53 RC, "Mandarin's Jade," end of Part 5.

53 *Ibid.*, Part 5.

53 RC, "Finger Man," Part 7.

Page
53   RC, "Spanish Blood," Part 13.
53   RC, "Smart-Aleck Kill," Part 10.
54   RC, "Blackmailers Don't Shoot," Part 1.
54   RC, untitled typescript, p. 2. RC files.
54   RC, "Red Wind," Part 6.
54   RC, "Pickup on Noon Street," Part 7.
54   RC, "Goldfish," Part 5.
54   *Ibid.*, Part 4.
54   RC, "Mandarin's Jade," Part 3.
55   RC to George Kull, February 3, 1948.
56   RC, "Nevada Gas," Part 1.
57   RC, "Bay City Blues," Part 7.
57   RC, "Red Wind," Part 1.
58   RC, "Bay City Blues," Part 8.
58   RC to Barris, March 18, 1949.
58   RC, "Bay City Blues," Part 5.
59   RC to Sandoe, December 15, 1948.
59   RC to William Gault, n.d. (February–March 1949).
60   RC, "A Couple of Writers," published in *Raymond Chandler Speaking* (1962).
60   RC to Hamilton, April 22, 1949.

CHAPTER 4.   THE BIG SLEEP

Apart from personal knowledge of Los Angeles and California generally, I have read several of the many books that have been written about Southern California. Among them are Cary McWilliams, *Southern California Country* (1946); Morrow Mayo, *Los Angeles* (1933); and Remi Nadeau, *Los Angeles* (1960).

The notes below reveal the principal sources of my information about Chandler at this time in his life.

61   RC to Charles Morton, July 17, 1944.
61   *Ibid.*
62   RC to James Keddie, March 18, 1948.
62   RC to George Harmon Coxe, June 27, 1940.
62   *Ibid.*
62   *Ibid.*
63   RC to James Sandoe, October 31, 1951.
63   RC to Keddie, March 18, 1948.
63   RC to Bernice Baumgarten, March 19, 1951.
63   RC to Baumgarten, March 11, 1949.
63   RC to Sandoe, May 20, 1949.
65   Ernest Hopkins, *Our Lawless Police* (1931), p. 152.
66   RC, *The Little Sister*, Chapter 26.
67   RC to Morton, March 26, 1945.
67   RC to Paul Brooks, July 19, 1949.
67   RC to Neil Morgan, August 30, 1956.
67   RC to H. R. Harwood, July 2, 1951.
67   RC to Baumgarten, May 14, 1952.

Page

68 RC to Sandoe, September 23, 1948.
68 RC, "The Curtain," Part 4.
69 RC, *The Big Sleep*, Chapter 3.
70 RC, "The Simple Art of Murder," *Atlantic Monthly*, December 1944.
70 RC to Sandoe, May 12, 1949.
70 RC to Leroy Wright, April 12, 1950.
70 RC to Sandoe, May 12, 1949.
71 Reply to questionnaire sent by Luther Nichols, *San Francisco Examiner*, 1958. RC files.
71 RC to Alfred Knopf, January 12, 1946.
71 RC, *The Big Sleep*, Chapter 12.
72 *Ibid.*, Chapter 30.
72 *Ibid.*, Chapter 32.
72 RC to William Koshland, November 2, 1938.
72 RC to H. N. Swanson, September 22, 1954.
73 RC to Hardwick Moseley, April 23, 1949.
73 *Ibid.*
73 *Ibid.*
73 RC to Alfred Knopf, February 19, 1939.
73 *Ibid.*
73 Frank Gruber, "Some Notes on Mystery Novels and Their Authors," a clipping from a newspaper preserved in one of Chandler's notebooks. Newspaper unknown, date probably during 1940s, since Chandler is mentioned.
74 RC, quoted in Paramount press release, 1944.
74 W. T. Ballard to the writer, March 6, 1975.
74 *Ibid.*
74 W. T. Ballard to the writer, September 14, 1974.
74 Dwight Babcock to the writer, March 9, 1975.
75 Ruth Babcock to the writer, April 8, 1975.
75 *Ibid.*
75 *Ibid.*
75 W. T. Ballard to the writer, March 21, 1975.
75 Ruth Babcock to the writer, April 8, 1975.
76 RC to Barris, April 16, 1949.
76 RC to Alfred Knopf, January 12, 1946.
76 RC to Sandoe, December 28, 1949.
77 RC to Coxe, October 17, 1939.
77 RC to James Howard, March 26, 1957.
77 RC to James Fox, February 5, 1954.
77 *Ibid.*
78 RC to Coxe, October 17, 1939.
78 RC to Carl Brandt, April 3, 1949.
78 RC to Brandt, October 18, 1948.
78 RC to Coxe, April 9, 1939.
79 RC to Alfred Knopf, February 19, 1939.
80 RC, Notebook, unpaginated. RC files.
81 RC to Sandoe, January 26, 1944.
84 RC, Notebook, unpaginated. RC files.
84 RC, notes quoted in letter to Leroy Wright, July 6, 1951.

Page
  85 *Ibid.*
  85 *Ibid.*
  85 Also RC affidavit made in San Diego, December 4, 1950.
  85 RC to Blanche Knopf, August 23, 1939.
  85 *Ibid.*
  86 *Ibid.*

CHAPTER 5.   LAW IS WHERE YOU BUY IT

Most of the biographical information contained in this chapter comes from the correspondence cited below, especially from Chandler's letters to Alfred and Blanche Knopf. I have also visited the places referred to in the chapter.

  87 RC to George Harmon Coxe, December 19, 1939.
  87 *Ibid.*
  87 RC to Blanche Knopf, January 17, 1940.
  88 *Ibid.*
  88 RC to Leroy Wright, July 7, 1951.
  88 *Ibid.*
  88 *Ibid.*
  88 RC to Alfred Knopf, April 3, 1942.
  89 RC to Blanche Knopf, May 31, 1940.
  89 Blanche Knopf to RC, October 1, 1940.
  81 RC to Blanche Knopf, October 9, 1940.
  89 Summary of reviews, Houghton Mifflin sales office. RC files.
  90 RC to Blanche Knopf, December 10, 1940
  90 Quoted in John Houseman, "Lost Fortnight," *Harper's Magazine*, August 1965, p. 61.
  90 RC to Blanche Knopf, December 10, 1940. Cumulative hardcover sales reached 11,000 by 1950.
  90 RC, *Farewell, My Lovely*, Chapter 28.
  90 *Ibid.*, Chapter 19.
  91 RC to Charles Morton, October 12, 1944.
  91 RC, *Farewell, My Lovely*, Chapter 24.
  91 *Ibid.*, Chapter 33.
  92 *Ibid.*, Chapter 28.
  92 *Ibid.*, Chapter 29.
  92 *Ibid.*, Chapter 28.
  92 *Ibid.*, Chapter 4.
  92 *Ibid.*, Chapter 3.
  92 *Ibid.*, Chapter 5.
  93 *Ibid.*
  93 *Ibid.*
  93 RC to Blanche Knopf, July 10, 1939.
  93 RC to Alfred Knopf, January 12, 1946.
  93 RC to Bernice Baumgarten, March 11, 1949.
  94 RC to Edgar Carter, February 5, 1951.
  94 RC to Coxe, November 5, 1940.
  94 RC to Dwight Babcock, December 4, 1940.
  94 RC to Erle Stanley Gardner, February 1, 1941.

Page
95   RC to Alex Barris, March 18, 1949.
96   RC to Blanche Knopf, March 15, 1942.
96   *Ibid.*
96   Blanche Knopf to RC, March 30, 1942.
96   RC to Blanche Knopf, April 3, 1942.
96   *Ibid.*
96   RC to Hamish Hamilton, October 6, 1946.
97   RC to Blanche Knopf, June 14, 1940.
97   RC to Alfred Knopf, July 16, 1942.
97   RC to Blanche Knopf, October 22, 1942.
97   *Ibid.*
97   RC, *The High Window*, Chapter 2.
98   *Ibid.*, Chapter 1.
98   *Los Angeles Times,* September 21, 1939.
98   RC, *The High Window*, Chapter 15.
98   *Ibid.*
99   *Ibid.*, Chapter 35.
100 RC to Alfred Knopf, February 8, 1943.
101 RC to Alfred Knopf, October 22, 1942.
101 RC to Alfred Knopf, February 8, 1943.
102 RC, *The Lady in the Lake*, Chapter 5.
102 *Ibid.*, Chapter 1.
102 *Ibid.*, Chapter 2.
102 *Ibid.*, Chapter 37.
103 *Ibid.*, Chapter 25.
103 Stanley Kunitz, ed., *Twentieth Century Authors, First Supplement* (1955), entry for RC.

CHAPTER 6.   THE GOLDEN GRAVEYARD

There are many books about Hollywood, but few of them are good. A large proportion are compendia of gossip. Some of the best are works of fiction like Scott Fitzgerald's *The Last Tycoon* (1941) and Nathanael West's *The Day of the Locust* (1939). As general background reading I have found Lillian Ross's *Picture* (1952) and John Dunne's *Studio* (1969) especially helpful. Daniel Stern's novel *Final Cut* (1975) suggests that the situation has changed little since Chandler's day.

Aside from the books cited below that deal directly with the films or individuals Chandler dealt with, I found useful Frank Gruber, *The Pulp Jungle* (1967); Harry Hossent, *Gangster Movies* (1974); and an article by Michael Desilets, "Raymond Chandler and Hollywood," in *Filmograph*, April 1972.

Information for this chapter comes through the cooperation of the studios Chandler worked for, especially the successor of Paramount, Universal City Studios, and MGM. The Academy of Motion Picture Arts and Sciences, the Screen Actors Guild, and the Writers Guild also provided useful information. Mainly, however, the chapter is based on conversations and letters with the men and women who knew and worked with Chandler in Hollywood, in particular, Miss Leigh Brackett, Mrs. Ruth Morse, Mrs. Meta Rosenberg, Mrs. Katherine Sistrom, and Messrs. Eric Ambler, James M. Cain, Teet Carle,

Whitfield Cook, William Dozier, José Ferrer, Steve Fisher, John Houseman, Robert Montgomery, E. Jack Neuman, Lloyd Nolan, Robert Presnell, Jr., H. Allen Smith, H. N. Swanson, Harry Tugend, Irving Wallace, Billy Wilder, and John Woolfenden.

Page

104 RC to Alfred Knopf, February 8, 1943.

105 RC to Dale Warren, May 22, 1950.

105 RC to Ray Stark, June 8, 1948.

107 RC to Hamish Hamilton, November 10, 1950.

107 RC to James Sandoe, May 23, 1949.

108 Quoted in Axel Madsen, *Billy Wilder* (1969), p. 91.

108 *Double Indemnity* folder. RC files.

108 Michael Desilets, "Raymond Chandler and Hollywood," *Filmograph*, April 1972, p. 2.

108 *Double Indemnity* folder. RC files.

108 Quoted in press release of Mystery Writers of America after Chandler's death, March 1959. RC files.

109 Quoted in John Houseman, "Lost Fortnight," *Harper's Magazine*, August 1965, p. 55.

109 Frank Capra, *The Name Above the Title* (1971), p. 253.

109 Teet Carle to the writer, December 20, 1974.

109 Robert Presnell, Jr., to the writer, November 7, 1974.

110 *Ibid.*

110 H. Allen Smith, *Lost in the Horse Latitudes* (1944), p. 111.

110 Robert Presnell, Jr., to the writer, November 7, 1974.

111 RC to Carl Brandt, November 26, 1948.

111 José Ferrer to the writer, February 22, 1974.

111 Quoted in Irving Wallace, "Murder for Money" typescript, p. 12. Custody FM.

111 RC to Warren, September 15, 1949.

111 James M. Cain to the writer, April 30, 1975.

113 RC to Sandoe, September 18, 1945.

113 RC to Alfred Knopf, November 13, 1943.

114 RC to Charles Morton, May 31, 1946. The scene occurs in *The Blue Dahlia*.

114 RC to Morton, January 1, 1945.

114 RC to Paul Ferris, January 31, 1945. The salary estimate of $1,000 is based on Chandler's statement in this letter that for the following year it would be increased to $1,250. In Chandler's range at this time, salaries were agreed to on multiples of $250.

115 RC to Morton, January 15, 1945.

115 RC to Morton, January 21, 1945.

115 RC to Morton, March 5, 1945.

116 Houseman, "Lost Fortnight," p. 59.

117 RC, Notebook, unpaginated. RC files.

117 RC to Sandoe, June 17, 1946.

117 Quoted in Frank Gruber, *The Pulp Jungle* (1967), p. 116.

118 RC to Sydney Sanders, February 19, 1945.

118 RC to Brandt, November 26, 1948.

118 RC to Sandoe, August 18, 1945.

Page
119   RC to Edward Weeks, June 10, 1957.
119   RC to Morton, October 13, 1945.
119   RC to Hamilton, January 9, 1946.
119   RC to Sandoe, May 30, 1946.
120   RC to Alex Barris, April 19, 1949.
120   RC to Morton, October 13, 1945.
120   Sanders to RC, June 4, 1945.
121   RC to Alfred Knopf, January 12, 1946.
121   RC to Hamilton, February 1, 1946.
121   RC to Warren, May 5, 1949.
122   RC to Knopf, January 12, 1946.
122   RC to Brandt, November 20, 1948.
122   RC to Morton, January 1, 1945.
122   Quoted in Wallace "Murder for Money" typescript, p. 7. Custody FM.
122   RC to Knopf, December 20, 1948.
122   RC to Morton, December 18, 1944.
123   *Ibid.*
123   *Ibid.*
123   RC to Erle Stanley Gardner, January 20, 1946.
123   RC to Sol Siegel, April 27, 1951.
123   RC to Brandt, September 1, 1949.
124   RC to Morton, December 12, 1945.
124   *Ibid.*
124   RC to Weeks, February 27, 1957.
124   RC to Morton, March 15, 1946.
124   RC to Blanche Knopf, March 27, 1946.
124   RC to Gardner, April 4, 1946.
124   *Ibid.*
124   RC to Morton, May 31, 1946.
124   RC to H. N. Swanson, August 4, 1946.
124   *Ibid.*
125   *Ibid.*
125   RC to Hamilton, May 30, 1946.
126   *Ibid.*
126   RC to Jean Bethel (Mrs. Erle Stanley) Gardner, April 20, 1947.
126   RC to Sandoe, October 2, 1946.
126   RC to Hamilton, March 21, 1949.
126   RC to Hamilton, January 9, 1946.
126   RC to Sandoe, May 30, 1946.
126   RC to Brandt, January 23, 1949.
127   C. A. Lejeune, "The Films," *Observer*, April 28, 1946. RC files.
127   Dilys Powell, "Films of the Week," *Sunday Times*, April 28, 1946. RC files.
128   RC to Morton, March 15, 1946.
128   *Ibid.*

CHAPTER 7. THE RELUCTANT SUBURB

Apart from the sources noted below, I have gathered information about this period of Chandler's life in La Jolla from conversations with Mrs. Juanita

Messick, Mrs. Katherine Sistrom, and Messrs. Jonathan Latimer, Neil Morgan, George Peterson, and H. N. Swanson. Mr. Bernard Siegan, the present owner of Chandler's house, allowed me to inspect it. Mr. Dale Warren gave me information about Chandler's switch from Knopf to Houghton Mifflin.

Page

129 RC, "Crosstown with Neil Morgan," guest appearance in this column in *San Diego Tribune,* March 1, 1957.

129 Quoted in Neil Morgan, interview with RC, *San Diego Journal,* 1946.

130 RC to Dale Warren, October 2, 1946.

130 *Ibid.*

130 *Ibid.*

131 Quoted in Morgan interview, *San Diego Journal,* 1946.

131 RC to Bernice Baumgarten, April 21, 1949.

132 RC to Carl Brandt, February 26, 1950.

132 RC to James Sandoe, November 18, 1948.

133 RC to Hamish Hamilton, January 9, 1951.

133 RC to Charles Morton, March 19, 1945.

133 RC to Warren, December 19, 1948.

134 Edmund Wilson, "Who Cares Who Killed Roger Ackroyd?," *New Yorker,* January 20, 1945; reprinted in Howard Haycraft, *The Art of the Mystery Story* (1946), p. 395.

134 W. H. Auden, "The Guilty Vicarage," *Harper's Magazine,* May 1948, p. 408.

134 RC to Morton, January 21, 1945.

134 RC, "Hollywood Bowl," *Atlantic Monthly,* January 1947, p. 108.

134 RC to Sandoe, August 10, 1947.

134 RC to Sandoe, December 16, 1944.

135 RC to Edward Weeks, January 18, 1947.

135 RC, "Lines to a Lady with an Unsplit Infinitive." RC files.

136 RC to Sandoe, October 14, 1949.

136 RC to Warren, January 8, 1948.

136 RC to Hamilton, May 16, 1945.

137 RC to Morton, January 8, 1947.

137 RC to Mrs. Robert Hogan, March 8, 1947.

138 RC to Sandoe, May 12, 1949.

138 RC to Sandoe, October 17, 1948.

139 RC to Sandoe, January 27, 1948.

139 RC, *The High Window,* Chapter 28.

139 RC to Miss Aron, January 11, 1945.

140 RC to Hamilton, January 11, 1950.

140 RC to Hamilton, October 13, 1950.

140 RC to Hamilton, November 10, 1950.

140 RC to Hamilton, June 22, 1949.

140 RC, "Oscar Night in Hollywood," *Atlantic Monthly,* March 1948, p. 24.

141 RC to Sandoe, October 2, 1947.

141 *Ibid.*

142 RC to Warren, April 20, 1949.

142 *Ibid.*

142 RC, "Oscar Night in Hollywood," p. 25.

142 RC to Baumgarten, March 31, 1949.

Page
143   RC, *Playback* story idea. UCLA.
143   RC to H. N. Swanson, attached to *Playback* story idea. UCLA.
144   RC to Swanson, June 23, 1947.
144   RC to Swanson, August 16, 1947.
144   RC to James Howard, March 26, 1957.
144   RC to Hamilton, October 27, 1947.
145   RC to Joseph Shaw, November 9, 1946.
146   RC to Alfred Knopf, July 16, 1953.
146   RC to Morton, January 1, 1948.
147   RC to Brandt, May 11, 1948.
147   RC to Brandt, June 1, 1948.
147   RC to Brandt, June 9, 1948.
148   RC to Warren, June 17, 1958.
148   RC to Warren, June 2, 1947.
148   RC to Sandoe, March 8, 1947.
148   RC to Hamilton, July 13, 1948.
148   RC to Hamilton, August 10, 1948.
149   RC to Frederick Lewis Allen, May 7, 1948.
149   RC to Hamilton, August 10, 1948.
149   RC to Hamilton, August 19, 1948.
149   RC to Mrs. Holton of Houghton Mifflin, April 3, 1949.
149   RC to Hamilton, June 22, 1949.
150   RC to Hamilton, October 5, 1949.
150   RC to Sandoe, May 20, 1949.
150   RC, "Hollywood Bowl," p. 109.
150   RC to Baumgarten, February 15, 1951.
150   RC, *The Little Sister*, Chapter 19. The character appears to be based on
      Y. Frank Freeman of Paramount.
150   *Ibid.*
151   *Ibid.*, Chapter 18.
151   *Ibid.*, Chapter 13.
151   RC to Helga Greene, May 25, 1957.
151   RC, *The Little Sister*, Chapter 13.
151   *Ibid.*
151   *Ibid.*
151   *Ibid.*
152   RC, "Notes on Homicide Bureau," January 25, 1945. RC files.
153   RC, *The Little Sister*, Chapter 29.
153   *Ibid.*, Chapter 24.
153   RC, Notebook, unpaginated. RC files.
153   RC to Baumgarten, April 17, 1950.
153   RC to Baumgarten, November 15, 1949.
153   RC to Swanson, October 15, 1948.
154   RC to Sandoe, October 14, 1949.

CHAPTER 8.   NO THIRD ACT

Most of the information for this chapter comes from the sources mentioned in
the notes below. Valuable additional facts were provided in correspondence
and conversations with Messrs. Edgar Carter, Whitfield Cook, Arthur Lovell,

Jonathan Latimer, Neil Morgan, S. J. Perelman, and H. N. Swanson. I am also indebted to Mrs. Judith Pfeiffer of Warner Brothers and especially to Mrs. Juanita Messick, Chandler's secretary for a number of years.

Page
155 Anthony Boucher, "Chandler, Revalued," *New York Times Book Review,* September 4, 1949.
156 J. B. Priestley, *New Statesman,* April 9, 1949; quoted in Houghton Mifflin publicity material, "To the Travelers," No. 62, July 15, 1949.
156 RC to Hamish Hamilton, October 5, 1949.
156 RC to Hamilton, August 31, 1949.
158 RC to Hamilton, June 17, 1949.
158 RC to Bernice Baumgarten, March 21, 1949.
158 RC to Baumgarten, April 21, 1949.
158 *Ibid.*
158 *Ibid.*
159 RC to Carl Brandt, February 3, 1949.
159 *Ibid.*
159 RC to Baumgarten, October 15, 1949.
159 RC to Dale Warren, December 22, 1949.
159 *Ibid.*
159 RC to Warren, October 15, 1949.
160 RC to Hamilton, April 4, 1949.
161 RC to Hamilton, September 19, 1951.
161 RC to Charles Morton, August 30, 1949.
161 RC to Brandt, November 12, 1948.
162 RC to H. N. Swanson, January 5, 1953.
162 Erle Stanley Gardner to RC, July 8, 1947.
162 John Crosby, *Los Angeles Daily News,* June 26, 1947. RC files.
162 Quoted in interview with Terry Nolan, *San Diego Journal,* July 1, 1947. RC files.
162 RC to Gardner, October 23, 1947.
162 RC to Brandt, January 23, 1948.
163 RC to Ray Stark, July 19, 1948.
163 RC to Stark, quoted in *Screen Writer,* October 11, 1948.
163 Notes by Gene Levitt for Marlowe series.
163 RC to James Sandoe, May 14, 1949.
164 RC to Brandt, September 10, 1949.
164 RC to Baumgarten, October 16, 1950.
164 RC to Brandt, December 1, 1950.
164 RC to Brandt, November 13, 1951.
165 RC to Gene Levitt, November 22, 1950.
165 RC to Edgar Carter, September 10, 1951.
166 RC to Hardwick Moseley, April 23, 1949.
166 RC to Hamilton, May 13, 1949.
166 *Ibid.*
167 RC to Baumgarten, October 15, 1949.
167 RC to Baumgarten, October 15, 1949.
167 RC to Baumgarten, November 17, 1949.
167 RC to Baumgarten, December 3, 1949.
167 RC to Baumgarten, July 7, 1949.

Page
167   RC to Moseley, February 6, 1955.
168   RC to Paul Brooks, July 19, 1949.
168   RC to E. Howard Hunt, November 26, 1952.
169   RC, "A Qualified Farewell" typescript, p. 3. RC files.
169   *Ibid.*, pp. 3 4.
169   *Ibid.*, p. 8.
169   Brandt to Stark, March 8, 1951.
169   RC to Warren, June 2, 1947.
169   RC to Paul Brooks, September 13, 1949.
169   RC to Brooks, May 29, 1952.
170   RC, "Ten Per Cent of Your Life," *Atlantic Monthly*, February 1952; reprinted in *Raymond Chandler Speaking* (1962).
170   *Ibid.*
170   Baumgarten to RC, March 21, 1951.
170   RC to Brandt, June 24, 1949.
170   RC to Hamilton, September 4, 1950.
171   RC to Stark, August 17, 1950.
171   Quoted in François Truffaut, *Hitchcock* (1967), pp. 142–143.
172   RC, note made while working on *Strangers on a Train*. RC files.
173   *Ibid.*
174   Quoted in Truffaut, *Hitchcock*, p. 143.
174   Quoted in Robin Wood, *Hitchcock's Films* (paperback; 1970), p. 50.
174   RC, first-draft screenplay for *Strangers on a Train*. RC files.
174   Quoted in Robin Wood, *Hitchcock's Films*, p. 51.
174   Quoted in Truffaut, *Hitchcock*, p. 147.
174   Finlay McDermid to RC, August 17, 1950.
174   R. J. Obringer to RC, August 23, 1950.
175   RC to Stark, August 17, 1950.
175   *Ibid.*
176   RC to McDermid, November 2, 1950.
176   RC to Hamilton, October 6, 1946.
176   RC to Ben Benjamin, December 1, 1950.
176   RC to Warren, October 4, 1950.
176   RC to Benjamin, December 11, 1950.
177   RC to Brandt, December 11, 1950.
177   RC to Warren, July 20, 1951.
177   RC to Hamilton, July 24, 1951.
178   RC to Hamilton, March 12, 1949.
178   RC to Brandt, February 13, 1951.
178   RC to Juanita Messick, n.d.
178   RC to Baumgarten, May 21, 1951.
179   RC to Baumgarten, June 5, 1951.
179   RC to Brandt, December 21, 1950.
179   RC to Hamilton, May 28, 1957.
179   RC to Hamilton, February 5, 1951.
180   RC to Hamilton, May 28, 1957.
180   RC to Hamilton, February 5, 1951.
181   Priestley, *New Statesman*, April 9, 1949.
181   RC to Messick, n.d.
181   RC to Hamilton, February 14, 1951.

Page
181 *Ibid.*
181 Quoted in "Raymond Chandler Speaking," produced by Robert Pocock for the Home Service of the BBC, transmitted July 4, 1962.
181 RC to Sandoe, February 20, 1951.
182 RC to Edgar Carter, December 13, 1951.
182 RC to Hamilton, February 27, 1951.
182 RC to Hamilton, December 4, 1949.
183 RC to Hamilton, January 5, 1950.
183 *Ibid.*
184 Somerset Maugham, *The Vagrant Mood* (1953), p. 129.
184 *Ibid.*, p. 131.
184 RC to Frank Francis, October 30, 1952.
184 RC to S. J. Perelman, September 4, 1951.
185 Perelman to RC, October 24, 1951.
185 RC to Perelman, January 9, 1952.
185 RC to Warren, August 6, 1951.
185 *Ibid.*
185 Perelman to the writer, March 10, 1974.

CHAPTER 9. THE LONG GOODBYE

The notes below identify all the main sources for this chapter with the exception of some observations on Chandler's domestic situation and behavior. This information was given to me by Mrs. Juanita Messick and Mr. Milton Philleo. My comments on Chandler's creative processes are indebted in part to work done by Professor Albert Rothenberg of the Yale Medical School, whose book *Studies in the Creative Process in Art and Science* is in preparation.

188 RC to James Fox, March 27, 1954.
189 RC to Bernice Baumgarten, November 8, 1949.
190 RC to Juanita Messick, n.d.
190 RC to Messick, n.d. (probably 1951 or 1952).
191 RC, "Advice to a Secretary." RC files.
191 *Ibid.*
191 RC, "Advice to an Employer." RC files.
191 RC to Messick, n.d.
191 RC to Hamish Hamilton, January 9, 1951.
192 RC, "A Qualified Farewell" typescript, p. 14. RC files.
192 RC to Baumgarten, January 3, 1952.
193 RC to Hamilton, October 5, 1951.
193 RC to Hamilton, May 21, 1952.
194 RC to Baumgarten, May 14, 1952.
194 Baumgarten to RC, May 22, 1952.
194 Carl Brandt to RC, May 22, 1952.
194 Baumgarten to RC, May 26, 1952.
194 RC to Baumgarten, May 25, 1952.
195 RC to Brandt, June 11, 1952.
195 RC to Baumgarten, June 15, 1952.
195 *Ibid.*

Page

195   Brandt to RC, October 20, 1952.
195   RC to Brandt and Brandt, November 26, 1952.
195   RC to Hamilton, February 26, 1945.
196   RC, *The Long Goodbye* typescript. RC files.
196   RC, corrections on *The Long Goodbye* typescript. RC files.
196   RC, *The Long Goodbye*, Chapter 53.
197   Donald Henderson, *Mr. Bowling Buys a Newspaper* (1944), p. 17.
197   *Ibid.*, p. 21.
197   *Ibid.*, p. 83.
197   *Ibid.*, p. 210.
198   RC to D. J. Ibberson, April 19, 1951.
198   *Ibid.*
200   RC, *The Long Goodbye*, Chapter 4.
200   *Ibid.*, Chapter 53.
200   *Ibid.*
200   *Ibid.*
201   *Ibid.*, Chapter 28.
201   *Ibid.*
201   RC, "Nocturne from Nowhere" typescript. RC files.
202   RC, *The Long Goodbye*, Chapter 24.
202   *Ibid.*, Chapter 23.
202   *Ibid.*
202   RC to Edgar Carter, June 3, 1957.
202   *Ibid.*
202   *Ibid.*
203   RC to Deirdre Gartrell, April 23, 1957.
203   RC to Jean de Leon, February 11, 1957.
203   RC to Hamilton, April 4, 1949.
203   RC, *The Big Sleep*, Chapter 25.
203   RC to Ibberson, April 19, 1951.
204   RC, *The Long Goodbye*, Chapter 20.
204   *Ibid.*, Chapter 29.
204   *Ibid.*
204   *Ibid.*, Chapter 49.
204   *Ibid.*
205   *Ibid.*, Chapter 50.
206   *Ibid.*, Chapter 13.
206   *Ibid.*, Chapter 38.
206   RC, "The Simple Art of Murder," *Atlantic Monthly*, December 1944.
206   RC to Hamilton, June 10, 1952.
206   RC, Notebook, unpaginated. RC files.
208   RC to James Sandoe, March 8, 1947.
208   RC to James Howard, March 26, 1957.
208   RC to Brandt, December 21, 1950.
209   RC to Hamilton, September 19, 1951.

CHAPTER 10.   NOCTURNE

Additional information to that mentioned below comes from talks and correspondence with a number of Chandler's friends and acquaintances at this time, in particular, Mrs. Juanita Messick, Mrs. Bruce Weston, Messrs. Nicolas Bentley, James Fox, Hamish Hamilton, Jonathan Latimer, Roger Machell, and Neil Morgan, Dr. Solon Palmer, Mr. J. B. Priestley, Dr. Francis Smith, and Messrs. Dale Warren and Hillary Waugh.

Page
210 RC to Hamish Hamilton, January 9, 1946.
210 RC to Charles Morton, January 1, 1948.
211 RC to Hamilton, January 24, 1949.
211 *Ibid.*
211 RC to Carl Brandt, January 23, 1949.
211 RC to Hamilton, January 24, 1949.
211 RC to Morton, February 13, 1948.
212 RC to H. F. Hose, January 6, 1953.
213 Quoted in "Raymond Chandler Speaking," produced by Robert Pocock for the Home Service of the BBC, transmitted July 4, 1962.
213 *Ibid.*
213 *Ibid.*
213 *Ibid.*
214 *Ibid.*
214 RC to Paul Brooks, September 28, 1952.
214 Alistair Cooke, "American Letter," No. 120, April 1, 1949.
214 Cyril Ray, *Sunday Times,* September 21, 1952.
215 RC to William Townend, November 11, 1952.
215 RC to Mr. Sheppard of Hamish Hamilton, November 14, 1952.
216 RC to Townend, November 11, 1952.
216 RC to Hamilton, November 5, 1952.
216 RC to Dale Warren, November 13, 1952.
216 RC to Hamilton, November 5, 1952.
216 *Ibid.*
217 *Ibid.*
217 RC to Hamilton, January 16, 1953.
217 RC to Hamilton, December 12, 1952.
217 RC to Leonard Russell, December 11, 1952.
218 RC to Dr. O. C. Helming, January 23, 1953.
218 RC to Juanita Messick, n.d. (1953).
218 *Ibid.*
218 RC to Hardwick Moseley, March 23, 1954.
218 RC to Messick, n.d.
219 RC to Roger Machell, March 15, 1953.
219 RC to Hamilton, May 11, 1953.
219 RC to Machell, September 8, 1953.
220 RC to Hamilton, October 24, 1953.
220 RC to Machell, October 9, 1953.
220 RC to Hamilton, January 7, 1954.
220 *Time,* March 29, 1954.
220 *New Yorker,* March 27, 1954.
220 RC to Hamilton, January 16, 1954.
221 RC to Moseley, March 23, 1954.
221 RC to Messick, n.d.
221 *Ibid.*

Page
221   RC to James Fox, March 27, 1954.
222   *Ibid*
222   RC to Fox, May 19, 1954.
222   *Ibid.*
222   RC to Hamilton, June 15, 1954.
222   RC to Hamilton, January 5, 1955.
224   *Ibid.*
224   RC to Jean de Leon, February 11, 1957.
225   RC to Hamilton, January 22, 1955.
225   *Ibid.*
225   RC to Machell, February 7, 1955.
226   RC to Machell, March 5, 1955.
227   Neil Morgan, "The Decline and Rise of Raymond Chandler" typescript,
        p. 7. Custody FM.
227   RC to Machell, March 5, 1955.
227   *Ibid.*
227   *Ibid.*
227   RC to Helga Greene, March 19, 1957.
227   RC to Russell, December 29, 1954.
228   RC to William Gault, n.d. (March 1955).
228   RC to Moseley, March 23, 1955.
228   RC to Neil Morgan, n.d. (March 1955).
228   RC to Machell, April 6, 1955.
228   RC to Fox, April 10, 1955.
230   RC, "Requiem" typescript. RC files. The poem was accepted by the
        Atlantic Monthly but never published.

CHAPTER 11.   ONCE IN A WHILE FOREVER

Much information about Chandler's last years was relayed to me personally.
I am indebted in particular to the following people, some of whom also wrote
to me extensively: Mrs. Kay West Beckett, Mrs. Nicolas Bentley, Miss Jean
de Leon, Miss Dorothy Gardiner, Mrs. Helga Greene, Dr. Evelyn Hooker,
Miss Alison Hooper, Mrs. Juanita Messick, Mrs. Marian Murray, Mrs. Sonia
Orwell, Miss Dilys Powell, Miss Jocelyn Rickards, Mrs. Stephen Spender,
Miss Jessica Tyndale, Messrs. Eric Ambler, Nicolas Bentley, W. E. Durham,
Michael Gilbert, Graham Carleton Greene, Maurice Guinness, E. T. Guymon,
Jr., Christopher Isherwood, Neil Morgan, E. Jack Neuman, Frank Norman,
George Peterson, J. B. Priestley, Stephen Spender, Julian Symons, Hillary
Waugh, and Leroy Wright.

For purposes of privacy, I have referred to one person in this chapter by
a different name. References to this person in Chandler's letters have therefore also been altered.

232   Mystery Writers of America folder. RC files.
232   Helga Greene, "Account of Meeting Raymond Chandler" typescript,
        June 1960, p. 1. RC files.
232   Quoted in *Daily Sketch*, April 27, 1955.
232   Patrick Doncaster, typescript of interview for *Daily Mirror*; never pub-
        lished because of newspaper strike.

Page

232 Ian Fleming, "Raymond Chandler," *London Magazine*, December 12, 1959, p. 43.

233 RC to Hamish Hamilton, April 27, 1955.

233 *Ibid.*

233 *Ibid.*

234 Quoted in "Raymond Chandler Speaking," produced by Robert Pocock for the Home Service of the BBC, transmitted July 4, 1962.

234 RC to Hardwick Moseley, April 24, 1955.

234 Quoted in BBC transcript, July 4, 1962.

234 Natasha Spender to the writer, November 20, 1975.

234 Jocelyn Rickards to the writer, November 26, 1975.

234 Natasha Spender to the writer, November 20, 1975.

234 Alison Hooper to the writer, November 29, 1975.

235 *Ibid.*

235 Jocelyn Rickards to the writer, November 26, 1975.

235 RC to J. B. Priestley July 29, 1955.

236 Natasha Spender to the writer, November 20, 1975.

236 RC to Hillary Waugh, reprinted in the *Third Degree*, the newsletter of the Mystery Writers of America, September–October 1955.

236 RC to Helga Greene, November 23, 1956.

236 Quoted in the *Evening Standard*, June 30, 1955.

238 RC to Neil Morgan, June 3, 1955.

238 Quoted in the *Daily Express*, April 25, 1955.

238 RC to Mrs. S. S. Tyler, June 30, 1956.

238 RC to Deirdre Gartrell, March 20, 1957.

239 Natasha Spender to the writer, November 20, 1975.

239 *Ibid.*

239 *Ibid.*

239 RC to Arthur Lovell, February 9, 1954.

240 RC to Moseley, June 20, 1956.

240 RC to Roger Machell, n.d. (October 1955).

240 RC to Hamilton, n.d. (October 1955).

240 RC to Michael Gilbert, October 27, 1955.

240 RC to Machell, October 27, 1955.

240 *Ibid.*

240 *Ibid.*

241 RC to Greene, November 13, 1955.

241 RC to Morgan, November 18, 1955.

242 RC to James Fox, January 7, 1956.

242 *Ibid.*

242 RC to Fox, December 16, 1955.

242 RC to Fox, January 7, 1956.

243 *Ibid.*

243 *Ibid.*

243 RC to Paul Brooks, March 10, 1957.

243 RC to Frank Francis, January 30, 1956.

243 RC to Neil Morgan, February 20, 1956.

243 Natasha Spender to the writer, November 20, 1975.

243 RC to Jessica Tyndale, April 28, 1957.

244 RC to Morgan, February 20, 1956.

Page
244 Fleming, "Raymond Chandler," p. 43.
244 RC to Gilbert, July 25, 1957.
244 RC to Dale Warren, July 9, 1949.
244 RC to Greene, June 21, 1956.
244 RC to Greene, May 5, 1957.
245 RC to Greene, May 15, 1956.
245 *Ibid.*
245 *Ibid.*
245 *Ibid.*
245 RC to Hamilton, June 10, 1956.
245 RC to Morgan, June 5, 1956.
245 *Ibid.*
245 RC to Greene, June 5, 1956.
246 RC to Greene, June 10, 1956.
246 RC to Greene, June 19, 1956.
246 RC to Greene, June 29, 1956.
247 RC to Greene, July 13, 1956.
247 RC to Leroy Wright, November 21, 1956.
247 RC to Gilbert, January 3, 1957.
247 RC to Tyndale, January 18, 1957.
247 *Ibid.*
248 RC to Greene, February 4, 1957.
248 RC to Greene, May 5, 1957.
248 RC to Natasha Spender, May 30, 1957.
248 RC to Greene, May 25, 1957.
248 RC to Michael Gilbert, June 19, 1957.
248 RC to Greene, July 25, 1957.
248 Natasha Spender to the writer, November 20, 1975.
249 RC, "Faster, Slower, Neither" typescript. RC files.
249 RC to Moseley, February 3, 1957.
249 RC to Wright, March 31, 1957.
249 *Ibid.*
250 RC to Greene, May 25, 1957.
250 RC to Greene, October 20, 1957.
250 RC to Greene, August 24, 1957.
250 RC to Gilbert, December 15, 1957.
251 RC to Greene, April 28, 1957.
251 RC to Greene, July 11, 1957.
251 RC to Greene, July 3, 1957.
251 RC to Greene, September 20, 1957.
251 RC to Hamilton, December 2, 1957.
252 RC to Brooks, December 28, 1957.
252 RC to Tyndale, February 3, 1958.
252 RC to Maurice Guinness, February 10, 1958.
252 RC to Gilbert, December 19, 1957.
253 RC to Greene, May 5, 1957.
253 Quoted in *Newsweek*, July 21, 1958.
253 RC to Charles Morton, October 9, 1950.
253 *Ibid.*
253 *Ibid.*

Page

254   RC to Gilbert, March 25, 1957.
254   *Ibid.*
255   RC to Greene, December 21, 1957.
255   RC to Wilbur Smith, October 16, 1958.
255   RC to Guinness, February 10, 1958.
255   RC to Greene, January 4, 1958.
255   RC to Guinness, February 10, 1958.
256   RC to Moseley, October 5, 1958.
256   RC to Greene, June 29, 1957.
256   RC to Greene, November 30, 1957.
256   *Ibid.*
256   RC to Greene, January 4, 1958.
256   RC to Greene, December 28, 1957
257   RC to Greene, February 23, 1958.
258   Luciano Lucania to RC, March 24, 1958.
258   Lucania to RC, May 8, 1958.
258   RC, "My Friend Luco" typescript, pp. 6–7. RC files.
259   RC to Jean de Leon, April 30, 1958.
259   Quoted in BBC transcript, July 4, 1962.
260   *Ibid.*
260   *Ibid.*
261   RC, "Foreword" to Frank Norman, *Bang to Rights* (1958).
261   RC to Greene, May 25, 1957.
261   *Ibid.*
261   RC to Anne Jameson, May 19, 1958.
262   RC to Anne Jameson, June 24, 1958.
262   RC to Greene, August 16, 1958.
262   RC to Greene, August 24, 1958.
262   RC to Greene, August 31, 1958.
262   RC to Greene, September 4, 1958.
263   RC to Greene, October 12, 1958.
263   RC, "The Pencil," Part 2.
263   RC to Juanita Messick, August 12, 1953.
263   RC to Warren, May 5, 1949.
264   RC to Bergen Evans, January 18, 1958.
264   RC to Greene, October 12, 1958.
264   RC to Greene, June 19, 1956.
264   RC to Greene, October 24, 1958.
264   RC to Greene, October 29, 1958.
265   RC to Greene, November 7, 1958.
265   RC to Gilbert, January 22, 1959.
266   RC to Marian Murray, March 4, 1959.
266   RC, notes for speech to Mystery Writers of America. UCLA.
267   *Ibid.*
267   RC to Greene, March 17, 1959.
267   *Times* (London), March 28, 1959. RC files.
267   *Los Angeles Times*, March 27, 1959. RC files.
269   RC to Alex Barris, April 16, 1949.

INDEX